International Law in Cyberspace

International Law in Cyberspace

The Nordic Perspective

Edited by

Marc Schack and Astrid Kjeldgaard-Pedersen

BRILL | NIJHOFF

LEIDEN | BOSTON

This is a spin-off book from the Nordic Journal of International Law (NORD), Volume 92 (2023) Issue 3: Special Issue: Nordic Perspectives on the International Legal Regulation of Cyberspace, edited by Marc Schack and Astrid Kjelgaard-Pedersen.

The Library of Congress Cataloging-in-Publication Data is available online at https://catalog.loc.gov

Typeface for the Latin, Greek, and Cyrillic scripts: "Brill". See and download: brill.com/brill-typeface.

ISBN 978-90-04-70392-6 (hardback)
ISBN 978-90-04-70393-3 (e-book)
DOI 10.1163/9789004703933

This book is printed on acid-free paper and produced in a sustainable manner.

Contents

Figures and Tables

Figures

Tables

CHAPTER 1

Introduction

It is almost becoming trite to claim that small, liberal democracies, like the Nordic states, have a vested interest in maintaining a rules-based international order. Nonetheless, this holds true as a general statement, and it is also true when it comes to the specific realm of cyberspace. In recent years, growing cyber threats have served as a stark reminder to the Nordics that their security and prosperity depend on a stable and predictable international environment. Not least the war in Ukraine has underscored the urgent need for clearer international legal regulation in the context of cyberspace. As the lack of clarity continues to be exploited by hostile actors, efforts by allied nations to develop cohesive cybersecurity strategies and policies, based on international legal norms, are complicated.

In this context, the Nordic states can have a crucial role to play in the ongoing international debates on the development of international law concerning cyberspace. The question is therefore not only *what* specific interests the Nordic states should promote but also *how* they should engage in these difficult discussions. Such critical issues were the focus of a conference held at the University of Copenhagen on September 28–29, 2022, titled "Nordic Perspectives on the Regulation of Cyberspace under International Law". The conference brought together legal scholars, civil servants, and other stakeholders to explore the current state of international law as it pertains to cyberspace, as well as the role that the Nordic states can and should play in shaping these legal frameworks.

The present edited volume builds on the discussions and findings of the Copenhagen conference, as well as a special issue of the *Nordic Journal of International Law* published in 2023. It seeks to provide a comprehensive overview of Nordic perspectives on the international legal regulation of cyberspace, through the inclusion of two types of contributions: Firstly, the official state position papers published by the governments of Denmark, Finland, Norway, and Sweden, expressing their views on the application of international law in cyberspace, and secondly, academic contributions that explore various specific issues that play a special role for the Nordic states, including through reflections on the Nordic contributions. Together, these contributions offer both an authoritative account of the official Nordic positions and a scholarly analysis of the key legal challenges and debates in this rapidly evolving field.

 | DOI:10.1163/9789004703933_002

1 Official Position Papers from the Governments of Finland, Norway, Sweden, and Denmark

The first chapters of this volume thus comprises, in addition to this introduction, the official position papers from the governments of Finland, Norway, Sweden, and Denmark on the application of international law in cyberspace. Together, these position papers provide invaluable insights into the official Nordic perspectives and reflect each country's approach to the interpretation and application of international law in the digital domain.

What becomes immediately clear when reading these statements is that the Nordics are fully aligned in their conviction that international law applies fully to cyberspace, and one of the most fundamental areas of consensus among the Nordic states is thus the basic recognition that international law, including the UN Charter, governs state behaviour in cyberspace. At this point in time, this is a position that the Nordics share with virtually all states and academics. The Nordics also agree that foundational international legal principles apply in cyberspace, and thus agree, for example, that sovereignty extends to cyber operations, meaning that states have jurisdiction over cyber infrastructure within their territories and must respect the sovereignty of other states in their cyber activities. This shared understanding reinforces the importance of the rule of law in maintaining peace and stability in the digital realm and pushes back against positions taken e.g. by the United Kingdom, which questions the application of the legal principle of sovereignty in cyberspace. The Nordic states also converge on e.g. the principle of non-intervention, which prohibits states from coercively interfering in the internal or external affairs of other states. They recognize that cyber operations that disrupt or manipulate essential governmental functions or political processes could constitute violations of this principle. Additionally, there is agreement that the prohibition on the use of force, a cornerstone of international law, applies to cyber operations. This means that cyber-attacks causing physical damage, injury, or significant disruption could be regarded as uses of force under international law, potentially triggering a state's right to self-defence, if the operation constitutes an 'armed attack'.

Despite such strong alignments and commonalities, however, the Nordic states do differ in some of their interpretations and/or emphases on certain issues. An example of the latter is the states' specific statements on the concept of the use of force. Here, as noted, all the Nordics believe that certain cyber operations can constitute use of force, and all of them also agree that an effect-based approach is appropriate for determining, whether a specific cyber operation violates the prohibition on the threat or use of force. Although

Finland only uses the specific language of 'scale and effect' in regards to its discussions of 'armed attacks', it considers factors that are very similar to the other three states, which all rely expressly on the 'scale and effect' formula when discussing the point at which cyber operations constitute use of force (Denmark, p 450; Finland, p 6; Sweden p 4; Norway p 5). All of the states also seem to agree that cyber operations that, as Denmark puts it, result in "injury, death, or significant physical damage" *prima facie* qualifies as use of force. What is noteworthy, however, is what each state adds to this conclusion regarding issues that are not as uncontroversial. Denmark notes, for example, that "it generally cannot be ruled out" that also "acts of economic or political coercion" can fall within the definition of use of force if, for example, the relevant cyber operation "leads to significant economic damage." (Denmark, p 451). As such, Denmark opens up the door for non-physical damage constituting use of force if a certain threshold is reached – but Denmark does not conclude clearly on the matter. Norway similarly considers cyber operations that cause "severe disruption to the functioning of the State" and "the use of crypto viruses or other forms of digital sabotage against a State's financial and banking system, or other operations that cause widespread economic effects and destabilisation, may amount to the use of force in violation of Article 2(4)." Norway thereby focuses on similar kinds of operations and concludes that such operations 'may' violate the prohibition on the use of force. In sum, Norway seems to agree with Denmark but frames its analysis a bit more broadly and concludes in a slightly more confident manner. When it comes to Finland, it is interesting to note that the discussions of these issues do not take place in the context of the concept of the use of force but rather in relation to the concept of 'armed attacks'. Finland notes that "[a] question has also been raised, whether a cyberattack producing significant economic effects such as the collapse of a State's financial system or parts of its economy should be equated to an armed attack. This question merits further consideration." Hence, Finland does not conclude on this question, noting only that the issue merits consideration, but given that the threshold of 'armed attacks' is (substantially) higher that 'use of force', Finland seemingly assumes that at least the same would apply to the question of use of force. On the one hand, Finland thus raises the bar by discussing armed attacks and self-defence, rather than use of force. Yet, on the other hand, Finland does not provide conclusions to the questions raised. Finally, Sweden does not go into much detail on these subjects in its statement. The Swedish position paper simply states that cyber operations would be considered as uses of force if they are "comparable to the scale and effects of kinetic use of force." Sweden adds that such assessments need to be made "on a case-by-case basis" (p 4). As such, variations in the level of specificity, focus and certainty illustrate some differences in each States emphasis and focus, but all in all the Nordics seem to strongly align on their views on the concept on the use of force in cyber space.

Similar differences in emphasis and focus can be found regarding other elements as well. For example, in discussions of the application of human rights norms in cyber space, Finland, Norway, and Sweden all include a separate human rights 'chapter' in their statement, where they discuss this area of law briefly. Finland emphasises, for example, that the rights of access to information and privacy are particularly important in the cyber domain (p 7), while Sweden emphasises the rights of "freedom of opinion, expression and information, freedom of association and assembly, and privacy" as being particularly relevant (p 8). Norway notes briefly that human rights law, including the rights of freedom of expression and privacy, applies to cyber activities (p 10). Denmark does not have a separate chapter on human rights in its statement but explains that "Denmark subscribes to the general view that also human rights obligations apply in cyberspace, but for the sake of brevity this paper does not elaborate further on that topic." (p 447).

In addition to these elements that represent largely common ground, but with variations on emphasis and focus, there are also a few elements where the national positions either differ quite clearly, or where statements of legal interpretations are made that do not necessarily align with the other Nordics states. An example of the latter is the Danish approach to countermeasures. Here, Denmark holds that, while the question on the legality of collective countermeasures has not been fully settled, Denmark is of the opinion that "there may be instances where one State suffers a violation of an obligation owed to the international community as a whole, and where the victim State may request the assistance of other States in applying proportionate and necessary countermeasures in collective response hereto." (p 454) The other three states note that injured states may employ countermeasures under certain conditions, but they do not take a position on the question on the legality of collective countermeasures.

Finally, an example of a specific point of disagreement can be found when comparing the Danish and Finish statement regarding the concept of digital 'objects' under international humanitarian law (a question also discussed in Chapter 7). The legal question here is whether the concept of 'objects' within this legal setting is to be understood as including or excluding (digital) data. Finland notes in this regard that "[c]onstant care shall be taken to ensure the protection of civilians and civilian objects, including essential civilian infrastructure, civilian services and civilian data." (p 7) Finland thus includes 'civilian data' in the concept of 'civilian objects'. Denmark, on the other hand, notes that "digital data cannot generally in and of itself be considered an object under IHL", although the destruction of data can lead to secondary effects that will constitute, for example, an attack under IHL (p 455). Neither Sweden nor Norway discusses this question in their statements – at least not explicitly – although Norway has expressed an opinion in its 2013 Norwegian Manual on the laws of war that resemble the Finish perspective (see discussion in Chapter 7).

In summary, while the Nordic countries share a strong foundation of agreement on the application of international law in cyberspace, their position papers reveal different national priorities and interpretations. These differences, however, mostly represent differences in emphasis and focus, and actual legal disagreements are relatively few and/or minor.

2 Academic Contributions

The second part of the volume features eight academic chapters that delve into some of the most pressing and unresolved issues in the interpretation and application of international law in cyberspace. These contributions reflect the cutting-edge scholarship presented at the Copenhagen conference and offer a range of perspectives on how international law can and should evolve to meet the challenges posed by the digital age.

In Chapter 6, "Virtual Groups and the Triggering of Armed Conflicts," Marie Thøgersen considers how/if virtual groups can trigger armed conflicts and thus the application of IHL. Thøgersen contends that the rise of non-State actors in cyberspace and the growing use of cyber operations in conflicts make regulating these actors an increasingly pressing concern. Specifically, the chapter analyses the organizational requirements in IHL's triggering provisions for non-State groups and identifies their underlying rationales. Thøgersen ultimately concludes that these provisions do not currently permit reinterpretation to accommodate the unique structures of virtual groups, thus making it difficult for such groups to trigger an armed conflict.

In Chapter 7, entitled 'Attacking Data: Moving beyond the Interpretative Quagmire of the 'Data as an Object'-debate', *Marc Schack & Katrine Lund-Hansen* explore a key contemporary IHL problem in regulating cyber operations: How to apply the law on 'attacks' under IHL when the target is neither a person nor a physical object in the traditional sense but rather purely (digital) data. Schack and Lund-Hansen consider the current state of this legal debate and explore ways of moving the debate forward. Thus, while critiquing the standard interpretative approach of either focusing on the 'ordinary meaning' of the term 'object', or on the 'object and purpose' of the rules, the authors argue that the debate could be advanced by adding an additional, contextual analysis. Doing so, the authors argue, would make it is possible to achieve a more coherent and meaningful outcome for this complex debate.

Pia Hüsch's contribution in Chapter 8, 'Non-Intervention Thresholds in Cyberspace – In the Shadow of the Sovereignty Debate?' explains that important questions about the functions and effects of the legal principle of non-intervention in the cyber domain have been overshadowed by debates about the application of the principle of sovereignty. On this basis, Hüsch takes the reader through the two parallel debates and considers how these have progressed. From here, Hüsch sets out the implications of the one-sided focus of the debate, noting for example that questions of the relevant legal thresholds have not been treated in the same level of detail by States, which could create problems as States begin to grapple more with the non-intervention principle. Given the need for clearer red lines, Hüsch emphasizes why Nordic states, in particular, should have an interest in advancing these discussions, and she notes that they could advance such interests either through more detailed state pronouncements on the matter, or through collective statements e.g., by the Nordic states.

Going somewhat in the other direction, *Peter Pijpers* argues, in his contribution in Chapter 9 entitled 'Careful What You Wish For: Tackling Legal Uncertainty in Cyberspace', that the increase in the number of State's expressions of legal opinions does not, as is commonly assumed, necessarily increase the level of legal certainty – rather it decreases it. Pijpers explains that while it is widely acknowledged that international law applies to cyberspace, there is an ongoing dispute about 'how' it applies, and the hope, he argues, that once we get more *opinio juris* and State practice, we will be able to clarify the rules, is ill-founded. Rather, Pijpers notes that the recent increase in the number of legal opinions has led to more differences and thus greater legal uncertainty, and that this may even result in a kind of legal asymmetry, where some States chose to comply with international law while others exploit the ambiguity to support their own strategic goals. Therefore, one should – as an international lawyer – in Peter Pijpers' words be 'careful what you wish for'.

Henning Lahmann argues in his Chapter 10 'The Plea of Necessity in Cyber Emergencies: Unresolved Doctrinal Questions' that while an increasing number of States recognize the plea of necessity in cyber emergencies, many important doctrinal questions remain underexplored. Lahmann focuses on three key issues: 1) the 'only way' requirement, 2) the non-contribution condition, and 3) the question of assistance by unaffected states in emergencies. He concludes that the necessity defence continues to present a range of problems in relation to all three of the issues considered. Specifically, Lahmann finds that it is still unclear, regarding the first requirement, if the dominant, strict understanding of the 'only way'-criterion could be softened, which makes reliance on the necessity defence difficult. On the non-contribution condition, he concludes that emerging norms obliging States to observe a certain standard of 'cyber hygiene' regarding domestic cyber infrastructures could influence legal assessments. Finally, in considering the question of assistance, Lahmann does not find clear guidance in the law. Thus, he notes several relevant policy perspectives and argues that it would be preferable if States would strive for more legal clarity.

In Chapter 11, entitled "Disinformation, Strategic Corruption, and International Law: The Indispensable Leadership by Nordic Countries in Combating Cyber-based Disinformation Campaigns Targeting Democratic Opinion-making", Kimberly Breedon and Christopher Bryant examines the role of disinformation in undermining democratic processes. The authors argue that the Nordic countries, with their strong democratic traditions and commitment to transparency, are uniquely positioned to lead international efforts to combat cyber-based disinformation.

In Chapter 12 on "The Human Rights and IHL Challenges of Private Military and Security Companies and Mercenaries in Cyberspace," Sorcha MacLeod and Daniel Wand explore the legal challenges posed by the increasing use of private military and security companies (PMSCs) and mercenaries in cyberspace. The chapter discusses the implications of these actors' involvement in cyber operations for both human rights and international humanitarian law, highlighting the need for clearer legal regulations and stronger oversight mechanisms.

Finally in Chapter 13, 'Cyber Espionage and the Nordics: Between Principles and Pragmatism', Asbjørn Thranov provides a detailed analysis of the legal and strategic challenges associated with cyber espionage, as viewed through the lens of Nordic legal pragmatism. Thranov discusses how the Nordic countries have approached the issue of cyber espionage, both in terms of national legislation and international cooperation. He considers how the Nordics have balanced the need for operational flexibility to conduct peacetime cyber espionage with the need to have normative guardrails for states' activities in cyberspace.

3 Conclusion

This edited volume represents a significant contribution to the ongoing debate on the international legal regulation of cyberspace from a Nordic perspective.

By bringing together official state positions and cutting-edge academic scholarship, the volume offers a comprehensive and nuanced understanding of the key legal challenges and opportunities in this rapidly evolving field.

As the digital domain continues to expand and cyber threats become increasingly sophisticated, the need for clear and effective international legal frameworks will only grow. The Nordic states, with their strong commitment to a rules-based international order, are well-positioned to lead these efforts. As such, this volume not only highlights the important contributions that the Nordic states have already made to the international legal regulation of cyberspace but also points the way forward for future engagement in this critical area.

Through the insights and analyses provided in this volume, readers will gain a deeper understanding of the complex legal landscape of cyberspace and the critical role that international law must play in ensuring security, stability, and justice in the digital age.

CHAPTER 2

Finland's views on International Law and Cyberspace

Marja Lehto

Introduction

In 2013, the Group of Governmental Experts (GGE) under the United Nations auspices reached agreement on the critical question that international law applies in cyberspace.[1] While this point of departure has since then been confirmed in successive reports of the GGE,[2] as well as by the Open-ended Working Group (OEWG) of the General Assembly,[3] further discussions on how international law applies in cyberspace, and where adjustments might be needed to accommodate the specific features of cyberspace, have proved challenging. The deadlock of the fifth GGE, which failed to adopt a report in 2017 because of fundamentally differing views on international law may have been decisive in triggering unilateral responses from individual States.[4] The

1 2013 Report of the Group of governmental experts on developments in the field of information and telecommunication in the context of international security (U.N. Doc. A/68/98).

2 2015 Report of the Group of governmental experts on developments in the field of information and telecommunication in the context of international security (U.N. Doc. A/70/174), para. 24; 2021 Report of the Group of governmental experts on developments in the field of information and telecommunication in the context of international security (U.N. Doc. A/76/135), para. 69.

3 Open-ended Working Group on developments in the field of information and telecommunication in the context of international security, Final Substantive Report (2021), (U.N.Doc. A/AC.290/2021/CRP.2), para. 34.

4 *See, for instance,* the national position papers of the United States (2016), available at https://cyberlaw.ccdcoe.org/wiki/National_position_of_the_United_States_of_America_(2016); United Kingdom (2018), available at https://www.gov.uk/government/speeches/cyber-and-international-law-in-the-21st-century and (2021), available at https://www.gov.uk/government/publications/application-of-international-law-to-states-conduct-in-cyberspace-uk-statement/application-of-international-law-to-states-conduct-in-cyberspace-uk-statement; The Netherlands (2019), available at https://cyberlaw.ccdcoe.org/wiki

 | DOI:10.1163/9789004703933_003

emerging practice of issuing national statements and position papers on international law and cyberspace has provided an alternative way to bring clarity to the contentious issues.

Finland's position paper that is reproduced below was issued in 2020 as a contribution to the ongoing debate.[5] As such, it comments on selected issues and does not provide a comprehensive compilation of Finland's legal views on cybersecurity. The limited scope of the paper reflects the mandate of the GGE, established by the General Assembly's First Committee, to address, *inter alia*, existing and emerging threats in cyberspace that may jeopardize international peace and security.[6] The paper confirms the applicability and essential role of international law in cyberspace, in line with the major GGE findings. It also comments on a number of topical issues such as sovereignty, State responsibility, prevention of transboundary harm, illegal intervention, use of force and armed attack, international humanitarian law and human rights law.

The position papers and statements issued so far, including the present one, share a lot of common substance, which is obvious as they generally have the same background and have been prepared by States belonging, in the context of the GGEs and the OEWG, to the Western 'like-minded' group. While the papers are consistent on most questions, there are also differences regarding how the legal limitations concerning State action in cyberspace are defined, most notably with regard to the legal nature of the principles of sovereignty and due diligence. These differences have given a further reason for Finland to articulate its own views in a public position paper.

/National_position_of_the_Netherlands_(2019); France (2019), available at https://documents.unoda.org/wp-content/uploads/2021/12/French-position-on-international-law-applied-to-cyberspace.pdf; New Zealand (2019), available at https://dpmc.govt.nz/publications/application-international-law-state-activity-cyberspace; Australia (2020), available at https://www.internationalcybertech.gov.au/our-work/annexes/annex-b; Israel (2020), available at https://cyberlaw.ccdcoe.org/wiki/National_position_of_Israel_(2020); Italy (2021), available at https://cyberlaw.ccdcoe.org/wiki/National_position_of_the_Italian_Republic_(2021); Estonia (2021), available at https://cyberlaw.ccdcoe.org/wiki/National_position_of_Estonia_(2021); Switzerland (2021), available at https://www.eda.admin.ch>eda>voelkerrecht.pdf; Poland (2022), available at https://www.gov.pl/web/diplomacy/the-republic-of-polands-position-on-the-application-of-international-law-in-cyberspace and Canada (2022), available at https://www.international.gc.ca/world-monde/issues_development-enjeux_developpement/peace_security-paix_securite/cyberspace_law-cyberespace_droit.aspx?lang=eng (all accessed on 27 February 2023). See also the position papers by Denmark, Norway and Sweden reproduced in the current issue of NJIL.

5 Also available at https://um.fi/documents/35732/0/Cyber+and+international+law%3B+Finland%27s+views.pdf/41404cbb-d300-a3b9-92e4-a7d675d5d585?t=1602758856859 (accessed on 27 February 2023). See also Michael Schmitt, 'Finland sets out key Positions on International Cyber Law', October 27, 2020, available at https://www.justsecurity.org/73061/finland-sets-out-key-positions-on-international-cyber-law/

6 *See, for instance*, A/RES/68/243, op. para. 4.

The statement that international law applies to State activities when they are using information and communication technologies may seem as little more than stating the obvious. While questions related to non-State actors increasingly occupy international lawyers and few would claim that States are the only subjects of international law, the one question that can be taken for granted is its applicability to State action. In spite of the self-evidence of the issue, the successive GGEs and the OEWG have so far not been able to clearly state, for instance, that international humanitarian law applies to the use of cyber means and methods of war in an armed conflict.[7] Whether this inability has something to do with the mystification of the concept of 'cyberspace', or rather reflects an attempt to circumscribe or put aside the existing rules, the debate has proved persistent. Finland's paper seeks, on its part, to make it clear that cyberspace is no lawless area.

For the reasons mentioned above, the issue of State sovereignty occupies a prominent place in the paper. Finland disagrees with the claim that no rights and obligations would flow from the principle of sovereignty as such, or that no rule prohibiting violations of sovereignty would have crystallized in respect of cyber activities. This contention seems to overlook the established status in international law of the rule that prohibits violations of sovereignty, confirmed both by State practice and international jurisprudence. Finland sees sovereignty as both a principle and a primary rule of international law, a breach of which amounts to an internationally wrongful act and triggers the wrongdoing State's international responsibility. Similarly, in response to the claim that there would be no legal obligation to exercise due diligence in cyberspace, the paper recalls "each State's obligation not to knowingly allow its territory to be used to harm the rights of other States" that the International Court of Justice called 'well-recognized' already in 1949.[8] According to the paper, the general principle of due diligence is applicable to any activity which involves the risk of causing significant transboundary harm.

The question of sovereignty as a rule or as a mere principle, and that of the binding nature of due diligence in cyberspace, are examples of legal disagreements that have important concrete implications. Should it be accepted that sovereignty cannot be violated, it would mean that there are no legal consequences for violations that fall below the notoriously high threshold of

---

7 See, however, Group of Governmental Experts on Advancing Responsible State Behaviour in Cyberspace in the Context of International Security, Final Report, 14 July 2021, U.N. Doc. A/73/135, para. 71(f), in which, referring to the principles of humanity, necessity, proportionality and distinction, "the group recognized the need to further study on how and when these principles apply to the use of ICTs by States".

8 *Corfu Channel case*, Judgment of April 9th, 1949: I.C.J. Reports 1949, P. 4, p. 22.

prohibited intervention in the internal affairs of a State. It is also not comprehensible that States would have no legal obligation to take efforts to ensure that cyber activities within their territory or jurisdiction do not seriously harm other States. It further seems politically unwise to question the applicability of such long-standing rules in cyberspace, as carving out a cyber-specific exception from their application may give credence to the claim that international law does not apply in cyberspace in the absence of specific regulation.

Two further questions addressed in the paper seem worth drawing attention to. First, regarding the use of force, like most if not all of the States that have pronounced on the issue, Finland agrees that for a cyberattack to be comparable to use of force, it must be sufficiently serious and have effects in the territory of the target State, or in areas within its jurisdiction, that are similar to those of the use of traditional armed force. To be equated to an armed attack, a cyberattack must further fulfil the requirements of scale and effects. The paper is open to the possibility that a cyberattack producing significant economic effects such as the collapse of a State's financial system or parts of its economy could possibly be comparable to an armed attack. Indeed, such a collapse would be likely to cause serious effects on the population.

In general, however, the paper underlines that any understanding of the use of force in cyberspace should respect the UN Charter, and not just the letter of the Charter but also its object and purpose, which is to prevent the escalation of armed activities. Particular issues concerning the use of force in cyberspace may need cyber-specific solutions but these should always be assessed in light of the more general understandings. It should also be kept in mind that many of the issues related to the use of force continue to be debated even in the physical, or kinetic context. The ILA Committee on the Use of Force, in its 2018 report, made a similar point stating that conclusions concerning cyber operations as a use of force "must be reached with great caution" because a wide interpretation of Articles 2(4) and 51 of the Charter in the cyber context "may affect the interpretation and debate surrounding other areas of the law of use of force".[9]

Second, regarding International Humanitarian Law (IHL), the paper does not only state that the use of cyber means and methods in the context of an armed conflict is subject to the rules of IHL, including the principles of distinction, proportionality and precautions, but also underlines that the foreseeable direct and indirect effects of cyber means and methods must be taken into account when assessing their capacity to cause prohibited harm. The paper

9 International Law Association, Sydney Conference (2018), Final Report on Aggression and the Use of Force, p. 26.

also takes a stand in favor of including data within the concept of object for the purposes of IHL in stating that there is an obligation to take constant care "to ensure the protection of civilians and civilian objects, including essential civilian infrastructure, civilian services and civilian data".

Since 2020, new questions have arisen in the ongoing exchange of views, both as regards the national statements and within the two UN working groups. Peaceful settlement of disputes is one of such new themes and one that would most likely have been addressed in Finland's paper, had it been issued later.[10] Indeed, if States abided by the fundamental Charter-based and customary obligation to settle their disputes peacefully and in a manner that does not endanger international peace and security, less attention would need to be paid to the intricacies of prohibited intervention, use of force, armed attack and application of IHL in cyberspace.

May, 2023

International Law and Cyberspace Finland's National Positions

Introduction

In line with its general support to rules-based international cooperation and respect for international law, Finland sees international law as an essential framework for responsible State behaviour in cyberspace. In the same vein, the UN Group of Governmental Experts (GGE) has reaffirmed that "international law, and in particular the Charter of the United Nations, is applicable and is essential to maintaining peace and stability and promoting an open, secure, stable, accessible and peaceful ICT environment".[1] As this formulation, reflecting the specific mandate of the GGE, focuses on questions of international

10 See the statement of the delegations of Finland and Sweden in the OEWG in March 2021, available at https://reachingcriticalwill.org/images/documents/Disarmament-fora/other/icts/oewg/statements/9March_FinlandSweden.pdf (accessed on 27 February 2023).

1 See Group of Governmental Experts on Developments in the Field of Information and Telecommunications in the Context of International Security, 2013 Report (UN Doc. A/68/98, para.20; 2015 report (UN Doc. A/70/174), para.

peace and security, there is reason to underline that the same applies to other rights and obligations of States, whether based on treaty law or customary international law.

While the existing rules and principles of international law are applicable in cyberspace, the application of certain provisions may give rise to practical problems due to the specific characteristics of cyberspace. Finland therefore welcomes the current exchange of views on particular questions regarding how international law applies to State use of information and communication technologies and wishes to contribute to the discussion by commenting on some of the issues that have been raised recently in this regard.

Sovereignty

It is undisputed that the principle of State sovereignty applies in cyberspace. While cyberspace as a whole cannot be subject to appropriation by any State, each State has jurisdiction over the cyber infrastructure and the persons engaged in cyber activities within its territory.[2] Sovereignty confers each State the exclusive right to exercise the functions of a State within a certain territory,[3] and protects its territorial integrity and political independence from interference by other States.[4] In this sense, sovereignty is a foundational principle of the international legal order.

The principle of State sovereignty has also given rise to a number of specific rules, such as those prohibiting the use of force and intervention in the internal affairs of other States. Below the threshold of prohibited intervention, all States have an obligation to refrain from acts that violate the territorial integrity or political independence of other States.

The International Court of Justice has consistently confirmed that it is a duty of every State to respect the territorial sovereignty of others. This applies

---

2 The Group of Governmental Experts has stated in this regard that "State sovereignty and international norms and principles that flow from sovereignty apply to State conduct of ICT-related and to their jurisdiction over ICT infrastructure within their territory". See GGE 2015 Report, para. 27. Other bases of jurisdiction may be applicable to cyber activities in accordance with international law.

3 As Judge Max Huber stated in the *Island of Palmas* arbitral award: "Sovereignty in the relations between States signifies independence. Independence in regard to a portion of the globe is the right to exercise therein, to the exclusion of any other State, the functions of a State." See *Island of Palmas (Netherlands v. the US)*, 2 UNRIAA 829, 838 (PCA 1928).

4 According to the International Court of Justice, "between independent States, respect for territorial sovereignty is an essential foundation of international relations." See *Corfu Channel Case (UK v. Albania)*, ICJ reports 1949, p. 4, at 35.

to unauthorized intrusions to physical spaces such as overflight of a State's territory by an aircraft belonging to another State or under its control,[5] penetration of territorial waters by foreign warships,[6] conducting of certain activities in another State's territory without its consent[7] but also to producing effects in another State's territory without physical intrusion.[8] According to the Court, it is "quite obvious that a State possesses a legal interest in the protection of its territory from **any form** of external harmful action".[9]

Similarly, a non-consensual intrusion in the computer networks and systems that rely on the cyber infrastructure in another State's territory may amount to a violation of that State's sovereignty. The prohibition of cyber operations violating the territorial sovereignty of another State protects, first of all, the cyber infrastructure located in the territory of that State, or otherwise under its jurisdiction, as well as computer networks and systems supported by such infrastructure, from material harm. The situation is the same irrespective of whether such infrastructure belongs to or is operated by governmental institutions, private entities or private individuals. In addition to material harm that may be caused by such an operation, other relevant considerations include whether an intrusion in the cyber infrastructure triggers a loss of functionality of the equipment relying on it, or modifies or deletes information belonging to the target State, or to private actors in its territory.

More generally, an unauthorized intrusion by cyber means may be seen as a violation of the target State's territorial sovereignty if it interferes with data or services that are necessary for the exercise of inherently governmental functions. This rule put forward in the Tallinn Manual 2.0[10] is consistent with the understanding of violations of sovereignty as unauthorized exercise of authority in another State's territory. Finally, cyber operations against objects that enjoy sovereign immunity (warships, ships owned by a State and used only for government or noncommercial service; State aircraft) can be characterized as violations of sovereignty.[11]

---

5 *Military and Paramilitary Activities in and against Nicaragua (Nicaragua v. United States of America)*, Merits, Judgment, I.C.J. Reports 1986, p. 14, paras. 251, 253, 292.

6 *Corfu Channel case (United Kingdom v. Albania), Judgment, I.C.J. Reports 1949, p. 4,* at 26, 35, 36.

7 *Certain Activities carried out by Nicaragua in the Border Area (Costa Rica v. Nicaragua) and Construction of a Road in Costa Rica along the San Juan River (Nicaragua v. Costa Rica)*, Judgment, I.C.J. Reports 2015, p. 665, paras. 67, 69, 93, 221-223 and 229.

8 *Nuclear Tests (Australia v. France)*, Judgment, I.C.J. Reports 1974, p. 253, para. 454.

9 *Ibid.* para 456, emphasis added.

10 Michael N. Schmitt (ed.), *Tallinn Manual 2.0*, Cambridge University Press 2017, Rule 4, para. 15.

11 Cf. *Ibid.*, Rule 5.

The argument has been raised recently that no legal consequences could be attached to sovereignty as a general principle, at least for the purposes of cyber activities. It is not only difficult to reconcile such an idea with the established status of the rule prohibiting violations of sovereignty in international law but it also gives rise to policy concerns. Agreeing that a hostile cyber operation below the threshold of prohibited intervention cannot amount to an internationally wrongful act would leave such operations unregulated and deprive the target State of an important opportunity to claim its rights.

Finland sees sovereignty as a primary rule of international law, a breach of which amounts to an internationally wrongful act and triggers State responsibility. This rule is fully applicable in cyberspace. Whether an unauthorized cyber intrusion violates the target State's sovereignty depends on its nature and consequences and is subject to a case-by-case assessment.

Illegal intervention

A hostile interference by cyber means may also breach the customary prohibition of intervention in the internal affairs of another State, provided that it is done with the purpose of compelling or coercing that State in relation to affairs regarding which it has free choice (so-called *domaine réservé*). The requirement of coercion leaves out lesser forms of influence and persuasion that are commonplace in international relations. The limitation to sovereign affairs – such as a State's political, economic or cultural system or the direction of its foreign policy[12]– further distinguishes prohibited intervention from measures, the purpose of which is to compel another State to comply with its international obligations.

For a cyber operation to amount to a prohibited intervention, both above-mentioned elements must be present. Most open questions relate to the element of coercion and to how it manifests itself in cyber operations. For instance, while the conduct of elections belongs undisputedly to the internal affairs of each State, all methods of electoral interference do not display the element of coercion.[13] Hacking of voter databases or manipulation of vote counts in order to alter the election results has nevertheless been recognized as a fairly clear case. To be comparable to a real world intervention, cyber interference must also be of a serious nature.

12 *Military and Paramilitary Activities in and against Nicaragua*, para. 205.

13 All methods of electoral interference are not coercive, see EU vs. disinfo, 10 *Methods of electoral interference* (2019).

According to the International Court of Justice, the element of coercion is particularly clear if force is used through means of military action, threats of such action, or through support to armed groups in another State.[14] Military or economic pressure may also qualify as coercion. Hostile cyber interference done with the purpose of promoting or supporting armed action in another State could constitute an example of prohibited intervention, provided that it seeks to force a certain policy change.[15]

Compared to a violation of sovereignty, the requirement of coercive nature and that of *domaine réservé* make the threshold of prohibited intervention considerably higher. This underlines the importance of continued understanding of sovereignty as not only a principle but also an independent primary rule of international law.

Transboundary harm

Another cardinal principle flowing from sovereignty, closely related to the obligation to respect the sovereignty of other States, is each State's obligation not to knowingly allow its territory to be used to cause significant harm to the rights of other States. It is widely recognized that this principle, often referred to as due diligence, is applicable to any activity which involves the risk of causing significant transboundary harm.[16] Due diligence is a variable standard in the sense that its content can change over time as a result of technological development or changes in risk assessment,[17] and as such fully applicable to cyber operations.

States may thus not knowingly allow their territory, or cyber infrastructure within a territory under their control, to be used to cyber operations that

---

14 *Military and Paramilitary Activities in and against Nicaragua*, para.247.

15 *Ibid.*, see also paras 241 and 242. See also Friendly Relations Declaration, UN Doc. A/RES/2625(XXV).

16 International Law Commission, Draft Articles on the *Prevention of transboundary harm from hazardous activities*, art. 3: "The State of origin shall take all appropriate measures to prevent significant transboundary harm or at any event to minimize the risk thereof", *Yearbook*... 2001, vol. II (Part Two), pp. 144–170; International Law Association, Second Report on Due Diligence in International Law, July 2016, p. 6: "This broad principle of due diligence can be understood as underlying more specific rules of due diligence. Hence, it can be viewed as a default standard that is triggered in operation if no more specific elaboration of due diligence or stricter standard is in existence."

17 International Tribunal for the Law of the Sea, Seabed Disputes Chamber, *Responsibilities and Obligations of States Sponsoring Persons and Entities with Respect to Activities in the Area*, Advisory opinion, 1 February 2011, List of Cases: No. 17, para. 117.

produce serious adverse consequences for other States. While only States can violate sovereignty, the sovereignty-based obligation of due diligence extends to private activities taking place in a State's territory. Significant harm caused to other States by private cyber activities may give rise to a State's international responsibility but only if the State in question has breached its due diligence obligations.

Some legal obligations are inherent in the principle of due diligence and apply to cyber activities even in the absence of cyber-specific elaborations of the principle. For instance, if a State knows about a planned cyber activity in its territory likely to affect another State adversely and seriously, it must notify that other State. In addition to actual knowledge of harmful acts emanating from the territory of a State, a State's responsibility may be engaged in situations in which it should have known about the activities in question. It is nevertheless clear that "it cannot be concluded from the mere fact of the control exercised [...] over its territory [...] that [a] State necessarily knew, or ought to have known, of any unlawful act perpetrated therein".[18]

If harmful cyber activity takes place and causes serious harm to another State, the State of origin must take appropriate action to terminate it, as well as to investigate the incident and bring those responsible to justice. In order to be able to do this, States should have the necessary procedural and legal mechanisms in place. It should nevertheless be recalled that due diligence is an obligation of conduct, not one of result. In general, what is required of States is that they take all measures that are feasible under the circumstances. A particular question in this regard is related to the position of transit States through which a particular harmful data is routed. Much depends on whether such a State has any knowledge of the ongoing operation, or ability to take feasible measures to terminate it.

Furthermore, while States must show due diligence in the control of the national territory, doing so does not release them from the observance of other international obligations such as those related to human rights.

State responsibility

The law of State responsibility consists of secondary rules that apply generally in the absence of clear specific rules that modify their effect. As there is no specific regulation concerning State activities in cyberspace that would constitute

18 International Court of Justice, *Corfu Channel case*, Judgment of April 9th, 1949, I.C.J. Reports 1949, p.4, at 18.

such *lex specialis*, it can be concluded that the normal rules of State responsibility apply in cyberspace.

When a State's cyber operation violates its obligations under international law, it constitutes an internationally wrongful act. An internationally wrongful act of a State entails its international responsibility and gives rise to an obligation to make full reparation for the damage that may be caused by the act.[19] This requires that the act is attributable to the State. The rules of attribution reflected in the UN International Law Commission's Articles on State Responsibility[20] remain fully valid in cyberspace. If State organs, or private groups or individuals acting on behalf of the State, can be identified as the authors of a cyber operation that violates the State's international obligations, its international responsibility is engaged. It is in this regard useful to distinguish identification as a technical operation from attribution as a legal operation. Identification may be technically challenging given the often covert nature of hostile cyber activities but this is without consequence to the legal rules of attribution.

An internationally wrongful act may justify recourse to countermeasures by the injured State if the State responsible for an internationally wrongful act declines to cease the wrongful conduct or pay reparation. Countermeasures may only be taken with the purpose of ensuring compliance, not for retaliation. Countermeasures may furthermore not breach the prohibition of the threat or use of force, or other peremptory norms of general international law, and must be consistent with other customary law requirements and limitations concerning countermeasures, most of which are reflected in the International Law Commission's Articles on State Responsibility.[21] Some of the procedural requirements concerning countermeasures may nevertheless require adjustment. For instance, it may be possible to attribute a hostile cyber operation only afterwards whereas countermeasures normally should be taken while the wrongful act is ongoing.

There is no general obligation for a State taking countermeasures to disclose the information on the basis of which the action is taken. At the same time, it is in each State's best interests to ensure that a decision to take countermeasures is based on solid evidence, given that recourse to countermeasures would otherwise constitute an internationally wrongful act. A State that responds to a hostile cyber operation must therefore have adequate proof of the source

---

19 International Law Commission, *Responsibility of States for Internationally Wrongful Acts* (2001), available at www.legal.un.org/ILC (ARSIWA).

20 *Ibid.*, arts. 4–11.

21 *Ibid.*, arts. 49–54.

of the operation and convincing evidence of the responsibility of a particular State.

Public attribution, as a sovereign choice, is primarily a question of political consideration. Public attribution may nevertheless have legal effects to the extent it includes determinations of conduct that constitutes an internationally wrongful act.

In addition to countermeasures, other circumstances precluding wrongfulness may justify taking of cyber measures that would otherwise constitute an internationally wrongful act.[22] This may be the case, for instance, if deviating from an international obligation is the only way for the State to safeguard an essential interest against a grave and imminent peril. Facing such an exceptional situation, a State may deviate from its international obligations within the limits specified in the law of State responsibility.[23]

Use of force/ armed attack

While there is currently no established definition of a cyberattack that would pass the threshold of "use of force" in the sense of article 2(4) of the UN Charter, or "armed attack" in the sense of article 51, it is widely recognized that such a qualification depends on the consequences of a cyberattack. For a cyberattack to be comparable to use of force, it must be sufficiently serious and have impacts in the territory of the target State, or in areas within its jurisdiction, that are similar to those of the use of force. A threat of such a cyberattack could also violate Article 2(4) of the Charter, if the threat is sufficiently precise and directed against another State.

Similarly, most commentators agree that when the scale and effects of a cyberattack correspond to those of an armed attack responding to the cyberattack is justifiable as self-defence. It is obvious that the attack must have caused death, injury or substantial material damage, but it is impossible to set a precise quantitative threshold for the effects, and other circumstantial factors must be taken into account in the analysis, as well. A widely discussed question is, to what extent the definition of a cyberattack comparable to an armed attack should take account of the indirect and long-term impacts of the attack. In any case, this would require that the impacts can be assessed with sufficient precision. A question has also been raised, whether a cyberattack producing significant economic effects such as the collapse of a State's financial system

22 ARSIWA, Chapter V, Circumstances precluding wrongfulness.

23 Ibid., art. 25. See also Tallinn Manual 2.0, Rule 26.

or parts of its economy should be equated to an armed attack. This question merits further consideration.

Any interpretation of the use of force in cyberspace should respect the UN Charter and not just the letter of the Charter but also its object and purpose, which is to prevent the escalation of armed activities. This would mean, for instance, that the distinction between armed attack as a particularly serious violation of the Charter, on the one hand, and any lesser uses of force, on the other, is preserved. Similarly, the conditions for the exercise of the right of self-defence apply in cyberspace as they do with regard to the use of armed force. The right of self-defence arises if a cyberattack comparable to an armed attack occurs and can be attributed to a particular State.[24] It is reasonable to think that a State victim to such an attack can respond with either cyber means or armed action. At the same time, the use of force must not be disproportionate or excessive.

International Humanitarian Law

International humanitarian law only applies to cyber operations when such operations are part of, or amount to, an armed conflict. Most so far known cyberattacks have not been launched in the context of an armed conflict or have met the threshold of armed conflict.At the same time, when cyber means are used in the context of a pre-existing armed conflict, as has been done in many current conflicts, there is no reason to deny the need for the protections that international humanitarian law provides.

This includes that cyber means and methods of warfare must be used consistently with the principles of distinction, proportionality and precautions, as well as the specific rules flowing from these principles. When assessing the capacity of cyber means and methods to cause prohibited harm, their foreseeable direct and indirect effects shall be taken into account. Constant care shall be taken to ensure the protection of civilians and civilian objects, including essential civilian infrastructure, civilian services and civilian data.

The unique characteristics of cyberspace, such as interconnectedness and anonymity, may affect how international humanitarian law is interpreted and applied with regard to certain cyber means and methods warfare.The related problems can nevertheless mostly be solved on the basis of existing rules. New

24 While the possibility of a cyberattack rising to the level of an armed attack without the involvement of any State is conceivable, the related questions of self-defence against non-State actors are too complicated to be discussed here.

technologies do not render the existing rules of international humanitarian law meaningless or necessarily require new legal regulation. Furthermore, while international humanitarian law is *lex specialis* in an armed conflict, it does not override other areas of international law,such as human rights law, which may continue to apply throughout the conflict.

Human rights law

A number of specific human rights such as the freedom of opinion and expression,including the right to access to information, and the right to privacy are particularly relevant in cyberspace.It should nevertheless be underlined that individuals enjoy the same international human rights with respect to cyber-related activities as otherwise and, accordingly, that States are bound by all their human rights obligations both online and offline. Furthermore,each State has to protect individuals within its territory and subject to its jurisdiction from interference with their rights by third parties.

Note from the publisher

The author mentioned at the start of this chapter, Marja Lehto, is only responsible for the introduction to this position paper. The position paper is a product of the government of Finland and available online: https://um.fi/documents/35732/0/Cyber+and+international+law%3B+Finland%27s+views.pdf/41404cbb-d300-a3b9-92e4-a7d675d5d585?t=1602758856859.

CHAPTER 3

Norway's Position Paper on International Law and Cyberspace

Vibeke Musæus

Introduction

Existing international law applies in cyberspace. There is a simple reason for that. International law regulates the conduct of states. Insofar as that conduct takes place in cyberspace, it may, just as conduct taking place in other domains of this world, be subject to international legal obligations. The application of international law in cyberspace was first recognised by the UN Group of Governmental Experts (GGE) in 2013,[1]and has been reconfirmed in subsequent consensus reports by the GGEs in 2015[2] and 2021,[3] and by the UN Open-ended Working Group (OEWG) in 2021.[4] The reports have been adopted by the UN General Assembly, and are thus supported by all UN member States.

It is important to be clear about this point, especially because certain States continue to argue that we need a new legally binding instrument to regulate State activity in cyberspace. In the view of Norway and likeminded States, there is no need for a new convention on cyber security to set out the rights and obligations of States in respect of activities in cyberspace. What is needed is an

1 2013 Report of the Group of Governmental Experts on Developments in the Field of Information and Telecommunications in the Context of International Security, (UN Doc. A/68/98).

2 2015 Report of the Group of Governmental Experts on Developments in the Field of Information and Telecommunications in the Context of International Security, (UN Doc. A/70/174).

3 2021 Report of the Group of Governmental Experts on Advancing Responsible State Behaviour in Cyberspace in the Context of International Security, (UN Doc. A/76/135).

4 2021 Report of the Open-ended working group on developments in the field of information and telecommunications in the context of international security, (UN Doc. A/AC.290/2021 /CRP.2).

 | DOI:10.1163/9789004703933_004

enhanced common understanding of *how* existing international law applies to cyberspace. And that is the issue on the international agenda today, in line with the mandate of the current OEWG (2021-2025).[5]

States should therefore develop and publish national positions on how they interpret the rules of international law as applied to state conduct in cyberspace. Only States are in a position to clarify any potential grey zones through their cyber practices and by expressing what they consider to be their rights and obligations vis-à-vis other States (*opinio juris*). The development of national positions is therefore also essential for meaningful engagement at multilateral level.

Only 4-5 years ago, very few States had publicly expressed their views on how international law applies in cyberspace. The situation has now changed. Position papers from fifteen States were annexed to the final report of the latest GGE.[6] And more position papers have followed. NATO has also contributed through political declarations setting out the common understanding of its (then) 30 allies. In addition, national statements from a broad range of States have been issued and made publicly available in connection with the previous and the current OEWG.

Norway published its position paper in May 2021 as part of the participation by a Norwegian expert in the GGE, and as a contribution to an enhanced common understanding among States.[7] The position paper was developed in cooperation between the Ministry of Foreign Affairs, the Ministry of Justice, the Ministry of Defence and the security services. As the title indicates, it sets out Norway's views on selected questions of international law relating to cyberspace. It was written in the context of international security, which was the focus of the parallel GGE and OEWG processes. It reflects the international legal debate, and has a particular focus on when a cyber operation is in violation of State sovereignty, the prohibition of intervention, and the prohibition on the use of force. It addresses State responsibility and the question of attribution of conduct to a State under international law, the obligation of due diligence and the response measures a targeted State is entitled to use under international law. Finally, it contains positions on the application of international humanitarian law, and on human rights in cyberspace. In order to

5 *See* UN Doc. A/RES/75/240, para. 1.

6 Official compendium of voluntary national contributions on the subject of how international law applies to the use of information and communications technologies by States submitted by participating governmental experts in the Group of Governmental Experts on Advancing Responsible State Behaviour in Cyberspace in the Context of International Security established pursuant to General Assembly resolution 73/266, (UN Doc. A/76/136).

7 Also available at https://www.regjeringen.no/contentassets/a8911fc020c94eb386a1ec7917bf0d03/norwegian_positions.pdf

make the paper easier to read and understand, it highlights key messages and includes practical examples.

Certain issues need particular emphasis, and State sovereignty is one of them. The obligation to respect other States' sovereignty is probably the rule of international law most likely to be violated by a State's cyber operations. It therefore generated debate when it was claimed that no rule prohibiting violations of sovereignty could be extrapolated from the principle of sovereignty in the context of cyberspace. In line with an increasing number of states, Norway has therefore considered it important to make it clear that in its view, sovereignty is both a principle and a primary rule of international law that is applicable in cyberspace. This in turn means that a breach of the rule amounts to an internationally wrongful act, and if attributable to a State, may also give rise to State responsibility. To argue otherwise would mean that State activity normally considered to be in violation of sovereignty, may have to come under the definition of a prohibited intervention or even a prohibited use of force to be in violation of international law in a cyber context. If the State activity does not amount to an intervention or a use of force, it would also preclude the use of countermeasures by the injured state, since such measures may only be taken in response to an internationally wrongful act.

Unlike most States that have addressed sovereignty, Norway has also expressly recognised that States can violate sovereignty in two ways. First, on the basis of territoriality, and second on the basis of interference with or usurpation of the inherently governmental functions of another State. As regards the latter, the paper makes clear that there is no requirement for there to be physical damage, injury, or loss of functionality. Whether or not a violation has occurred must be determined by a case-by-case assessment.

As a consequence of the right to exercise sovereignty over cyber infrastructure located on their territory, States also have a corresponding obligation not to knowingly allow their territory to be used for cyber operations that target third States, known as the obligation to exercise due diligence. This obligation is particularly relevant in a cyber context, and could to some extent compensate for the difficulties of attributing cyber operations to specific States. Similarly, since certain otherwise likeminded States have been unwilling to categorise due diligence as a legal obligation, Norway has considered it important to express its own view clearly: that there is a customary international law obligation to exercise due diligence, which also applies in cyberspace.

As regards international humanitarian law (IHL), Norway states clearly that it applies to cyber operations in connection with an armed conflict.

The reluctance of certain States to recognise the applicability of IHL to state conduct in cyberspace in the event of an armed conflict has had an effect on both the GGE and the OEWG processes, and was one of the main reasons why the GGE failed to adopt a consensus report in 2017. However, agreement on an explicit reference to the applicability of IHL as such, and not only to the fundamental principles of IHL, was reached in the 2021 GGE report [8] and reiterated in the first annual progress report of the current OEWG in 2022.[9] Now that consensus has been reached on the basics, there is an urgent need to discuss further *how* IHL applies to cyber operations. For instance, a common understanding should be sought as to whether digital data enjoys legal protection against damage and destruction similar to that afforded to physical objects. Strengthening a common understanding of the law would also weaken certain States' narrative that there is a need for a new cyber-specific convention.

Finally, State responsibility and the issue of attribution is another important topic that may be highlighted. Unsurprisingly, it is controversial at the multilateral level, and particularly sensitive for states that are known to use cyber operations in violation of international law. For the same reason, it is also often presented as complex and unclear, without there necessarily being any intention to engage constructively in order to bring the discussions forward. In Norway's view, and as clearly stated in the paper, the general rules on State responsibility under international law apply to cyber operations just as they apply to other activities by States. It may be technically challenging to establish the facts of a case, for instance whether a relationship between a State and a non-State actor amounts to direct instructions, direction or effective control. However, this is a question of obtaining the evidence, and not of a lack of clarity in international law.

International law is the foundation for peaceful co-existence. Upholding the international legal order is in the interest of all States. This applies to all areas of interstate relations, and cyberspace is no exception. An alleged need for a new cyber convention cannot be used as justification for non-compliance with existing international law. The Nordic countries, like all UN member states, should therefore continue to develop and share their interpretations (*opinio juris*) of how existing international law applies to practical situations in a cyber context, in order to promote common understanding. This is also capacity building in practice.

May, 2023

8 UN Doc. A/76/135, *Supra note* 3, para. 71(f).

9 The first annual progress report of the open-ended working group on security of and in the use of information and communications technologies 2021-2025 OEWG, (UN Doc. A/77/275) p. 10, para. 15(b)(ii).

Norwegian Positions on Selected Questions of International Law relating to Cyberspace May 2021

1 Introduction

International law applies in cyberspace. This has been recognised by the international community. The 2012-2013 United Nations Group of Governmental Experts (GGE)[1] concluded as much in its consensus report, and wrote as follows:

> International law, and in particular the Charter of the United Nations, is applicable and is essential to maintaining peace and stability and promoting an open, secure, peaceful and accessible ICT environment.[2]

This was reconfirmed in the subsequent consensus report by the 2015 GGE, which also underscored that the UN Charter applies in its entirety.[3] The UN General Assembly welcomed the 2015 report of the GGE in its resolution 70/237 and called upon Member States to be 'guided in their use of information and communications technologies' by the report.

In the Final Substantive Report of the Open-ended Working Group on developments in the field of information and telecommunications in the context of international security (OEWG), all UN Member States reaffirmed the conclusions of previous GGEs that international law applies in cyberspace.[4] Moreover, the report called upon States 'to avoid and refrain from taking any measures not in accordance with international law, and in particular the Charter of the United Nations.' The report also concluded that 'further common understandings need to be developed on how international law applies to State use of ICTs.'

Compliance with international law is fundamental for preserving international peace and security in cyberspace. In this paper, Norway sets out its views on the concrete application of certain rules of international law to State conduct in cyberspace, including practical examples, to contribute to a common understanding among States.

---

1 UN Group of Governmental Experts (UN GGE) on Developments in the Field of Information and Telecommunications in the Context of International Security.

2 See UN Doc., 24 June 2013, A/68/98*, para. 19.

3 See UN Doc., 22 July 2015, A/70/174.

4 See UN Doc., 12 March 2021, A/AC.290/2021/CRP.2 para. 34.

The focus of this paper is on cyber activity that threatens international peace and security, and on issues of State sovereignty. However, numerous bilateral and multilateral treaties are also binding on States, and cyber activity perpetrated by or attributable to a State also has the potential to violate such obligations.

2 The Application of International Law in Cyberspace

> *Key message*:
> *International law applies in cyberspace.*

Existing international law, that is customary international law and international treaties, has not been developed with cyberspace in mind. However, the application of the rules of international law to new areas, for example in response to technological developments, is nothing new. If the law in certain areas is perceived as unclear when applied to activities in cyberspace, this must be resolved in the usual way through interpretation. This applies both to general international law, for instance the rules that relate to sovereignty and state responsibility, and to the specialised regimes of international law, such as international human rights law and international humanitarian law.

Norway is of the view that there is no need for specific legal instruments to set out rights and obligations of States in respect of activities in cyberspace.

3 Cyber Operations in Violation of International Law

> *Key message:*
> *One of the conditions for holding a State internationally responsible for a cyber operation is that the operation, or the failure to react against the operation, constitutes a breach of an international obligation of the State.*

Cyber operations can vary widely in scope and intensity, from minor digital disruptions to armed attacks on a State. One of the conditions for holding a State internationally responsible for a cyber operation is that the operation, or the failure to react against the operation, constitutes a breach of an international obligation of the State.[14] The obligation in question may follow from customary international law or be treaty-based. A cyber operation is thus not unlawful *per se* but may become so when carried out to the detriment of the rights of other States.

In the following, Norway gives its interpretation of certain obligations of international law as they apply to cyber operations.[15] The focus in Section 3 is on sovereignty, non-intervention and the prohibition on the use of force. The question of attribution of conduct to a State, which is the other condition for holding a State internationally responsible for a cyber operation, is dealt with in Section 4 (*State responsibility*). The measures a targeted State is entitled to use in response under international law are dealt with in Section 5 (*Response measures*). Section 6 discusses international humanitarian law as it applies to cyber operations in armed conflict, and Section 7 deals with the application of international human rights obligations in cyberspace.

3.1 *Sovereignty*

Key message:
Sovereignty is not just a principle, but also a primary rule of international law.
A State must not conduct cyber operations that violate another State's sovereignty.
Whether a cyber operation violates the target State's sovereignty depends on the nature of the operation, the scale of the intrusion and its consequences, and must be assessed on a case-by-case basis.

The principle of sovereignty is one of the fundamental principles of international law and applies in cyberspace.[16] It refers to the supreme authority of

14 This is set out as one of two conditions in Article 2 of the International Law Commission's Articles on State Responsibility (ILC ASR). The Article is considered to express customary international law.

15 This position paper does not contain any specific analysis of cyber espionage, that is cyber operations whose purpose and effect is limited to the mere collection of information for use by the authorities, which is not in itself illegal under international law. However, certain aspects of such intelligence operations could violate specific rules of international law.

16 *Island of Palmas case* (*USA v Netherlands*), arbitral award, 4 April 1928: '*Sovereignty in the relations between States signifies independence. Independence in regard to a portion of the*

every State within its territory to the exclusion of other States, and also in its relations with other States.

The internal dimension of a State's sovereignty includes the exclusive right to exercise jurisdiction within its territory, including over the information systems located on its territory, and to exercise independent State powers. The external dimension includes the right of the State to decide its foreign policy and to enter into international agreements. Both dimensions of sovereignty apply in cyberspace, subject only to obligations under international law.

Norway is of the view that sovereignty constitutes both an international law *principle* from which various rules derive, such as the prohibition of intervention and the prohibition of the use of force, and a primary *rule* in its own right capable of being violated.[17] Thus, cyber operations that do not amount to a prohibited intervention or a prohibited use of force may nevertheless amount to a violation of a State's sovereignty under international law.

The International Court of Justice (ICJ) has consistently held that States have an obligation to respect the territorial integrity and political independence of other States as a matter of international law. In a cyber context this means that a State must not conduct cyber operations that violate another State's sovereignty.

A cyber operation that manifests itself on another State's territory may, depending on its nature, the scale of the intrusion and its consequences, constitute a violation of sovereignty.

Causing physical damage by cyber means on another State's territory may easily qualify as a violation of territorial sovereignty. For example, a cyber operation against an industrial control system at a petrochemical plant that led to a malfunction and a subsequent fire would constitute a violation of the State's territorial sovereignty. In addition to physical damage, causing cyber infrastructure to lose functionality may also be taken into consideration and may amount to a violation. This includes the use of crypto viruses to encrypt data and thus render them unusable for a substantial period of time.

The principle of sovereignty encompasses cyber infrastructure located in a State's territory irrespective of whether it is governmental or private.

---

globe is the right to exercise therein, to the exclusion of any other State, the functions of a State', p. 838.

17 *Military and Paramilitary Activities in and against Nicaragua (Nicaragua v. United States of America), 'Nicaragua case'*, International Court of Justice (ICJ), judgment 27 June 1986, paras. 15, 212-213 and 292.

Similarly, a cyber operation that interferes with or usurps the inherently governmental functions of another State may constitute a violation of sovereignty.[18]

This is based on the premise that a State enjoys the exclusive right to exercise within its territory, 'to the exclusion of any other State, the functions of a State'.[19] Accordingly, what matters is not whether physical damage, injury, or loss of functionality has resulted, but whether the cyber operation has interfered with data or services that are necessary for the exercise of inherently governmental functions. Cases in point would include altering or deleting data or blocking digital communication between public bodies and citizens so as to interfere with the delivery of social services, the conduct of elections, the collection of taxes, or the performance of key national defence activities. Another example could be the manipulation of police communications so that patrol cars are unable to communicate with police dispatch/operation centres. In this context it is irrelevant whether the inherently governmental function is performed by central, regional or local governments and authorities, or by non-governmental bodies in the exercise of powers delegated by such governments or authorities. Conducting elections is a clear example of an inherently governmental function. In contrast to the case of a cyber operation in breach of the prohibition of intervention, there is no requirement for the interference to reach to the level of coercion.

The precise threshold of what constitute a cyber operation in violation of sovereignty is not settled in international law, and will depend on a case-by-case assessment.

3.2 *The Prohibition of Intervention*

> *Key message:*
> *Cyber operations that compel the target State to take a course of action, whether by act or omission, in a way that it would not otherwise voluntarily have pursued (coercion) in matters relating to its internal or external affairs (domaine réservé), will constitute an intervention in violation of international law.*

18 See Tallinn Manual 2.0, commentary to Rule 4, p. 21-22, paras. 15-16.

19 *Island of Palmas* arbitral award, p. 838.

The prohibition of intervention applies to a State's cyber operations as it does to other State activities.[20] Accordingly, a State must not carry out cyber operations in breach of the prohibition of intervention, according to customary international law.[21]

A cyber operation must therefore not be carried out to compel the target State to take a course of action, whether by act or omission, in a way that it would not otherwise voluntarily have pursued (coercion) in matters relating to its internal or external affairs (*domaine réservé*) – such as a State's political, economic, social or cultural system or the formulation of its foreign policy.[22] The constituent element of coercion means that cyber activities that are merely influential or persuasive will not qualify as illegal intervention.

Holding elections is an example of a matter within a State's *domaine réservé*. Thus, carrying out cyber operations with the intent of altering election results in another State, for example by manipulating election systems or unduly influencing public opinion through the dissemination of confidential information obtained through cyber operations ('hack and leak'), would be in violation of the prohibition of intervention. Another example is a cyber operation deliberately causing a temporary shutdown of the target State's critical infrastructure, such as the power supply or TV, radio, Internet or other telecommunications infrastructure in order to compel that State to take a course of action.

3.3 *Prohibition on the Use of Force*

Key message:
A cyber operation may, depending on its scale and effects, violate the prohibition on the threat or use of force in Article 2(4) of the UN Charter.
A cyber operation that is in violation of the prohibition on the threat or use of force may, depending on its scale and effects, constitute an armed attack under international law. An armed attack is the gravest form of the use of force.

20 Norway recognises that no State seems to object to the application of the prohibition on intervention (or rule of non-intervention) in the cyber context. Reference is made to the GGE 2015 report, para. 26 and 28(b), subsequently endorsed by the GA. However, Norway is aware that there are differences of opinion as to where the threshold for breach lies.

21 *Nicaragua* judgment, para. 202.

22 *Nicaragua* judgment, para. 205.

Article 2(4) of the UN Charter prohibits the threat or use of force by a State against the territorial integrity or political independence of another State, or in any other manner inconsistent with the purposes of the UN. The prohibition is a norm of customary international law.[23] It applies to any use of force, regardless of the weapons or means employed.[24]

There are only three exceptions to the prohibition on the use of force in the sense that using force would not be in violation of international law: if the state on whose territory the use of force takes place consents; if it is authorised by the Security Council under Chapter VII of the UN Charter; or in the case of self-defence, in response to an armed attack as recognised in Article 51 of the UN Charter.

Whether a cyber operation violates the prohibition on the threat or use of force in Article 2(4) of the UN Charter depends on its scale and effects, physical or otherwise.[25] Depending on its gravity, a cyber operation may also constitute an armed attack under international law.[26,27] In accordance with the case law of the International Court of Justice (ICJ), an armed attack is the gravest form of the use of force.[28]

A cyber operation may constitute use of force or even an armed attack if its scale and effects are comparable to those of the use of force or an armed attack by conventional means. This must be determined based on a case-by-case assessment having regard to the specific circumstances. A number of factors may be taken into consideration, such as the severity of the consequences (the level of harm inflicted), immediacy, directness, invasiveness, measurability, military character, State involvement, the nature of the target (such as critical infrastructure) and whether this category of action has generally been characterised as the use of force.[29] This list is not exhaustive.

---

23 *Nicaragua* judgment, paras. 188-190.

24 See *Legality of the Threat or Use of Nuclear Weapons*, ICJ, advisory opinion 8 July 1996, para. 39.

25 *Nicaragua judgment,* para. 195, where ICJ stated that the 'scale and effects' are to be considered when assessing whether particular actions constitute an 'armed attack'. The factors are equally useful and logical when determining whether a cyber operation constitutes the use of force according to Article 2(4) of the UN Charter.

26 *Nicaragua* judgment, para. 195.

27 A cyber operation that constitutes an armed attack on a State under international law triggers the right to self-defence under Article 51 of the UN Charter. See *Section 5 Response measures* in this paper.

28 *Nicaragua* judgment, para. 191: '[...] it will be necessary to distinguish the most grave forms of the use of force (those constituting an armed attack) from other less grave forms'.

29 Tallinn Manual 2.0., commentary to Rule 69, p. 333-337, paras. 9-10.

Cyber operations that cause death or injury to persons or physical damage to or the destruction of objects could clearly amount to the use of force. Likewise, a cyber operation causing severe disruption to the functioning of the State such as the use of crypto viruses or other forms of digital sabotage against governmental or private power grid- or telecommunications infrastructure, or cyber operations leading to the destruction of stockpiles of Covid-19 vaccines, could amount to the use of force in violation of Article 2(4). Similarly, the use of crypto viruses or other forms of digital sabotage against a State's financial and banking system, or other operations that cause widespread economic effects and destabilisation, may amount to the use of force in violation of Article 2(4).

A cyber operation that severely damages or disables a State's critical infrastructure or functions may furthermore be considered as amounting to an armed attack under international law. Depending on its scale and effect, this may include a cyber operation that causes an aircraft crash.

4 State Responsibility

Key message:
In order for a State to be held internationally responsible for a cyber operation, the operation has to be attributable to the State under international law.
A State may also be held responsible under international law if it possesses knowledge of a cyber operation that is being carried out from its territory and causing serious adverse consequences with respect to a right of the target State under international law, and fails to take reasonably available measures to terminate the cyber operation.

The general rules on State responsibility under international law apply to cyber operations just as they apply to other activities.

In order for a State to be held responsible for a cyber operation under international law, it is a condition that the cyber operation is attributable to the State under international law.[30] Both State and non-State actors conduct cyber operations. Even if a cyber operation is not conducted by someone acting

30 The condition is set out in Article 2 ILC ASR. The other condition, that the act or omission must constitute a breach of an international obligation of the State, is dealt with in Section 3.

directly or indirectly on behalf of a State, the State may nevertheless be held responsible under international law if it fails to take adequate measures against cyber operations that target third States from or via its territory.

4.1 *Attribution under International Law*

A State may be held responsible under international law for cyber operations conducted by an organ of the State or by actors exercising governmental authority on behalf of the State.[31]

A State may be held responsible under international law for cyber operations conducted by non-State actors if these are conducted on the direct instructions of the State or under its direction or effective control.[32] It may be technically challenging to establish that a relationship between a State and a non-State actor amounts to direct instructions, direction or effective control. However, this is a question of evidence, and not of lack of clarity of international law.

4.2 *Due Diligence*

Furthermore, a State may be held responsible under international law if it knows or should have known that cyber operations that target third States are being carried out from or via its territory, and fails to take adequate measures.[33]

As a consequence of the right to exercise sovereignty over cyber infrastructure located on its territory, States also have a corresponding obligation not to knowingly allow their territory to be used for acts causing significant harm to the rights of other States under international law. This customary international law obligation, often referred to as the due diligence principle, was recognised by the ICJ in the 1949 *Corfu Channel* judgment,[34] and is reflected in numerous rules in specialised regimes of international law. Norway is of the view that the due diligence obligation applies in situations where there is a risk of transboundary harm from hazardous activities, regardless of the nature of the activity, and accordingly also applies to cyber operations.

Accordingly, if a State possesses knowledge of a cyber operation being carried out from or via its territory causing serious adverse consequences with

31 Cf. ILC ASR, in particular Articles 4, 5 and 7.

32 See Article 8 ILC ASR. See also *Nicaragua* judgment, para 115, and *Application of the Convention on the Prevention and Punishment of the Crime of Genocide*, ICJ, judgment 27 February 2007, para. 400.

33 See Article 2 ILC ASR, which explicitly states that a State's conduct may consist of 'an action or omission'. See also *Corfu Channel*, ICJ, judgment 9 April 1949, p. 18.

34 *Corfu Channel* judgment, 9 April 1949, p. 22

respect to a right of the target State under international law, it is required to take adequate measures to address the situation.

The due diligence standard is the conduct that is generally considered to be appropriate and proportional to the degree of risk of transboundary harm in the particular instance. It is an obligation of conduct, not of result. Applied to cyber activities, what is required is for the State to take all reasonably available measures to terminate the cyber operation. A breach of the obligation consists not of failing to achieve the desired result, but of failing to take the necessary, diligent steps towards that end. It is irrelevant whether the cyber operation in question is conducted by a third State or a non-State actor. Likewise, it is irrelevant whether the cyber operation in question is conducted by an actor physically present on the State's territory or by an actor making remote use of ICT infrastructure on the State's territory.

In addition to actual knowledge of the use of cyber infrastructure within its territory for harmful cyber operations against another State, a State may also violate its due diligence obligation if it is in fact unaware of the activities in question but objectively should have known about them and fails to address the situation.[35] Accordingly, knowledge also encompasses those situations in which a State in the normal course of events would have become aware that its territory was being used for harmful cyber operations.[36] This implies that the criterion that a State 'should have known' is more likely to be met if for instance the operation used publicly known and easily detected malware, as opposed to highly sophisticated and previously unknown malware.

There is currently no legal basis for a general obligation to prevent cyber operations, and States are consequently not under an obligation to monitor all cyber activities on their territories.[37]

Norway considers the due diligence obligation to be of particular importance in a cyber context. In situations where a targeted State cannot directly attribute (technically and legally) a wrongful cyber operation – for instance election interference – to the State from whose territory it is being carried out, the territorial State may nevertheless still be held accountable on the basis of a breach of the due diligence obligation.

35 *Corfu Channel* judgment, 9 April 1949, p. 18.

36 See also Tallinn Manual 2.0, commentary to Rule 6, p. 41.

37 A general obligation of full control and prevention in the cyber context could be problematic in relation to a State's obligations under international human rights law.

5 Response Measures

The response measures an injured State may take under international law depend on the severity and nature of the cyber operation and on whether the legally responsible actor behind it is another State or a non-State actor.

5.1 *Retorsion*

A State may respond to any form of cyber operation by retorsion. Retorsion refers to the taking of measures that are lawful but unfriendly, directed against another State. Retorsion may therefore be used regardless of whether international law has been violated and regardless of whether State responsibility applies. Examples of acts of retorsion are breaking off or limiting diplomatic relations, for instance by declaring a diplomat persona non grata, or the imposition of sanctions. Publicly declaring that another State is responsible for a cyber operation is in itself an act of retorsion.

5.2 *Countermeasures*

If a State is the victim of an internationally wrongful cyber operation and another State can be held responsible under customary international law on State responsibility, the injured State may, depending on the circumstances, be entitled to take countermeasures.

A countermeasure is an act that would otherwise be contrary to international law, but where the injured State can invoke the prior internationally wrongful act[38] as a ground for precluding wrongfulness.[39] If there is doubt regarding the attribution of a cyber operation to a State under international law, it may be preferable for the injured State to make use of acts of retorsion rather than countermeasures in order to avoid the possibility of incurring State responsibility for its response.

Countermeasures may only be taken to induce a State to cease an internationally wrongful act or resume its compliance with an international obligation. They are not to be used for punishment and retaliation. Countermeasures must be limited to what is considered necessary and proportional, and may only target the State to which the cyber operation or internationally wrongful act can be attributed. There is no requirement for countermeasures to be of the same nature as the internationally wrongful acts to which they are a response,

38 In this document, 'internationally wrongful acts' must be understood as including both actions and omissions, *see* Articles 1 and 2 ILC ASR.

39 See Articles 22 and 49–54 ILC ASR.

and countermeasures in response to cyber operations may therefore be carried out within or outside cyberspace. Countermeasures must not violate the prohibition on the threat or use of force or international humanitarian law.

The State held responsible should be notified of both the violation of international law and the grounds for attribution, as well as of the intention to introduce countermeasures.[40] Countermeasures may only be taken if a State has sufficient grounds for attributing the conduct in question to a particular State under international law. What constitutes sufficient grounds will be fact-specific and case-specific, and can be particularly challenging to determine in the case of cyber operations. The State taking countermeasures must be confident in its attribution before resorting to countermeasures. However, the State taking countermeasures need not publish detailed grounds for its attribution or give a detailed technical account of this to the State identified as responsible as this might reveal sensitive methods of interception and detection or offensive and defensive capabilities.

Countermeasures may be taken without prior notification to the responsible State if providing such notification might reveal sensitive methods or capabilities or prevent the countermeasures from having the necessary effect. For example, the injured State could carry out a cyber operation to disrupt the capability of the aggressor State conducting the internationally wrongful cyber operation such as election interference. This countermeasure would in other circumstances be in violation of the aggressor State's sovereignty.

5.3 *Necessity*

In a situation of necessity, a State may be able to respond to a cyber operation in a way that is in principle in breach of an international obligation and nevertheless not incur responsibility for its actions under international law.

Necessity refers to those exceptional situations where the only way a State can safeguard an essential interest threatened by a grave and imminent peril, whether cyber in nature or not, is by temporary non-compliance with international obligations of lesser weight or urgency. For instance, if infrastructure in a third country is used in an internationally wrongful cyber operation, the injured State may under certain conditions launch a cyber operation to destroy or disrupt the internationally wrongful cyber operation, even if this violates the territorial sovereignty of the third State.

It is not a requirement that the preceding cyber operation must be attributable to a particular State.

---

40 ILC ASR Articles 43 and 52.

It should be emphasised that, according to customary law on state responsibility, a number of conditions must be fulfilled before necessity can be invoked as a ground for precluding wrongfulness.[41]

5.4 *Self-defence*

A State that is the victim of a cyber operation that qualifies as an armed attack under international law, may exercise its inherent right of individual or collective self-defence under Article 51 of the UN Charter.

The right of self-defence as reflected in Article 51 is a norm of customary international law. It must be exercised subject to the requirements of necessity and proportionality[42], and may involve both digital and conventional means.

6 Cyber Operations during Armed Conflicts – International Humanitarian Law

> *Key message:*
> *International humanitarian law applies to cyber operations in connection with an armed conflict.*

International humanitarian law (IHL) applies in the event of an armed conflict. Whether an (international or non-international) armed conflict exists will depend on the specific circumstances.

This specialised regime of international law, also called *jus in bello*, governs actions, including cyber operations, when they are conducted in connection with an armed conflict.

International humanitarian law aims to minimise the human suffering caused by armed conflict. It thus regulates and limits cyber operations during armed conflicts, just as it regulates and limits the use of any other weapons, means and methods of warfare in an armed conflict.

IHL does not legitimise the use of force in cyberspace. Any use of force by States – either by digital or by conventional means – remains governed by the Charter of the United Nations and the relevant rules of customary international law, also called *jus ad bellum*. Of particular relevance is the prohibition

---

41 See Article 25 ILC ASR.

42 See e.g. *Nicaragua* judgment paras. 176, 194, and *Oil Platforms*, ICJ, judgement 6 November 2003, paras. 43, 73-74, 76.

against the use of force. International disputes must be settled by peaceful means, in cyberspace as in all other domains.

The general rules for legitimate military targets are the same regardless of whether conventional or digital means are used. A cyber operation conducted in connection with an armed conflict must be assessed according to its consequences, and may qualify as an attack under international humanitarian law. 'Attack' is a key concept of international humanitarian law, and is understood to mean 'acts of violence against the adversary, whether in offence or defence'.[43] Cyber attacks during armed conflicts are subject to the same restrictions and regulations under international humanitarian law as conventional attacks, including the principles of humanity, military necessity, proportionality and distinction. The concept of attack is particularly relevant to the rules and principles on the selection of targets and precautions. Attacks against civilians or civilian objects are for example prohibited.[44]

Under IHL, medical services must be protected and respected, including when carrying out cyber operations during armed conflict.[45] IHL also prohibits attacking, destroying, removing or rendering useless objects indispensable to the survival of the population, including through cyber means and methods of warfare.[46] 'Objects indispensable to the survival of the civilian population' include ICT infrastructure for food production or drinking water installations.

7 Human Rights in Cyberspace

> *Key message:*
> *States must comply with their human rights obligations in cyberspace, just as they must in the physical world. States must both respect and protect human rights.*

---

43 Additional Protocol I to the Geneva Conventions of 12 August 1949 relating to the protection of victims of international armed conflict (AP I), Article 49(1).

44 AP I, Article 51(2) and 52(1).

45 See, for instance, Convention (I) for the Amelioration of the Condition of the Wounded and Sick in Armed Forces in the Field (GCI), Article 19; Convention (II) for the Amelioration of the Condition of Wounded, Sick and Shipwrecked Members of Armed Forces at Sea (GCII), Article 12; Convention (IV) relative to the Protection of Civilian Persons in Time of War (GCIV), Article 18; AP I, Article 12; AP II, Article 11; ICRC Customary IHL Study, Rules 25, 28, 29.

46 AP I, Article 54; Protocol Additional to the Geneva Conventions of 12 August 1949, and relating to the Protection of Victims of Non-International Armed Conflicts (AP II), Article 14; ICRC Customary IHL Study, Rule 54.

International human rights law applies to cyber activities just as it does to any other activity. States must comply with their human rights obligations also in cyberspace, as they must in the physical world. States must both respect and protect human rights, including the right to freedom of expression and the right to privacy.

Neither the individuals that are subject to a State's jurisdiction, nor the concept of jurisdiction, is altered by the fact that the activity attributed to the State is a cyber activity. In this respect, cyber activity is no different from other means that States may use to violate their human rights obligations towards their citizens.

Note from the publisher

The author mentioned at the start of this chapter, Vibeke Musæus, is only responsible for the introduction to this position paper. The position paper is a product of the government of Norway and available online: https://www.regjeringen.no/contentassets/a8911fc020c94eb386a1ec7917bf0d03/norwegian_positions.pdf

CHAPTER 4

Sweden's Position Paper on the Application of International Law in Cyberspace

Ola Engdahl

Introduction

The question of cyber and international law has been discussed for many years in UN forums, primarily within Groups of Governmental Experts (GGE:S) but also later on in the Open-ended Working Group (OWEG).[1] These discussions have focused on developments in the field of information and telecommunication in the context of international security. International law has been one important part, but the mandate is also addressing other areas such as existing and emerging threats, norms, rules and principles (which are understood to be of a non-binding character), confidence-building measures and capacity-building. The focus on international security has also formed the international law topics that have been on the agenda in these forums. So far, the work has clearly concluded that international law applies in cyberspace and that the question now is rather *how* international law applies.

A number of states have published position papers on the application of international law in cyberspace. The OEWG also encouraged the sharing of national views in its 2021 Report, and the 2021 GGE Report included an annex of voluntary contributions of participating governmental experts on

1 Reports of these groups include, 2010 Report of the Group of Governmental Experts on Developments in the Field of Information and Telecommunications in the Context of International Security, UN Doc. A/65/201, 2013 Report of the Group of Governmental Experts on Developments in the Field of Information and Telecommunications in the Context of International Security, UN Doc. A/68/98, 2015 Report of the Group of Governmental Experts on Developments in the Field of Information and Telecommunications in the Context of International Security, UN Doc. A/70/174, 2021 Report of the Group of Governmental Experts on Advancing Responsible State Behaviour in Cyberspace in the Context of International Security, UN Doc., A/76/135 and 2021 Report of the Open-ended working group on developments in the field of information and telecommunications in the context of international security UN Doc. A/AC.290/2021/CRP.2.

 | DOI:10.1163/9789004703933_005

the subject of how international law applies to the use of Information and Communications Technologies (ICTs) by states.

Sweden published its position paper in July 2022.[2] By presenting its view on some of the areas of international law that are relevant to international security, Sweden aims to promote deeper understanding on how international law applies in cyberspace. The areas covered in the position paper reflect the subjects discussed in the UN forums and those which are commonly covered in other states' position papers. Like other likeminded states, Sweden finds it important to share its views on international law and cyber to counter an emerging narrative that new binding rules are needed to regulate the use of cyberspace.

Although Sweden does not see a need for new rules of international law in this area, the cyber technology can, however, give rise to specific questions that may require further clarification. The position papers published so far are mainly from states sharing the view that there is no need for new binding rules in relation to ICTs. There are, however, some areas of difference between otherwise likeminded states.

One of those areas concerns the sovereignty of states, where it has been argued that sovereignty is not considered a rule of international law in cyberspace. This sparked a need for many states, including Sweden, to state their positions on this issue. Sweden clarified that states have an obligation to respect the sovereignty of other states in cyberspace as well, and a breach of this obligation would amount to a wrongful act and give rise to state responsibility.

Another debated area of international law related to cyberspace is the question of due diligence. Some states regard due diligence to be a non-binding norm in cyberspace. This is also how due diligence has been treated in the GGE, where it is considered under the heading of rules, norms and principles. Sweden – together with many other states, including the Nordic states – instead regards due diligence to also be a rule of international law in cyberspace.

A third area of great interest, which several states also address in their national position papers, is the application of international humanitarian law (IHL). So far, this topic has met some resistance in the work of the GGE and the OEWG, although some progress has been seen in recent years. Sweden finds it important to make clear that IHL also applies to cyber operations conducted in the context of armed conflict.

May, 2023

2 Position Paper on the Application of International Law in Cyberspace - Government.se

Position Paper on the Application of International Law in Cyberspace

Introduction

The applicability of existing international law, including the UN Charter, in cyberspace has been confirmed by the United Nations Group of Governmental Experts (UN GGE) and by the United Nations Open-ended Working Group (OEWG).[1] The Reports of both groups have been adopted by the UN General Assembly.[2] UN Members have thus unequivocally reaffirmed the applicability of international law in cyberspace. The current discussion focuses primarily on *how* international law applies.

State behaviour based on compliance with international law fosters stability in international relations. A better understanding of how international law applies in cyberspace contributes to the strengthening of an open, secure, stable, accessible and peaceful cyber environment. In this respect, and based on its commitment to an international rules-based order, Sweden presents its general position on some of the areas of central importance to a safe and secure cyberspace. Sweden does not see a need for new rules regulating cyber activities. However, cyber technology may give rise to specific questions requiring further clarification.

Sovereignty

The principle of sovereign equality of States is also applicable to cyberspace. Within their territories, States have jurisdiction and the right to exercise authority within the framework of international law. At international level, States are independent and enjoy sovereign equality in relation to other States.

---

1 *Report of the Group of Governmental Experts on Developments in the Field of Information and Telecommunications in the Context of International Security*, UN Doc. A/68/98 (2013), adopted by the UNGA Resolution A/RES/68/243; *Report of the Group of Governmental Experts on Developments in the Field of Information and Telecommunications in the Context of International Security*, UN Doc. A/70/174 (2015), adopted by the UNGA Resolution A/RES/70/237; *Report of the Open-ended working group on developments in the field of information and telecommunications in the context of international security*, UN Doc. A/75/816 (2021); *Report of the Group of Governmental Experts on Advancing Responsible State Behaviour in Cyberspace in the Context of International Security*, UN Doc. A/76/135 (2021).

2 Both Reports of 2021 were adopted by the UNGA Resolution A/RES/76/19.

State sovereignty provides a basic foundation for other principles and rules such as those governing the prohibition of intervention and the prohibition of the use of force. However, States also have an obligation to respect the sovereignty of other States, and a breach of this obligation would amount to a wrongful act and give rise to State responsibility.

A State's jurisdiction and authority apply to persons and objects within its territorial borders, including cyber-related activities. A State has a right to protect persons and objects within its territory, or otherwise under its jurisdiction, against interference by cyber means. A State's authority and jurisdiction include a responsibility not to allow knowingly its territory to be used for acts contrary to the rights of other States.

In general, Sweden is of the view that violations of sovereignty may arise from cyber operations that result in damage or loss of functionality. Altering and interfering with data without causing physical harm may also violate sovereignty.[3] Such acts include those directed against cyber infrastructure belonging to private individuals or entities. Interference with a State's inherently governmental functions may also constitute a violation of State sovereignty, including when undertaken with cyber means.

Whether an intrusion has in fact resulted in a violation of sovereignty needs to be assessed on a case-by-case basis taking into consideration the nature and character of the intrusion.

Non-intervention

The principle of non-intervention is a fundamental principle of international law also applicable in cyberspace. It is not expressly mentioned in the UN Charter but is a corollary of the sovereign equality of all States. In the Friendly Relations Declaration, the principle of non-intervention is explained as "No State or group of States has the right to intervene, directly or indirectly, for any reason whatever, in the internal or external affairs of any other State."[4]

The prohibition of intervention is generally understood to include two elements: intervening in matters in which each State is permitted to decide freely, and the involvement of coercion. These elements were confirmed by the

3 A view expressed in Rule 4 of the Tallinn Manual. Michael N. Schmitt, *Tallinn Manual 2.0 on the International Law Applicable to Cyber Operations*, 2nd ed., 2017.

4 *General Assembly Declaration on Principles of International Law concerning Friendly Relations and Co-operation among States in accordance with the Charter of the United Nations*, UNGA Resolution 2625 (XXV) 1970. The principle of non-intervention may also be derived from a reading of articles 2(4) and 2(7) of the UN Charter.

International Court of Justice (ICJ) in the *Nicaragua case.*[5] With regard to the latter, the Court held that the "element of coercion, which defines, and indeed forms the very essence of, prohibited intervention, is particularly obvious in the case of an intervention which uses force, either in the direct form of military action, or in the indirect form of support for subversive or terrorist armed activities within another State."[6] The prohibition of intervention is applicable between States and does not apply directly to non-state actors.

While coercion is not defined in international law, it must be distinguished from other acts that would not qualify as coercion, such as criticism or other ways of influencing through diplomatic means. What constitutes coercion in the cyber context may not be easy to determine, requiring a case-by-case assessment that takes the specific circumstances into account.

Use of force

The prohibition of the use of force is a cardinal rule of customary international law, also applicable in relation to cyber operations. In the UN Charter, Article 2(4) stipulates a prohibition of the threat or use of force. The only exceptions in the UN Charter are the inherent right of individual or collective self-defence if an armed attack occurs, or acts taken pursuant to a decision of the UN Security Council authorising the use of force.

Acts that constitute the use of force are not clearly defined in international law. The ICJ has declared that the provisions on the use of force are not dependent on the choice of means, but rather apply to any use of force regardless of the weapons employed.[7] The Court has furthermore distinguished the most grave forms of the use of force (those constituting an armed attack) from other less grave forms based on scale and effects.[8] A similar assessment of scale and effects may be made in relation to whether an act constitutes a breach of the prohibition of the use of force. While most cyber operations would not constitute use of force, such operations would be considered as such if comparable to the scale and effects of kinetic use of force. An assessment needs to be made on a case-by-case basis.

5 ICJ, *Military and Paramilitary Activities in and against Nicaragua (Nicaragua v. United States of America)*, Merits, Judgment, ICJ Reports 1986, p. 14, para. 205.

6 *Ibid.*

7 ICJ, *Legality of the Threat or Use of Nuclear Weapons*, Advisory Opinion, ICJ Reports 1996, p. 226, para. 39.

8 ICJ, *Military and Paramilitary Activities in and against Nicaragua (Nicaragua v. United States of America)*, Merits, Judgment, ICJ Reports 1986, p, 14, para.195.

Under Article 51 of the UN Charter, States have a right of self-defence if an armed attack occurs. It is not a requirement under the right of self-defence that the armed attack use kinetic means, nor that the use of force in self-defence is limited to such means. An attack by cyber means may have the potential to constitute an armed attack if its scale and effects are comparable to an armed attack by kinetic means. The exercise of the right of self-defence needs to be reported to the Security Council. Any use of force in the exercise of self-defence, including through cyber means, needs to adhere to principles of necessity and proportionality.

Due diligence

As a corollary to their sovereignty, States have an obligation to not knowingly allow their territory to be used for acts contrary to the rights of other States. This well-established rule of international law, described by the ICJ in the *Corfu Channel case*, also applies to cyber operations.[9] A State's obligation to ensure that its territory is not used to harm other States has often been referred to as an obligation of due diligence.

Due diligence is a standard of conduct and not of result, requiring a State to act responsibly and to do anything feasible to fulfil this obligation. States must use all reasonable means to prevent its territory to be used for acts causing serious adverse consequences to other states.

The difficulties involved in discovering cyber activities by non-state actors may affect what a State knows or should have known about such activities. Taking these difficulties into account, Sweden believes that this obligation, in principle, includes situations in which a State should have known about harmful activities taking place from its territory.

State responsibility

An internationally wrongful act by a State entails the responsibility of that State under international law. The articles on State responsibility drafted by the International Law Commission constitute secondary norms of international law, identifying conditions when a State is internationally responsible

9 ICJ, *Corfu Channel case* (United Kingdom of Great Britain and Northern Ireland v. Albania), Judgement of 9 April 1949, ICJ Reports 1949, p.4, p. 22.

for wrongful acts and the effects thereof.[10] The general norms on State responsibility apply also in relation to wrongful acts in the cyber context.

Technical difficulties pose new challenges in identifying those responsible for cyber operations, compared with kinetic operations, but the rules on attribution under the law of State responsibility also apply in a cyber context. Cyber operations conducted by State organs are attributed to the State, as are cyber operations conducted by persons empowered to exercise elements of governmental authority if acting in that particular capacity. A State is normally not responsible for the conduct of individuals not empowered to exercise governmental authority. However, in situations where non-state actors act on the instructions or under the direction or control of a State, that conduct is attributed to the State. Conduct not attributed to a State may nevertheless be considered an act of that State if that State acknowledges and adopts the conduct as its own.

Legal attribution must be distinguished from public attribution. Legal attribution is an integral part in the process to establish and characterise an act in legal terms, and there is no legal requirement to disclose any evidence in relation to the assessment of attribution of conduct. Publicizing a decision on attribution is the prerogative of sovereign States and is not a requirement under international law.

A State responsible for a wrongful act is under an obligation to cease its behaviour and to make full reparation for the injury caused. When a State is injured by an internationally wrongful act it may respond by a variety of measures. Such measures include countermeasures against the responsible State to ensure compliance with its international obligations. Recourse to countermeasures is subject to strict requirements under the law of State responsibility and includes measures otherwise prohibited by international law. Countermeasures must *inter alia* be proportionate in character and cannot include the use of force. There is no requirement for responsive measures to be similar in kind and they may include non-cyber means. Before resorting to countermeasures, the injured State must notify the responsible State. It should be noted that this rule also allows for countermeasures without prior notification when urgent measures are needed to preserve the rights of the injured State. This rule also applies to cyber operations.

Under certain strict conditions, a State is allowed to employ measures that would otherwise be in breach of an international obligation in order to safeguard an essential interest against a grave and imminent peril. This would also

10 International Law Commission, *Responsibility of States for Internationally Wrongful Acts* (2001).

apply in a cyber context. Necessity will, however, only rarely be available to excuse non-performance of an obligation.

International humanitarian law[11]

Sweden is of the view that international humanitarian law (IHL) applies to cyber operations conducted in the context of armed conflict. An armed conflict may be of an international or non-international character, depending on the nature of the parties to the armed conflict. The application of the law of armed conflict is not limited to kinetic force. However, to fall within the scope of IHL, a cyber operation must show a sufficient nexus with the armed conflict. IHL is not concerned with the legality of war and does not as such legitimise the use of force between States. IHL aims to regulate the conduct of hostilities and to protect those who are not, or no longer, participating in hostilities, thereby reducing risks and potential harm to civilians and civilian objects as well as persons recognised to be *hors de combat*.

IHL requires parties to an armed conflict to distinguish between civilians and civilian objects on the one hand and military objectives on the other. The conduct of hostilities obligates parties to the armed conflict *inter alia* to comply with the principles of distinction, proportionality and precaution. Compliance with these principles in a cyber context may require specific considerations as the infrastructure in cyberspace is often used for both military and civilian purposes.

In the framework of IHL, 'attack' is defined as an act of violence against the adversary whether in offence or in defence. The determination of an act of violence should be based on its effects rather than the means used. A cyberattack in the context of IHL would at least include cyber operations that are reasonably expected to cause injury or death to persons or damage or destruction to objects.[12] Civilians are protected against attacks but only as long as they do not take a direct part in hostilities. A civilian may thus become a military target if taking a direct part in hostilities by the use of cyber means. In case of doubt whether a person is a civilian, that person shall be considered to be a civilian.

Cyber operations in the context of an armed conflict need to comply not only with rules governing the conduct of hostilities; certain persons, objects and activities are subject to special protection, such as medical personnel and

11 This section does not include the laws of Occupation and Neutrality.

12 *Tallinn Manual 2.0*, Rule 92. Michael N. Schmitt, *Tallinn Manual 2.0 on the International Law Applicable to Cyber Operations*, 2nd ed., 2017.

units, including their cyber infrastructure, and religious or humanitarian personnel and objects.

International human rights law

Human rights apply online as they do offline. It is a well-established principle, first expressed in the 2012 Human Rights Council resolution on *The promotion, protection and enjoyment of human rights on the Internet*.[13]

The same human rights responsibilities and obligations that States have in the physical world also apply in the digital world. Although human rights are universal and indivisible, some are particularly relevant to the use of the internet, including (but not limited to) freedom of opinion, expression and information, freedom of association and assembly,and privacy. To enable the full enjoyment of human rights online, it is crucial that the internet remains open, free and secure with equal access and inclusiveness for all. The digital divides, including the gender digital divide, need to be closed. The internet should be governed through a multi-stakeholder approach.

Note from the publisher

The author mentioned at the start of this chapter, Ola Engdahl, is only responsible for the introduction to this position paper. The position paper is a product of the government of Sweden and available online: https://www.government.se/contentassets/3c2cb6febd0e4ab0bd542f653283b140/swedens-position-paper-on-the-application-of-international-law-in-cyberspace.pdf

13 HRC Resolution, *The promotion, protection and enjoyment of human rights on the Internet*, A/HRC/RES/20/8 (2012), and subsequent resolutions, adopted by consensus.

CHAPTER 5

Denmark's Position Paper on the Application of International Law in Cyberspace

Jeppe Mejer Kjelgaard and Ulf Melgaard

Introduction

A number of States have published national position papers on the application of international law in cyberspace to further the common understanding of the interpretation of international law in this domain. Denmark fully supports these efforts and is pleased to now share its own paper.

The focus of the Danish position paper is on cyberspace in the broad context of international law, including issues pertaining to state sovereignty, non-intervention, the prohibition on the use of force and international humanitarian law. The position paper supplements Denmark's views already expressed in the UN Open-ended Working Group on Information and Communication Technologies and through the annual reporting to the UN Secretary General.

May, 2023

 | DOI:10.1163/9789004703933_006

Denmark's Position Paper on the Application of International Law in Cyberspace

1 Introduction

The UN General Assembly has endorsed the conclusions set out in the reports from the Group of Governmental Experts (GGE) and the Open-ended Working Group on Information and Communication Technologies (OEWG) affirming that international law, including the UN Charter, applies in cyberspace. Denmark is an unwavering supporter of this view and continues to support efforts to develop the rules, norms and principles of responsible State behaviour in cyberspace. As a strong proponent of the rules based international order Denmark is fully committed to international law as the fundamental framework for responsible state behaviour in cyberspace. With a view to contributing to clarifying that framework this paper sets out Denmark's official position on selected issues of international law in relation to cyberspace. The aim of the paper is to strengthen the interpretation of international law in relation to cyberspace and to clarify the basis upon which Denmark will respond to unlawful acts from other States and non-State actors in cyberspace.

It is the view of Denmark that the application of international law does not depend on the particular technological means employed. Treaty obligations, customary law, and general principles of law apply across domains, which includes operations conducted in cyberspace.

However, unanswered questions remain regarding the precise interpretation of international law with respect to cyberspace operations. This lack of clarity stems from general issues of interpretation of international law, from limited State practice in cyberspace, and from the unique characteristics of cyberspace. Consequently, the understanding of how international law applies to cyberspace is, and will continue to be, a complex and evolving process.

The focus of this paper is on cyberspace in the broad context of international peace and security and general issues of international law such as state sovereignty, use of force, countermeasures and international humanitarian law (IHL). Denmark subscribes to the general view that also human rights obligations apply in cyberspace, but for the sake of brevity this paper does not elaborate further on that topic. In addition, the paper does not deal with sector specific issues such as law enforcement cooperation, intelligence gathering and telecommunications law, nor does it address the many treaty obligations that Denmark is subject to, and which would necessarily be part of a legal analysis of any particular cyber operation.

It should also be noted that international law does not regulate all cross border cyber activities undertaken by States. Some cyber acts might be unfriendly, or even hostile, but not as such regulated by international law and will accordingly be subject to policy considerations.

2 Sovereignty

Sovereignty denotes each State's authority to exercise within its territory the functions of a State, to the exclusion of any other State. Denmark is of the view that sovereignty is not only a principle but a primary rule of international law a breach of which amounts to an internationally wrongful act and if attributable to a State it may give rise to State responsibility.

Denmark shares the view that sovereignty applies to States' cyber activities as has been widely endorsed by other States who have voiced their national positions on international law in cyberspace.

Sovereignty has both an internal and external dimension. Internal sovereignty signifies the independent right of a State to exercise the functions of a State in regard to a given territory to the exclusion of any other State. It pertains to a State's jurisdiction over all persons, entities, and objects within its territory and some manifestations of the State outside its territory.

It follows that all States may exercise sovereignty over any cyber infrastructure located on their territory and all activities associated with that infrastructure – irrespective of whether such infrastructure or activity is of a public or private character. In the exercise of governmental authority, the State may promulgate and enforce domestic laws or protect cyber infrastructure and cyber activity located or taking place in its territory unless prohibited from doing so by its international legal obligations such as the limitations set out in international human rights conventions and international law on State and diplomatic immunity. A State's internal sovereignty also encompasses an obligation for the State not to allow its territory to be used for acts contrary to the rights of other States (as further elaborated under section 6 on due diligence).

External sovereignty pertains to the international equal rights and duties of a State in its relations to other States. It derives from the principle of sovereign equality of States as recognized in article 2(1) of the UN Charter and requires all States to respect the territorial integrity and political independence of other States. Other principles and rules of international law such as the prohibition of the use of force, the prohibition on intervention, and the right of self-defence are based on this principle.

As sovereignty is a primary rule under international law States are obliged to respect the sovereignty of other States and must not conduct activities that violate another State's sovereignty. Whether or not a given act in cyberspace is done in violation of another State's sovereignty requires a case-by-case assessment of all relevant factors, in particular the nature of and the effects caused by the cyber operation. Denmark supports the view that the lawfulness of a cyber operation should be assessed based on two different bases: the degree of infringement upon the target State's territorial integrity, and whether there has been an interference with or usurpation of inherently governmental functions. Unlike the prohibition on intervention, a breach of sovereignty is not contingent on a coercion element.

With respect to infringements on a State's territory Denmark generally shares the view that cyber operations which result in physical damage or injury constitute a violation of a State's sovereignty and may also violate the principle of non-intervention, or the prohibition of the use of force, cf. section 3 and 4. In addition to physical damage or injury loss of functionality may also, depending on its nature, scale, and effects, constitute such a violation. Cyber operations that alter or delete data without necessarily resulting in physical damage or loss of functionality may also, based on a case-by-case assessment of the nature, scale, and effects of the operation in question, constitute a violation. Cyber activities causing negligible physical effects or loss of functionality would generally not be considered a violation of sovereignty.

Furthermore, interference with or usurpation of a State's inherently governmental functions may constitute a violation of a State's sovereignty or prohibited intervention. This assessment is not contingent on whether physical damage, injury, or loss of functionality have occurred, but rather if a cyber operation has interfered with data or services necessary for the exercise of inherently governmental functions. This applies irrespective of whether such inherently government functions are performed by the State itself (either by central, regional or local government) or have been delegated to non-governmental entities.

3 Non-intervention

The principle of non-intervention is a fundamental principle of international law. It is a corollary of the principle of sovereignty, and more specifically the aspect that provides for the sovereign equality of States as set forth in article 2(1) of the UN Charter.

Denmark is of the view that the prohibition of intervention is a rule of international law forming part of customary international law. This was established by the ICJ in the *Nicaragua* v. *United States of America* case where the Court held that States are prohibited from intervening directly or indirectly in internal or external affairs of other States.[1]

In order for an action to qualify as an unlawful intervention it must qualify as an intervention in matters that are the sovereign prerogative of a State, the so-called *domaine réservé*, and it must involve an element of coercion.[2]

The scope of activities falling within the *domaine réservé* include but are not limited to " (...) the choice of a political, economic, social, and cultural system, and the formulation of foreign policy."[3] The range of activities covered by the non-intervention rule largely overlap with the activities reserved to States under the rule of sovereignty.

The term coercion is not defined in either treaty law or customary international law. Denmark takes the view that an act may be considered of a coercive nature when the act of interference has a potential for compelling the target State to engage in an action that it would otherwise not take. However, a distinction must be drawn between activities that merely involve influencing, as opposed to compelling, the voluntary actions of a target State. Acts of influence, such as persuasion, criticism, and public diplomacy are insufficient to qualify as an intervention. To be coercive the effort to intervene must be designed to have a decisive impact on outcomes or conduct with respect to a matter reserved to the target State. As emphasized by the Court in the Nicaragua judgment coercive acts involving the use of force are particularly obvious examples of unlawful interventions.[4] Denmark considers that coercion is not limited to means of direct or indirect use of force and that also measures below this threshold may constitute coercion. Cyber activities that do not amount to use of force can therefore also be coercive.

An example of unlawful intervention in the cyber domain could be where a State coercively interferes in the internal political process of another. In the cyber context this could potentially occur by using cyber technology to alter electronic ballots and thereby affecting the results of a political election.

4 Use of force and self-defence

Cyber operations may violate the prohibition on the threat or use of force, which primarily depends on the physical scale and effects of the cyber operation in question. It requires an individual assessment of the specific circumstances

1 Military and Paramilitary Activities in and against Nicaragua (*Nicaragua* v. *United States of America* case). Merits, Judgment. ICJ Reports 1986, p. 14, para. 205.

2 *Ibid.*

3 *Ibid.*

4 *Ibid.*

in each case to determine whether the scale and effects of a cyber operation correspond to what would qualify as use of force had they resulted from conventional weapons.

Article 2(4) of the UN Charter sets out that all Member States shall refrain in their international relations from the threat or use of force against the territorial integrity or political independence of any State, or in any other manner inconsistent with the purposes of the United Nations. Numerous other international documents and State practice contribute to the understanding of the principle of the non-use of force. It is, however, fair to assert that there are still significant grey areas and divergent views among States as to the precise content of the law.

Generally, Denmark subscribes to the notion that where a cyber operation results in injury, death, or significant physical damage, this prima facie qualifies as use of force.

With regard to the precise interpretation of the term force and the question as to whether economic or political coercion can qualify as use of force, Denmark considers that it generally cannot be ruled out that acts of economic or political coercion can fall within the purview of Article 2(4) of the UN Charter if, for example, a cyber operation resulting in the malfunctioning of a State's financial system leads to significant economic damage.

It has been suggested that States should apply the following non-exhaustive factors for determining if a cyber operation reaches the level of use of force: Severity, immediacy, directness, invasiveness, measurability of effects, military character, State involvement, presumptive legality.[5] While few States in their public positions have endorsed these particular factors, Denmark is of the view that these factors are useful reference points for further understanding and discussing the definition of use of force in cyberspace.

In certain instances, use of force may due to its scale and effects reach the level of an armed attack and thus give rise to a right to self-defence of the target State, cf. article 51 of the UN Charter. In its Nicaragua judgment the ICJ defined an armed attack as the most grave form of the use of force.[6] Denmark subscribes to the understanding that not all illegal use of force under article 2(4) of the UN Charter necessarily amounts to an armed attack under article 51 of the Charter.

Denmark takes the view that a cyber attack may qualify as an armed attack under article 51 of the UN Charter if the effects generated are comparable to

5 M. N. Schmitt (ed.), *Tallinn Manual 2.0 on the International Law Applicable To Cyber Operations*, (Cambridge University Press, 2017), pp. 334-336.

6 *Nicaragua* v. *United States of America* case, *supra* note 1, para. 191.

effects resulting from an action, which would otherwise qualify as an armed attack. Thus, Denmark considers that a cyber operation, which e.g. leads to serious injury or death, or which causes significant physical damage, may qualify as an armed attack. This could be the case if a cyber attack leads to the disabling of an air traffic control system which causes planes to crash or an interference with the operating system of a power station, which causes serious physical damage.

Certain States take the view that an armed attack can only be undertaken by State actors or entities acting under the control or instruction of States, and thus no right to self-defense exists against an armed attack by a non-State actor. Denmark does not share this view, but contends that State practice supports that a State might in some instances and under certain conditions be permitted to exercise self-defence against an armed attack by a non-State actor.

5 State responsibility

Denmark is of the view that the general rules of State responsibility apply in cyberspace. A State bears international responsibility if it breaches an international obligation owed to another State. A State may be responsible under international law for acts undertaken by an organ of the State or by actors exercising government authority on behalf of that State. Acts by a non-State actor may be attributable to a State where the non-State actor carries out a cyber operation under the instruction of, or under the direction or control of that State, or where the State actor acknowledges and adopts the operations carried out by the non-State actor as its own.

Each State may decide whether to publicly attribute cyber acts to other States or not. There is no obligation under international law for States to share documentation or other evidence supporting an attribution. The application of international law and State responsibility does not depend on public attribution.

6 Due diligence

Denmark is of the view that a State may bear international responsibility where a State fails to take adequate measures against a non-State actor - or third State - that conducts harmful cyber operations against another State from its territory or other cyber infrastructure under its effective control.

As the ICJ Stated in the *Corfu Channel* Case[7], States are under an "obligation not to knowingly allow its territory to be used for acts contrary to the right of other States". This obligation is a natural corollary of a State's sovereignty over persons and cyber infrastructure on its territory.

As a general rule due diligence requires States to take all reasonable measures to prevent, eliminate and mitigate potentially significant harm to legally protected interests of another State, or the international community as a whole. The general principle of due diligence has developed with some variation in different fields of international law, including international environmental law, transboundary harm, and human rights. Similarly, Denmark believes that the precise contours of the due diligence obligation in cyberspace will continue to develop and crystalize in the coming years. It is, however, possible to set out some key features.

Due diligence is an obligation of conduct, not of result. A State is obliged to take all reasonable measures to stop or prevent a given cyber act from occurring. Not all harmful cyber operations emanating from another State's territory entail due diligence obligations and corresponding rights of the target State. While there is still scope for State practice to clarify the precise threshold, Denmark subscribes to the view that the harm suffered must be significant and not merely amount to inconveniences or minor disruptions.

The lack of compliance with a State's due diligence obligations may lead another State to take countermeasures if the conditions set out below in section 7 are fulfilled.

7 Countermeasures

States may be subject to unfriendly or hostile cyber acts or omissions that do not rise to the level of illegality under international law. These may be met with responses of a diplomatic, economic, or political nature intended to deter and hold accountable such States, irrespective of the fact that those acts are not illegal under international law. Such responses are generally termed retorsions. However, where one State breaches its obligations under international law towards another State, the victim State may respond with countermeasures. A State injured by an internationally wrongful act may be justified in taking non-forcible countermeasures in order to procure the cessation of the wrongful act and to achieve reparation for the injury.

7 *United Kingdom of Great Britain and Northern Ireland* v. *Albania* (merits), p. 22.

Breaches of international obligations, whether cyber or non-cyber in nature, may be responded to by both cyber and non-cyber countermeasures. Countermeasures must be necessary and proportionate. Thus, countermeasures may not go beyond what is necessary to bring the illegal conduct to an end. Countermeasures must be taken with the intention of compelling the offending State to change its behaviour. That being the case countermeasures may only be taken for the period where the other State continues its illegal acts. To the extent possible countermeasures should be reversible although the precise meaning of this concept in a cyber-context is not clear.

Countermeasures may only be taken in response to an internationally wrongful act. That raises the question of when such an act may be considered to have been completed and whether a target State may, for example, take countermeasures in response to an unsuccessful cyber operation that has not been completed e.g. due to defensive mechanisms from the target State. It is the view of Denmark that States cannot be presumed to have to suffer actual harm before taking countermeasures.

Denmark accepts the existence of general procedural requirements when taking countermeasures including an obligation to notify, but also supports the view put forward by a number of States that observance of these obligations may not be feasible in all circumstances in a cyber-context.

Countermeasures must be directed against State organs or other entities acting on behalf of, or whose acts are attributable to, a State as it is the State that is in breach of its obligations vis-à-vis the target State. This, however, does not necessarily exclude that actions may in some circumstances be directed against non-State actor as part of countermeasures.

The question of collective countermeasures does not seem to have been fully settled in state practice and needs careful consideration. As a general observation Denmark finds that there may be instances where one State suffers a violation of an obligation owed to the international community as a whole, and where the victim State may request the assistance of other States in applying proportionate and necessary countermeasures in collective response hereto.

8 International humanitarian law and cyber operations

Denmark concurs with the view put forward by a number of States that international humanitarian law (IHL) applies to cyber operations undertaken in the context of armed conflict. This is the case regardless of whether the cyber operation takes place during an international or a non-international armed conflict.

With regard to the application of IHL in the cyber domain one key issue concerns the definition of attack and under which circumstances a cyber operation can amount to an attack.

Denmark is a party to the four Geneva Conventions and Additional Protocols and defines cyber-attack within the meaning of Article 49 of Additional Protocol I. Denmark takes the view that a cyber operation may be considered an attack in the context of an armed conflict where it produces effects akin to those of a kinetic attack. Consequently, a cyber operation will constitute an attack if it can be reasonably expected to cause injury, death, or physical damage to individuals or objects. This definition also includes activity where substantial destruction is caused as a foreseeable secondary effect. For instance, if a military air traffic control system through a cyber operation is taken out of operation which causes foreseeable loss of human life or substantial damage to or destruction of physical objects.

Although digital data cannot generally in and of itself be considered an object under IHL, the destruction of data may have such adverse secondary effects on individuals or physical objects that the operation may nonetheless qualify as an attack. This may be the case where the destruction of data foreseeably results in injury, death or physical damage, in which case the objects or individuals subject hereto can be considered the object of the attack. Similarly, an operation targeting data upon which the functionality of an object relies could qualify as an attack depending on the nature and scale of the damage foreseeably resulting from the operation in question.

Where a cyber operation amounts to an attack it is subject to the same rules and requirements as those applicable to attacks conducted in the physical domain. These include, inter alia, the principles of military necessity, distinction, proportionality, and humanity.

In situations where a cyber operation does not amount to an attack the relevant rules of IHL that address conducts or effects falling below the threshold of an attack nevertheless apply. This includes but is not limited to the obligation of constant care by which States are required to take all reasonable precautions to spare the civilian population as well as civilian individuals and objects, including essential civilian infrastructure, services, and data, when planning or conducting cyber operations in the context of hostilities.

Note from the publisher

The authors mentioned at the start of this chapter, Jeppe Mejer Kjelgaard and Ulf Melgaard, are only responsible for the introduction to this position paper. The position paper is a product of the government of Denmark.

CHAPTER 6

Virtual Groups and the Triggering of Armed Conflicts

Marie Thøgersen

Abstract

The chapter examines how virtual groups can trigger an armed conflict, and thus, the application of international humanitarian law (IHL). The emergence of non-State actors as central players in cyberspace, together with the increasing use of cyber operations in conflicts, makes the regulation of non-State actors in armed conflicts a topical issue. The triggering provisions in IHL require a level of organization of non-State groups, which do not necessarily resonate with the realities among virtual groups. To determine if the triggering provisions allow for a reinterpretation to fit better the potentially differently structured virtual groups, the chapter scrutinizes the legal bases for the organization requirements in the respective provisions and identities the underlying rationales. The chapter concludes that the legal bases for the organization requirement in the three provisions are distinct, but that none of them currently allows for reinterpretation.

Keywords

non-State armed groups – cyber warfare – triggering of armed conflicts

 | DOI:10.1163/9789004703933_007

1 Introduction

Cybersecurity plays an inevitable role in contemporary conflicts. As States increasingly rely on digital technology and infrastructure, their cyber vulnerabilities also increase. This makes technologically advanced States particularly vulnerable to malicious cyber operations. In general, non-State actors have emerged as central players in the cyber domain, with the capacity to mount cyber operations that can profoundly affect States' security.[1] Full-blown cyber warfare is a phenomenon that is yet to be seen, but cyber vulnerabilities are frequently exploited in the context of conflicts along with kinetic means as part of broader military strategies. In this rapidly developing landscape, it is essential to consider the legal consequences of digital warfare.

While some have suggested the need to adopt new treaty law to ensure a legal framework that fits the new realities of cyberspace,[2] most scholars consider this unrealistic.[3] There appears to be a consensus among the majority of States, including the Nordic States, that it is both possible and preferable to respond to the developments occurring in cyberspace through an interpretation of existing international law. Accordingly, existing international legal norms are considered to provide a sufficient regulatory framework to govern this new and rapidly changing reality.[4] This approach requires that the current legal framework be interpreted and applied to remain responsive to the new reality occurring.

The emergence of non-State actors as central players in cyberspace, together with the increasing use of cyber operations in conflicts, makes the regulation of non-State actors in armed conflicts a topical issue. International law, including international humanitarian law (IHL), primarily governs the

1 M.N. Schmitt and S. Watts, 'Beyond State-Centrism: International Law and Non-State Actors in Cyberspace' 21 Journal of Conflict and Security Law (2016) p. 595.

2 'The Hypocrisy of Russia's Push for a New Global Cybercrime Treaty' Lowy Institute <https://www.lowyinstitute.org/the-interpreter/hypocrisy-russia-s-push-new-global-cybercrime-treaty> accessed 22 August 2023; 'A Digital Geneva Convention to Protect Cyberspace' Microsoft Cybersecurity <https://www.microsoft.com/en-us/cybersecurity/content-hub/a-digital-geneva-convention-to-protect-cyberspace> accessed 22 August 2023.

3 M. Waxman, 'Self-Defensive Force Against Cyber Attacks: Legal, Strategic and Political Dimensions' 89 Int'l L. Stud. (2013) p. 109; C. Droege, 'Get off My Cloud: Cyber Warfare, International Humanitarian Law, and the Protection of Civilians' 94 International Review of the Red Cross (2012) p. 533; M.N. Schmitt, 'The Law of Cyber Conflict: Quo Vadis 2.0?' <https://papers.ssrn.com/abstract=4260951> (28 January 2022) accessed 7 February 2023; M. Schack, 'Folkeret i cyberspace: Udfordringer og muligheder' in *Cybertrusler: Det digitale samfunds skyggeside* (2022) p. 297.

4 This was the attitude of the speakers from Denmark, Norway, Sweden and Finland, at the conference: Nordic Perspectives on the International Legal Regulation of Cyberspace (28 September 2022).

relationships between States.[5] To the extent that IHL regulates the engagement of non-State actors, the regulation often relies on certain assumptions about the characteristics of the actors, which do not necessarily resonate with the realities amongst non-State actors in the digital domain. For example, some non-State groups solely have a virtual existence – group members do not meet frequently, they do not have formal hierarchies or command structures, and the entire coordination of their activities is conducted on the internet. Notably, cyber operations conducted by such groups have so far been safely below the severity required for the Geneva Conventions to be even remotely relevant. As such, the topic of this chapter – the question of how such virtual groups can trigger an armed conflict – and thus, trigger the application of IHL – is, admittedly, of a hypothetical nature. However, developments in the cyber realm tend to happen at a faster pace than in the traditionally conservative realm of law. Thus, there is good reason to explore the plasticity in our legal norms to predict their suitability for the regulation of new types of actors with different characteristics.

The focus of the chapter is on the application of the triggering provisions in IHL to a new type of *actors* existing in cyberspace, rather than to a new type of *weaponry*. In reality, those two assessments are connected; as this chapter demonstrates, the legal regulation of the actors may also depend on their capacities to do harm. Therefore, considerations regarding the capacities of virtual non-State groups are included to a limited extent where relevant, but general questions as to the prospects of cyber operations reaching particular thresholds of severity in IHL is beyond the scope of this chapter. Instead, and despite the fact that the majority of cyber operations have so far been safely below the level of hostilities required for the existence of an armed conflict, the chapter assumes that such a scenario cannot be rejected as unrealistic and that it is therefore relevant to consider how virtual groups fit into the legal framework of IHL.

The chapter is structured as follows. To lay the groundwork, the following section introduces the legal framework that determines when an armed conflict is triggered by a non-State group. As the section demonstrates, the triggering provisions of the four Geneva Conventions (common article 2 (CA2) and common Article 3 (CA3)) have been interpreted as requiring a certain level of organization, and an explicit organization requirement is contained in Additional Protocol II to the Geneva Conventions relating to the Protection of Victims of Non-International Armed Conflicts (APII). Section 3 provides some reflections on the consequences of applying a requirement of organization to virtual groups. Concluding that virtual groups fall short of meeting such

5 Schmitt and Watts, *supra* note 1.

requirement, the foundation has been established for a scrutiny in section 4 of the plasticity of the organization requirement under the three provisions. Thus, the section dissects the legal bases for the organization requirements in the provisions to identify the underlying rationales and, on that basis, assess the relevance of the organization requirement for virtual groups. This analysis leads to a conclusion as to the possible room for reinterpretation of the legal norms due to the new reality occurring.

2 The Legal Framework: Non-State Groups Triggering Armed Conflicts

IHL regulates the conduct of hostilities and seeks to ensure a minimum level of humanitarian safeguards in conflict situations. While States have traditionally been the main international actors, including in warfare, it was recognized in the Geneva Conventions that a non-State armed group might also be a party to a conflict. Thus, with the introduction of CA3, States agreed for the first time on regulating, in an international treaty framework, what was at the time considered by States as being exclusively their domestic affair: the non-international armed conflict (NIAC).[6] Compared with the number and detail of the provisions governing international armed conflicts (IACs) in the Geneva Conventions, CA3 is far less elaborate and was already at the 1949 Diplomatic Conference described as a "convention in miniature".[7] To a significant extent, IAC norms have now migrated into the NIAC realm, but differences still prevail. In particular, the NIAC regime does not provide for prisoner-of-war status and contains no equivalent to the occupation law regime. Moreover, unlike CA2, CA3 requires a level of sustained hostilities between the parties – the existence of "protracted armed violence" taking place within a certain defined area – before an armed conflict exists.[8] As such, the same hostile conduct may trigger an IAC if perpetrated by a State against another, but might not trigger a NIAC if conducted by a non-State actor.[9] This is particularly relevant in a cyber-context, where attacks often fall below the required threshold, or where there is uncertainty as to the exact scope of consequences of an attack. The legal

6 ICRC, *Commentary on the First Geneva Convention: Convention (I) for the Amelioration of the Condition of the Wounded and Sick in Armed Forces in the Field* (2nd edn, 2016) para. 351, 356.

7 *Ibid* para. 355.

8 M. Milanovic and V. Hadzi-Vidanovic, 'A Taxonomy of Armed Conflict' in N. White and C. Henderson (eds.), *Research Handbook on International Conflict and Security Law* (Edward Elgar Publishing 2013) p. 270 <http://www.elgaronline.com/view/9781849808569.00013.xml> accessed 24 February 2023.

9 *Ibid* 274.

regulation of NIACs has been further developed and supplemented with APII, which entails more extensive obligations on the conflict parties, but which also contains higher criteria for its application.[10] To conclude, the classification of a conflict remains the first step in any analysis under IHL.[11] Section 2.1 examines the organization requirement in the legal framework for the triggering of NIACs, *i.e.* CA3 and APII, Article 1. Section 2.2 examines the organization requirement in the legal framework for the triggering of IACs, *i.e.* CA2.

2.1 *Non-State Groups Triggering* NIACs

The text of CA3 defines a NIAC in the negative, as the provision simply establishes that the minimum humanitarian standards proscribed by the provision apply in the case of an armed conflict "not of an international character".[12] As such, the provision contains no explicit criterion or delimitation as to what type of armed group is capable of triggering a NIAC. In its decision on jurisdiction in the case of *Tadić*, the Appeals Chamber of the ICTY articulated what has now become widely accepted as a test of two criteria, namely (i) the intensity of the conflict and (ii) the organization of the parties to the conflict.[13] The criteria were later further developed in the case law of international tribunals. It is now established that the armed group is required to have some degree of organization, but that it does not necessarily need to be as organized as the armed forces of a State.[14] Indicative factors for whether a sufficient level of organization is reached include the existence of a command structure and disciplinary rules and mechanisms within the group; the existence of a headquarters; the control over a certain territory; the ability to gain access to weapons, other military equipment, recruits and military training; its ability to plan, coordinate and carry out military operations, including troop movements and logistics; its ability to define a unified military strategy and use military tactics; and its ability to speak with one voice and negotiate and conclude agreements such as cease-fire or peace accords.[15] As such, the provision has

10 M.M. Bradley, 'Additional Protocol II: Elevating the Minimum Threshold of Intensity?' 102 International Review of the Red Cross (2020), p. 1131.

11 M.N. Schmitt, 'Classification of Cyber Conflict' 17 Journal of Conflict and Security Law (2012), p. 245.

12 ICRC, *Commentary on the First Geneva Convention: Convention (I) for the Amelioration of the Condition of the Wounded and Sick in Armed Forces in the Field* (1st edn, 1952) p. 49.

13 *Prosecutor v Duško Tadić* (Appeals Chamber of the ICTY, Decision on the Defence Motion for Interlocutory Appeal on Jurisdiction) para. 70.

14 *Prosecutor v Boškoski and Tarčulovski*, 2008, ICTY, Trial Chamber II Judgment, IT-04-82, para. 197.

15 *Prosecutor v Ramush Haradinaj, Idriz Balaj & Lahi Brahimaj*, 3 April 2008, ICTY, Trial Chamber II Judgment, IT-04-84, para. 60; *Prosecutor v Fatmir Limaj, Haradin Bala & Isak Musliu*, 30 November 2005, ICTY, Trial Chamber II Judgment, IT-03-66, para. 102.

been interpreted as requiring a certain level of organization of the armed group. Consequently, the organizational structure of a group is imperative for the application of CA3.

The legal regulation of NIACs has been further developed and supplemented with Protocol Additional to the Geneva Conventions of 12 August 1949, and relating to the Protection of Victims of Non-International Armed Conflicts (APII), which entails more extensive obligations on the conflict parties.[16] However, not all conflicts triggering a NIAC under CA3 will suffice to trigger the application of APII. First, the intensity threshold for the application of APII is higher; the application of the convention requires "sustained and concerted military operations", which elevates the minimum threshold of protracted armed violence in CA3.[17] Second, and more relevant for the present purpose, the protocol applies in a situation where a the armed forces of a State confront dissident armed forces or fight against organized armed groups, the latter more often being the case.[18] Thus, for armed groups, the provision contains an explicit requirement on organization. In addition, for both dissident armed forces and organized armed groups, the provision requires that the group operate under responsible command. This further implies some degree of organization of the insurgent armed group or dissident armed forces. While it does not necessarily require a hierarchical system of military organization similar to that of regular armed forces, the organization must be capable, on the one hand, of planning and carrying out sustained and concerted military operations, and on the other, of imposing discipline in the name of a de facto authority.[19] The provision further requires that the group exercise such control over a part of its territory as to enable them to carry out sustained and concerted military operations and to implement APII.

As such, both CA3 and APII contain an organization requirement. In contrast to the organization requirement in CA3, for APII, this requirement can be deduced directly from the text of the convention.

2.2 *Non-State Groups Triggering IACs*

Despite CA2 defining an IAC as an armed conflict between two or more States, international tribunals have accepted that the armed activities of non-State groups may also trigger an IAC. Thus, an armed conflict between an armed

16 Bradley, *supra* note 10, p. 1131.

17 *Ibid* 1152.

18 ICRC, *Commentary on Protocol Additional to the Geneva Conventions of 12 August 1949, and Relating to the Protection of Victims of Non-International Armed Conflicts (Protocol II)*, 8 June 1977 (1st edn, 1987) para. 4460.

19 *Ibid* 4463.

group and a State, *prima facie* resembling a NIAC, may turn international if the armed group is acting on behalf of a State. The imperative question is what degree of authority or control must be wielded by a State over armed forces fighting on its behalf in order to trigger an IAC.[20] This question became relevant for the International Criminal Tribunal for the Former Yugoslavia (ICTY) when it had to determine whether the regime of grave breaches under IHL, only applicable in IACs, applied to the war crimes committed by Tadić, a prison guard in a Bosnian Serb prison camp. As such, the Appeals Chamber had to determine whether the *prima facie* non-international conflict between the Bosnian Muslims, the Croats and the Serbs would turn international because of the involvement of the Federal Republic of Yugoslavia (FRY) in the conflict. The ICTY found that this question should be informed by Article 4A of the Geneva Convention Relative to the Treatment of Prisoners of War of 12 August 1949 (GCIII), establishing when members of militias or paramilitary groups may obtain combatant status. The provision implies that members of such groups may obtain combatant status if the group belongs to a State, provided that certain additional requirements are fulfilled. The ICTY found that the term "belonging to" implicitly refers to a test of control. However, it did not find any relevant criteria in IHL for establishing when a group of individuals was under such control.[21] Because of the lack of specific rules, the court found it necessary to examine the notion of control by a State over individuals laid down in general international law. The ICTY found this notion in the customary rules on State responsibility, which set out the legal criteria for attributing acts of non-State actors to a State.[22] According to the ICTY, logically, the conditions on which under international law an individual may be held to act as a *de facto* organ of a State must be the same, regardless of whether the question at stake is about attributing acts of the individual to the State for the purpose of State responsibility, or about determining whether non-State actors act as *de facto* State officials, rendering a conflict international.

This approach triggered a jurisprudential dispute between the ICTY and the International Court of Justice (ICJ). The ICJ had previously considered the question of attribution for State responsibility in the case of *Nicaragua*, in which it had to determine whether the acts of *the contras*, an armed non-State opposition group, could be attributed to the United States government because of State support for the operations of the group.[23] In broad terms, the

20 *Prosecutor v Duško Tadić,* 15 July 1999, ICTY, Appeals Chamber Judgment, para. 97.

21 *Ibid* para. 98.

22 *Ibid* para. 99, 105.

23 *Case Concerning Military and Paramilitary Activities in and against Nicaragua,* 27 July 1986, ICJ, Judgment on the merits, para. 109.

judgment articulates two coexisting tests of control leading to the attribution of acts of non-State actors to a State. The first test, which Milanovic names the test of complete control, implies that the relationship between a State and a non-State group must be so much one of dependence on one side and control on the other that it would be right to equate the group either with an organ of the State or as acting on its behalf.[24] The judgment suggests a list of criteria indicating whether this requirement is met, which essentially revolves around the requirement that the dependent group have no real autonomy from the controlling State.[25] If this test is met, then the actions of the group are generally attributable to a State. Consequently, no assessment of the degree of State involvement in specific operations is necessary. The second test articulated by the ICJ is subsidiary in nature, as it becomes relevant once the test of complete control is not fulfilled. It sets up criteria for the establishment of State control over the conduct of a specific operation in the course of which violations have been committed. The test implies a high threshold of control; State participation in the financing, organizing, training, supplying and equipping of the non-State actor, the selection of its targets and the planning of the whole of its operation is insufficient in itself for the purpose of attribution. The Court emphasizes that these measures do not imply that the acts of the non-State actor could not have been committed without the assistance of the State and, against this background, articulates the need for *effective control*.[26]

In the case of *Tadić*, when the ICTY was to consider the substantial requirements of attribution for the purpose of State responsibility, with a view to applying those requirements for conflict classification, it initially looked toward the approach taken by the ICJ in *Nicaragua*. In contrast to the analysis laid out above,[27] the ICTY does not read the *Nicaragua* judgment as containing two tests of control. Rather, it interprets the propounding of effective control as the substantial requirements under the first test, that is, that of dependence and control (in the terminology of Milanovic, the test of complete control[28]). Based on this reading, the ICTY found the approach of the ICJ unpersuasive.[29] Instead, it articulated its own test. The ICTY found that the degree of control

24 *Ibid* 109–110; M. Milanovic, 'State Responsibility for Genocide' 17 European Journal of International Law (2006) p. 553, 577; M. Milanovic, 'Special Rules of Attribution of Conduct in International Law' 96 International Law Studies (2020), p. 318.

25 Milanovic, *supra* note 24, p. 577.

26 *Nicaragua, supra* note 23, para. 115.

27 This reading is in accordance with the reading of the Prosecution and of dissenting Judge McDonald. *See Tadić (Appeals Chamber judgment), supra* note 20, para. 111; Milanovic, *supra* note 24.

28 Milanovic (n 24) 577.

29 *Tadić, supra* note 20, para. 115.

that the State should have over a non-State actor for the internationalization of the conflict may vary according to the factual circumstances of each case. For individuals, and for groups that are not militarily organized, it is necessary to prove not only that the State exercised some measure of authority over those individuals but also that it issued specific instructions to them concerning the performance of the acts at issue, or that it *ex post facto* publicly endorsed those acts.[30] In contrast, for individuals making up an organized and hierarchically structured group, such as a military unit or, in case of war or civil strife, armed bands of irregulars or rebels, it suffices to prove that the State wields *overall control* over the group, not only by equipping and financing the group, but also by coordinating or helping in the general planning of its military activity. The ICTY elaborates that this comprises more than the mere provision of financial assistance or military equipment or training, but does not go so far as to include the issuing of specific orders by the State, or its direction of each individual operation.[31] As such, it is not necessary that, in addition, the State should issue, either to the head or to members of the group, instructions for the commission of specific acts.[32] With this approach, the level of organization of the armed group becomes vital for the degree of involvement required from a State over the group before the actions of the group can trigger an IAC.

In the case of *Genocide*, the ICJ rejects the conceptual basis on which the ICTY has built its argumentation, as it finds that logic does not require the same test to be adopted in resolving the question of State involvement required to establish State responsibility and the question of State involvement in an armed conflict for the conflict to be characterized as international.[33] Moreover, substantially, the ICJ rejects the Tadić-approach for attribution for State responsibility, as it finds that it broadens the scope of State responsibility well beyond the fundamental principle governing the law of international responsibility.[34] As for the utility of the Tadić-approach for conflict classification, the ICJ holds that "it may well be that the test is applicable and suitable". As such, while rejecting the conceptual basis on which the approach was articulated, the ICJ leaves open the question of the substantial appropriateness of the criteria for conflict classification.

30 *Ibid* 118, 137.

31 *Ibid* 137.

32 *Ibid* 121, 131.

33 *Case Concerning Application of the Convention on the Prevention and Punishmen of the Crime of Genocide* (*Bosnia and Herzegovina v Serbia and Montenegro*) 11 July 1996, ICJ Judgment, para. 404.

34 *Ibid* para. 405.

Since then, the majority of scholars and States have substantially accepted the approach of the ICTY for conflict classification, while resorting to the approach of the ICJ for State responsibility. Therefore, relevant for the present purpose is the substantial approach taken by the ICTY, according to which the organizational structure of the group is decisive for the level of control required from the State over the non-State group for the triggering of an IAC.

In conclusion, non-State armed groups have the ability to trigger either a NIAC or an IAC. Classifying the conflict in question is the first step in any analysis under IHL, since the nature of the conflict determines the applicable legal regime. Both the triggering provisions of the Geneva Conventions, that is, CA2 and CA3, have been interpreted as requiring a certain level of organization of a non-State group. Moreover, APII, which extends the rules applicable to NIACs, contains an organization requirement in the text of the Convention. In contrast to the explicit organization requirement in APII, the requirements on organization in the application of CA2 and CA3 are not rooted in the text of the provisions, but have been developed in the jurisprudence of international tribunals. Notably, it is somewhat inaccurate to speak of a *requirement* on organization under CA2, since a non-organized group may also trigger an IAC if it acts under the specific instructions of a State. Apart from this nuance, the requirements appear remarkably similar. The Tallinn Manual 2.0 on the International Law Applicable to Cyber Operations (the Tallinn Manual 2.0) has suggested that the considerations regarding the nature of virtual groups in relation to the requirement on organization in CA3 are equally relevant in the context of GCIII Article 4A, out of which the CA2-criterion was arguably born.[35] Whether the same considerations are indeed relevant with regards to the application of the organization requirement under the different triggering provisions to virtual groups are explored in section 4.

3 Applying a Requirement on Organization to Virtual Groups

As section 2 demonstrates, the organizational structure of a non-State group is decisive for its ability to trigger an armed conflict. However, non-State groups operating in cyberspace have the potential to implement fundamentally different organizational structures than kinetic groups: Virtual groups may have the technical capacity to coordinate and conduct operations without their members meeting physically. This does not mean that no coordination

35 MN. Schmitt, *Tallinn Manual 2.0 on the International Law Applicable to Cyber Operations* (Second edition, University Press 2017) r 87, para. 10.

of activities take place in virtual groups; with the words of professor in anthropology Gabriella Coleman:

> Cooperation, fellowship, mutual aid, and even institution building are quotidian to the hacker experience – even among the most subversive, rule-breaking practitioners. ... Whether acknowledged or not by hackers themselves, all types of hacking embody profound forms of social entanglement and feelings of communion. These elements are established by a mutual adoration of technical pursuits and the pragmatic need to secure the help of others; crucially, the collective development of technology is bolstered by social spaces, and hackers have long had and continue to build and inhabit many of these – mailing lists and image boards, code repositories, free software projects, hacker and maker spaces, Internet chat relays, and developer and hacker conferences.[36]

Thus, virtual groups often find ways of collaborating, motivated by the potential to increase capacity through the help of others. Such collaboration may take the form of hacking collectives or networks of likeminded individuals. At the same time, this type of collaboration by no means ensures predictability or entails any measures of control over individual members. Cyberspace enables the quick formation of virtual groups with the ability to coordinate and conduct collective activities without leadership, a formal hierarchy, or a chain of command, and with no geographical boundaries. Those features imply that virtual groups carrying those characteristics are unlikely to be perceived as organized in the sense of CA2, CA3 and APII. Therefore, upholding an emphasis on organization for those groups implies that they are unlikely to trigger an armed conflict.

From an operational perspective, a challenge when applying an organization criterion in cyberspace is that it is technically difficult – and sometimes maybe impossible – for the victim of a hostile operation to gain sufficient knowledge on the organizational structure of the author group to determine whether it meets the required threshold to trigger a conflict.[37] The attribution problem in cyberspace is generally well known, but the emphasis on organization for the triggering of an armed conflict implies a further challenge for military commanders and legal advisers, as they must have intelligence on the organizational structure of the attacker to know what legal framework the operations must conform to. For these reasons, upholding the organization

36 G. Coleman, 'From Internet Farming to Weapons of the Geek', 58 Current Anthropology (2020) p. 91.

37 ICRC, *supra* note 6, para. 437.

criterion could hamper the civilian protection that the body of law was put in the world to ensure.

4 Testing the Plasticity: Room for Reinterpretation of the Triggering Provisions?

International legal norms necessarily evolve over time to ensure that the applicable normative architecture remains responsive to the context in which it applies.[38] The aim of this section is to explore how the organization requirements inherent in the triggering provisions, as examined above, could be interpreted and applied to virtual groups. It does so by testing the plasticity in the requirements, that is, the extent to which the legal norms allow for modifications of the requirements when reality changes. International law must be interpreted in accordance with the principles laid out in Article 31 of the Vienna Convention on the Law of Treaties.

Thus, the triggering provisions must be interpreted in good faith in accordance with the ordinary meaning to be given to the terms of the treaty in their context and in the light of its object and purpose. The context includes any subsequent agreement and any subsequent practice in the application of the treaty establishing the agreement of the parties regarding its interpretation. CA2 and CA3 are distinguishable from APII Article 1(1) in that no organization requirements are contained in the former two provisions, but have been subsequently developed in the application of the provisions. Thus, they are the result of an interpretation of the treaty, and the room – and need – for a reinterpretation depends on whether the link between the organization requirements and the legal sources are still valid in the light of a rapidly changing reality among non-State groups in cyberspace. Answering this question requires a dissection of the legal norms to understand the rationales behind the requirements on organization.

4.1 *The Plasticity in the Organization Requirement in CA3*

As is apparent from the analysis in section 2.1, no organization requirement is present in the text of CA3. Instead, it was developed by international tribunals in their interpretation of the provision. The Tallinn Manual 2.0 reiterates the requirement on organization in its application of CA3 to cyberspace. A majority of the IGE agreed that the failure of the members to meet physically does not alone preclude groups operating purely virtually from having the requisite degree of organization. With reference to the ICRC commentary on

38 Schmitt, *supra* note 3.

CA3, the manual states the rationale behind the requirement on organization is that it must be possible for the group to comply with IHL. No other possible rationales for organization are explicitly considered (although some of the indicating factors taken into consideration in the assessment of the organization requirement indeed point to other rationales). However, in fact, not only one but three possible rationales for an organization requirement can be deduced from the text of the Convention and identified in the practice of international tribunals. The rationales are reflected in different indicative factors for organization.

4.1.1 The First Rationale: Intensity of the Conflict

One rationale for the requirement of organization can be deduced from the text of the provision, as the term "armed conflict" has in itself been interpreted to suggest the existence of hostilities of a certain intensity.[39] The requisite intensity of hostilities may depend on the armed group being organized to a certain degree.[40] The ICTY has found the criteria of organization and intensity to be closely related, and in the ICRC commentary to CA3 both criteria are considered sub-criteria to determine whether the hostilities are above the requisite threshold.[41] The 2008 Report of the International Law Association's Use of Force Committee suggests that "[t]he criteria of organization and intensity are clearly related and should be considered together when assessing whether a particular situation amounts to an armed conflict. It seems that the higher the level of organization the less degree of intensity may be required and vice versa."[42] Based on this rationale, relevant indicia for organization include the ability of the group to gain access to weapons, other military equipment, recruits and military training; its ability to plan, coordinate and carry out military operations. In the same vein, the Tallinn Manual 2.0 emphasizes the ability to conduct sustained military operations as relevant indicia for organization.[43] Measuring virtual groups based on indicia for organization pointing to the intensity of operations, some virtual groups may have good prospects for meeting them. Indeed, cyber operations usually occur

39 *Prosecutor v Jean-Paul Akayesu*, 2 September 1998, ICTR, Chamber 1 Judgment ICTR-96-4-T, para. 620.

40 S. Sivakumaran, *The Law of Non-International Armed Conflict* (Oxford University Press 2012).

41 ICRC, *supra* note 6, para. 414 *et seq.*

42 Committee on the Use of Force, International Law Association, *Initial Report on the Meaning of Armed Conflict in International Law,* (2008) p. 22; R. Geiss, 'Cyber Warfare: Implications for Non-international Armed Conflicts', *International Law Studies, U.S. Naval War College* (2013). vol. 89.

43 Schmitt, *supra* note 35, rule 83.

at much lower levels of severity than kinetic operations. However, the scenario of highly destructive cyber operations meeting the threshold of protracted armed violence cannot be rejected as entirely unrealistic. A hacker's level of sophistication ultimately depends on expertise, not equipment.[44] As such, a small group of individuals, or even a single individual, can potentially cause considerable levels of harm through malicious hacking.[45] What is more, the flexibility that comes with a virtual and networked group structure may also help a group spreading across the globe.[46] Thereby, those very features may enable the group to overcome the problem of a general shortage of skilled labour in the cyber field.[47] Accordingly, based on indicative factors for organization pointing to the intensity of operations, the virtual, networked groups could well be treated as organized for the purpose of CA3.

4.1.2 The Second Rationale: Ability to Be a Party

However, the intensity-rationale does not stand alone. A second possible rationale may be deduced from the requirement that there are "parties" to the conflict. In assessing whether a non-State group constitutes a party, a certain level of organization may provide an indication that the violence is of a collective character, rather than being carried out by random individuals; thus, a requirement on organization is a way of distinguishing an armed conflict from banditry, unorganized and short-lived insurrections, or terrorist activities, which are not subject to IHL.[48] The ICTY has held that an armed conflict can exist only between parties that are sufficiently organized to confront each other with military means. State governmental authorities have been presumed to dispose of armed forces that satisfy this criterion.[49] On the other hand, for non-State armed groups, it must be concretely assessed whether the criterion is fulfilled. Assuming such a correlation between a certain level of organization and the ability to constitute a party, an organization requirement can arguably be deduced from the notion of "party".[50] With this rationale for organization, relevant indicative factors for the level of organization are: the existence of

---

44 T. Maurer, *Cyber Mercenaries: The State, Hackers, and Power* (1st edn, Cambridge University Press 2018), p. 13 <https://www.cambridge.org/core/product/identifier/9781316422724/type/book> accessed 15 February 2023.

45 *Ibid.*

46 G. Coleman, *Hacker, Hoaxer, Whistleblower, Spy: The Many Faces of Anonymous* (Verso Books 2015), p. 16.

47 Maurer, *supra* note 44, p. 38.

48 *Prosecutor v Duško Tadić* [1997] Trial Chamber II of the ICTY, Opinion and Judgment IT-94-I-T, para. 562; *Boškoski supra* note 14, para. 175; Sivakumaran *supra* note 40, p. 177.

49 *Haradinaj et al* (n 15) para. 60.

50 Sivakumaran, *supra* note 40, p. 177; ICRC, *supra* note 6, para. 423.

headquarters; the control of territory; and the ability to speak with one voice and negotiate and conclude agreements such as cease-fire or peace accords.[51] If emphasis is placed on those indicative factors, networked and virtual groups are unlikely to be considered sufficiently organized to constitute a party, and thereby to meet the criterion on organization.

4.1.3 The Third Rationale: Ability to Comply with IHL

The notion of parties to the conflict also brings with it responsibility on both sides.[52] This condition points to a third possible rationale for the requirement of organization, which is also, as mentioned above, the only rationale explicitly emphasized in the Tallinn Manual 2.0. A certain level of organization is assumed necessary for the non-State party to be able to comply with the obligations of CA3.[53] The International Law Association Committee on the Use of Force has noted that the "underlying theme" within the requirement of organization "is that there must be a sufficient level of organization through a command structure in order for the basic requirements of [CA3] to be implemented".[54] CA3 can only be applied to a particular factual situation if it can be applied by both parties to the armed conflict, namely the State and the armed group or both armed groups. This is a key feature of IHL, and is rooted in the principle of equality.[55] The requirement that the non-State group must have some form of responsible command and the capacity to implement IHL arguably precludes virtual groups from qualifying as organized armed groups. Members of virtual groups may be dispersed all over the globe,[56] and it would be difficult to establish an effective system of discipline within such a group to ensure respect for IHL.[57] The IGE in the Tallinn Manual 2.0 was divided as to whether the difficulty in complying with the requirement that the organization must be able to implement the law of armed conflict would bar qualification as an organized armed group.[58] Presumably, if the emphasis is put on indicative factors for organization pointing to the ability to comply with IHL, such as the existence of some form of responsible command, the existence of internal

---

51 *Haradinaj, supra* note 15, para. 60; *Limaj, supra* note 15, para. 102.

52 Sivakumaran, *supra* note 40.

53 *Ibid* 177.

54 International Law Association on the Use of Force, *Final Report on the Meaning of Armed Conflict in International Law*, The Hague Conference (2010) p. 29.

55 R. Bartels and K. Fortin, 'Law, Justice and a Potential Security Gap: The "Organization" Requirement in International Humanitarian Law and International Criminal Law' 21 Journal of Conflict and Security Law (2016), p. 38.

56 Droege, *supra* note 3, p. 550; Geiss, *supra* note 42, p. 630.

57 Droege, *supra* note 3, p. 550.

58 Schmitt, *supra* note 35, r 83, para. 14.

disciplinary systems and the capacity to implement IHL, networked and virtually organized groups are precluded from qualifying as organized armed groups. However, it cannot be excluded that it would be possible to establish a virtual system of discipline that would enable the group to comply with IHL. Some virtual organizations already have systems in place for democratic decision-making, allowing group members who have conducted operations of a certain level of sophistication, to gain influence on the direction of the group.[59] Perhaps it is, theoretically, equally possible to establish a virtual system of internal sanctioning for wrongful conduct. Whether such systems would suffice to meet the criterion of having a disciplinary system that enables the compliance with IHL is uncertain.

To conclude, three rationales for the requirement on organization can be deduced from CA3. The first rationale is based on an assumption about a correlation between organization and intensity of hostilities. This rationale may allow for some plasticity in the organization requirement; for cyber operations, the level of organization is not necessarily the most relevant indicator for the ability of the group to conduct highly destructive operations. On the contrary, a loose, networked group structure may enable a group to spread across the globe and attract skilled individuals. However, this rationale does not stand alone. A second rationale is based on an assumption about a correlation between organization and the ability to be party to a conflict; a third rationale is based on an assumption about a correlation between organization and ability to ensure compliance with IHL. These two rationales are equally valid in the context of virtual groups, and applying the indicia for organization pointing to these rationales to virtual groups would lead to the conclusion that they could not be considered organized. As all three rationales can be deduced from the provision and have been applied by international criminal tribunals. Therefore, they must all be taken into consideration in the interpretation and application of CA3 to virtual groups. This leads to the conclusion that there is not room for a reinterpretation of CA3. As such, the requirement on organization must be upheld for virtual groups, and it is unlikely that such groups will be able to trigger a NIAC.

4.2 *The Plasticity in the Organization Requirement in* APII

In APII, the organization requirement can be directly deduced from the ordinary meaning of the terms of the treaty; APII, Article 1(1) establishes that to trigger the application of the Convention, the non-State party must be "dissident armed forces or other organized armed groups". Already for this

59 Coleman, *supra* note 46.

reason, the plasticity of the requirement is presumably limited. Moreover, interestingly, all three rationales behind the organization requirement in CA3 are reflected in the wording of APII. Thus, the requirement on organization appears to be highly similar in the two provisions, albeit their legal bases are different. For the reasons stated in section 4.1, and due to the safe legal basis in the text of the Convention, there is no room for reinterpretation of the organization requirement in APII, Article 1(1).

4.3 *Plasticity in the Organization Requirement in CA2*

As is apparent from the analysis in section 2.2, the road to the development of a criterion on organization in the jurisprudence on CA2 is slightly less straightforward than for CA3. As of today, the *Tadić*-approach is widely acknowledged by States and in the jurisprudence of international courts and tribunals for the assessment of the existence of an IAC and must be considered state-of-the-art. However, the ICJ's subsequent rejection of the conceptual basis on which the approach was built makes the legal nature of the *Tadić*-approach uncertain. Does the approach, despite being articulated as an (erroneous) identification of the rules on State responsibility, constitute an interpretation of CA2? Alternatively, does it constitute a specific IHL rule of customary international law? To the extent that the approach constitutes an interpretation of treaty law, the subsequent endorsement of the approach may be perceived as subsequent practice in the application of the treaty, which should be taken into account in the interpretation of the treaty. To the extent that the approach constitutes a rule of customary international law, it constitutes a binding legal source in its own capacity.

Regardless of the perception of the approach as subsequent practice or customary international law, it constitutes an IHL -specific rule. Moreover, several treaty rules under IHL have the status of customary law, and attempting to make a clear distinction between the evolvement of the two types of legal norms is beyond the scope of this chapter. The continued relevance of organization depends, either way, on whether the rationale behind the emphasis holds in the context of cyberspace. Accordingly, the next step is to identify the rationale behind the emphasis on organizational structures, which must be found in the argumentation of the Appeals Chamber. As noted above, it found that the question of when a non-State armed group was fighting on behalf of a State should be informed by the standard laid out in Article 4A of the Third Geneva Convention, establishing when members of non-State armed forces participating in an IAC may gain combatant status. This provision requires that the group "belongs to" a State, which according to the ICTY implies a test of control. The ICTY resorts to the rules on State responsibility to determine the substance of this test of control. With its finding that the rules on State responsibility require a distinction between organized and non-organized groups, the ICTY deviates from the test of control articulated by the ICJ, which is today widely acknowledged for State responsibility. Regardless of the perception of the ICTY that it was a reflection of general international law on State responsibility, reality is that the test, and its logic, is IHL -specific. The rationale behind the distinction between organized and hierarchically structured groups and, on the other hand, individuals and groups not sufficiently organized is that IHL is a "realistic body of law", not grounded on formalistic postulates.[60] This notion implies that a formal position of authority is not crucial for the legal characterization of a certain act.[61] An organized group differs from an individual in that the former normally has a structure, a chain of command and a set of rules as well as the outward symbols of authority. Members of the group normally do not act on their own but conform to the standards prevailing in the group and are subject to the authority of the head of the group.[62] Regardless of the absence of formal recognition as a State organ, if a non-State armed group *resembles* as a group forming part of the State's armed forces, the acts of such a group should be treated in the same way under IHL as the act of the State. As such, the rationale behind the delimitation of the scope of application of the test of overall control to organized armed groups is that individuals and insufficiently organized groups do not resemble a group forming part of the State's armed forces. This rationale is closely connected to the nature of IHL and is, as such, a relevant consideration, regardless of whether one considers the *Tadić*-approach an interpretation of treaty law or an IHL -specific rule of customary international law. Consequently, despite the conceptual confusion that the complicated jurisprudential history has brought with it, the rationale of the Appeals Chamber for the emphasis on organization remains relevant.

Applied to cyberspace, the rationale implies that a general change in the way that non-State actors organize in the digital domain is not sufficient to allow for plasticity in the organization requirement. What matters is that the non-State group resembles a group of the State. As such, as long as the State's armed forces remain organized, so must non-State groups for the test of overall control to be applicable. However, in the case of States' armed forces, in particular their cyber armies, starting to loosen their organizational structure,

60 *Tadić, supra* note 20, para. 96.

61 *Ibid.*

62 *Ibid.*, para. 120.

the organization requirement for non-State actors for the applicability of the test of overall control should be affected.

5 Conclusion

This chapter has examined how virtual groups can trigger an armed conflict in light of the emphasis in the triggering provisions on the organizational structure of non-State groups. To set the scene, section 2 introduced the legal framework determining when an armed conflict is triggered. In the NIAC realm, which has the most obvious relevance when a non-State group is involved, two categories of NIACs exist. It was concluded that in both categories, a certain level of organization of the non-State group is required for the triggering of a conflict. As for the first category of NIACs, that is, those regulated in CA3, the organization requirement has been developed in the case-law of international criminal tribunals. As for the second category of NIACs, that is, those NIACs that (moreover) satisfy the requirements for the application of APII, an organization requirement appears directly in the text of the APII, Article 1(1). Despite CA2 defining an IAC as an armed conflict between two or more States, the hostile activities of a non-State group against a State may also trigger an IAC. This requires that the group is acting on behalf of a State. In this determination, the organizational structure is decisive: an organized armed group is only required to be under the overall control of a State, whereas an individual or a non-organized armed group must receive specific instructions from the State. As such, in all categories of armed conflicts, the organizational structure of a non-State group is decisive for its ability to trigger a conflict.

Section 3 reflected on the characteristics of virtual groups and on the consequences of applying an organization requirement to those groups. It was concluded that virtual groups often fall short of meeting these requirements. Against this background, section 4 examined the plasticity in the organization requirement under the triggering provisions by dissecting their legal foundations. Under CA3, three rationales for organization were identified: the ability to conduct operations of a certain intensity; the ability to be a party to the conflict; and the ability to ensure compliance with IHL. While the first rationale could potentially be challenged by virtual groups, the latter two rationales were equally valid for virtual groups. As such, there was no room for a reinterpretation of the organization requirement in CA3. The organization requirement under APII, Article 1(1) was deduced directly from the text of the Convention, which also contained rationales similar to CA3. Thus, there was no room for reinterpretation this provision either. The examination of the plasticity in CA2 was complicated by the intricate jurisprudential history leading to the approach now constituting state-of-the-art. However, the section concluded that the rationale behind the emphasis on organization is that the group should resemble an organ of the State. The factual change that would be needed before the emphasis on organization could not be upheld is a change in the organization of the States' cyber organs, which is yet to be seen.

CHAPTER 7

Attacking Data: Moving beyond the Interpretative Quagmire of the 'Data as an Object'-Debate

Marc Schack and Katrine Lund-Hansen

Abstract

A key contemporary challenge for international lawyers is to determine how international humanitarian law (IHL) applies to cyberoperations. This involves determining how IHL-language – devised for the physical world – can be translated into usable concepts for the digital age. Often, this is done largely by balancing the 'ordinary meaning' of specific IHL-concepts against the 'object and purpose' of IHL-treaties. This, at least, has been the case in the debate on whether the concept of 'objects' include or exclude (digital) data. Contributors to this debate often emphasize this balancing act, but also seem guided by what they consider acceptable outcomes. Specifically, they argue that what is legal in the analogue, physical world should not be rendered illegal through digitisation and vice versa. This chapter argues that this approach is unhelpful as it leads to conflicting results. Instead, we argue that the addition of a contextual analysis could help move the debate forward.

Keywords

cyber – international humanitarian law – legal interpretation – objects – data

1 Introduction

The fundamental function of international humanitarian law (IHL) is to balance the military necessity of using violence during armed conflict with considerations of humanity.[1] This aim permeates throughout the written and unwritten rules of IHL, which regulate namely how parties to an armed conflict can fight, whom and what they can lawfully target, and how vulnerable

1 M. N. Schmitt, 'Military Necessity and Humanity in International Humanitarian Law: Preserving the Delicate Balance' 50:4 *Virginia Journal of International Law* (2010).

 | DOI:10.1163/9789004703933_008

persons are to be spared from unnecessary danger, harm, and suffering. A key rule in this regard is article 52(2) of the Additional Protocol I to the Geneva Conventions (API),[2] which regulates attacks on objects. The rule states that:

> Attacks shall be limited strictly to military objectives. In so far as objects are concerned, military objectives are limited to those objects which by their nature, location, purpose or use make an effective contribution to military action and whose total or partial destruction, capture or neutralization, in the circumstances ruling at the time, offers a definite military advantage.

This rule makes clear, firstly, that only military objectives can be lawfully targeted, and secondly, that in so far as 'objects' are concerned, this includes only objects that can be considered legitimate military targets because of their particular nature, location, purpose, or use. As such, enemy weaponry and armored vehicles can generally be considered military objectives because of their core nature, while a particular bridge or landing strip might be a military objective because of its specific use. Conversely, 'civilian objects' are defined in the negative in API, article 52(1), simply as "all objects which are not military objectives".[3] These objects are protected from attack. While this system is spelled out quite clearly in the legal text, the margins of the system become less clear when we consider that, since its inception, a new kind of military objective has appeared, which does not fit neatly within the language used, but can nevertheless be targeted directly by the modern weaponry of armed forces: Data.

It has long been a subject of debate whether data in itself could be considered an 'object' within the meaning of IHL, and thus protected as such, or if some or all data fall outside the scope of this system and is thus largely unregulated in IHL. Many of the core arguments put forward in this debate are, we believe, based on overly simplistic interpretative approaches that focus on preserving the *status quo* rather than engaging constructively with the problem. As such, this chapter reviews the core tenets of these approaches to the 'data as an object'-problem, explain their shortcomings, and suggests a way forward for the debate. As such, the focus of this chapter is the question of whether data is to be included in the general rules protecting objects under IHL, without a need for a physical component to the military operation. As there is general agreement that once a cyberoperation that targets data results in physical

2 Protocol Additional to the Geneva Conventions of 12 August 1949, and relating to the Protection of Victims of International Armed Conflict (Protocol 1), 8 June 1977 (API).

3 *Ibid.*, article 52(1), second sentence.

damage or injury, it will be covered by IHL-regulation, we will not be covering these kinds of attacks. Rather, we focus exclusively on attacks on data that do not lead to physical damage – at least immediately and foreseeably. This problem, we believe, is of major importance to the future of IHL, as the answer can have major implications to future conflicts. Indeed, if data is included in the concept of 'objects', it will be protected by general rules on targeting in IHL, but also create a myriad of interpretative problems. If data is not included in this concept, it will result in a situation where data largely fall outside the scope of general IHL protection, thus leaving civilians vulnerable to a range of cyberoperations during armed conflict.

Two further notes should be made in terms of the delimitations of this chapter: Firstly, this chapter covers the general protection of objects under IHL. It does not deal with specific protections under IHL, such as the more specific rules on e.g., medical data. Secondly, for the purposes of this chapter, 'data' is understood simply as information that is stored, processed, or transmitted digitally, irrespective of its function. This definition includes so-called 'operational level-data', such as operating systems, applications, and individual lines of code, as well as 'content-level data', such as digital texts, images, or banking information.[4] In other words, data is all digital information that can, in principle, be reduced to its binary form.

The chapter starts out in part 2 by considering the rules of interpretation of the Vienna Convention on the Law of Treaties (VCLT).[5] From there, it presents the different modes of interpretation that are most prominent in the current literature. In part 3, the chapter presents highlights from an emerging State *opinio juris* on the matter, while in part 4, the chapter argues for the addition of the interpretative perspective of contextualisation to the current debate. The chapter concludes in part 5.

2 Solving the Problem through Interpretation

2.1 *Rules on Interpretation*

Article 31 of the VCLT contains general rules on treaty interpretation. Most notably, article 31(1) determines that "A treaty shall be interpreted in good faith in accordance with the ordinary meaning to be given to the terms of the treaty in their context and in the light of its object and purpose." This rule is usually read as containing four core elements of legal analysis: a 'good faith'-requirement,

4 See further considerations on the separation between operational data and content-level data in H. A. H. Dinniss, 'The Nature of Objects: Targeting Networks and the Challenge of Defining Cyber Military Objectives, 48:1 *Israel Law Review* (2015).

5 United Nations, *Vienna Convention on the Law of Treaties*, Treaty Series vol. 1155 (1969), p. 331.

an 'ordinary meaning'-textual analysis, a 'contextual'-analysis, and the consideration of 'object and purpose' (teleological). Although all four elements are, in principle, on equal footing and closely connected principles of interpretation, the most prominent components are surely the textual and teleological approaches. These emphasise either the specific language used in the rule being interpreted, or its overall object and purpose. This prominence is evident in most analyses of the 'data as an object'-problem.

As such, some participants in the 'data as an object'-debate focus on the ordinary meaning of the words used in Additional Protocol I. This textual approach has the advantage of being clearly based on the text itself without relying on potentially controversial modes of interpretation that extrapolates meaning from other circumstances surrounding it. A textual approach to interpretation is thus a sensible choice when the ordinary meaning of the words leads to a conclusion that is clear and non-ambiguous: This is what the authors wrote and, therefore, what they meant.

On the other hand, other participants in this debate tend to favour the teleological approach, which allows for an interpretation that can be described as 'dynamic', in that it makes it possible to consider changes in the society surrounding the rule, if such a dynamic approach best befits the aim of achieving the object and purpose of the rule. Thus, focusing on determining the object and purpose of a treaty as the main interpretative approach offers perspectives that consider the evolution of social, political, and, not least, technological circumstances in order for the rule to be relevant for the areas it was intended to regulate.

While these interpretative principles are, of course, meant to work in tandem, they are often employed as opposing views in legal deliberations. That is also true within this debate. Accordingly, while the two approaches should not necessarily lead legal interpreters to arrive at opposing conclusions, this seems to be the case when applied to the question of 'data as an object', as will be seen below.

2.2 *Modes of Interpretation in the Current Debate*

As established, the question under debate is whether data can be considered an 'object', and thus potentially afforded protection from hostilities under IHL-rules if deemed a 'civilian object'. This question is, to an extent at least, a 'yes or no'-proposition. Those that answer the question in the negative – and reject the idea that data can be considered an object – are understood in this chapter as representatives of a 'traditionalist' camp. This is because their arguments tend to favour a highly cautious approach to legal interpretation. Conversely, the contributors to the debate that answer the question in the positive – and thus accept data as an object (in some cases) – are considered representatives of an 'evolutionist' camp, as they allow for progressive developments in their legal interpretation. The following section outlines the main arguments of these two camps and posits that, while both camps argue in good faith and arrive at legally defensible conclusions, their approach exposes a key fault in their logic. As such, while both camps ostensibly represent legal approaches that simply emphasise different elements of commonly accepted principles of interpretation (textual versus teleological interpretations), they nevertheless seem guided by the same underlying logic. And as this parallel logic leads the two camps to diametrically opposing results, it is suggested that this reveals a fundamental flaw in these approaches. It should be noted, however, that some contributors to the debate do not fall neatly into these categories. This includes, for example, Robin Geiß and Henning Lahmann, who apply an approach that moves beyond existing IHL to push the conversation forward.[6] Such approaches are, however, quite rare.

2.2.1 The Traditionalist Camp

As noted, the traditionalists seek to solve the issue of the status of civilian data in IHL largely through a textual approach. This camp is most prominently represented by the majority of the International Group of Experts behind the Tallinn-manual (2.0). In the manual their view on the matter is summarised as follows:

> The majority of the International Group of Experts agreed that the law of armed conflict notion of 'object' is not to be interpreted as including data, at least in the current state of the law. In the view of these Experts, data is intangible and therefore neither falls within the 'ordinary meaning' of the term object, nor comports with the explanation of it offered in the ICRC Additional Protocols 1987 Commentary. Therefore, an attack on data *per se* does not qualify as an attack.[7]

As such, their argument is generally based on the basic logic that it has been clear since API was devised that the authors meant for an object to be interpreted as something visible and tangible. This follows from a simple textual interpretation of article 52, as set out in the 1987 ICRC Commentary on the Additional Protocol.[8] In this commentary, it is established that the dictionary

6 R. Geiß and H. Lahmann, 'Protection of Data in Armed Conflict', 97 *International Law Studies* (2021).

7 M. N. Schmitt (ed.), *Tallinn Manual 2.0 on the International Law Applicable to Cyber Operations* (Cambridge University Press, Cambridge, 2017) p. 437 (Tallinn Manual 2.0).

8 Y. Sandoz et al., *Commentary on the Additional Protocols of 8 June 1977 to the Geneva Conventions of 12 August 1949* (ICRC, 1987), pp. 633–634, (ICRC Commentary).

definitions of the chosen words of both the English and French versions of the text – "objects" and "biens" – only refer to physical things. Therefore, it is considered "clear that in both English and French the word means something that is visible and tangible."[9] The same requirement of tangibility applies to the concept of "military objectives", thus excluding an interpretation of such objectives as referring to a general aim or purpose – although it is noted that a French dictionary meaning of the term 'objective' gives it such an extended meaning.[10]

The view that only visible and tangible things can be considered civilian objects protected from attack is further supported by the definition of an attack as established in API article 49(1), where attacks are "acts of violence against the adversary whether in offence or in defence." The ICRC Commentary establishes that "in the sense of the Protocol an attack … refers simply to the use of armed force to carry out a military operation at the beginning or during the course of armed conflict."[11] Thus while a strict textual interpretation of article 49(1) could suggest that attacks require the use of violence in the execution of an act, it is broadly accepted that acts of violence not only encompasses acts that are carried out by violent means, but also those that have violent consequences.[12] This understanding is supported by the fact that non-kinetic acts such as employing biological and chemical agents have always been included in the definition of attack, on account of their violent consequences, whereas non-kinetic acts without violent consequences, such as psychological operations, are not considered attacks.[13] Therefore, the traditionalists argue, for something to be an attack, it must have violent consequences for something that is visible and tangible, i.e. death or injury to civilians or damage or destruction to civilian objects.[14]

9 *Ibid.*, p. 634.
10 *Ibid.*, p. 634.
11 *Ibid.*, p. 603.
12 *See* C. Droege, 'Get Off My Cloud: Cyber Warfare, International Humanitarian Law, and the Protection of Civilians', 94:886 *International Review of the Red Cross* (2012), p. 557; *and* L. Gisel, T. Rodenhäuser and K. Dörmann, 'Twenty Years On: International Humanitarian Law and the Protection of Civilians Against the Effects Of Cyber Operations During Armed Conflicts', 913 *International Review of the Red Cross* (2021), p. 2.
13 M. Bothe, K. J- Partsch and W. A. Solf, *New Rules for Victims of Armed Conflicts: Commentary on the Two 1977 Protocols Additional to the Geneva Conventions of 1949* (Martinus Nijhoff, The Hague, 1982), p. 289.
14 M. N. Schmitt, 'The Notion Of 'Objects' During Cyber Operations: a Riposte in Defence of Interpretive and Applicative Precision', 48:1 *Israel Law Review* (2015), p. 86.

When it comes to the issue of data, therefore, the traditionalists argue that, as data is neither tangible nor visible, it cannot be seen as a protected civilian object in itself. Any operation that results in the destruction of only civilian data would thus not be an attack. Rather, what determines whether an attack on civilian objects has taken place would be any associated damage and destruction to actual visible, tangible objects.[15]

Importantly, the traditionalists bolster their argument by noting that if data were to be included as protected objects, it would afford protection to areas that were never intended to be protected. As an example, the blocking of television signals as a psychological operation against a civilian population has always been permitted, they argue.[16] The fact that most television signals are now digitised should not impact the legality of such an operation, even if such a blocking action would now require the deletion or damage to data that is, in essence, civilian. The inclusion of all civilian data as protected objects would thereby lead to an overly broad interpretation of API, article 52, and would lead to absurd and unreasonable results. Indeed, Michael N. Schmitt notes that these considerations – and not the purely textual interpretation – was "a more influential factor" for the majority of the International Group of Experts, and namely that the experts were unprepared to accept such outcomes.[17] Thus, the idea of preserving the *status quo* of legality became the key factor that aided the experts in defining the concept of objects within API.

As should be clear, the traditionalists undoubtably have a point in noting that the ordinary meaning of words like 'object' and 'violence' point towards considerations of physicality and tangibility. Indeed, the Oxford Dictionary of English defines the word 'violence' namely as "behaviour involving physical force intended to hurt, damage, or kill someone or something", while it defines the word 'object' namely as "a material thing that can be seen and touched". These definitions obviously point towards an element of tangibility. However, as will be seen below, a question remains as to whether the ordinary meaning of these words should be determinative for the interpretation of the rule in today's modern, digitised society – especially given the reliance on the consequences of this interpretative approach, rather than its purely textual origins.

2.2.2 The Evolutionist Camp

The evolutionist side of the debate employs a teleological logic to determine that data should, at least in some cases, be considered objects within the

15 *Ibid.*, p. 97.

16 *Ibid.*, p. 93–94.

17 *Ibid.*

meaning of IHL. This camp is most prominently represented by the minority of the International Group of Experts behind the Tallinn-manual (2.0), and in response to the above quoted arguments by the majority, the minority argued that:

> [F]or the purposes of targeting, certain data should be regarded as an object. In [the minority's] view, the majority position is under inclusive in the sense that failure to include cyber operations targeting data *per se* in the scope of the term 'attack' would mean that even the deletion of essential civilian datasets such as social security data, tax records, and bank accounts would potentially escape the regulatory reach of the law of armed conflict, thereby running counter to the principle (reflected in Article 48 of Additional Protocol I) that the civilian population enjoys general protection from the effects of hostilities. For these Experts, the key factor, based on the underlying object and purpose of Article 52 of Additional Protocol I, is one of the severity of the operation' s consequences, not the nature of harm. Thus, they were of the view that, at a minimum, civilian data that is 'essential' to the well-being of the civilian population is encompassed in the notion of civilian objects and protected as such.[18]

Accordingly, the evolutionists essentially argue that the object and purpose of API is to protect civilians and civilian items, and that it would thus run counter to the aspirations of API, if the concept of objects is understood as excluding data. Indeed, it is evident from the very name of the protocol that it relates to the 'protection of victims of international armed conflict', and it would thus make little sense to employ an interpretative approach that effectively hinders such protection. Given this object and purpose, the rules of API regarding the protection of civilian objects should be interpreted to ensure that the same protection is always afforded, regardless of societal or technological developments. As such, the evolutionists also employ a logic that focuses largely on the consequences of employing a certain interpretative logic. They cannot accept a narrow understanding of the concept of an object, simply because this would unreasonably limit the protections afforded to civilians by IHL. This argument can be understood as an attempt to hinder that civilians lose more and more protections as society digitises. Indeed, the minority refers to an argument put forward by the International Committee of the Red Cross

18 Tallinn Manual 2.0, *supra* note 7, p. 437.

(ICRC), which essentially attempts to straddle the divide between the contemporary definition of 'attacks' under IHL and other acts that do not constitute attacks in the physical domain – such as acts of espionage, or the jamming of radio communications or television broadcasts.[19] This argument was later picked up in another ICRC publications, where it was emphasised that "[i]n the ICRC's view, the conclusion that deleting or tampering with essential civilian data would not be prohibited by IHL in today's ever more data-reliant world seems difficult to reconcile with the object and purpose of this body of law."[20] The argument made for this conclusion strongly resembles the argument put forward by Michael N. Schmitt (and by extension, the majority of the International Group of Experts behind the Tallinn Manual 2.0) – although the focus is not on keeping certain military operations lawful, but on keeping certain military operations unlawful in a digitised world. The ICRC thus argue that "[p]ut simply, the replacement of paper files and documents with digital files in the form of data should not decrease the protection that IHL affords to them."[21] This logic entails that, for example, as it has always been unlawful to attack public archives, such as libraries or government registries, where civilian information is stored in the form of physical documents, it makes little sense to make the targeting of such documents lawful simply because they have been digitised. Not including civilian data as civilian objects in this sense would therefore vastly expand the types of permissible targets in armed conflict, far beyond what the authors of the API envisioned.[22] Indeed, it could be posited that the reasoning behind defining 'objects' in the ICRC commentary to Additional Protocol I as something tangible and visible was not to delimit the concept in the way argued by the traditionalist. Rather, the commentary can be seen, firstly, as simply a product of its time, where it was not considered or foreseen that data could play the major role that it does in modern society. Secondly, as argued by Heather A. Harrison Dinniss, the chosen definition could be seen as making the basic point that one should separate specific 'things' from abstract notions of, for example, the 'aim or purpose' of a military operation.[23] In support of this idea that the authors of API had not

---

19 International Committee of the Red Cross, *International Humanitarian Law and the Challenges of Contemporary Armed Conflict* (2015), p. 41–42.

20 International Committee of the Red Cross, *International Humanitarian Law and the Challenges of Contemporary Armed Conflict* (2019), p. 28.

21 *Ibid.*

22 K. Mačák, 'Military Objectives 2.0: The Case For Interpreting Computer Data As Objects Under International Humanitarian Law' 48:1 *Israel Law Review* (2015), p. 79.

23 Dinniss, *supra* note 4, p. 43.

made a conscious decision that should be read as a rejection of the notion that data can be understood as an object within this system, Dinniss highlights the fact that the ICRC Commentary merely refers to dictionary definitions of the concept in English and French, but does not refer "to any specific discussions that occurred in either the working committees or the Diplomatic Conference regarding the matter."[24]

From the above review of the arguments of the two camps, both sides are clearly intent on ensuring that the law covers what it did before the advent of the digital age: What was permissible before should still be permissible, and what was prohibited shall still be prohibited. In this light, we posit that interpretations that aim at conserving the legal *status quo* have little interpretative merit, as the same logic can be applied to reach completely opposite results. While these arguments ostensibly represent either a logic based on the ordinary meaning of the words used or the object and purpose of the legal framework interpreted, the chosen interpretative approach often seems to reflect a desired result rather than an unbiased conclusion. As such, strictly textual or teleological interpretations, as employed, fail to solve the problem.

3 *Emerging State* opinio juris

One way of finding a solution to this problem could be to consider how States have interacted in this area and to identify State-positions on this matter. However, at present, there is a lack of clear practice within this area, and the available expressions of *opinio juris* are both too limited and too diverse to enable us to settle the matter. As such, most States have up until now remained quiet about their views on the matter. Of the States that have chosen to comment, most seem to support the evolutionist camp, while fewer States choose to endorse the traditionalist approach. Chile, Denmark, and Israel have thus expressed explicit support for the traditionalist approach, while namely Costa Rica, Finland, France, Germany, Ireland, Norway, Peru, and Rumania have expressed explicit support for the evolutionist approach.[25] For the purposes

24 *Ibid.*

25 Chile, *'Response submitted by Chile to the OAS Inter-American Juridical Committee Questionnaire'*, quoted in OAS, Improving Transparency: International Law and State Cyber Operations: Fifth Report, OAS Doc. CJI/doc. 615/20 rev.1 (7. august 2020), para. 36; Danish Ministry of Defence/Defence Command Denmark, Military Manual on International Law Relevant to Danish Armed Forces in International Operations (2016 – English version published in 2020), p. 292, 310 (Danish Military Manual); Danish Ministry of Foreign Affairs, Denmark's Position Paper on the Application of International Law in

of exemplifying the types of statements represented here, we describe four of statements, which cover both the traditionalist and evolutionist perspectives and encompass all of the Nordic contributions to this debate. Thus, we focus on the Norwegian and Danish contributions, which represent mainly reflections presented in these States' military manuals, which predate most of the cyber-specific statements made on international law in general, while the two others represent reflections made more recently in cyber-specific statements on international law, where one is quite detailed, while the other is quite vague.

3.1 *Norway*

In the 2013 Norwegian Manual on the laws of war, the issue of data as a civilian object is broached in the review of whether an attack on data in itself can constitute a cyber-attack.[26] In setting the scene, the Manual notes that cyberattacks are covered by the same rules as other types of attack, and that cyber-attacks are defined as cyber operations that are expected to cause death or harm to persons or harm or destruction to objects.[27] The manual goes on to argue that "[I]n target selection, data must be considered objects and can

Cyberspace, Nordic Journal of International Law (2023), p. 10 (Denmark's cyber statement); R. Schöndorf, 'Israel's Perspective on Key Legal and Practical Issues Concerning the Application of International Law to Cyber Operations' (2021), 97 International Law Studies, p. 401; Costa Rica, *Position on the Application of International Law in Cyberspace* (2023), p. 13; Finland's Ministry of Foreign Affairs, *International law and cyberspaces, Finland's national positions* (2020), p. 7 (Finland's cyber statement); Ministère Des Armées, *Droit International Appliqué Aux Opérations Dans Le Cyberespace* (2019), p. 14 (France's cyber statement); The Federal Government of Germany, *On the Application of International Law in Cyberspace* (marts 2021), p. 8; Ireland Department of Foreign Affairs, *Position Paper on the Application of International Law in Cyberspace* (2023), p. 7–8; Forsvarets høgskole/Forsvarets stabsskole, *Manual i Krigens Folkerett* (2013), p. 190–191 (Norwegian Military Manual); Peru, '*Response submitted by Peru to the OAS Inter-American Juridical Committee Questionnaire*', quoted in OAS, Improving Transparency: International Law and State Cyber Operations: Fifth Report, OAS Doc. CJI/doc. 615/20 rev.1 (2020), para. 36; Rumanian statement in UN General Assembly, *Official compendium of voluntary national contributions on the subject of how international law applies to the use of information and communications technologies by States submitted by participating governmental experts in the Group of Governmental Experts on Advancing Responsible State Behaviour in Cyberspace in the Context of International Security established pursuant to General Assembly resolution 73/266*, UN Doc. A/76/136 (2021), p. 78. Some more indirect support for the evolutionist approach can also be found in International Committee of the Red Cross, Regional Consultation of Central and Eastern European States, 8 December 2021, International Humanitarian Law and Cyber Operations During Armed Conflicts (ICRC, Geneve, December 2022), p. 7.

26 Norwegian Military Manual, *supra* note 25, p. 191.

27 *Ibid.*, p. 190.

only be attacked directly if they meet the criteria for being a lawful target."[28] Whether the targeting of data is considered an 'attack', however, must be decided in view of the consequences of the operation.[29] As such, while attacks on military data is always permissible, the Manual explains that, "[o]perations against civilian data that entail violent consequences in the sense of a certain destruction, damage, neutralization, conquest, or similar effects that can be compared to kinetic attacks are, on the other hand, prohibited."[30] Similarly, the Manual explains that the principle of proportionality applies to incidental but unavoidable deletion or modification of civilian data in a cyber-attack against another, legitimate target – that is, the principle applies to the act of deleting or modifying civilian data, not any violent consequences that should be the result thereof. As codified in API, article 51(5)(b), the principle of proportionality places limitations on incidental damage to civilian objects, determining that such incidental damage may not be excessive in relation to the concrete and direct military advantage of an attack. On this basis, it seems clear that Norway considers data as an object within the context of targeting decisions, although several elements of the Norwegian approach remain unclear.

3.2 *Denmark*

Published in 2016, the Danish Military Manual posits that digital data "do not in general constitute an object."[31] This comment is made almost in passing, as the Manual defines the concept of an 'object' within the meaning of IHL, and it does so simply though a brief reference to the Tallinn Manual (1.0).[32] Later in the Military Manual, in a section that deals with collateral damage to objects, it is noted that "[a]s previously mentioned, data are not regarded as "objects" under IHL."[33] In this second mention of the issue, the statement is not cushioned with the "in general" qualifier – a qualifier which in the Danish-language version actually translates more precisely to "as a point of departure". The reasoning behind the exclusion of a qualifier is unclear. Indeed, directly following this statement, the Manual explains that:

---

28 *Ibid.* (our translation).

29 *Ibid.* 26, p. 191.

30 *Ibid.* (our translation).

31 Danish Military Manual, *supra* note 25, p. 292.

32 *Ibid.*; M. N. Schmitt (ed), *Tallinn Manual on the International Law Applicable to Cyber Warfare* (Cambridge University Press, Cambridge, 2013) (Tallinn Manual 1.0).

33 Danish Military Manual, *supra* note 25, p. 310.

> Damage to or deletion of certain types of data, however, may have the same impact on civilians as damage to an object. This may be of relevance, for instance, in the case of irreplaceable data that can be directly translated into a valuable asset (typically, money) or are in themselves irreplaceable, such as digital art. When the loss of – or damage to – such data is foreseeable, Danish armed forces are required to recognise this as collateral damage in their *Collateral Damage Estimation* (CDE).[34]

As such, Denmark recognizes that damage to data may have as harmful effects as damage to (other types of) objects, although Denmark does not consider data as an object within the meaning of IHL. However, given such potential harm, the Manual requires Danish armed forces to take this harm into account when considering collateral damage. This requirement is not a legal one, however. It forms part of a construction of addendums to IHL contained in the Manual, which are defined as "deliberate addendum[s] to the explicit obligations of the Danish armed forces under international law."[35] It is stressed in the Manual that an addendum "cannot be seen as an indication that Denmark or the Danish Defence feels obliged under international law to act in this way."[36] As such, Denmark notes – both with and without the qualifier "in general" – that data is not considered an object under IHL, but acknowledges that damage to data can have very harmful effects and thus obliges Denmark's own armed forces to act as though data in itself is worthy of protection under IHL-rules on proportionality. Recently, it seems, Denmark doubled down on this position. Within the 2023 special issue of the *Nordic Journal of International Law*, the Ministry of Foreign Affairs of Denmark published Denmark's position on the application of international law in cyberspace, where it touches upon this issue briefly. In this document, it is noted that "digital data cannot generally in and of itself be considered an object under IHL".[37] As such, while this statement includes a qualifier ("generally"), the Danish position remains the same as the one presented in the 2016-military manual.

3.3 *France*

France declared its position on data as an object in a 2019 Ministry of Armed Forces report on international law in cyberspace. The Ministry formulates its stance by referencing the majority position in the Tallinn Manual, declaring

34 *Ibid.* (emphasis removed).

35 *Ibid.*, p. 704 (emphasis removed).

36 *Ibid.* (emphasis removed).

37 Denmark's cyber statement, *supra* note 25, p. 10.

that it disagrees with several of its conclusions. Regarding the definition of an attack, the Ministry notes the following:

> Contrary to the Tallinn Manual, France considers that an attack within the meaning of Article 49 of AP I may occur even if there is no human injury or loss of life, or physical damage to goods. Thus, a cyberoperation constitutes an attack if the targeted equipment or systems can no longer provide the service for which they were implemented, including temporarily or reversibly, where action by the adversary is required in order to restore the infrastructure or the system.[38]

Accordingly, there is no need for physical damage, in the Ministry's view, for a cyber operation to be qualified as an attack within IHL, and the Ministry further highlights that most cyberoperations carried out by France during armed conflicts remain below this threshold, "since they mostly involve information-gathering and the jamming of the adversary's influence capabilities."[39] Furthermore, commenting specifically on the concept of objects, the Ministry argues that "[g]iven the current state of digital dependence, content data (such as civilian, bank or medical data, etc.) are protected under the principle of distinction."[40] France is thus seemingly endorsing a position where both the concept of an 'attack' and the concept of an 'object' within IHL is to be understood broadly, encompassing attacks on data with certain serious non-physical consequences.

3.4 *Finland*

Finland published its official national positions on public international law in cyberspace in 2020, which includes the position that civilian data is a protected civilian object. With this document, Finland is the only State thus far to express the view that there are no exceptions to civilian data's status as a protected civilian object, stating that "[c]onstant care shall be taken to ensure the protection of civilians and civilian objects, including essential civilian infrastructure, civilian services and civilian data."[41] The only qualifier seems to be that the relevant data should be essential. The document does not elaborate on how Finland arrived at this position, but the inclusion of data along with

38 France's cyber statement, *supra* note 25, p. 13–14 (translated).

39 *Ibid.*, p. 14 (translated).

40 *Ibid.*, p. 15 (translated).

41 Finland's cyber statement, *supra* note 25, p. 7.

civilian infrastructure and services makes it clear that Finland considers data *per se* covered by IHL rules on e.g. precautions in attack.

In sum, these four States have very different approaches to the legal question and arrive at very different positions on the 'data as an object'-question. Denmark is the only State that rejects the idea of defining at least some data as objects outright, although inconsistencies in language makes it unclear if this position is as unambiguous as it seems. As noted above, positions similar to the Danish perspective can also be found in statements made by Israel and Chile. Norway, on the other hand, clearly considers at least some data as objects within the context of targeting decisions, but imprecise language makes several elements of the Norwegian position unclear. France is quite clear that it considers several kinds of data to be objects within IHL, but its use of the term 'content data' could imply that other types of data – such as operational-level data[42] – are not necessarily covered in the same manner. Finally, Finland seems to take the position that data *per se* is considered an object within IHL, and thus generally protected as a civilian object if it cannot be considered a military objective. As mentioned above, similar support for a broad interpretation of the IHL-concept of 'objects' can be found in official statements from Costa Rica, Germany, Ireland, Peru and Romania. Accordingly, while it seems easiest to find State support for the view that at least some data can be considered as objects in at least some aspects of IHL, and while a trajectory of views does seem to favour this 'evolutionist' position, the differences in approach make it difficult to draw clear conclusions. This is not least the case in terms of identifying the proper method of legal interpretation. Therefore, we suggest bolstering the legal logic applied to this debate by emphasising the context of the rules under IHL which aims to protect civilians and civilian objects.

4 Contextualisation

As should be clear, the approaches to legal interpretation discussed above, which highlight almost exclusively either the 'ordinary meaning' of the term 'object' in article 52(2) of API and related IHL-rules, or the 'object and purpose' behind this body of law, is of limited utility if used in isolation. The reason is simple: On their own, these approaches can lead to diametrically opposing results, based purely on the weight given to each element, and thus, if one

42 See Dinniss, supra note 4, for the more on the difference between operational-level data and content-level data.

can simply choose between these focuses, the stability and predictability of the rules are undermined. Furthermore, the approach of simply adding to this analysis considerations about the value of keeping the *status quo* intact suffers from the same basic problem. These modes of analysis simply lead to diverging results, based on the analysts' particular perspective, rather than the strength of the argument itself. To solve this problem, we propose conducting a more comprehensive legal analysis, that takes all the arguments presented above seriously, but adds an often-underappreciated element to the interpretative effort: The contextual analysis.

4.1 *Adding Context to the Textual and Teleological Approaches*

As noted above, the contextual analysis forms an integral part of the interpretative system presented in article 31 of the VCLT. Indeed, as explained by Richard Gardiner:

> [T]he primary reason for looking to the context is to confirm an ordinary meaning if a single contender emerges or to assist in identifying the ordinary meaning if two or more possibilities come forward. In performing these roles, the context, once linked with one or more ordinary meanings, is to be considered under the guidance provided by the object and purpose of the treaty.[43]

In other words, considerations about the ordinary meaning of words and phrases, the object and purpose of the relevant treaty, and the context of the provision are closely connected elements in a 'system' of legal interpretation. Usually, contextual analysis involves simply making sure that a particular word or phrase is not interpreted in isolation. The idea would be, for example, to ensure that a particular rule is not understood in a way that would divorce its meaning from the whole of the treaty of which it is a part. Therefore, as explained by Oliver Dörr, "the interpreter of any phrase in a treaty has to look at the treaty as a whole and ... even beyond that."[44] Indeed, Dörr goes on to state that "[t]he systematic structure of a treaty is thus of equal importance to the ordinary linguistic meaning of the words used, in order to determine its true meaning".[45] Thus, elements such as titles, headings, grammar, and syntax, can all form the basis of a contextual analysis, as can the basic structure

43 R. Gardiner, *Treaty Interpretation* (Oxford University Press, Oxford, 2015), p. 198.

44 O. Dörr, 'Article 31. General rule of interpretation', in O. Dörr and K. Schmalenback (eds.), *Vienna Convention on the Law of Treaties: A Commentary* (Springer, Berlin, 2012), p. 543.

45 *Ibid.*, p. 543 (emphasis removed).

and function of a treaty, or sections thereof.[46] In particular, the aspect of the contextual analysis that we find most useful in this situation is the idea, as articulated by Richard Gardiner, that "context may be taken as including any structure or scheme underlying a provision or the treaty as a whole".[47] In this regard, an analysis of the 'structure' behind a particular provision can include considerations about the arrangement of, or relations between, the individual elements that surrounds the provision, while an analysis of the 'scheme' underlying a provision can include considerations about the overall plan or idea behind this arrangement. In our case, this would mean considering the structure of rules within API that aim to protect the civilian population against the effects of hostilities, and analysing the basic legal construct erected for this purpose.

4.1.1 The Structure

The main treaty under interpretation regarding the question of whether 'data' can be considered as an object within IHL is Additional Protocol I to the Geneva Conventions. This treaty supplements the Geneva Conventions – it is 'additional' to them – and is formally entitled 'Protocol Additional to the Geneva Conventions of 12 August 1949, and relating to the protection of Victims of International Armed Conflicts (Protocol I), 8 June 1977'. As such, it encompasses the protection of all kinds of victims of armed conflict, including the wounded, sick, and shipwrecked members of armed forces and prisoners of war, which are specifically protected in the First, Second, and Third Geneva Conventions. Article 52 of the Protocol is found, however, in Part IV of the Convention, which deals – like the Fourth Geneva Convention – with the protection of civilians. As such, the heading used is simply "Civilian population". Part IV is further subdivided into sections, where article 52 is found within the subsections 1 which affords "General protection against the effects of hostilities" to the civilian population. As such, the legal structure is defined as concerning:

1) The civilian population (as opposed to e.g., the wounded, sick, and shipwrecked, or prisoners-of-war, who are regulated elsewhere in the treaty)
2) The rules are of a general character (as opposed to the more specialised rules found elsewhere in the treaty)

46 *Ibid.*, p. 543–535.
47 Gardiner, *supra* note 49, p. 202.

3) The idea is to protect the civilian population as such against the effects of hostilities.

If we dive a bit deeper into this structure, it is notable that the opening provision of Part IV (article 48) articulates the principle of distinction, highlighting the need to divide the world into (lawful) military targets and (unlawful) civilian targets. Specifically, the rule states that:

> In order to ensure respect for and protection of the civilian population and civilian objects, the Parties to the conflict shall at all times distinguish between the civilian population and combatants and between civilian objects and military objectives and accordingly shall direct their operations only against military objectives.

The rules that follow then go on to define key concepts in article 48, including the terms 'civilian population' and 'civilian objects'. The core feature of the chosen definitory approach is, importantly, to define the terms in the negative: Accordingly, civilians are defined as persons that fall outside of other definitions in IHL that provide persons with combatant-status (the civilian population comprises all persons who are civilian), and civilian objects are defined as those that fall outside the definition of a military objective. These negative definitions ensure that the concepts are mutually exclusive, meaning that the structure of the rules facilitates an order where there is no "undistributed middle".[48] The rules were thus made with the clear intention of covering everything, and leaving nothing to fall through the cracks or be defined as neither a civilian object nor a military objective. Indeed, the rules even stipulate that "in case of doubt" as to the status of a particular person or object (see article 50(1) and 52(3), respectively), the person or object shall be presumed to be entitled to protection.

This structure suggests that the intent has been to create a general system of protection for civilians that aims to protect the civilian population from harm, and which deals with this issue comprehensively. The structure also underscores that the aim has been to avoid disputes or a lack of clarity as to whether particular persons or objects plausibly fit within the definition of a civilian – and are thus protected from attack. This is clear from the decision to use negative definitions and the inclusion of a presumptions-clause.

48 Y. Dinstein, *The Conduct of Hostilities under the Law of International Armed Conflict* (Cambridge University Press, Cambridge, 2016), p. 142.

4.1.2 The Scheme

Building on this structure, we can attempt to define the basic legal construct erected for this purpose. What seems immediately evident is that the structure aims to confirm and operationalize the principle of distinction under IHL. The commentary to article 48 makes this point clear, and it notes that this principle "is the foundation on which the codification of the laws and customs of war rests: the civilian population and civilian objects must be respected and protected in armed conflict, and for this purpose they must be distinguished from combatants and military objectives."[49] With this aim in mind, it becomes clear that the primary function of the rules are to divide the world into four categories. These are:

1) Persons that *can* be lawfully targeted during armed conflict (combatants)
2) Persons that *cannot* be lawfully targeted during armed conflict (civilians)
3) Objects that *can* be lawfully targeted during armed conflict (Object which by their nature, location, purpose, or use make them lawful military objectives)
4) Objects that *cannot* be lawfully targeted during armed conflict (Civilian objects).

The question then becomes: What is the defining feature of the world created through these four categories. The most obvious and logical answer would seem to be that the world represents all things that can be targeted or 'attacked' within the meaning of IHL. Therefore, it seems logical to conclude that this world consists of things that are targetable by armed forces. Similarly, it would seem the authors of these rules – and thus the architects of this system – considered the world defined therein as exhaustive. They envisioned no fifth categories of targetable things that fall outside of its scope. Outside fall only things that cannot logically be considered directly targetable within the meaning of IHL. This would, for example, be an 'idea' or the 'spirit' of a population, which cannot logically be put under attack within the meaning of IHL. This notion is supported by the method of defining objects as military objectives to the extent they have a nature, location, purpose, or use, that makes them worthy of destruction, capture, or neutralization. It seems self-evident that data can have, at least, a nature or (potential) use that makes it a legitimate military target. As such, in regards to the idea of data having a particular nature that

49 ICRC Commentary, *supra* note 8, p. 598.

makes it a legitimate military target, the ICRC Commentary provides a list of relevant objects which are "directly used by the armed forces", including "communication centres".[50] It does not seem much of a leap to suggest that the individual components of such a military communication centre, including relevant buildings, servers, antennas, and – yes – the software which runs the entire operation, as objects which by their nature may be considered legitimate military targets. Similarly, if the adversary is in possession of a piece of software that could undermine the military capabilities of its opponent, its potential use would seem to make it fit within the definition of an object that can be considered a military objective. Thus, turning this argument on its head, it could simply be argued that if certain pieces of data can plausibly be considered to be (targetable) military objectives, it makes little sense to suggest that such data fall outside the category of an object – given that the IHL definition of a military objective encompasses persons and objects that can be lawfully targeted. Furthermore, it seems similarly evident that the targeting of such data can, at least, have the effect of neutralizing the danger posed, and thus offer a definite military advantage. As such, there is nothing inherent in the targeting of data that makes it unsuitable for the definition of an object which can be considered a military objective within the definition provided in article 52(2). Thus, as digital systems and infrastructure are surely things that can be directly targeted by modern armed forces, and as it is broadly accepted that such forces are heavily engaged in both the development and employment digital weapons, it would seem most consistent with this scheme to include data within its scope, and thus define the concept of an 'object' to include data.

5 Conclusions

The question of whether data can be considered an 'object' within IHL is one where reasonable people can disagree. This is because the written rules on the matter do not provide an obvious answer, and the employment of generally accepted principles of interpretation lead to different results, depending on the analyst's particular emphasis and perspective. Moreover, current State practice and *opinio juris* do not provide definitive answers. On that basis, we do not believe that we can definitively answer the question posed in this chapter, but we do, however, believe that we can, firstly, draw some important conclusions about the logic applied in much of the current literature, and secondly, that we can add important perspectives to further the debate.

50 *Ibid.*, p. 636.

Accordingly, as to the first element, it seems evident to us that the approaches taken in much of the current literature cannot solve the problem. In a situation where the ordinary meaning of a term under interpretation stands so starkly in contrast to the object and purpose of the rule in which it is placed, it seems overly simplistic to employ modes of interpretation that lean heavily on either a textual or teleological analysis. Indeed, the result of the analysis will largely be determined through the choice of interpretative approach, which is obviously unsatisfactory. Similarly, it seems unhelpful to add to such analyses an interpretative approach that aims mainly to ensure that what is legal in the analogue, physical world is not rendered illegal through digitisation and vice versa. As is the case with the overly textual versus the overly teleological approach, the chosen point of departure on this issue largely determines the result.

On the second element, we believe that only tentative conclusions can be reached at this point on the 'data as an object'-question. However, the debate should reflect a more nuanced approach to interpretation, utilizing the rules found in the VCLT. Thus, while the current debate largely reflects opposing views based on the textual versus the teleological approach, this chapter argues that the addition of a good faith contextual analysis provides a more solid basis for conclusions. As such, we note that the structure of the relevant section of Additional Protocol I aims to provide an exhaustive legal construct to deal with the principle of discrimination under IHL, which is built around the idea that the rules leave no room for an undistributed middle. This construct is built, it seems, for the purpose of dividing the world into four categories: Objects and people that can lawfully be targeted, and objects and people that cannot be lawfully targeted. As such, the defining feature of this scheme seems to be that it comprises things that can be targeted or 'attacked' within the meaning of IHL. As digital objects seem to fit neatly into these categories, the contextual analysis leans towards accepting the idea that data can be considered an object within IHL. This notion leaves open the possibility that certain acts that are lawful in the physical domain become unlawful in the digital domain. However, we believe that this is less of a problem than often assumed in the literature. Indeed, several types of cyber operations that affect civilian data would not plausibly fit within the definition of an 'attack' under IHL, namely if they simply lead to mere "[i]nconvenience, annoyance, awkwardness, or diminution of the quality of life".[51] Only operations that lead to more significant harm would likely qualify and thus be covered by IHL-rules on precautions in attack.

51 W. H. Boothby, *The Law of Targeting* (Oxford University Press, Oxford, 2012), p. 386.

CHAPTER 8

Non-Intervention Thresholds in Cyberspace – In the Shadow of the Sovereignty Debate?

Pia Hüsch

Abstract

State practice and international legal scholarship have paid detailed attention to the question of how international law can be applied to cyberspace. More specifically, it is the regulation of low-intensity cyber operations under the principle of state sovereignty and in particular the principle vs. rule debate that have been addressed in depth. In contrast, discussions around the principle of non-intervention have not received the same amount of attention from states, and scholarly debates on reinterpreting applicable thresholds have not been mirrored in state statements. This chapter examines how the discussion on each principle's application to cyberspace is approached in scholarship and state statements. It compares and contrasts the two approaches and sets out the implications that follow from such approaches, emphasising why Nordic countries should have a particular interest in advancing the discussions on non-intervention thresholds further and how they can bring them out of the shadow of the sovereignty debate.

Keywords

principle of sovereignty – principle of non-intervention – low-intensity cyber operations – coercion

 | DOI:10.1163/9789004703933_009

1 Introduction

In the first two decades of the 21st century, state practice and international legal scholarship have paid detailed attention to the question of how international law can be applied to cyberspace. More specifically, it is the regulation of low-intensity cyber operations[1] under the principle of state sovereignty that has been the focus of many scholarly debates. In this context, international legal scholars have been engaging in fundamental debates, primarily on whether state sovereignty constitutes a rule or a principle of international law.[2] From this "principle vs. rule debate" follows a second important question, i.e. that where sovereignty is understood as a primary rule of international law, what constitutes the applicable threshold to determine when such rule has been violated.[3] Although this debate has allowed for meaningful discussions on the subject, it has arguably monopolised the discourse on the application of international law to cyberspace to the detriment of other norms, such as the principle of non-intervention.

Unlike sovereignty, which has continuously been a much-debated topic of international legal scholarship, the principle of non-intervention was less relevant after the end of the Cold War. However, with the 2016 Russian interference in the U.S. presidential election, the principle of non-intervention has firmly regained the attention of international legal scholarship.[4] The Russian interference and the lawfulness thereof under public international law was widely discussed in international legal scholarship. While some exceptions

1 Defined as cyber operations "taken short of destructive or violent attacks", S. Watts, 'Low intensity cyber operations and the principle of non-intervention' (2014) <https://papers.ssrn.com/sol3/papers.cfm?abstract_id=2479609>, visited on 12 January 2023, p. 2.

2 See e.g. G. P. Corn and R. Taylor, 'Sovereignty in the Age of Cyber', 111 *AJIL Unbound* pp. 207–212; M. N. Schmitt and L. Vihul, 'Respect for Sovereignty in Cyberspace' 95 *Texas Law Review* (2017) pp. 1639–1676.

3 I.a. discussed in P. Roguski, 'Violations of Territorial Sovereignty in Cyberspace – an Intrusion-based Approach' in D. Broeders and B. van den Berg (eds.), *Governing Cyberspace – Behavior, Power, and Diplomacy* (Rowman & Littlefield, 2020).

4 J. D. Ohlin, 'Did Russian Cyber-Interference in the 2016 *Election* Violate International Law?', No 17–15 *Cornell Legal Studies Research Paper* (2016); M. N. Schmitt, 'Foreign Cyber Interference in Elections' 97 *International Law Studies* (2021) pp. 739–764; S. Wheatley, 'Foreign Interference in Elections under the Non-Intervention Principle: We Need to Talk about "Coercion"' 31 *Duke Journal of Comparative International Law* (2020) pp. 161–198; M. N. Schmitt, '"Virtual" Disenfranchisement: Cyber Election Meddling in the Grey Zones of International Law' 19 *Chicago Journal of International Law* (2018) pp. 30–67; R. Goodman, 'International Law and the US Response to Russian Election Interference' 5 January 2017, Just Security, <www.justsecurity.org/35999/international-law-response-russian-election-interference/>, visited on 13 January 2023.

exist,[5] the majority of legal interpretations concluded that the Russian election interference was not unlawful,[6] but at the very least it remains "genuinely unclear"[7] whether Russian interference amounted to coercive intervention. The incident thus demonstrated that many low-intensity cyber operations fall below the existing thresholds, leading to a range of academic proposals on how to reinterpret the principle of non-intervention in cyberspace, some of which will be explored in more detail in this chapter. However, this chapter also demonstrates that such academic attention has not been mirrored in state practice. Instead, states' statements on non-intervention largely remain vague, merely paying lip-service to the norm by confirming its application to cyberspace and the relevance of the *domaine réservé* and coercion requirements. However, there has been little further clarification by states on the question of what exactly constitutes these requirements and their relevant thresholds.

This chapter zooms out of the question of how these respective principles can be applied exactly, but instead examines the way in which the legal analysis of their application is approached more broadly. It considers what implications follow from such approaches for international legal scholarship more generally but also for Nordic states in particular. To this end, this chapter explores and contrasts these different levels of attention each principle and its application to cyberspace have received in state statements and considers what implications follow from the different ways to approach each principle. Therefore, it looks at both, scholarship and legal practice for the principle of sovereignty (section 2) and the principle of non-intervention (section 3), paying special attention to the question of the applicable threshold that determines a violation of each principle. The chapter continues with a comparative section 4 considering the implications that follow from the approaches set out in the previous sections.

Throughout the analysis, special attention is paid to state statements setting out national approaches to how international law applies to cyberspace. In light of the lack of many examples of state practice in cyberspace that is either attributed to states or meets the relevant thresholds of international law, these statements have become key documents to determine states' *opinio juris* around international law's application to cyber operations in recent years. However, the following chapter will also demonstrate that the level of detail

5 S. J. Barela, 'Cross-Border Cyber Ops to Erode Legitimacy: An Act of Coercion' 12 January 2017, Just Security, <www.justsecurity.org/36212/cross-border-cyber-ops-erode-legitimacy-act-coercion/>, visited on 14 January 2023.

6 See e.g. Goodman, *supra* note 4; Schmitt (2018) *supra* note 4, pp. 49–50; Ohlin *supra* note 4, p. 19.

7 Ohlin, *supra* note 4, p. 18.

and clarity advanced in these statements differs significantly, pointing to different levels of depth reached in statements serving as an example.

2 The Debate on the Application of the Principle of Sovereignty in Cyberspace

One of the most prominent topics discussed when examining the application of international law to cyberspace is the principle of sovereignty. Sovereignty is a historically contentious and illusive concept. Its interpretation and understanding has changed over time and depends on the historical, legal, societal but also technological context it is applied in. As a consequence, it currently has no authoritative definition in public international law. Interpretations and academic suggestions for definitions come from Oppenheim, who speaks of "the power of a state to exercise supreme authority over all persons and things within a territory",[8] or Besson, who similarly considers sovereignty to be "supreme authority within a territory".[9] But whereas these interpretations show a certain tendency for definitions to evolve around the ideas of control and territory, they also underline different nuances and approaches to the question of what constitutes sovereignty. Simultaneously, they also already raise awareness for potential difficulties applying these attributes around control and territory in cyberspace which is often perceived as a-territorial.

Next to the lack of an authoritative definition – and with it perhaps more importantly the lack of a common understanding – of the principle of sovereignty, it is also the principle's broad scope that augments the challenges experienced when trying to reach agreement on its application in cyberspace. What is meant when referring to sovereignty? For example, some consider that the principle of sovereignty is a collection of rights and obligations, spanning from the right to the integrity of territorial sovereignty and the right to exercise jurisdiction to the right to independence and sovereign equality.[10] This interpretation was also advanced in the *Corfu Channel* case, when Judge

8 R. Jennings and A. Watts (eds.), *Oppenheim's International Law,* vol 1 (9 edn, Addison Wesley Longman, 1996), p. 382.

9 S. Besson, 'Sovereignty', Max Planck Encyclopedias of Public International Law (Oxford University Press, Oxford, 2011), para. 1.

10 H. Moynihan, 'The Application of International Law to State Cyberattacks – Sovereignty and Non-Intervention', 2019, Research Paper – Chatham House, <www.chathamhouse.org/sites/default/files/publications/research/2019-11-29-Intl-Law-Cyberattacks.pdf>, visited on 16 January 2023, pp. 11 *et seq.*

Alvarez stressed that with respect to sovereignty "we understand the whole body of rights and attributes which a State possesses in its territory".[11]

In more concrete terms, this means that the question of how exactly sovereignty applies in cyberspace can be held with many different angles in mind. One focus point is the question of governance of cyberspace, and in particular Information and Communications Technology (ICT) infrastructure forming the very essence of the internet. The approach to governance of cyberspace raises points that illustrate how authority can play out in cyberspace. Here, the assumption that authority is traditionally presumed to be exclusively retained by states is challenged given the strong role held by the private sector.[12] Yet the question of governance is also a very practical one in so far as it "is also a reflection of power struggles over internet governance amongst the world's major rival military powers".[13] While some states, primarily the U.S. and like-minded states, favour a multi-stakeholder approach that includes non-state actors like NGOs, private sector companies and civil society in the governance of cyberspace,[14] others support a traditional multilateral approach to cyberspace governance, envisaging a state-centred, intergovernmental process in which cyberspace governance is provided by the International Telecommunications Union (ITU) and is further complimented by national regulation.[15]

Another angle that lends itself as a lens through which the sovereignty in cyberspace debate can be approached is the question of how matters of jurisdiction play out in cyberspace.[16] Generally, where a state exercises jurisdiction, it is manifesting its supreme authority as it demonstrates "the legal competence of a State … to make, apply, and enforce legal rules"[17] – not necessarily over territory but more often than not jurisdiction is directly

11 *Corfu Channel Case* (UK v Albania), (Merits) [1949] ICJ Rep 4, Separate Opinion of Judge Alvarez, p. 43.

12 What the role of non-state actors means for the relationship between states and non-state actors under international law in cyberspace is examined in M. N. Schmitt and S. Watts, 'Beyond State Centrism: International Law and Non-state Actors in Cyberspace', 21 *Journal of Conflict and Security Law* (2016), pp. 595–611.

13 M. L. Mueller, 'Against Sovereignty in Cyberspace' *International Studies Review* (2019), pp. 1–23, p. 8.

14 P. Cornish, 'Governing Cyberspace through Constructive Ambiguity' 57 *Survival* (2015), pp. 153–176, p. 161.

15 S. Myers West, 'Globalizing Internet Governance: Negotiating Cyberspace Agreements in the Post-Snowden Era', *TPRC* (2014), pp. 1–27, p. 6.

16 See generally U. Kohl, 'Jurisdiction in Cyberspace' in N. Tsagourias and R. Buchan (eds.), *Research Handbook on International Law and Cyberspace* (Edward Elgar Publishing, 2015).

17 G. I. Hernández, *International Law* (Oxford University Press, Oxford, 2019), p. 194.

linked to territory.[18] When addressing the question of how jurisdiction can be established in cyberspace it becomes evident that this involves physical components which are located within a territory, such as servers or cables. With respect to these physical components, the UN GGE has confirmed that "States have jurisdiction over ICT infrastructure located within their territory".[19] In contrast, other key elements required to make cyberspace workable such as code or data are often considered to be a-territorial. Challenges arise with respect to questions of how to establish jurisdiction over the selling of items online[20] as well as how to establish extraterritorial jurisdiction over data. Here, territoriality is no longer at the centre of the debate but it is the control over data that is decisive.[21] As a consequence, extraterritorial jurisdiction over data remains a contentious issue particularly between the U.S. and European states and also in the UN GGE.[22]

While these two issues are certainly not ignored within the sovereignty in cyberspace debate, it is the so-called "principle vs. rule" debate that has manifested its position at the core issue that arises when discussing how sovereignty applies to cyberspace exactly. Since the Tallinn Manual 1.0 came out in 2013[23] and the Tallinn Manual 2.0 stated in 2017 that "[a] state must not conduct cyberoperations that violate the sovereignty of another state",[24] several states have – more or less directly – positioned themselves in relation to such a statement. Thereby, they have been providing fuel to the debate on whether the principle of sovereignty is exactly that – merely a principle of international law – or whether it has to be interpreted as a rule of international law.[25]

---

18 See e.g. Schmitt and Watts, *supra* note 12, arguing that "[a] State's sovereignty seldom extends beyond its territory", 597.

19 Group of Governmental Experts on Developments in the Field of Information and Telecommunications in the Context of International Security (UN GGE), 22 July 2015, Report 2015, UN Doc A/70/174, para. 28(a).

20 Kohl, *supra* note 16, p. 38 *et seq.*

21 N. Kushwaha, P. Roguski and B. W. Watson, 'Up in the Air: Ensuring Government Data Sovereignty in the Cloud' (23th International Conference on Cyber Conflict: 20/20 Vision: The Next Decade), pp. 43–61, p. 48.

22 *Ibid,* p. 45.

23 M. N. Schmitt (ed.), *Tallinn Manual on the International Law Applicable to Cyber Warfare* (Cambridge University Press, Cambridge, 2013).

24 M. N. Schmitt (ed.), *Tallinn Manual 2.0 on the International Law Applicable to Cyber Operations,* (Cambridge University Press, Cambridge, 2017), Rule 4.

25 See e.g. C. Nordström, 'The Regulation of Cyber Operations Below the Threshold of Article 2(4) of the Charter – An Assessment of Rule 4 of the Tallinn Manual 2.0', *Master Thesis* (Uppsala University, 2019).

Whereas the U.K. remains an outlier in the sense that it is the only state that has so far clearly and repeatedly positioned itself in the sovereignty as a principle only camp,[26] multiple other states including France,[27] Germany,[28] and New Zealand[29] have all confirmed that they understand that the principle of sovereignty is also a primary rule of international law.

With almost all states who have published their interpretation on international law in cyberspace supporting the sovereignty as a rule camp, it has been argued that the debate no longer is one of principle vs. rule but that instead the decisive and contentious question has become one of threshold.[30] Indeed, amongst the supporters of the principle as a rule interpretation, crucial differences in nuances remain, particularly with respect to the threshold question. Whereas France is joined by Iran and Switzerland in a stringent interpretation that considers every intrusion of their networks a violation of their sovereignty,[31] other states require a certain threshold to be met so that the cyber operation in question amounts to a violation of sovereignty and as a consequence also to an international wrongful act. However, states do not agree on what exactly qualifies as the relevant threshold. Here, some states provide a range of examples illustrating the necessary threshold that needs to be met, like the Czech Republic has done,[32] or they expand on possible interpretations, as done by Germany. Germany positioned itself with respect to both the interpretation and the discussion advanced by the Tallinn Manual 2.0, supporting its interpretation focussing on physical effects yet also pointing to

26 J. Wright, *Cyber and International Law in the 21st century*, 2018, <www.gov.uk/government/speeches/cyber-and-international-law-in-the-21st-century>, visited on 17 January 2023; S. Braverman, *International Law in Future Frontiers*, 2022, <www.gov.uk/government/speeches/international-law-in-future-frontiers>, visited on 17 January 2023.

27 French Ministère des Armées, *International Law Applied to Operations in Cyberspace*, 2019, pp. 6–7.

28 The Federal Government of Germany, *On the Application of International Law in Cyberspace*, 2021, pp. 3–4.

29 New Zealand Ministry of Foreign Affairs and Trade, *The application of International Law to State Activity in Cyberspace*, 2020, para. 12.

30 K. J. Heller, 'In Defense of Pure Sovereignty in Cyberspace' 97 *International Law Studies* (2021), pp. 1432–1499, p. 1454 *et seq.*

31 Although it remains unclear whether this intrusion approach also sees DDoS attacks or espionage as a violation of the targeted state's sovereignty, e.g. M. N. Schmitt, 'France's Major Statement on International Law and Cyber: An Assessment', 16 September 2019, Just Security, <www.justsecurity.org/66194/frances-major-statement-on-international-law-and-cyber-an-assessment/>, visited on 15 January 2023.

32 Czech Republic, *Statement at the 2nd Substantive Session of the Open-Ended Working Group on Developments in the Field of Information and Telecommunications in the Context of International Security*, 2020, pp. 2–3.

support for an interpretation that also considers that "functional impairments" may amount to a violation of sovereignty.[33] Similarly, the Netherlands has also explicitly supported the Tallinn Manual's approach including the need to reach a certain threshold, but do not further discuss what exactly constitutes such a threshold.[34]

Unsurprisingly, the Nordic countries of Finland, Norway and Sweden have clearly positioned themselves as supporters of the sovereignty as a rule interpretation. Finland, for example, provides a detailed account of its interpretation of sovereignty in cyberspace, considering that "a non-consensual intrusion in the computer networks and systems that rely on cyber infrastructure in another State's territory may amount to a violation of that State's sovereignty".[35] More clearly, Finland stresses that "an unauthorized intrusion by cyber means may be seen as a violation of the target State's territorial sovereignty if it interferes with data or services that are necessary for the exercise of inherently governmental functions", and continues to state that this interpretation directly supports that advanced by the Tallinn Manual 2.0.[36] In case any doubts remained, Finland again repeats that it "sees sovereignty as a primary rule of international law, a breach of which amounts to an internationally wrongful act and triggers State responsibility" and that the "rule is fully applicable in cyberspace".[37] But Finland is not only clear and direct in its statement, it also adds to the discourse by adding nuances to the debate, providing examples and details in his analysis, letting Schmitt conclude that Finland's statement is one of "normative sophistication".[38]

The Norwegian statement on international law in cyberspace also addresses the application of sovereignty, and, much like Finland, Norway confirms that "[s]overeignty is not just a principle, but also a primary rule of international

33 The Federal Government of Germany, *supra* note 28, p. 4.

34 Dutch Minister of Foreign Affairs, *Letter to Parliament: International Law in Cyberspace,* 2019, p. 3.

35 Finnish Ministry of Foreign Affairs, *International Law and Cyberspace – Finland's National Positions*, 2020, p. 2.

36 *Ibid,* p. 2, referencing Schmitt, *supra* note 24, rule 4, para. 15.

37 Finnish Ministry of Foreign Affairs, *supra* note 35, p. 3.

38 M. N. Schmitt, 'Finland Sets Out Key Positions on International Cyber Law', 27 October 2020, Just Security, <www.justsecurity.org/73061/finland-sets-out-key-positions-on-international-cyber-law/>, visited on 14 January 2023.

law",[39] again supporting the sovereignty as a rule approach. Norway's statement is relatively detailed and supports an interpretation that foresees that a certain threshold has to be met for a violation to have occurred. For example, Norway states that "[a] cyber operation … may, depending on its nature, the scale of the intrusion and its consequences, constitute a violation of sovereignty".[40] The relevant threshold is met where cyber operations cause physical damage as a consequence of a cyber operation but also where the functionality of cyber infrastructure is affected.[41] Furthermore, Norway considers that a violation of sovereignty may be established where a cyber operation "interferes with or usurps the inherently governmental function of another State", again relying on the Tallinn Manual 2.0 here and providing examples such as the blocking of digital communication between a government and its citizens as well as the interference with tax collection.[42] By providing such examples and also clarifying that a violation of sovereignty requires no level of coercion, Norway's interpretation of the application of sovereignty in cyberspace adds practical examples to the debate.

Finally, Sweden's statement on sovereignty in cyberspace remains somewhat limited compared to Norway and Finland's statements but also confirms the interpretation that sovereignty constitutes a primary rule of international law. Furthermore, Sweden also considers that a violation of sovereignty can occur where a cyber operation results in damage or loss of functionality as well as where data is altered or where it interferes with inherently governmental functions.[43] Iceland and Denmark have at the time of writing not yet published national positions on the application of sovereignty in cyberspace.

The interpretations advanced by both the three Nordic countries but also several other states are of varying degrees of detail, yet often clearly position themselves in one of the two camps of the principle vs. rule debate. Whereas some states provide a range of examples and give insights on where they consider the relevant threshold lies for a violation of sovereignty to be established, these issues are also addressed in detail in relevant scholarship. In fact, the principle

39 Official compendium of voluntary national contributions on the subject of how international law applies to the use of information and communications technologies by States submitted by participating governmental experts in the Group of Governmental Experts on Advancing Responsible State Behaviour in Cyberspace in the Context of International Security established pursuant to General Assembly resolution 73/266, UN DOC A/76/136, submission of Norway (hereafter: Norway), pp. 67–74, p. 67.

40 *Ibid*, p. 67.

41 *Ibid*, p. 67.

42 *Ibid*, p. 68.

43 Government Offices of Sweden, Position on the Application of International Law in Cyberspace, July 2022, p. 2.

vs. rule debate has gained a prominent position in scholarship with a range of academics debating whether the interpretation of sovereignty as a principle or as a rule is more adequate or where the relevant threshold lies.[44] However, little attention has been paid to the question why the principle vs. rule debate has become such a focus point[45] and what implications follow from such a narrow approach to the discussion of the principle of sovereignty in cyberspace. More specifically, the sovereignty debate is often contrasted with the discussion on how the principle of non-intervention applies to cyberspace. Therefore, the following section takes a closer look at the discourse of non-intervention in cyberspace before offering insights on the implications that follow from the way both principles are approached.

3 The Debate on the Application of the Principle of Non-Intervention in Cyberspace

Closely related to the principle of sovereignty – and often mentioned in the same breath – is the principle of non-intervention. At its core, it refers to the idea that states, as sovereign equals, must not intervene in the affairs of another state. The most clear-cut example of a violation of the principle of non-intervention is a military intervention. However, since after the Second World War the principle is no longer equivalent to an armed intervention. Instead, it has become increasingly common to expand the definition of an unlawful intervention beyond the use of force paradigm to include other forms of interference that can, under certain circumstances, amount to an unlawful intervention.[46] An example of such more indirect means of intervention could therefore be intervention through economic, diplomatic or political means.[47]

44 See e.g. Corn and Taylor, *supra* note 2; Schmitt and Vihul, *supra* note 2; Heller, *supra* note 30.

45 One exception is H. Lahmann, 'On the Politics and Ideologies of the Sovereignty Discourse in Cyberspace', 32 *Duke Journal of Comparative and International Law* (2021), pp. 61–107.

46 C. Tomuschat, International Law: Ensuring the Survival of Mankind in the Eve of a New Century, General Course on Public International law (Volume 281), Collected Courses of the Hague Academy of International Law, Brill 1999), 231.

47 P. Kunig, 'Prohibition of Intervention', Max Planck Encyclopedias of Public International Law (Oxford University Press, Oxford, 2008), para 18.

The principle of non-intervention is considered to form part of customary international law[48] and is reflected in the UN Charter.[49]

Non-intervention often seems straightforward in its application, in particular when contrasted to the principle of sovereignty.[50] Unlike for sovereignty, there is widespread consensus that the principle of non-intervention also constitutes a rule of international law.[51] As such, all violations thereof conducted by or attributed to a state and in the absence of circumstances precluding wrongfulness constitute an international wrongful act.[52] The question remains what constitutes an unlawful intervention under public international law? The ICJ's landmark *Nicaragua* case sheds light on the issue. Here, the ICJ established two requirements that have to be fulfilled in order for an interference to constitute an unlawful intervention. Firstly, the activity in question must target another state's *domaine réservé*, and secondly, such interference must be conducted in a coercive manner.[53] As such, the application of the principle of non-intervention seems relatively straightforward – a narrative that often seems reflected in states' statements on the application of international law to cyberspace. Here, the principle of non-intervention, as a seemingly clear-cut rule of international law which benefits from widely agreed upon requirements that have to be met, is contrasted with the vague notion of sovereignty. In relation to the latter, its status as a rule is contested and no such requirements can be identified.[54]

However, practice confirms that the application of the principle of non-intervention is far from straightforward. To the contrary, its application is highly complex, inconsistent and determined by significant grey zones and ambiguities. This is reflected in the language used to describe the activities

48 Nicaragua Case, para 202.

49 E.g. indirectly reflected in Art. 1(2), 2(4), and 2(7) UN Charter, see L. Fisler Damrosch, 'Politics Across Borders: Nonintervention and Nonforcible Influence over Domestic Affairs' American Journal of International Law, (1989), p. 8.

50 See e.g. Wright, *supra* note, 26.

51 This is particularly true in the cyber context, where non-intervention is contrasted with sovereignty, where the question of rule vs. principle remains open. More generally, Oppenheim famously said "[t]hat intervention is, as a rule, forbidden by international law there is no doubt", see Jennings and Watts, *supra* note 8, p. 428.

52 International Law Commission, Responsibility of States for Internationally Wrongful Acts, 2001, Annex to General Assembly Resolution 56/83, art. 2, arts. 20–26.

53 *Case Concerning the Military and Paramilitary Activities in and Against Nicaragua* (Nicaragua v United States of America) (Merits) [1986] ICJ Rep 14, hereafter: *Nicaragua* Case, para. 205.

54 Again, compare Wright, *supra* note 26, but also the absence of detailed elaboration on non-intervention in statements by other states, e.g. the Czech Republic, see below.

in question, as well as its inconsistent invocation by states.[55] Indeed, states sometimes do not comment on an activity that in other circumstances may be considered unlawful and then again, is described as perfectly legal where the state itself seeks such influence in another state. The lines between what is considered mere influence, perhaps an unwanted interference, and what amounts to an unlawful intervention are thus not clearly defined in state practice.[56] Similarly, the language applied in scholarship is equally inconsistent. And whereas the principle has only received limited attention since the end of the Cold War, it has regained prominence in international legal scholarship since the 2016 U.S. presidential elections.

In this context, it has been widely debated whether the Russian interference into the U.S. elections amounts to an unlawful intervention.[57] To recall, Russian activities included the hacking of emails of the Democratic National Committee as well as the release of such emails and other confidential information in addition to disinformation operations,[58] primarily conducted via social media platforms like Facebook. Holding elections is considered a prime example of an activity that falls within a state's *domaine réservé*,[59] i.e. matters "which are not regulated by international treaty, customary international law, or other international rules".[60] As such, Russian election interference in the U.S. elections clearly took this first hurdle to establish an unlawful intervention. However, it is less clear whether these activities also fulfilled the second requirement of an unlawful intervention, i.e. that they must be coercive in nature. Coercion is a requirement of non-intervention that is extremely difficult to define, yet is crucial to distinguish mere influence from

55 M Jamnejad and M. Wood, 'The Principle of Non-Intervention', 22:2 *Leiden Journal of International Law* (2009), pp. 345–381, p. 352.

56 *Ibid*, p. 352.

57 A. Denton, 'Fake News: The Legality of the Russian 2016 Facebook Influence Campaign', 37 *Boston University Law Journal* (2019), pp. 183–210; Ohlin, *supra* note 4; Goodman, *supra* note 4; D. B. Hollis, 'Russia and the DNC Hack: What Future for a Duty of Non-Intervention?', 25 July 2016, Opinio Juris, <opiniojuris.org/2016/07/25/russia-and-the-dnc-hack-a-violation-of-the-duty-of-non-intervention/>, visited on 12 January 2023; Schmitt, *supra* note 4.

58 N. Tsagourias, 'Electoral Cyber Interference, Self-Determination and the Principle of Non-Intervention in Cyberspace' in D. Broeders and B. van den Berg (eds.), *Governing Cyberspace – Behavior, Power, and Diplomacy* (Rowman & Littlefield 2020), pp. 48–49, referencing U.S. Office of the Director of National Intelligence, *Background to "Assessing Russian Activities and Intentions in Recent US Elections": The Analytic Process* and Cyber Incident Attribution (2017), <www.dni.gov/files/documents/ICA_2017_01.pdf>, visited on 12 January 2023, pp. 2–5.

59 Schmitt (2021), *supra* note 4, p. 746.

60 Kunig, *supra* note 47, para. 3.

intervention, as it "goes to the core of the mischief that the non-intervention principle seeks to address".[61] As such, it is no surprise that the ICJ is of the opinion that coercion "forms the very essence" of intervention.[62] But despite the requirement's central role, its definition remains uncertain. Some have referred to it as "imperative pressure",[63] while Oppenheim refers to it as the subordination of the will of another state.[64] Just like the academic definitions remain unclear, equally uncertain is therefore the principle's application in practice. The Russian interference in the 2016 U.S. presidential elections illustrate this point. On the one hand, some scholars argue that these activities were not coercive because they did not force the U.S. into a specific outcome, as the meddling with the vote count might have done which, in turn, would have amounted to an unlawful intervention.[65] On the other hand, some considered the various activities from hacking emails to information operations via social media in combination and concluded that when taken together they did fulfil the necessary characteristics of a coercive intervention.[66] In conclusion, it is perhaps most accurate to refer to the existing grey zones around the legality of election interference in international law[67] and to conclude that it is unclear whether the activities in question amounted to an unlawful intervention.[68]

Against this backdrop and the rather unsatisfactory results encountered when applying the principle of non-intervention and the ICJ's restrictive interpretation thereof in a cyber context, scholarship has advanced several efforts to redefine the notion of the *domaine réservé* as well as the coercion requirement. Such reinterpreting and the lowering of the applicable thresholds aims to address the specific low-intensity but persistent nature of activities in cyberspace. For example, Moulin suggested to reinterpret the *domaine réservé* as the "*domaine privilégie*", which includes vital interests like national security and public safety, but is not purely restricted to areas where there is no international regulation at all – a requirement that Moulin does not even see fulfilled with respect to elections.[69] His suggestion seeks to remedy his criticism of the *domaine réservé*, e.g. for not including cyber operations

61 Jamnejad and Wood, *supra* note 55, p. 348.

62 *Nicaragua Case*, para. 205.

63 W. M. Reismann, *Nullity and Revision: The Review and Enforcement of International Judgments and Awards* (Yale University Press, Yale, 1971), pp. 839–849.

64 L. Oppenheim, *International law: A Treatise* (Longmans, Green and Co, 1995), p. 305.

65 Schmitt (2018), *supra* note 4, pp. 49–50; Ohlin, *supra* note 4.

66 Barela, *supra* note 5.

67 Schmitt (2018), *supra* note 4.

68 Ohlin, *supra* note 4, p. 18.

69 T. Moulin, 'Reviving the Principle of Non-Intervention in Cyberspace: The Path Forward', 25 *Journal of Conflict and Security Law*, pp. 423–447, pp. 425 *et seq.*

exclusively directed at the private sector.[70] As such, his suggestion aims to significantly widen the restrictive scope of the *domaine réservé*.

Similarly, other authors have suggested to broaden the interpretation of what constitutes coercive behaviour. Kilovaty, for example, proposes that instead of applying the notion of coercion, the activity in question should merely constitute a *disruption* in order to amount to an unlawful intervention.[71] His proposal is attractive in so far as it puts less emphasis on the intent of the acting state, which is extremely difficult to establish in the first place, but instead, focusses more on the effects felt by the targeted state. However, by lowering the relevant threshold, such proposal also comes at the risk of blurring the lines of what is considered an unlawful intervention and mere influence. A similar observation can be made with regards to a proposal stemming from Watts, who suggests that an unlawful intervention should not only be established where the targeted state is coerced into a specific behaviour but instead that it suffices if the targeted state's choice of action is restricted.[72] Again, such proposal seems plausible as it shifts attention to the effects of the targeted states rather than the intervening state's intention and further because it might be easier to establish whether a targeted state's choices were limited rather than it being forced into a specific behaviour. Nevertheless, Watts' suggestion and the lowering of the applicable threshold again risks blurring the line that distinguishes between unlawful intervention and accepted interference.

Finally, some authors have suggested a reconceptualization of the principle of non-intervention in line with the principle of self-determination. This line of thought is advanced by Tsagourias who considers that where a state seeks external interference, for example through cyber-enabled disinformation operations, the free will of people to self-determine their political development is undermined.[73] Similarly, Ohlin argues that the Russian interference in the 2016 U.S. presidential elections is better assessed through the principle of self-determination, as "there are situations and cases where the best legal categories for understanding the situation are not sovereignty and intervention but rather the frustratingly imprecise notion of self-determination".[74]

70 *Ibid*, p. 432.

71 I. Kilovaty, 'Doxfare: Politically Motivated Leaks and the Future of the Norm on Non-Intervention in the Era of Waponized Information', 9 *Harvard National Security Journal* (2018), pp. 146–179, pp. 169 *et seq.*

72 Watts, *supra* note 1, p. 12.

73 Tsagourias, *supra* note 58, p. 51; Ohlin, *supra* note 4.

74 Ohlin, *supra* note 4, pp. 3–4.

However, these efforts remain purely academic at this point. States have not mirrored the same level of discourse as experienced in scholarship. To the contrary, their state statements often remain of a limited nature when it comes to the application of the principle of non-intervention to cyberspace. For example, the Dutch letter to Parliament setting out the Dutch position on international law in cyberspace generally introduces the principle of non-intervention in broad terms and concludes that "[t]he precise definition, and thus of unauthorised intervention, has not yet fully crystallised in international law".[75] However, while the Dutch letter "dealt extensively with sovereignty",[76] the position does not set out any concrete examples nor does it offer meaningful insights into the Dutch understanding thereof. The Czech statement does not refer to intervention all together, despite the fact that it covers several other principles of international law including sovereignty and due diligence.[77] Whereas the Japanese statement refers to sovereignty and non-intervention in the same section, the vast majority of said section is dedicated to the principle of sovereignty, not intervention.[78] The speech by U.K. Attorney General Braverman in 2022, however, constitutes somewhat of an exception in this context. In the speech, the U.K. position explicitly addresses non-intervention, setting out several examples and aiming at addressing the nuances of understanding.[79] Whereas some argue that the U.K. did not actually clarify what it means by non-intervention,[80] the speech nevertheless stood out for its focus on non-intervention and rightly highlighted the need for further discussion on the matter.

Whereas certainly not the only countries subject to information operations and influence seeking through other states, small and rich – and therefore technologically advanced but also technology dependent – states like the Nordic countries are particularly vulnerable to further influence seeking from hostile states such as Russia. For example, Russia has previously targeted the

75 Dutch Minister of Foreign Affairs, *supra* note 34, p. 3.

76 Lahmann, *supra* note 45, p. 88.

77 Czech Republic, *supra* note 32.

78 Ministry of Foreign Affairs of Japan, Basic Position of the Government of Japan on International Law Applicable to Cyber Operations, 28 May 2021, pp. 2–3.

79 Braverman, *supra* note 26.

80 A. Dwyer and C. Martin, 'A Frontier Without Direction? The U.K.'s Latest Position on Responsible Cyber Power', 1 August 2022, Lawfare, <www.lawfareblog.com/frontier-without-direction-uks-latest-position-responsible-cyber-power>, visited on 12 January 2023.

Norwegian Parliament by hacking email accounts of Norwegian politicians.[81] In the past, the Finnish Ministry of Foreign Affairs has also been hacked, an instance which a security company attributed to Russia.[82] More recently, in April 2022, Finnish government websites were taken down by an unattributed Denial-of-Service attack while the Ukrainian President Zelenskyy addressed the Finnish members of Parliament, shortly before Finland submitted its application for NATO membership.[83] Having also submitted an application for NATO membership, Sweden equally fears an increase of Russian cyber attacks.[84]

As highly digitalised, technology-dependent countries subject to considerable Russian (and other) influence seeking, setting out the exact boundaries of lawful influence and unlawful intervention is thus in the interest of the Nordic countries. Finland, for example, reconfirms the importance of both the coercion requirement and the targeting of another state's *domaine réservé* before addressing how these elements apply to cyberspace. With respect to election interference, Finland points out that whereas not "all methods of electoral interference … display the element of coercion", "[h]acking of voter databases or manipulation of vote counts in order to alter the election results has nevertheless been recognized as a fairly clear case".[85] Furthermore, Finland stresses the coercion requirement's function as a *de minimis* threshold when underlining that "[t]o be comparable to a real world intervention, cyber interference must also be of a serious nature".[86] While Finland acknowledges that "[m]ost open questions relate to the element of coercion and how it manifests itself in cyber operations",[87] the statement and its examples limited to the election context do not significantly advance the conversation either. The reference to economic pressure, for example, could have been expanded.

81 Aljazeera, 'Norway says Russia behind cyberattack against its parliament', 13 October 2020, <www.aljazeera.com/news/2020/10/13/norway-says-russia-behind-cyber-attack-against-its-parliament>, visited on 18 January 2023.

82 R. Windrem, NBC News, 'Timeline: Ten Years of Russian Cyber Attacks on Other Nations', 18 December 2016, <www.nbcnews.com/storyline/hacking-in-america/timeline-ten-years-russian-cyber-attacks-other-nations-n697111>, visited on 18 January 2023.

83 J. Lyons Hardcastle, The Register, 'Finnish govt websites knocked down as Ukraine President addresses MPs', 9 April 2022, <www.theregister.com/2022/04/09/dos_attacks_finland_russia/>, visited on 18 January 2023.

84 E. Lehto, Reuters, 'Finnish, Swedish security services warn of Russian meddling over expected NATO bids', 27 April 2022, <www.reuters.com/world/europe/finnish-swedish-security-services-warn-russian-meddling-over-expected-nato-bids-2022-04-27/>, visited on 18 January 2023.

85 Finnish Ministry of Foreign Affairs, *supra* note 35, p. 3.

86 *Ibid*, p. 3.

87 *Ibid*, p. 3.

Norway similarly sets out its interpretation on non-intervention in cyberspace by providing examples relating to election interference. Here, Norway considers that "manipulating election systems or unduly influencing public opinion through dissemination of confidential information obtained through cyber operations ('hack and leak'), would be in violation of the prohibition of intervention".[88] Similarly, taking down a state's critical infrastructure also amounts to an unlawful intervention according to Norway.[89] Despite these examples, the Norwegian interpretation remains somewhat limited when it comes to the definition of coercion and the scope of the *domaine réservé*. For coercion, Norway considers the requirement fulfilled if the targeted state is compelled "to take a course of action, whether by act or omission, in a way that it would not otherwise voluntarily have pursued".[90] Furthermore, Norway understands the *domaine réservé* as "matters relating to its internal or external affairs" but does not provide an analysis or insights on the applicable scope thereof.

A similar level of (missing) depth is also encountered in the Swedish statement. Again, Sweden confirms the application of the principle of non-intervention to cyberspace and refers to the ICJ *Nicaragua* judgment for the requirements of the element of coercion and the targeting of a state's *domaine réservé*.[91] In the statement, no further analysis or examples of application are provided so that the statement fails to advance the discussion further, but merely points out that "[w]hat constitutes coercion in the cyber context may not be easy to determine, requiring a case-by-case assessment", without clarifying what factors or considerations inform such assessment.[92]

So far, Denmark and Iceland have not yet published their interpretations on how non-intervention applies to cyberspace. To constitute a meaningful contribution, their statement would have to go beyond the reconfirmation of the dual approach of *domaine réservé* and coercion though and provide concrete examples, especially outside an election context.

88 Norway, *supra* note 39, p. 69.

89 *Ibid*, p. 69.

90 *Ibid*, p. 68.

91 Government Offices of Sweden, *supra* note 43, p. 3.

92 *Ibid*, p. 3.

4 Reflecting on the One-Sided Debate of the Legality of Low-Intensity Cyber Operations

Several implications follow from the way the application of both principles to cyberspace is discussed in both scholarship and in state statements. This section aims to point out and compare and contrast the narratives that have been identified in the previous analysis and reflects on their implications for how sovereignty and non-intervention can be understood in cyberspace. These implications include observations on this chapter's argument that the threshold debate of the non-intervention principle sits in the shadow of the rule vs. principle debate. Furthermore, this section explores how the debate could be advanced in the future to contribute to further clarification of the principles' application.

Firstly, this chapter set out that the discourse on how sovereignty applies to cyberspace is primarily dominated by the principle vs. rule debate. As a consequence, the analysis of how sovereignty applies to cyberspace is rather narrow minded in two ways. Firstly, the focus on the rule vs. principle debate means that other aspects of sovereignty, such as detailed matters of jurisdiction or governance, receive less attention. This is certainly not to say that these topics are not addressed at all – in fact, they are often raised, yet not necessarily to the detail and granularity that the principle vs. rule debate has experienced. For example, both the UN GGE and several states have confirmed that jurisdiction applies in cyberspace and that states enjoy jurisdiction over ICT infrastructure in their territory, but the nuances thereof, including questions of extraterritorial jurisdiction over data, are often not explicitly discussed in state statements where more attention is paid to the principle vs. rule argument. Furthermore, the narrative of the principle vs. rule debate is essential a binary one when putting states in either one or the other category. And whereas this might technically not be incorrect, such narrative at the same time implies there is a clear-cut distinction to be made between the two and that the question of the application of sovereignty in cyberspace can be solved where a state places itself in one or the other category.

Such impression is wrong for two reasons. Firstly, scholars like Heller have pointed out that the discussion is not just one that questions whether sovereignty is a rule or a principle but that the question of applicable threshold as outlined above is essential to the debate[93] – if not more important than the question of principle vs. rule. Secondly, such narrow focus on the principle vs. rule debate fails to take into account the complex historical development

93 Heller, *supra* note 30, p. 1454 *et seq.*

and the ideological complexities that form part of the discussions when understanding and applying sovereignty – not just in cyberspace but in any context. Sovereignty is an incredibly broad and difficult to grasp concept and its role in an interconnected world is a contested one.[94] When narrowing down the application of sovereignty in cyberspace to the categorical distinction between rule and principle, differences in nuances when referring to "sovereignty" are lost and fundamental questions about the role, origin and understanding of sovereignty more broadly are rendered irrelevant, despite the fact that these aspects potentially shed far more light on the complex task of understanding states' interpretations of state sovereignty than a short state statement on international law in cyberspace might. Reducing sovereignty to the principle vs. rule debate is thus a significant shortcoming, while a tempting one, as skipping many of the otherwise frustratingly complex but also vague conceptual debates may not seem as goal oriented as the principle vs. rule debate. The two-fold distinction, in contrast, seems capable of providing a long longed for clarity, a yes or no answer, a left or right decision as if the decades, if not centuries, long discussions trying to grasp the meaning of sovereignty could have been solved if only one had asked previously if sovereignty is a rule or a principle and for states to allocate themselves into one camp or the other. Finally, through his angle, sovereignty is no longer "hypocrisy"[95] or "a funny thing"[96] but first and foremost it is a simple yes or no question – that surely cannot be that difficult to answer – only that it is exactly that.

Despite these shortcomings of this principle vs. rule centric approach to the application of sovereignty to cyberspace, one also has to notice that the debate on the application of international to cyberspace is – on the whole – still in its infancy. If other areas of international, such as space law or the law of the sea, are any indication, the debates on the boundaries of sovereignty can take a long time – if there is an authoritative answer to these questions at all. Limited state practice in the cyber field further slows down this already complex debate. Admittedly, the initial focus on the sovereignty vs. rule debate, however, also has a positive side as it has produced a relatively advanced debate on the relevant thresholds establishing a violation of sovereignty. After all, practical considerations naturally mean that states have to prioritise certain topics and cannot address all issues with the same level of detail within the first few years of the debate.

94 See e.g. Krasner calling it "organized hypocrisy", S. D. Krasner, *Sovereignty: Organized Hypocrisy,* (Princeton University Press, 1999); M. Koskenniemi. 'What Use for Sovereignty Today?', 1 *Asian Journal of International Law* (2011), pp. 61–70.

95 Krasner, *supra* note 94.

96 Ohlin, *supra* note 1, p. 1.

The previous analysis has also demonstrated that some states, while acknowledging the need for a threshold, also leave the question of exact threshold open, many other states have gathered consensus on at least some of the relevant aspects, e.g. where there is wider support for the physical effects approached advanced by the Tallinn Manuals.[97] Such limited consensus does of course not mean that there is no need for any further clarifications. To the contrary, further clarification on the legality of disruptive cyber operations and DDoS attacks as well as cyber espionage would be appreciated. Equally, state statements would generally benefit from more detailed examples of cyber operations. These caveats granted, Heller's analysis has nevertheless demonstrated that it is possible to "rank" states from thresholds that are strict like the French approach to those who do not even see sovereignty as a rule but merely a principle as the U.K. does.[98] Whereas the principle vs. rule debate thus has not answered all questions, it has provided an opportunity for states to position themselves across a spectrum of interpretations. Here, the ends of the spectrum are currently occupied by the U.K. and France, successfully illustrating the wide range of interpretation of how sovereignty can be understood in cyberspace. Although not flawless and coming at the price of neglecting some of the complexities around the application of sovereignty, this is nevertheless a first achievement which – as will be seen below – is not yet mirrored in the non-intervention discussion.

Indeed, the debate on the application of the principle of non-intervention starts on a completely different premise. Here, the debate demonstrates that even where there is widespread agreement that the "principle" in question is indeed also a primary rule of public international law, the practice around applying such rule both in and outside cyberspace is by no means less ambiguous. With respect to debate on the application of non-intervention in cyberspace, it becomes evident that state practice has not yet reached the same level of detail, particularly on the question of thresholds, as the sovereignty debate has. Instead, many state statements merely repeat the application of the concept of *domaine réservé* and the coercion requirement without providing the level of detail appropriate to further the debate on the applicable thresholds. Whether this shortage of detail, which is not mirrored in academic approaches to the subject matter, can be changed by the 2022 speech of the then U.K. Attorney General Braverman, which may incentivise other states to issue more non-intervention centric statements, remains to be seen.

---

97 As explicitly supported by e.g. the Dutch Minister of Foreign Affairs, *supra* note 34 and The Federal Government of Germany, *supra* note 28, referencing Schmitt, *supra* note 24.

98 Heller, *supra* note 30, pp. 1458 *et seq.*

From the Nordic perspective, the principle of non-intervention is extremely relevant, as was previously demonstrated by the examples of Russian cyber attacks against Nordic political bodies. While states' desire for retaining ambiguity between influence and intervention is often understandable, the parameters shift in cyberspace. In an age of systematic information campaigns that reach new levels of scale and effect with the help of social media, AI and other technologies, and which seek to influence the wider population and their process of forming opinions, clarifying the red lines distinguishing influence and unlawful intervention is crucial.

It is therefore desirable that those states who have not yet published a comprehensive position on their interpretation of the application of international law to cyberspace do so in a clear and detailed manner, including a nuanced discussion on the application and thresholds of the principle of non-intervention. However, it is also upon those states who have previously positioned themselves in perhaps limited or unclear fashion to advance the conversation further, for example by providing more examples in their statements. A similar approach has been followed by the U.K., when updating its position in form of a second Attorney General speech which heavily focused on non-intervention.[99] Here, the former U.K. Attorney General's initiative must be seen as laudable, but also as one that has failed to live up to its own standards and expectation to considerably advance the conversation on responsible behaviour in cyberspace.[100]

In contrast, future additions to the debate could significantly contribute to the clarification of how non-intervention applies to cyberspace in two ways. Firstly, states could provide examples of permitted cyber operations merely constituting influence and not amounting to non-intervention. Whereas it is atypical for debates in international law to draw out permissive behaviour rather than sticking to the familiar exercise of "drawing red lines", such approach could significantly advance the discourse. It is of course not expected that any of these examples would amount to an exhaustive list of permissible behaviour as it is obvious that states cannot be expected to limit their behaviour in such fashion. However, even non-exhaustive examples of permissive behaviour would nevertheless enlighten the debate from a new angle.

A second way to advance the conversation further would be in the form of a collective statement on this particular legal principle. Whereas voices calling for a global cyber treaty based on international consensus have long been dismissed as too ambitious and unfeasible, a collective statement on a

99 Braverman, *supra* note 26.

100 Dwyer and Martin, *supra* note 80.

particular topic rather than one that follows a comprehensive approach does not seem unattainable. This is especially true for a group of states such as the Nordic countries. A common statement of the Nordic countries would be in line with other mutual efforts, like the Nordic Defence Cooperation.[101] Here, consensus for a common interpretation on non-intervention in cyberspace does not seen unreachable. A non-intervention focused statement could then be replicated by other groups of states or be submitted for future working groups as a conversation started instead of continuing the somewhat limited exercise of each state individually proposing its interpretation. A group statement could be seen as the next logical step to reach more meaningful consensus on the matter beyond a certain group. Together, both paths could take the question of non-intervention thresholds out of the shadows of the principle vs. rule debate and ignite new impetus for a more nuanced debate.

5 Conclusion

This chapter has introduced and situated the debates around the application of two cornerstone principles of international law to cyberspace. Whereas the discussion around the complex principle of sovereignty is all too often limited to the principle vs. rule debate, such a simplified approach raises the impression that the application of sovereignty in cyberspace can be approached in a binary manner. However, this chapter has emphasised that the application of sovereignty to cyberspace relates to more than just the principle vs. rule debate and that other aspects such as jurisdiction or governance of cyberspace but also its complex historical, conceptual and legal backdrop also form part of the question how sovereignty can be understood in cyberspace. Furthermore, even where focus rests on the principle vs. rule debate, it is crucial to understand that even where there is wider agreement on the interpretation that sovereignty constitutes a rule of international law, the question of what threshold is required to establish a violation thereof remains. In these details lie decisive nuances for the understanding and interpretation of sovereignty in cyberspace.

101 For example, Nordic cooperation includes the Nordic Defense Cooperation seeking to develop a common cyber security strategy, see G. O'Dwyer, DefenseNews, 'Nordic states to develop common cyberscecurity strategy', 17 January 2023, <www.defensenews.com/global/europe/2023/01/17/nordic-states-to-develop-common-cybersecurity-strategy/>, visited 18 January 2023.

In contrast, this chapter has demonstrated that a similarly nuanced discussion of relevant thresholds is not mirrored in state statements on non-intervention in cyberspace. While the consensus on the principle of non-intervention's status as a primary rule of international law and the existence of the two requirements, i.e. the targeting of the *domaine réservé* and the element of coercion, may raise the impression that the application of non-intervention is in comparison to that of sovereignty straightforward, reality paints a different picture. And while state statements have not engaged on discussions of these thresholds in great depth, scholarship has outlined the need to discuss the suitability of existing thresholds to the cyber context. Similarly, the U.K. has also echoed the need for greater attention to detail on the non-intervention thresholds in its U.K. Attorney General speech in 2022.

The contemporary lack of such nuanced debate means that the sovereignty in cyberspace debate currently overshadows other equally nuanced debates on the application of relevant thresholds in cyberspace. Effectively, this means that the tool of non-intervention to determine the lawfulness of inter-state cyber operations is currently underdeveloped. This is a missed opportunity for those states, particularly for Nordic countries, that as small but highly digitalised countries are particularly vulnerable to foreign (election) interference. It would be in their interest to create further impetus for a nuanced debate on the thresholds of non-intervention in cyberspace, building upon the former U.K. Attorney General's speech or in the form of individual, but clear, statements with examples of both permissible and unlawful cyber operations under the principle of non-intervention, as well as through collective statements, for example together with other Nordic countries.

CHAPTER 9

Careful What You Wish For

Tackling Legal Uncertainty in Cyberspace

Peter B.M.J. Pijpers

Abstract

It is commonly acknowledged that international law applies to cyberspace. But "how" it applies is still a matter of dispute; a matter that was hampered by the limited number of legal opinions by States. It was assumed that an increase in *opinio iuris* and State practice would crystalize how international law applies to cyberspace. However, the recent surge in legal opinions has had a contrary effect, i.e. increasing rather than decreasing the differences – and hence the legal uncertainty. This development could even create legal asymmetry: while some States will comply with international law, others will exploit the ambiguity and cherry-pick the interpretation that supports their strategic goals.

Keywords

cyberspace – sovereignty – non-intervention – influence operations – legal uncertainty – legal asymmetry

1 Introduction

The Cold War era saw numerous Russian and American (US) interferences in each other's sphere of influence, mainly within the legal grey areas of espionage and covert actions. The nature of these influence activities changed fundamentally with the emergence of cyberspace. Current influence operations go well beyond traditional espionage. Russian agents and

 | DOI:10.1163/9789004703933_010

State-sponsored media (e.g. RT and Sputnik) have actively been interfering with elections and disseminating antagonistic narratives and manipulated information via social media in order to sow doubt and discord.[1] In a research on Sweden, Wagnsson argued that influence operations endanger democracy, social cohesion and national security,[2] which echoes earlier research by Kragh c.s.[3]

The Russian endeavour to affect voters during the 2016 British (UK) EU referendum and the 2016 US presidential elections were examples of such influence operations making use of cyberspace. Though Russia was exposed after the 2016 US presidential elections,[4] the number of digital influence operations has not declined.[5] In the run-up to the 2020 US presidential elections, Russia shifted its cyber operation primarily towards digital influence, leaving out the cumbersome acts of sabotage and hacks on the digital infrastructure (hardware and software).[6] The intensified use of digital influence operations is also witnessed in the prelude to and during the current Russian invasion of Ukraine.[7]

Influence operations via cyberspace are not activities that use force or amount to an armed attack,[8] this in contrast to cyberattacks on the digital

---

1 C. Wagnsson and C. Barzanje, 'A Framework for Analysing Antagonistic Narrative Strategies: A Russian Tale of Swedish Decline', 14:2 *Media, War and Conflict* (2021) pp. 251–253.

2 C. Wagnsson, 'What Is at Stake in the Information Sphere? Anxieties about Malign Information Influence among Ordinary Swedes', 29:4 *European Security* (2020) p. 403.

3 M. Kragh and S. Åsberg, 'Russia's Strategy for Influence through Public Diplomacy and Active Measures: The Swedish Case', 40:6 *Journal of Strategic Studies* (2017) pp. 806–808.

4 R.S. Mueller, *Report On The Investigation Into Russian Interference In The 2016 Presidential Election* (US Department of Justice 2019); *United States v Internet Research Agency LLC* 16 February 2018, United States District Court of Colombia, Indictment (2018) <https://www.justice.gov/opa/pr/grand-jury-indicts-thirteen-russian-individuals-and-three-russian-companies-scheme-interfere> accessed 7 August 2023.

5 M.N. Schmitt, 'Foreign Cyber Interference in Elections', 97:739 *International Law Studies* (2021) pp. 740–741.

6 Office of the Director of National Intelligence, 'Foreign Threats to the 2020 US Federal Elections' (Intelligence Community Assessment 2021) pp. 1–2.

7 M.N. Schmitt, 'Russian Cyber Operations and Ukraine: The Legal Framework', *Articles of War* (2022).

8 Referring to Articles 2(4) resp. 51 of the United Nations, 'Charter of the United Nations' (1945).

infrastructure that affect cyberspace itself, such as the 2010 Stuxnet attack on the nuclear facilities in Natanz.[9]

The fact that influence activities remain below these thresholds does not render them lawful. States executing foreign influence operations via cyberspace may violate sovereignty and non-intervention.[10] Still, States are reticence in their response to such a breach since the threshold of violations is ambiguous. The UK and US response after the 2016 UK EU referendum and the US presidential elections respectively was marginal. Even the Russian violations of sovereignty in the months before the invasion on 24 February 2022 were hardly reacted to.[11]

While ambiguity in the interpretation of international law is not new, the emergence of cyberspace appears to have increased legal uncertainty.[12] The assumption was that the issuance of legal opinions (*opinio iuris*), combined with evolving State practice, would fill the gaps in how to interpret international law in cyberspace. States were encouraged to share their *opinio iuris* which, paradoxically enough, has widened rather than narrowed divergence in interpretation. Some States still stay silent on how to interpret international law;[13] Israel and the US are powerful and prominent examples of States that have not yet put forward their *opinio iuris*.[14] Others did articulate their legal opinions, but the views expressed were far from aligned.

The problem of the resulting legal uncertainty is that States show restraint in responding to alleged internationally wrongful acts in cyberspace; after all, invoking a countermeasure in response to a dodgy State activity could itself be unlawful. While the legal ambiguity *ipso facto* means room to manoeuvre, which is useful when confronted with novel developments, legal ambiguity could also be used as an instrument of power; States might pick and choose

---

9 M.N. Schmitt, *Tallinn Manual on the International Law Applicable to Cyber Warfare*, (Cambridge University Press, Cambridge 2013) Rule 10 (9), p. 45.

10 P.A.L. Ducheine, 'Militar Cyber Operations', in T.D. Gill and D. Fleck (eds) *The Handbook of the International Law of Military Operations* (Oxford University Press, Oxford, 2015) pp. 465–470.

11 B.M.J. Pijpers and E.H. Pouw, 'Sovereignty in Cyberspace: Lessons from the Ukrainian Case', 46:3 *Atlantisch Perspectief* (2022) pp. 36–41.

12 M.N. Schmitt, 'The Law of Cyber Warfare: Quo Vadis?', *Articles of War* (2022).

13 Which can very well be a calculated decision, see: R. Alcala, 'Opinio Juris and the Essential Role of States', *Articles of War* (2021).

14 R. Schondorf, 'Israel's Perspective on Key Legal and Practical Issues Concerning the Application of International Law to Cyber Operations', *European Journal of International Law* Blog (2021); B.J. Egan, 'International Law and Stability in Cyberspace', 35:1 *Berkeley Journal of International Law* (2017) p. 174.

the one interpretation that supports their strategic rationale. These diverging avenues will create an unwanted legal asymmetry.[15]

The objective here is to explore how legal uncertainty in cyberspace emerges, why this leads to legal asymmetry and how to tackle it. To answer these questions, first a brief explanation on the case study of the chapter, i.e. influence operations in cyberspace (section 2), is given, after which the standards of sovereignty and non-intervention (section 3) are explained. This is followed by an analysis of how sovereignty and non-intervention apply to (influence operations in) cyberspace (section 4) and how this can result in legal uncertainty (section 5). Legal uncertainty might be inducive to an asymmetrical application of international law, and the question is how to tackle this (section 6).

2 The Concept of Influence Operations in Cyberspace

Influence operations, whether they are described as Active Measures or Political Warfare, are nothing new.[16] The inception of cyberspace has, however, changed the dynamics and characteristics of influence operations, not least by adding new digital layers in our information environment in which influence can be exerted.[17]

Cyberspace is a man-made domain encompassing the virtual dimension (the logical and the virtual persona layer) and part of the physical dimension (the physical network layer) (figure 1). Operations in cyberspace can target the layers in cyberspace but can also use them as a vector to affect the cognitive dimension. Activities involving the use of cyberspace can entail (i) digital

15 B.A. White, 'Reordering the Law for a China World Order: China's Legal Warfare Strategy in Outer Space and Cyberspace', 11:2 *Journal of National Security Law & Policy* (2021) pp. 475–476.

16 T. Rid, *Active Measures: The Secret History of Disinformation and Political Warfare* (Profile Books, London, 2020). L. Robinson et al., *Modern Political Warfare: Current Practices and Possible Responses*, (Rand Cooperarion, Santa Monica, 2018).

17 T. Paterson and L. Hanley, 'Political Warfare in the Digital Age: Cyber Subversion, Information Operations and "Deep Fakes"', 74:4 *Australian Journal of International Affairs* (2020) pp. 439–442.

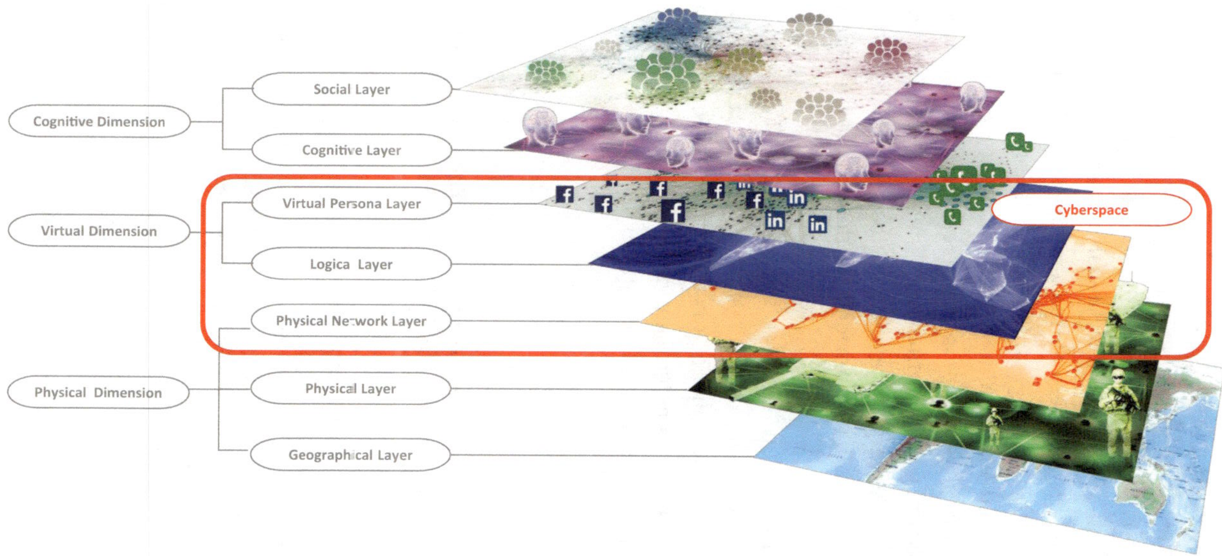

FIGURE 9.1 Information Environment and Cyberspace[18]

18 J. van Haaster, *On Cyber: The Utility of Military Cyber Operations During Armed Conflict* (Thesis, University of Amsterdam 2019) p. 173; P.A.L. Ducheine, J. van Haaster, and R. van Harskamp, 'Manoeuvring and Generating Effects in the Information Environment', in P.A.L. Ducheine, & F.P.B. Osinga (eds.), *Winning Without Killing: The Strategic and Operational Utility of Non-Kinetic Capabilities in Crises* (Asser Press The Hague 2017).p. 162.

espionage, or Computer Network Exploitation (CNE),[19] extracting data confined in virtual repositories; (ii) operations that undermine or subvert cyberspace itself (Computer Network Attacks (CNA)) with binary code, in order to modify or manipulate data, and to degrade or destroy the ICT infrastructure, resulting in (virtual and physical) effects *in* cyberspace;[20] or (iii) influence operations that use cyberspace as a vector,[21] and target the cognitive dimension, using content, words, memes and footage as a "weapon".[22]

Not only has cyberspace widened the engagement area by allowing numerous actors (State and non-State) to enter at low cost, but it has also made communication faster and more diffusional.[23] Digital influence operations surgically target specific audiences with bespoke messages based on algorithms and big data analysis, in order to gain insight into the correlation (rather than causality) between activity and effect. Manipulative influence operations lure audiences away from rational decision-making processes towards biased judgements using techniques (e.g. disinformation,[24] trolling or the leaking of sensitive data) that render the targeted audiences unable to validate the authority of the data provided. This in turn prevents the deliberate verification of the information.[25]

The main characteristics of digital influence operations are the absence of the threat or use of force, the focus on the cognitive dimension, and the objective to change the behaviour of other actors directly or indirectly via a change in attitude. These activities can potentially violate sovereignty and the prohibition to intervene in the affairs of another State.

---

19 W.O. Owens, K. Dam, and H. Lin, 'Technology, Policy, Law, and Ethics Regarding U.S. Acquisition and Use of Cyberattack Capabilities' *The National Academies* (2009) pp. 1–2.

20 B.M.J. Pijpers and K.L. Arnold, 'Conquering the Invisible Battleground', 44:4 *Atlantisch Perspectief* (2020) pp.12–14.

21 C. Whyte and B.M. Mazanec, *Understanding Cyber Warfare: Politics, Policy and Strategy* (Routledge, London 2017) pp. 100–101.

22 M. Lupion, 'The Gray War of Our Time: Information Warfare and the Kremlin's Weaponization of Russian-Language Digital News', 31:3 *Journal of Slavic Military Studies* (2018) pp. 329–330; C. Walton, 'What's Old Is New Again: Cold War Lessons for Countering Disinformation', 5:4 *Texas National Security Review* (2022) pp. 50–51.

23 F. Tansino, 'Analysing Strategic Communications through Early Modern Theatre', 6 *Defence Strategic Communications* (2019) p. 57.

24 A. Lanoszka, 'Disinformation in International Politics', 4:2 *European Journal of International Security* (2019) p. 229.

25 J. Nye Jr., Protecting Democracy in an Era of Cyber Information War (Belfer Center Paper 2019) p. 4.

3 Infringements of State Sovereignty

In general, there are different forms of infringement of the integrity of a State related to the use of force, coercion or milder forms of interference (see figure 2). These infringements are often interrelated. The unauthorised use of (armed) force is not only a violation of a peremptory norm, it also breaches the prohibition of intervention and violates the sovereignty of the State. In the 1986 *Nicaragua* Case,[26] it was stated that the "effects of the principle of respect for territorial sovereignty inevitably overlap with those of the principles of the prohibition of the use of force and of non-intervention".[27] The reverse, however, is not the case: a violation of sovereignty, such as unauthorised overflight or the exercise of jurisdiction on foreign territory without permission,[28] does not in itself constitute a breach of the prohibition of the use of force. Moreover, the lawful response to an armed attack differs fundamentally from response options related to violations of sovereignty or non-intervention.[29]

Digital influence operations are predominantly executed below the threshold of the (threat or) use of force. Consequently, this analysis focuses

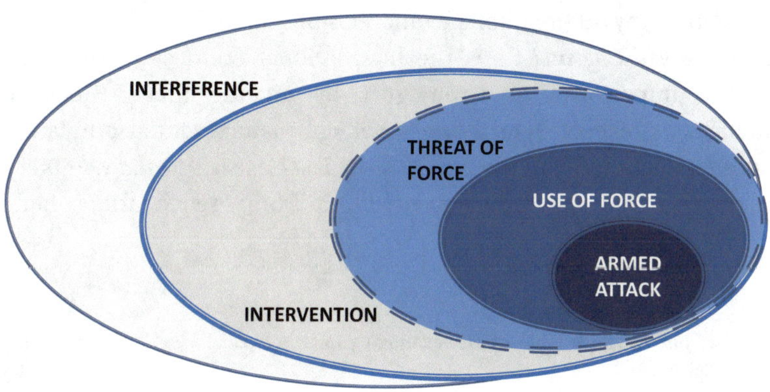

FIGURE 9.2 Infringement Overlaps

26 *Case Concerning Military and Paramilitary Activities in and against Nicaragua*, 27 June 1986, ICJ, Judgment, para 195, <https://www.icj-cij.org/public/files/case-related/70/070-19860627-JUD-01-00-EN.pdf>, visited on 7 August 2023.

27 *Ibid.*, para 251; See also: *Case Concerning Armed Activities on the Territory of the Congo (DRC v Uganda)*, 19 December 2005, ICJ, Judgment, para 165, <https://www.icj-cij.org/sites/default/files/case-related/116/116-20051219-JUD-01-00-EN.pdf>, visited 7 August 2023.

28 R. Jennings and A. Watts, *Oppenheim's International Law*, 9th edition (Longman, London 1998) para 119, pp. 385–390.

29 P.A.L. Ducheine and B.M.J. Pijpers, 'The Missing Component in Deterrence Theory: The Legal Framework' in F.P.B. Osinga and T. Sweijs (eds) Deterrence in the 21st Century – Insights from Theory and Practice (TMC Asser, The Hague, 2021), pp. 488–495.

on interferences of sovereignty and interventions caused by digital influence operations.

3.1 *Sovereignty*

The legal basis for sovereignty as a primary rule of customary international law is found in State practice and *opinio iuris*, as reflected in decisions of international courts and tribunals,[30] multilateral conventions,[31] and resolutions of the UN General Assembly.[32]

The UN Charter safeguards several aspects of sovereignty: the sovereign equality of States is referred to in Articles 2(1) and 78; and the territorial integrity and political independence in Article 2(4) of the UN Charter.

Case law on sovereignty is substantial. The 1927 *Lotus* Case argues that, if there are no permissive rules, a State "may not exercise its power in any form in the territory of another State" alluding to the territorial integrity, the political independence and sovereign equality of States[33] which are elements most prominently articulated in the 1928 *Island of Palmas* Arbitral Award: "Sovereignty in the relations between States signifies independence. Independence in regard to a portion of the globe is the right to exercise therein, to the exclusion of any other State, the functions of a State."[34]

In the 1949 *Corfu Channel* Case, the International Court of Justice (ICJ) highlights the importance of sovereignty by arguing that "[B]etween independent States, respect for territorial sovereignty is an essential foundation of international relations".[35] In the 1974 *Nuclear Test* Case (*Australia* v. *France*), Australia claimed that the radioactive fall-out from French atmospheric

30 M.N. Schmitt and L. Vihul, 'Respect for Sovereignty in Cyberspace', 95:7 *Texas Law Review* (2017) pp. 1650 ff.

31 See e.g.: OAS, *Charter of the Organization of American States* (1948), Article 1; ICAO, *Convention on International Civil Aviation* (1944) Article 1; UN *Convention on the Law of the Sea* (1982), Article 2.

32 United Nations General Assembly, *Declaration on Principles of International Law Concerning Friendly Relations and Co-Operation among States in Accordance with the Charter of the United Nations* (Resolution 2625(XXV) 1970).

33 *Case of the S.S. Lotus (France v. Turkey), 7 September 1927*, PCIJ, Judgment, p. 18, <https://www.icj-cij.org/public/files/permanent-court-of-international-justice/serie_A/A_10/30_Lotus_Arret.pdf>, visited on 7 August 2023.

34 *Island of Palmas Case (The Netherlands v United States)*, 4 April 1928, PCA, Arbitral Awards, p. 838, <https://legal.un.org/riaa/cases/vol_II/829-871.pdf>, visited on 7 August 2023.

35 *Corfu Channel Case (United Kingdom v Albania)*, 9 April 1949, ICJ, Judgment, p. 35, <https://www.icj-cij.org/sites/default/files/case-related/1/001-19490409-JUD-01-00-EN.pdf>, visited on 7 August 2023.

nuclear testing landed on Australian soil, violating its territorial integrity and, hence breaching international law.[36]

The 1986 *Nicaragua* Case referred to territorial integrity and sovereignty numerous times, including the obligation under customary international law not to violate these norms. Although in this case violation of sovereignty is often a consequence of a breach of the prohibition of intervention or use of force, sovereignty is also breached as a stand-alone legal obligation in the case of laying mines in Nicaraguan territorial waters,[37] and in relation to unauthorised overflights by US military aircraft in Nicaraguan airspace.[38]

The legal obligation of respect for the sovereignty of States in customary international law is echoed in numerous declarations of the UN. The 1970 UN General Assembly (UNGA) Declaration on Friendly Relations emphasises the importance of sovereign equality of States.[39] The sovereign equality entails not only the judicial equality of States but also highlights the inviolability of territorial integrity and political independence of States and their right to freely choose and develop political, social, economic and cultural systems.[40]

Based on the 1928 *Island of Palmas* Arbitral Award, sovereignty of a State is violated if one of its core elements – territorial integrity and political independence – is infringed.[41]

3.2 *Non-Intervention*

The prohibition of intervention is the corollary to every State's right to sovereignty.[42] Non-intervention not only safeguards States from unlawful interference but also gives substance to the concept of sovereign equality

36 *Nuclear Tests (Australia. v. France), 20 December 1970, ICJ*, Judgment, paras 58–59.

37 *Case Concerning Military and Paramilitary Activities in and against Nicaragua, supra* note 26, para 213. The prohibited use of force regarding the laying of mines is discussed in para 227.

38 *Case Concerning Military and Paramilitary Activities in and against Nicaragua, supra* note 26, para 251; P. Spector, 'In Defense of Sovereignty, in the Wake of Tallinn 2.0', 111 *AJIL Unbound* (2017) p. 222.

39 United Nations General Assembly, *supra* note 32, under 'the principle of sovereign equality of States'.

40 See e.g.: United Nations General Assembly, *Declaration on the Inadmissibility of Intervention in the Domestic Affairs of States and the Protection of Their Independence and Sovereignty* (Resolution 2131 (XX) 1965) bullet 5.

41 Q. Wright, 'Subversive Intervention', 54:3 *The American Journal of International Law* (1960) p. 522; S.K. Blay, 'Territorial Integrity and Political Independence' in *The Max Planck Encyclopedia of Public International Law* (2010) para 1.

42 Jennings and Watts, *supra* note 28 p. 428.

among States.[43] An unlawful intervention breaches a legal obligation and constitutes an internationally wrongful act if attributable to a State.[44]

The prohibition of intervention is widely considered to be both a principle and a rule of customary international law.[45] The legal basis for this primary rule between States vis-à-vis each other can be found in (regional) treaties[46] and in customary international law.[47] Article 2(7) of the UN Charter contains an element of non-intervention stipulating that the UN – not States – should refrain from any form of interference in matters that are essentially within the domestic jurisdiction of the States.[48]

Non-intervention as a customary rule is reflected in case law. In the 1949 *Corfu Channel* Case, the ICJ rejected the alleged right to intervene.[49] The 1986 *Nicaragua* Case is a seminal judgment related to the legal interpretation of non-intervention. The ICJ stated that the prohibition of intervention is "part and parcel" of customary international law,[50] and argued (echoing the 1970 UNGA Declaration on Friendly Relations) explicitly that the principle of non-intervention forbids States from intervening directly or indirectly in internal or external affairs of other States.[51]

---

43 As mentioned in: United Nations, *Charter of the United Nations*. Article 2(1); See also Vienna Convention on the Law of Treaties, Article 52; S. Watts, 'Low-Intensity Cyber Operations and the Principle of Non-Intervention' in J.D. Ohlin, K. Govern, and C. Finkelstein (eds) *Cyber Wars: Law and Ethics for Cyber Conflicts* (Oxford University Press, Oxford 2015) p. 250; M.N. Schmitt (ed), *Tallinn Manual 2.0 on the International Law Applicable to Cyber Operations* (Cambridge University Press, Cambridge 2017) Rule 66(1), p. 312.

44 T.D. Gill, 'Non-Intervention in the Cyber Context', in K. Ziolkowski (ed.) *Peacetime Regime for State Activities in Cyberspace* (International Relations and Diplomacy, NATO CCD COE Publication, Tallinn 2013) pp. 226–228.

45 Jennings and Watts, *supra* note 28 pp. 428–430; *Case Concerning Military and Paramilitary Activities in and against Nicaragua, 27 June 1986*, ICJ, Dissenting Opinion of Judge Jennings, p. 524 <https://www.icj-cij.org/sites/default/files/case-related/70/070-19860627-JUD-01-10-EN.pdf> visited 7 August 2023.

46 See e.g. International Conference of American States, *Montevideo Convention on the Rights and Duties of States*, Articles 3 and 8; OAS, *Charter of the Organization of American States*. Articles 9 and 13; *Vienna Convention on Diplomatic Relations*, Article 41.

47 O. Pomson, 'The Prohibition on Intervention Under International Law and Cyber Operations', 99:180 *International Law Studies* (2022).

48 Gill, *supra* note 44 pp. 219–220; P. Kunig, 'Prohibition of Intervention' in *The Max Planck Encyclopedia of Public International Law* (2008) paras 11–12, pp. 3–4; Schmitt, *supra* note 43 Rule 67(1) p. 325.

49 *Corfu Channel Case supra* note 35 p. 35.

50 *Case Concerning Military and Paramilitary Activities in and against Nicaragua, supra* note 26 p. 106.

51 Case Concerning Military and Paramilitary Activities in and against Nicaragua, *supra* 26 para 205. On this topic, see also the *Case Concerning Armed Activities on the Territory of the Congo, supra* note 27 para 165.

The UNGA has issued several resolutions related to non-intervention,[52] most importantly the 1970 Declaration on Friendly Relations[53] mentioned above. UNGA resolutions are non-binding, but they can be seen as a confirmation of customary international law.[54]

Deriving from customary international law, an intervention contains two elements:[55] the interference impacts upon the domestic jurisdiction – *domaine réservé* – of another State, and is coercive in nature.[56]

4 International Law on Influence Operations in Cyberspace

In general, international law – including the principles of sovereignty and non-intervention – applies to cyberspace.[57] Ample legal opinions of States underpinning this have been provided via unilateral statements,[58] reports by international organisations, and ad hoc declarations.[59] Nonetheless, there is room for interpretation. The question *how* international law applies to cyberspace is still subject to legal discourse.[60]

---

52 Including the United Nations General Assembly, *Declaration on the Inadmissibility of Intervention and Interference in the Internal Affairs of States* (A/Res/36/103 1980)).

53 United Nations General Assembly, see *supra* note 32.

54 M. Jamnejad and M. Wood, 'The Principle of Non-Intervention', 22:2 *Leiden Journal of International Law* (2009) p. 352.

55 M.N. Schmitt, '"Virtual" Disenfranchisement: Cyber Election Meddling in the Grey Zones of International Law', 19:1 *Chicago Journal of International Law* (2018) p. 48; S.J. Barela, 'Cross-Border Cyber Ops to Erode Legitimacy: An Act of Coercion', *Just Security* (2017) 3rd paragraph; Moynihan, *The Application of International Law to State Cyberattacks – Sovereignty and Non-Intervention* (Research Paper Chatham House, London, 2019) p. 27.

56 *Case Concerning Military and Paramilitary Activities in and against Nicaragua*, *supra* note 26 para 205; Jennings and Watts, *supra* note 28 p. 430.

57 See United Nations GGE *Group of Governmental Experts on Developments in the Field of Information and Telecommunications in the Context of International Security* (A/68/98 (2013)); United Nations General Assembly, *Final Substantive Report Open-ended working group on developments in the field of information and telecommunications in the context of international security* (A/AC.290/2021/CRP.2 (2021)) pp. 5–6.

58 Government Offices of Sweden, *Position Paper on the Application of International Law in Cyberspace* (2022) pp. 2–3 <https://www.government.se/contentassets/3c2cb6febd0e4ab0bd542f653283b140/swedens-position-paper-on-the-application-of-international-law-in-cyberspace.pdf> accessed on 9 August 2023.

59 Internet Governance Forum, *Paris Call for Trust and Security in Cyberspace* (2018) <https://pariscall.international/en/> visited on 7 August 2023.

60 N. Tsagourias, 'Electoral Cyber Interference, Self-Determination and the Principle of Non-Intervention in Cyberspace', in D. Broeders and B. van den Berg (eds.) *Governing Cyberspace: Behaviour, Power and Diplomacy* (Rowman, Lanham, London 2020) p. 45.

4.1 *Sovereignty in Cyberspace*

Sovereignty has a firm foundation in international law, a violation of which is a wrongful act and open to redress. Sovereign equality is one of the cornerstones of the system of international law and it is recognised in Article 2(1) of the UN Charter.[61] To assess the characteristics of a non-coercive violation of sovereignty, this contribution assesses territorial integrity and political independence separately.

Territorial integrity relates to the territory of the State. Territorial integrity signifies the exclusive authority and power the State has over its territory and its public and private residents.[62] This encompasses the inviolability of, and respect for, the territorial boundaries and connected territorial sea and airspace.[63] Cyberspace is partially linked to that territory. The physical network layer,[64] (the computers) that supports the Internet and activities in cyberspace, is generally located on the sovereign soil of a State.[65]

The nature of the incursion is related to the State's control of the territory but also to the authority and protection of persons, materiel and infrastructure in the territory of the State.[66] An infringement that damages the ICT infrastructure, whether held in public or private hands,[67] could constitute a

---

61 B. Fassbender, 'Purposes and Principles, Article 2 (1)', in B. Simma, D. Khan, G. Nolte, A. Paulus, N. Wessendorf (eds.), *The Charter of the United Nations: A Commentary, Volume I* (3rd Edition) para 73, p. 164.

62 J.R. Crawford, 'Sovereignty as a Legal Value' in J.R. Crawford and M. Koskenniemi (eds), *The Cambridge Companion to International Law* (Cambridge University Press, Cambridge 2015) pp. 131–132, which is in line with the wording used in the iterations of the Tallinn Manual, when related to cyberspace See e.g. Schmitt, *supra* note 9 Rule 1, pp. 15–18.

63 J.R. Crawford, *Brownlie's Principles of Public International Law*, 9th ed. (Oxford University Press, Oxford 2019). p. 192; A. Watts, 'Sovereignty', *Encyclopedia Princetoniensis*, 2019. p. 5 <https://pesd.princeton.edu/node/671#:-:text=sovereignty> visited 8 August 2023.

64 P. Roguski, 'Layered Sovereignty: Adjusting Traditional Notions of Sovereignty to a Digital Environment', in T. Minárik, S.Alatalu, S.Biondi, M.Signoretti, I.Tolga, G.Visky (eds.), *International Conference on Cyber Conflict: Silent Battle* (Cycon, Tallinn 2019) pp. 357–358.

65 E. Jensen, 'Cyber Sovereignty: The Way Ahead' 50:2 *Texas International Law Journal* 2015 pp. 277 & 296; B. Pirker, 'Territorial Sovereignty and Integrity and the Challenges of Cyberspace', in K. Ziolkowski (ed.), *Peacetime Regime for State Activities in Cyberspace* (International Relations and Diplomacy, NATO CCD COE Publication, Tallinn 2013) pp. 194–196.

66 W. Heintschel von Heinegg, 'Territorial Sovereignty and Neutrality in Cyberspace' 89:123 *International Law Studies* 2013 pp. 124–134.

67 Schmitt, *supra* note 43 Rule 4 (5), p. 18.

violation of territorial integrity,[68] since sovereignty "protects all infrastructure within a state".[69]

Though sovereignty is a legal rule in all domains of engagement, including cyberspace,[70] the challenge is how to apply the notion of territorial integrity to the virtual dimension of cyberspace[71] that – with its dematerialised, detemporalised and deterritorialised[72] characteristics – differs from other domains (land, sea, air) in scale, reach and effect.

Activities in cyberspace can be executed from within the territory of the targeted State, which constitutes a (physical) violation of sovereignty by unauthorised access of foreign State agents.[73] During the 2016 US presidential elections, Russian agents executed digital influence activities from within the US without the latter's consent, thereby violating its territorial integrity.

Cyber activities can also be executed remotely – from abroad – in which case no border is physically crossed[74] and a violation of territorial integrity is more difficult to substantiate. The most prominent scholarly work qualifying the impact on sovereignty is the second iteration of the Tallinn Manual (*Tallinn Manual 2.0*).[75] The *Tallinn Manual 2.0* lists three criteria for a remotely executed cyber operation violating territorial integrity: physical damage, functional damage and infringements falling below the threshold of functional damage.

68 Heintschel von Heinegg, *supra* note 66 p. 129; M.N. Schmitt and L. Vihul, 'Sovereignty in Cyberspace: Lex Lata Vel Non?', 111 *AJIL Unbound* (2017) p. 216.

69 D. Hollis and J. Neutze, 'Defending Democracies via Cybernorms' in D. Hollis and J. Ohlin (eds), *Defending Democracies: Combating Foreign Election Interference in a Digital Age* (Oxford University Press, Oxford 2021) p. 321.

70 See Schmitt, *supra* note 43 pp. 11–13. But also, the UN GGE reports, e.g. the United Nations GGE Report, *Group of Governmental Experts on Developments in the Field of Information and Telecommunications in the Context of International Security* (A/70/174 (2015)).

71 Moynihan, *supra* note 55 pp. 13–14.

72 J. Adams and M. Albakajai, 'Cyberspace: A New Threat to the Sovereignty of the State', 4:6 *Management Studies* (2016) p. 256; N. Tsagourias, 'The Legal Status of Cyberspace', in N. Tsagourias and R. Buchan (eds) *Research Handbook on International Law and Cyberspace* (Edward Elgar, Cheltenham, 2015) p. 21.

73 See the analogous1960 Eichmann abduction, Schmitt and Vihul, *supra* note 30 p. 1659; or the Russian attempt to hack the OPCW from within Netherlands' territory, see: Government of the Netherlands, *Russian Cyber Operations Disrupted* <https://english.defensie.nl/topics/cyber-security/russian-cyber-operation> visited 8 August 2023.

74 Schmitt, *supra* note 43 Rule 4 (5),(10),(21) pp 18, 20 & 23.

75 P. Roguski, 'Violations of Territorial Sovereignty in Cyberspace – an Intrusion-Based Approach', in D. Broeders and B. van den Berg (eds.) *Governing Cyberspace: Behaviour, Power and Diplomacy* (Rowman, Lanham, London 2020) p. 76.

First, causing physical damage by remote means may qualify as a violation of sovereignty.[76] Damage to the physical network layer of public or private ICT infrastructure can result from the malfunctioning of systems due to malware.

Second, functional damage could also qualify as a violation of territorial integrity. Where physical damage relates to the physical network layer, the loss of functionality relates to the logical and the virtual persona layers of cyberspace and is at the core of cyber-related interference with sovereignty (especially undermining activities or CNA). Although the experts of the *Tallinn Manual 2.0* could not agree on exact thresholds, permanent functional impairment stems from the degradation, destruction, or disruption of data and is an infringement of the confidentiality, integrity or availability (CIA) of the data or of the system as a whole.[77]

Due to the lack of a demarcation of functional impairment, activities that do not result in physical or permanent functional damage of systems in cyberspace are difficult to define. Examples are the temporary loss of functionality, CNE including data theft (by copying) or port scanning (reconnaissance) with malicious intent, and the creation of a backdoor for future cyberattacks. Within this remit, there are two interpretations. Either *every* cyberattack on, or exploitation of, the cyber infrastructure by another State is a violation of sovereignty – what Roguski has called the penetration-based approach.[78] This is the French[79] and Iranian[80] view and in line with Heller's notion of "pure sovereignty".[81] Or an attack requires at least a minimum impact,[82] which is in line with the German position – what Roguski named the intrusion-based

76 M. Milanovic and M.N. Schmitt, 'Cyber Attacks and Cyber (Mis)Information Operations During a Pandemic', 11:1 *Journal of National Security Law & Policy* (2020) p. 7. See also: Case Concerning Military and Paramilitary Activities in and against Nicaragua, *supra* note 26 para 205.

77 See also: Roguski, *supra* note 75 p. 79.

78 P. Roguski, *Application of International Law to Cyber Operations: A Comparative Analysis of States' Views* (The Hague Program For Cyber Norms Policy Brief 2020) pp. 5–6; Roguski, *supra* note 75 p. 75.

79 Ministère des Armées, *Droit International Appliqué Aux Opérations Dans Le Cyberespace* (2019) pp. 6–7 <https://www.defense.gouv.fr/sites/default/files/ministere-armees/Droit%20international%20appliqué%20aux%20opérations%20dans%20le%20cyberespace.pdf> visited on 9 August 2023.

80 Armed Forces of the Islamic Republic of Iran, 'Declaration Regaring International Law Applicable to the Cyberspace', *Nour News* (2020).

81 K.J. Heller, 'In Defense of Pure Sovereignty in Cyberspace', 97:1432 *International Law Studies* (2021) p. 1436.

82 The maxim of *de minimis non curat lex*, i.e. "the law is not concerned with trivial things". See also: Jensen, *supra* note 65 pp. 302–303.

approach, arguing that not all infringements violate sovereignty. Regular use of ICT infrastructure located in other States would not, referring to international law, be an unlawful intrusion, neither would unauthorised access.[83] Related to the CIA-trigram, Roguski argues that if the integrity (not the availability or confidentiality) of the data is compromised that would constitute a violation.[84] This interpretation in essence introduces a minimum impact threshold, hence a qualified threshold to assess violations of sovereignty in cyberspace. While this distinction has merit for attacks undermining cyberspace itself, it does not encompass digital influence operations.

The *Tallinn Manual 2.0* criteria largely relate to digital undermining operations (CNA) raising the question whether any remotely executed digital influence operation could violate territorial integrity.[85] The remotely executed influence operations during the 2016 UK EU referendum or the 2016 US presidential elections did not meet the criteria of violation of territorial integrity as stipulated in the *Tallinn Manual 2.0*. The disinformation and trolling campaigns, the fabricated content, misleading media sources or information deluges due to political advertisements did not cause physical damage or (permanent or temporary) loss of functionality[86] to (persons or materiel on) the territory of the State. Furthermore, the digital influence operations did not infringe upon the confidentiality, availability or integrity of ICT system since data were not deleted or altered. The Russian influence operation as such did not violate territorial integrity.[87]

Violation of territorial integrity traditionally relates to physical incursions into the territory of the State.[88] Though remote cyberattacks could cause physical damage or injury and subsequently violate the territorial integrity (and sovereignty) of the State,[89] digital influence operations seldom cause functional impairment, let alone physical damage.

---

83 Without stating that these intrusions, even in the form of political or economic espionage, will never violate international law, see also: R. Buchan, *Cyber Espionage and International Law* (Bloomsbury, London, 2019) pp. 53–54.

84 Roguski, *supra* note 75 p. 79.

85 Moynihan, *supra* note 55 pp. 21–24.

86 M.N. Schmitt, 'Taming the Lawless Void: Tracking the Evolution of International Law', 3:3 *Texas National Security Review* (2020) pp. 38–39.

87 A. Xiao, 'Responding to Election Meddling in the Cyberspace: An International Law Case Study on the Russian Interference in the 2016 Presidential Election', 30:2 *Duke Journal of Comparative & International Law* (2020) p. 371.

88 Spector, *supra* note 38 p. 222.

89 Milanovic and Schmitt, *supra* note 76 p. 253.

Political independence, on the other hand, can be violated by digital influence operations. Political independence refers to the authority States have over their "inherently governmental functions",[90] including collecting taxes, defending the State and holding elections.[91]

The State functions can be meddled with (also in cyberspace) via interference or – more severely – usurpation. Usurpation means taking over and performing governmental functions of another State.[92] In cyberspace, a foreign State can usurp the electoral process by changing the results of the voting machines, as was the case in Ukraine in the May 2014 presidential elections.[93]

Interference with the inherently governmental functions means tampering with or frustrating the State's functions – physical or functional damage is not a requirement. Not all forms of digital influence operations (using social media platforms) interfere with the inherently governmental functions of another State.[94] Unwelcome propaganda[95] and even fabricated information is not unlawful per se.[96] However, when a State uses subterfuges to propagate misleading content – factual or fabricated – or impersonate national citizens,[97] to dissuade voters,[98] or manipulate their ability to make a free and fair appreciation, their political choice is severely impaired. While the Russian influence operation did not violate territorial integrity, political independence was breached during the 2016 UK EU referendum and the 2016 US presidential election.

90 Schmitt, *supra* note 55 p. 45; Schmitt, *supra* note 43 p. 20 rule 4(10, 16, 17).

91 Other State functions are conducting diplomacy, enforcing the law, managing crises or establish a system of social welfare official and public communication (e.g. on Covid-19), see also Milanovic and Schmitt, *supra* note 76 p. 255.

92 As stated in the 1927 *Case of the S.S. Lotus, supra* note 33 p. 18.

93 D.E. Sanger, *The Perfect Weapon: War, Sabotage, and Fear in the Cyber Age* (Broadway Books, New York, 2019). pp. 90–98.

94 Xiao, *supra* note 87 p. 372.

95 Schmitt, *supra* note 43 Rule 4 (29), p. 26; A. Denton, 'Fake News: The Legality of the Russian 2016 Facebook Influence Campaign', 37:1 *Boston University International Law Journal* (2019) pp. 201–202.

96 Schmitt, *supra* note 55 p. 46.

97 *United States v Netyksho,* United States District Court, Indictment (2018). p. 3 <https://www.justice.gov/file/1080281/download> visited on 8 August 2023.

98 F.N. Ribeiro et al., 'On Microtargeting Socially Divisive Ads: A Case Study of Russia-Linked Ad Campaigns on Facebook' *Proceedings of the Conference on Fairness, Accountability, and Transparency* (2019) pp. 142–143.

4.2 *Non-Intervention in Cyberspace*

An intervention is a coercive incursion in the reserved domain of another State. The prohibition of intervention is considered to be both a principle and a rule of customary international law,[99] also in cyberspace.[100]

The *domaine réservé,* or reserved domain,[101] is the area "in which each State is permitted, by the principle of State sovereignty to decide freely. This area is the choice of a political, economic, social and cultural system, and the formulation of foreign policy."[102] The *domaine réservé* relates to the jurisdiction of a sovereign State,[103] a jurisdiction that is not unrestricted.[104] The size of the reserved domain of the State is "a relative question",[105] as alluded to in the 1923 *Nationality Decrees* Case, and the 1923 *Wimbledon* Case,[106] and dependent on the international obligations of the State (figure 3).

The domain of non-intervention is not an uncontested notion. Kilovaty rhetorically questions whether the *domaine réservé* still is distinctive in "a world where social media platforms have transformed online communications and political campaigning?"[107] Moreover, are there still domestic areas that are

---

99 Jennings and Watts, *supra* note 28 pp. 428–430; *Case Concerning Military and Paramilitary Activities in and against Nicaragua supra* note 45 p. 524.

100 R. Buchan, 'Cyber Attacks: Unlawful Uses of Force or Prohibited Interventions?', 17:2 *Journal of Conflict and Security Law* (2012) p. 221; Schmitt, *supra* note 5 p. 744; Hollis and Neutze, *supra* note 69 p. 317.

101 *Nationality Decrees in Tunis and Morocco,* 7 February 1923, PCIJ, Advisory Opinion, p. 24 <https://www.icj-cij.org/sites/default/files/permanent-court-of-international-justice/serie_B/B_04/Decrets_de_nationalite_promulgues_en_Tunisie_et_au_Maroc_Avis_consultatif_1.pdf> visited on 8 August 2023.

102 *Case Concerning Military and Paramilitary Activities in and against Nicaragua, supra* note 26 para 205; Pirker, *supra* note 65 p. 191.

103 Gill, *supra* note 44 p. 217; Kunig, *supra* note 48 para 3.

104 Crawford, *supra* note 63 pp. 191–200; Netherlands Ministry of Foreign Affairs, *Letter to the President of the House of Representatives on the International Legal Order in Cyberspace – Appendix: International Law in Cyberspace* (2019). p. 2 <https://www.government.nl/documents/parliamentary-documents/2019/09/26/letter-to-the-parliament-on-the-international-legal-order-in-cyberspace>, accessed on 8 August 2023.

105 *Nationality Decrees in Tunis and Morocco supra* note 101 p. 24.; Kunig, *supra* note 48 para 3, p. 1; K. Ziolkowski, 'General Principles of International Law as Applicable in Cyberspace', in K. Ziolkowski (ed), *Peacetime Regime for State Activities in Cyberspace, International Law* (2013). p. 164.

106 *Case of the SS Wimbledon* (*Great Britain v. Germany*), 17 August 1923, PCIJ, Judgment, pp. 30 & 33 <https://www.icj-cij.org/sites/default/files/permanent-court-of-international-justice/serie_A/A_01/03_Wimbledon_Arret_08_1923.pdf>, visited 8 August 2023.

107 I. Kilovaty, 'The International Law of Cyber Intervention', in N. Tsagourias and R. Buchan *Research Handbook on International Law and Cyberspace* (2nd Ed) (Edward Elgar, Cheltenham, 2021) p. 100.

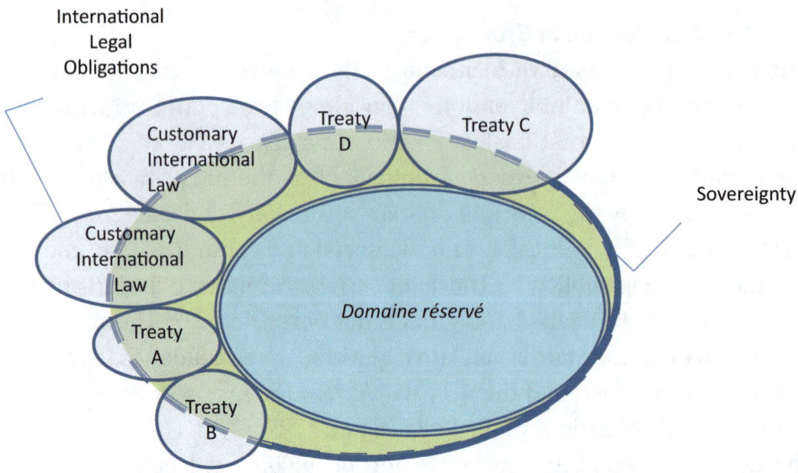

FIGURE 9.3 Domaine réservé

exempt from the effects of international law,[108] especially taking international human rights law into account? However, most ambiguity is connected to the nature of the incursion: coercion.

Intervention is perceived to be wrongful when it "uses methods of coercion in regard to such choices, which must remain free ones".[109] Coercion is "the very essence of prohibited intervention".[110] Or as Joyner states: "Coercion in inter-State relations involves the government of one State compelling the government of another State to think or act in a certain way by applying various kinds of pressure, threats, intimidation or the use of force."[111]

Coercion has been described in different ways in legal writing and case law.[112] Though it "has not yet fully crystallised in international law",[113] it has legal consequences.[114] In the *Nicaragua* Case, the ICJ mentioned that coercion

108 See Article 40 of the 'The Charter of Fundamental Rights of the European Union' articulating the ' Right to vote and to stand as a candidate at municipal elections.'

109 *Case Concerning Military and Paramilitary Activities in and against Nicaragua*, supra note 26 para 205.

110 *Ibid.* para 205.

111 C. Joyner, 'Coercion', *Max Planck Encyclopedia of International Law* (2006). para A; see also Schmitt, *supra* note 43. rule 66 (18) p. 317.

112 See also Gill, *supra* note 44 p. 219, providing an outline of the different forms of coercion.

113 Netherlands Ministry of Foreign Affairs, *supra* note 104 p. 3.

114 Kunig, *supra* note 48 para A.1.(b); A. Tzanakopoulos, 'The Right to Be Free from Economic Coercion', 4:3 *Cambridge Journal of International and Comparative Law* (2015) p. 623.

"is particularly obvious in the case of an intervention which uses force in the direct form of military action".[115] Aside from the coercive use of force,[116] coercion can be "otherwise coercive"[117] when it deprives another State of control, broadening the concept to diplomacy, the economy and other means if they are coercive in nature.[118] Coercion can also have a more subtle and psychological dimension, manipulating the opponent's choices and reducing the number of options to choose from by applying subversive, psychological or manipulative means.[119]

Apart from deliberately undermining control, the coercer must also pursue a change of policy,[120] or intend to effectuate a particular course of action. The intent of the coercer is pivotal,[121] as it objectifies the pursuit of a change to the policy. Therefore, coercive interferences that fail to reach a desired outcome still breach the prohibition of intervention.[122]

While coercion traditionally relates to the threat (or use) of force,[123] in cyberspace coercive behaviour will most likely take the shape of non-violent, manipulative, subversive threats through informational means.[124] The *Tallinn Manual 2.0*-experts also struggled with this topic.[125] Disseminating foreign propaganda or even fabricated news during elections will not immediately qualify as an intervention, but when digital influence operations (during elections) have the purpose to undermine faith in the integrity of the electoral process, or to alter or manipulate the perceptions and beliefs of the audience

115 Case Concerning Military and Paramilitary Activities in and against Nicaragua, *supra* note 26 para 205.

116 Watts, *supra* note 43 p. 258.

117 Jennings and Watts, *supra* note 28 p. 432.

118 Jamnejad and Wood, *supra* note 54 pp. 367–377.

119 S. Wheatley, 'Regulating the Frontiers of Hybrid-Warfare: The International Law on Foreign State Cyber' *Conference Paper from the New Technologies: New Challenges for Democracy and International Law, 2019-03-21, Cambridge University* (unpublished) pp. 6–7 <https://eprints.lancs.ac.uk/id/eprint/133957/> visited on 8 August 2023; Tsagourias, *supra* note 60 p. 53.

120 Schmitt, *supra* note 43 Rule 66 (19) p. 318; Wheatley, *supra* note 119 p. 5.

121 Wheatley, *supra* note 119 p. 18.

122 Schmitt, *supra* note 43 Rule 66 (29) p. 322; Schmitt, *supra* note 55 p. 52.

123 Barela, *supra* note 55.

124 L. Maschmeyer, 'The Subversive Trilemma: Why Cyber Operations Fall Short of Expectations', 46:2 *International Security* (2021) pp. 53–54.

125 As do other academics, see: Watts, supra note 43; J. Ohlin, *Election Interference: International Law and the Future of Democracy* (Cambridge University Press, Cambridge 2020); S.J. Barela, 'Zero Shades of Grey: Russian-Ops Violate International Law' *Just Security* (2018).

in another State,[126] they might well qualify as intervention, since these coercive efforts are "designed to influence outcomes in … matters reserved to a target State".[127]

The question that remains is: When are (manipulative) digital influence operation coercive? Though different in magnitude, it can be argued that the influence operations during the 2016 UK EU referendum and the 2016 US presidential elections amounted to interventions. The Russian influence operations entailed manipulative activities against the reserved domain – the ability to conduct popular votes – which could amount to coercion, as they constituted a deliberate act to undermine the decision-making process of the targeted States with the aim of policy changes (for the UK leaving the EU, and for the US not to have Clinton elected). Russia sought ways to lure voters into making decisions they might otherwise not have made, using deceitful and manipulative techniques including bots, repetitive social media utterances and political advertising. In the US case, the Internet Research Agency (IRA)[128] "created fake Facebook accounts and purchased politically charged advertisements intending to influence the outcome of a U.S. election".[129] Schmitt argues that the "covert nature of the troll operation deprived the American electorate of its freedom of choice".[130]

Manipulation is not coercive per se. However, if coercion can be defined as having the deliberate intent to change the policy of another State by denying the target State its autonomous decision-making capability, then some manipulative influence operations are coercive in nature.

All in all, digital influence operations can violate the prohibition of intervention, as well as political independence, but they are more difficult to align with the notion of territorial integrity since they lack a physical or tangible component.

126 A. Reynolds (ed), *Social Media As a Tool of Hybrid Warfare*, (NATO Strategic Communication Centre of Exellence, Latvia 2014). p. 8.

127 Schmitt, *supra* note 43. Rule 66 (19) p. 318.

128 United States Senate Committee on Intelligence, *Report on Russian Active Measures Campaigns and Interference in the 2016 U.S. Election – Volume 2: Russia's Use of Social Media* (2019) p. 5; *United States v Internet Research Agency LLC*, *supra* note 4, 1:18–32. pp. 2–11.

129 Denton, *supra* note 95 p. 199.

130 Schmitt, *supra* note 55 p. 51.

5 Legal Uncertainty

Digital influence operations with malign intent feed the growing distrust in traditional media and governmental institutions and increase cynicism, which can take shape in unwillingness to accept election results and scepticism toward public announcements.[131] Digital influence operations do not solely create unwanted societal effects, they also amplify ambiguity and legal uncertainty.

5.1 *Uncertainty regarding Sovereignty in Cyberspace*

International law is not set in stone, and legal leeway provides room to absorb new developments.[132] However, the lack of clarity, conducive to several interpretations of the law, can also lead to unwanted ambiguity. A case in point is the debate on whether sovereignty is a rule in cyberspace or not.

While most States agree that sovereignty is a primary rule of law in any domain including cyberspace, not all are convinced. In 2018 the UK argued it is not persuaded that a specific rule on sovereignty exists for cyber activities beyond a prohibited intervention.[133] Academics participated in the debate: Corn and Tayler state that there are sufficient proscriptions against unlawful uses of force and interventions in treaty law and customary international law, but that "below these thresholds there is insufficient evidence of either state practice or *opinio juris* to support assertions that the principle of sovereignty operates as an independent rule of customary international law that regulates states' actions in cyberspace".[134]

Despite the silence of some, a growing number of States have since provided their legal opinions on the applicability of international law, including sovereignty, in cyberspace. These States not only include Western States

131 N. Jankowicz and H. Collis, 'Enduring Information Vigilance: Government after COVID-19', 50:3 *Parameters* (2020) p. 22.

132 L. Lessig, 'The Law of the Horse: What Cyberlaw Might Teach', 113:2 *Harvard Law Review* (1999) pp 534–548.

133 J. Wright, 'Cyber and International Law in the 21st Century', Speech delivered at the *Chatham House* (2018) <https://www.gov.uk/government/speeches/cyber-and-international-law-in-the-21st-century> visited on 8 August 2023.

134 G. Corn and R. Taylor, 'Sovereignty in the Age of Cyber', 111 *AJIL Unbound* (2017) p. 208.

such as France,[135] the Netherlands,[136] Germany,[137] Switzerland,[138] Canada,[139] Finland[140] and Sweden,[141] but also China, Russia and Iran.[142]

Unfortunately, many of them use generic terms that reiterate existing law without expounding on how international law applies to cyberspace. The Australian legal opinion "recognises that activities conducted in cyberspace raise new challenges for the application of international law, including issues of sovereignty".[143] Estonia argues that the "violation of sovereignty through cyber means can breach international law, and therefore may give the victim

135 Ministère des Armées, *supra* note 79.

136 Netherlands Ministry of Foreign Affairs, *supra* note 104.

137 German Ministry of Foreign Affairs, *On the Applicability of International Law in Cyberspace* (2021) pp. 2–4, <https://www.auswaertiges-amt.de/blob/2446304/32e7b2498e10b74fb17204c54665bdf0/on-the-application-of-international-law-in-cyberspace-data.pdf> visited on 8 August 2023.

138 Swiss Ministry of Foreign Affairs, *Position Paper on Switzerland's Participation in the UN OEWG and UNGGE* (2020) <https://unoda-web.s3.amazonaws.com/wp-content/uploads/2020/02/switzerland-position-paper-oewg-gge-final.pdf> visited on 8 August 2023.

139 Government of Canada, *International Law Applicable in Cyberspace* (2022), <https://www.international.gc.ca/world-monde/issues_development-enjeux_developpement/peace_security-paix_securite/cyberspace_law-cyberespace_droit.aspx?lang=eng> visited on 8 August 2023.

140 J. Sareva, Statement by Finland on Behalf of the Nordic Countries (2021) <https://documents.unoda.org/wp-content/uploads/2021/12/Nordic-Statement-OEWG-First-Substantive-Session-Monday-13-December-2021.pdf> visited on 8 August 2023; Finland Ministry of Foreign Affairs, Finland Published Its Positions on Public International Law in Cyberspace (2020) <https://um.fi/current-affairs/-/assetpublisher/gc654PySnjTX/content/suomi-julkisti-n-c3-a4kemyksens-c3-a4-kansainv-c3-a4lisest-c3-a4-oikeudesta-kyberymp-c3-a4rist-c3-b6ss-c3-a4> visited on 8 August 2023.

141 Government Offices of Sweden, *supra* note 58.

142 Iran Minstry of Foreign Affairs, *Intervention by Delegation of the Islamic Republic of Iran on International Law* (OEWG second informal virtual meeting 2020) <https://ceipfiles.s3.amazonaws.com/pdf/CyberNorms/UNGGE/+Intervention+by+Delegation+of+the+Islamic+Republic+of+Iran+on+International+Law.pdf> visited on 8 August 2023. Also American states have provided legal opinions, see: D. Hollis, B. Vila, and D. Rakhlina-Powsner, *Elaborating International Law for Cyberspace* (Directions Cyber Digital Europe 2020); D. Hollis, *Improving Transparency International Law and State Cyber Operations* (OAS – Fourth Report 2020) para 52, p. 19; and the overview of national positions on the CCDCOE Cyberlaw <https://cyberlaw.ccdcoe.org/wiki/List_of_articles#National_positions> visited on 8 August 2023.

143 Australian Government, *Australia's Position on the Application of International Law to State Conduct in Cyberspace – Annex B* (2020) <https://www.internationalcybertech.gov.au/our-work/annexes/annex-b> visited on 8 August 2023.

state the right to take measures, including countermeasures. Views on what constitutes a breach of sovereignty in cyberspace differ."[144]

Apart from the UK legal opinion, which was not a one-off,[145] also within the group of States accepting that sovereignty is a rule, differences in interpretation exist. A case in point is the interpretation of sovereignty as a rule by France and Switzerland that favour a purist approach to sovereignty, versus Germany, Canada and the Netherlands who argue that "activities causing negligible or *de minimis* effects would not constitute a violation of territorial sovereignty".[146]

Russia and Iran take a different perspective highlighting the legal vacuum existing at the moment.[147] China further argues that cyberspace sovereignty is a "natural extension of state sovereignty in cyberspace",[148] whereby cyberspace is governed by domestic law and no distinction is make between virtual and physical elements of cyberspace.

The lack in alignment between and granularity of legal opinions, and the divergence between these opinions and actual State practice fuel ambiguity.

The uneasy fit between digital influence operations and the notion of territorial integrity furthers ambiguous interpretations. Digital influence operations executed remotely by foreign agents do not violate the territorial integrity of the targeted State because no borders are physically crossed. Furthermore, digital influence operations that target the cognitive dimension are unlikely to cause damage and are therefore unlikely to affect the territorial integrity of another State.

Interference with political independence is a more suitable threshold for assessing violations of sovereignty by digital influence operations, although it is not devoid of ambiguity. Defining interference with inherently governmental

144 United Nations General Assembly, *Official Compendium of Voluntary National Contributions on the Subject of How International Law Applies to the Use of Information and Communications Technologies* (A/76/136," no. July (2021)). p. 25.

145 S. Braverman, *International Law in Future Frontiers*, Speech delivered at the *Chatham House* (2022) <https://www.gov.uk/government/speeches/international-law-in-future-frontiers> visited on 8 August 2023.

146 Government of Canada, *supra* note 139 bullet 17.

147 Russian Delegation to the OEWG, *Statement by the Representative of the Russian Federation at the Online Discussion of the Second 'Pre-Draft' of the Final Report of the UN Open-Ended Working Group*, (2020) <https://ceipfiles.s3.amazonaws.com/pdf/CyberNorms/UNGGE/Statement+by+the+Representative+of+the+Russian+Federation+at+the+Online+Discussion+of+the+Second+"Pre-Draft"+of+the+Final+Report+of+the+UN+Open-Ended+Working+Group+on+Developments+in+the+Field+of+Information+and+Communications+in+the+Co.pdf> visited on 8 August 2023.

148 Z. Xinbao and X. Ke, 'A Study of Cyberspace Sovereignty', 4:5 *China Legal Science* (2016) p. 34.

functions is challenging, since both interference and State functions "lack granularity".[149]

5.2 *Uncertainty Regarding Non-Intervention in Cyberspace*

Ambiguity is not limited to the interpretation of sovereignty.[150] Contrary to sovereignty, the legal opinions regarding non-intervention are aligned though not always explicit in "how" the rule applies. The Australian legal opinion argues that interventions are prohibited. Estonia states that the principle of non-intervention applies to state conduct in cyberspace but is more explicit in how the reserved domain and coercion applies to cyberspace.[151]

The reserved domain – the domestic jurisdiction that is not regulated by international law – is an inherently relative notion. When applied to cyberspace, the question arises whether the virtual realm erodes this notion even further.[152]

The essential element for an intervention, i.e. coercion, is ill-defined,[153] and it becomes even more intangible when applied to cyberspace.[154] Coercion is obvious when an intervention uses force, but digital influence operations are characteristically below the level of threat (or use) of force. An unwanted development is that the elusiveness of cyberspace has increased the complexity of coercion in cyberspace and the criteria needed to establish it.[155] Cyberspace has significantly increased coercive potential, not only due to the increasing number of (non-State) actors but also because its attributes facilitate the use of covert and subconscious activities. Finally, the veiled operating methods that States use make it difficult to uncover the true purpose and intent of an alleged intervention. The elusive and intangible nature of influence operations

---

149 Schmitt, *supra* note 55 p. 45.

150 The application of due diligence – an acknowledged rule of customary international law – has been demoted to a voluntary norm for activities in cyberspace. See: United Nations GGE Report, *Group of Governmental Experts on Developments in the Field of Information and Telecommunications in the Context of International Security* (A 76/135 (2021)) para 13 c, p. 10.

151 United Nations General Assembly, *supra* note 144 p. 25.

152 See section 4.2.

153 Lahmann, 'Information Operations and the Question of Illegitimate Interference under International Law' 53:2 *Israeli Law Review* (2020) p. 197.

154 Denton, *supra* note 95 p. 196; C. Joyner and C. Lotrionte, 'Information Warfare as International Coercion: Elements of a Legal Framework' 12:5 *European Journal of International Law* (2001) p. 849.

155 See deliberations on this topic by Xiao, *supra* note 87 pp. 373–379; Denton, *supra* note 95 p. 202; I. Kilovaty, 'The Elephant in the Room: Coercion', 113 *AJIL Unbound* (2019) pp. 89–91.

in cyberspace, combined with the need for (legal) clarity, could significantly raise the threshold for establishing coercion. Following this rationale, coercion will only apply when activities bear the semblance of the threat or use of force. This approach – combined with the discourse on sovereignty in cyberspace – does not limit but rather facilitates manipulative influence operations.

6 Tackling Legal Uncertainty

The more States act in cyberspace without a common interpretation of sovereignty and non-intervention, the greater the normative uncertainty will be. This ambiguity could even lead to legal asymmetry.

6.1 *From Legal Uncertainty to Asymmetry*

Although the grey area[156] of ambiguity may be unwanted from a legal point of view, it could be beneficial from a political point of view. Differing interpretations of international law concerning cyberspace are conducive to "cherry-picking".[157] States can apply international law in a manner that is beneficial to their interests.[158] The "uneasy fit"[159] between traditional State-based international law and the a-territorial cyberspace creates tension between States due to the desire to preserve freedom of action for oneself while developing rules to restrict the others.[160]

The ambiguity surrounding the application of international law in cyberspace is not only "susceptible to exploitation when conducting cyber operations";[161] the variations in interpretation also have legal ramifications. After all, a violation of international law, or internationally wrongful act,[162] implies the

156 Schmitt, supra note 55 p. 33.

157 Schmitt, supra note 86 p. 33.

158 Which is sometimes called Lawfare or legal warfare, see: C. Dunlap, 'Lawfare 101 A primer' 97 *Military Review* pp 8–17; T. Grossman, *Norms vs. Realities: Cyber at the UN* (CSS Analyses in Security Policy 2022); P. Charon and J.-B. Jeangène Vilmer, *Chinese Influence Operations: A Machiavellian Moment*, (IRSEM, Paris, 2021). pp. 51–55.

159 Kilovaty, *supra* note 155 p. 89.

160 C. Keitner, 'Foreign Election Interference and International Law', in D. Hollis and J. Ohlin (eds), *Defending Democracies: Combating Foreign Election Interference in a Digital Age* (Oxford University Press, Oxford 2021) pp. 180–181.

161 M.N. Schmitt, 'Grey Zones in the International Law of Cyberspace' 42:2 *The Yale Journal of International Law* (2017) p. 3.

162 J. Crawford, *The International Law Commission's Articles on State Responsibility: Introduction, Text and Commentaries* (Cambridge University Press, Cambridge 2002). p. 81.

breach of a primary rule of law, not of non-obligatory principles. Perceiving sovereignty as a non-binding principle implies that it does not constitute an international obligation and that, even if the act can be attributed, the injured State cannot invoke an internationally wrongful act and consequently demand reparation including a reset of the system of international law.[163] If sovereignty is not a rule of international law, interferences of a non-coercive nature are not unlawful.

6.2 *Tackling Legal Uncertainty and Asymmetry*

Legal uncertainties can be reduced through awareness, resilience and reactive actions. Being aware of uncertainties and analysing how they originate constitutes the first step towards their acceptance and acknowledgement. We could, on the one hand, accept that not all States recognise sovereignty as a binding rule of international law in cyberspace. While on the other we should persistently underline that though territorial integrity might not be a perfect fit with the virtual dimension,[164] political independence can be violated in cyberspace just as in other (physical) domains. Political independence is the short-term lever for acceptance of sovereignty in cyberspace as a customary rule of international law in the long run. After all, uncertainty will be reduced if States align their interpretations regarding sovereignty, or better yet, recognise sovereignty – based on political independence – as a primary rule of law in cyberspace.

Adherents of the interpretation that political independence is a binding notion in cyberspace can facilitate advocacy of that interpretation by speaking with one voice at international conferences including the OEWG – following the example of the Scandinavian block. The idea of aligning the legal interpretation of like-minded States can grow incrementally both in areas of law and in number of States.[165]

Resilience can be defined as the capacity to recover or adapt.[166] This ability is facilitated by redundancy: if one avenue is cut off, another should remain

163 Schmitt, *supra* note 55 p. 41.

164 B.M.J. Pijpers and B. van den Bosch, 'The 'Virtual Eichmann": On Sovereignty in Cyberspace' *Amsterdam Law School Research Paper* (unpublished) pp. 19–20 <https://papers.ssrn.com/sol3/papers.cfm?abstract_id=3746843> visited on 8 August 2023; Schmitt, *supra* note 43 Rule 4 (21), p. 23.

165 See also: F. Delerue, 'Reinterpretation or Contestation of International Law in Cyberspace?', 52:3 *Israel Law Review* (2019) pp. 310–312.

166 T. Brinkel, 'The Resilient Mind-Set and Deterrence', in P.A.L. Ducheine, & F.P.B. Osinga (eds.), *Winning Without Killing: The Strategic and Operational Utility of Non-Kinetic Capabilities in Crises* (Asser Press The Hague 2017) pp 28–31.

open. If a State is unable or reticent to invoke a breach of sovereignty due to the uncertainty surrounding this notion, other justifications for responses can be found in the *force majeure* and distress, but particularly in a plea of necessity.[167] Necessity should not be invoked lightly and will only preclude wrongfulness if invoked to protect a State's essential "interest against a grave and imminent peril" without violating the rules or interests of other States. However, if sovereignty is not accepted as a binding legal norm, the threshold for a plea of necessity is lowered while at the same time the sovereignty of other States is not violated. Redundancy in legal avenues partially takes away the asymmetry.

The legal asymmetry will obviously vanish once all States lower their norms, which is an untenable slippery slope for rule-of-law States. Legal asymmetry can, however, also be addressed using non-legal instruments. If sovereignty (or any other notion of international law) is breached in cyberspace, and wrongfulness cannot be invoked since the target State does not recognise sovereignty as a binding legal rule, the victim State can counter the act with measures that are informational (narratives, propaganda), economic (sanctions) or diplomatic (*démarche*), comparable to the EU's nascent Diplomatic Cyber Toolbox – all unfriendly but lawful measures to take.

7 Conclusions and Reflections

The objective of this chapter was to explore how legal uncertainty in cyberspace arises, why it leads to legal asymmetry, and how to tackle it.

While it is generally accepted that international law applies to cyberspace;[168] "how" it applies is still subject to interpretation.[169] The expectation was that an increase in legal opinions and State practice would provide clarity.[170] Paradoxically, with the increase in legal opinions the differences have grown, intensifying rather than lessening uncertainty. The effect of the diverging interpretations of legal norms is that some are reluctant to respond to possible

167 L. Arimatsu and M.N. Schmitt, 'The Plea of Necessity: An Oft Overlooked Response Option to Hostile Cyber Operations' 97:1171 *International Law Studies* (2021) p. 1187.

168 United Nations GGE 2013 Report, *supra* note 57; United Nations GGE 2015 Report, *supra* note 70.

169 Schmitt, *supra* note 86 p. 34; D. Broeders, 'The (Im)Possibilities of Addressing Election Interference and the Public Core of the Internet in the UN GGE and OEWG: A Mid-Process Assessment' 6:3 *Journal of Cyber Policy* (2021) pp. 277–278.

170 Moynihan, *supra* note 55 p. 61.

internationally wrongful acts, while others see opportunities to exploit the ambiguity, creating legal asymmetry.

The main reasons for uncertainty can be summarised as follows. On sovereignty: some States refrain from sharing their *opinio iuris* altogether, while those that do are not aligned on whether sovereignty is a binding rule *and* a principle in cyberspace or solely a principle. Moreover, in their *opinio iuris*, many States regurgitate standards of international law without articulating how to apply them to cyberspace, and those that are outspoken differ in how to apply sovereignty as a rule in cyberspace. This is understandable as territorial integrity is difficult to apply to activities in the virtual dimension, especially related to remotely executed digital influence operations. Political independence, however, can be breached in cyberspace, which forms a basis for the existence of sovereignty in cyberspace; but still the notions of interference and State functions also lack clarity. On non-intervention: though non-intervention is an accepted rule in cyberspace, it is not without ambiguity. The virtual dimension has made the reserved domain of the State more intangible, and coercion is ill-defined in legal terms. Furthermore, international law is struggling to apply these standards to non-State (cyber) actors. Lastly, the covert and elusive methods employed by malign actors make it difficult to grasp the purpose and intent of their actions.

The effects of legal uncertainty can be mitigated by awareness and analysing how and why they emerge, but also by acceptance of the current state of (legal) affairs. From there pre-aligned block of like-minded nations could advocate those rules that are applicable in cyberspace (such as political independence) and build from there, expanding in legal rules and States involved. Creating resilience in international law will also ease the asymmetry. The plea of necessity which could serve as a redundancy in case sovereignty is too ambiguous as a legally binding rule of cyberspace. Finally, non-legal countermeasure can be taken if principles of international law are violated and States are reticent to invoke legal means.

All in all, given the current geopolitical turmoil, it is better to find satisfactory grassroot fixes than perfect but unrealistic universal solutions.

CHAPTER 10

The Plea of Necessity in Cyber Emergencies

Unresolved Doctrinal Questions

Henning Lahmann

Abstract

Although an increasing number of states has explicitly acknowledged the plea of necessity as a circumstance precluding wrongfulness to be applicable in situations of cyber emergencies, important doctrinal questions remain underexposed in both official expressions of opinio juris and in the literature. The chapter closes this gap by giving an account of three of the most salient issues in the context of the necessity defence: the "only way" requirement, the condition of non-contribution, and assistance by unaffected states to defensive measures taken in emergencies. It concludes that while recently growing academic criticism of the prevailing strict understanding of the "only way" criterion might be less relevant in the cyber context, states should consider more explicitly how emerging norms obliging states to observe a certain standard of cyber hygiene in regard to domestic cyber infrastructures could influence legal assessments as to a possible contribution to a situation of cyber emergency, potentially precluding the necessity defence. Finally, long-running doctrinal debates surrounding the exact legal nature of the defence within the larger context of the customary rules on state responsibility are revisited to examine whether third states could be permitted to come to the help of imperilled states even if the defence does not apply to them individually.

Keywords

necessity – cyber emergency – state responsibility – assistance – hack-back

 | DOI:10.1163/9789004703933_011

1 Introduction

Let us assume the following, fictitious scenario: In the early hours of the morning of 13 December 2024, the Norwegian operators monitoring the major natural gas pipeline from the Troll gas field in the North Sea to the Kollsnes processing plant in the Øygarden archipelago northwest of Bergen suddenly start noticing sudden and severe pressure fluctuations. The technicians estimate that without quick and effective intervention, the pipeline will exceed the pressure-bearing capacity of its material within hours,[1] and as a result likely burst and start releasing massive amounts of methane into the sea and then into the atmosphere. This will not only seriously compromise gas supply for the Norwegian population right at the beginning of winter but also pose a considerable climate hazard.[2] Called-in IT security specialists discover that the pressure abnormalities are being caused by remotely controlled malware placed in the pipeline's control systems. They trace the dataflow to a server located in a town near Moscow but are unable to make any further determinations as to its precise technical features or ownership. They assess, however, that it would be possible to destroy the server by injecting their own malware into the system. Doing so would most likely disrupt the ongoing operation and prevent the cybersecurity incident from escalating further.

It is a situation like this one that the Norwegian representatives at the United Nations Group of Governmental Experts on Advancing Responsible State Behaviour in Cyberspace in the Context of International Security (UN GGE) might have had in mind when they put on record their state's official position that

> [i]n a situation of necessity, a State may be able to respond to a cyber operation in a way that is in principle in breach of an international obligation and nevertheless not incur responsibility for its actions under international law.
>
> Necessity refers to those exceptional situations where the only way a State can safeguard an essential interest threatened by a grave and imminent peril, whether cyber in nature or not, is by temporary non-compliance with international obligations of lesser weight or urgency. For instance,

1 J. Zhou et al., 'Experimental Study on Pressure Pulses in Long-Distance Gas Pipeline during the Pigging Process', 1 *Science Progress* (2020) p. 1.

2 See K. McVeigh and P. Oltermann, 'Nord Stream Gas Leaks May Be Biggest Ever, with Warning of "Large Climate Risk"', *The Guardian*, 28 September 2022, <www.theguardian.com/environment/2022/sep/28/nord-stream-methane-gas-leaks-may-be-biggest-ever-with-warning-large-climate-risk>.

> if infrastructure in a third country is used in an internationally wrongful cyber operation, the injured State may under certain conditions launch a cyber operation to destroy or disrupt the internationally wrongful cyber operation, even if this violates the territorial sovereignty of the third State.[3]

Prudently adding that "a number of conditions must be fulfilled before necessity can be invoked as a ground for precluding wrongfulness", Norway made the notion's principal allure explicit: As opposed to other concepts such as self-defence or countermeasures, for necessity to work as a legal defence "[i]t is not a requirement that the preceding cyber operation must be attributable to a particular State".[4] In other words, for Norway to act lawfully in remotely destroying the command-and-control server located on Russian territory with the aim of bringing the malicious cyber operation directed against its pipeline infrastructure to an end, it does not need to demonstrate that the activity is attributable to the Russian Federation or even, for that matter, that the latter is responsible for a violation of its due diligence obligation to prevent such conduct from emanating from territory under its control.[5]

Norway is not the only state to have publicly recognised the doctrine's potential relevance in the cyber context. In its *Position Paper on the Application of International Law in Cyberspace* from July 2022, Norway's neighbour Sweden noted, albeit more cautiously:

> Under certain strict conditions, a State is allowed to employ measures that would otherwise be in breach of an international obligation in order to safeguard an essential interest against a grave and imminent peril. This would also apply in a cyber context. Necessity will, however, only rarely be available to excuse non-performance of an obligation.[6]

A handful of other states have since 2019 expressed the official legal view that the customary necessity defence as reflected in Article 25 of the Draft Articles on State Responsibility (ASR) is applicable in principle when a state is faced

3 UNODA, *Official compendium of voluntary national contributions on the subject of how international law applies to the use of information and communications technologies by States*, UN Doc. A/76/136 (August 2021), p. 73.

4 *Ibid.*

5 See on this A. Coco and T. de Souza Dias, '"Cyber Due Diligence": A Patchwork of Protective Obligations', 32 *European Journal of International Law* (2021) p. 771.

6 Government Offices of Sweden, *Position Paper on the Application of International Law in Cyberspace*, July 2022, p. 6.

with a serious cybersecurity incident that calls for a quick reaction which would *prima facie* be in conflict with one of the state's international obligations, namely France,[7] Germany,[8] Japan,[9] the Netherlands,[10] and Switzerland.[11] The second iteration of the Tallinn Manual on the International Law Applicable to Cyber Operations, compiled by an International Group of Experts, likewise acknowledged necessity as appliable to cyber emergencies in principle.[12]

Despite techniques to identify the origin and agents of adversarial cyber operations evidently having made considerable progress over the past decade, with the consequence that public attributions of cybersecurity incidents to states have started to become more frequent,[13] the plea of necessity as a customary circumstance precluding wrongfulness might well retain its relevance in transnational cybersecurity, as the states' official positions signal. For one, even if successful attribution appears to have become more likely, such processes will continue to take time in order to be carried out with a sufficient degree of certainty, in particular in terms of their forensic aspects.[14] Aside from identifying the immediate source of the incident, there is the further issue of demonstrating a link to the territorial state in accordance with Article 8 ASR, as Norway's statement notes: "It may be technically challenging to establish that a relationship between a State and a non-State actor amounts to direct instructions, direction or effective control."[15] Although it is correct that "this is a question of evidence, and not of lack of clarity of international law",[16] in a crisis situation such as the one outlined above, proper attribution might simply not be feasible ahead of initiating steps to prevent or mitigate harm. If

7 Ministry of Defense of France, *International Law Applied to Operations in Cyberspace*, September 2019, p. 8.

8 Federal Government of Germany, *On the Application of International Law in Cyberspace, Position Paper*, March 2021, p. 14.

9 Ministry of Foreign Affairs of Japan, *Basic Position of the Government of Japan on International Law Applicable to Cyber Operations*, June 2021, p. 5.

10 Government of the Kingdom of the Netherlands, *Appendix: International Law in Cyberspace*, September 2019, p. 7.

11 Swiss Federal Department of Foreign Affairs, *Switzerland's Position Paper on the Application of International Law in Cyberspace*, May 2021, p. 7.

12 M.N. Schmitt (ed.), *Tallinn Manual 2.0 on the International Law Applicable to Cyber Operations* (Cambridge University Press, Cambridge, 2017), Rule 26.

13 See F.J. Egloff and M. Smeets, 'Publicly Attributing Cyber Attacks: A Framework', *Journal of Strategic Studies*, DOI: 10.1080/01402390.2021.1895117.

14 T. Rid and T. Buchanan, 'Attributing Cyber Attacks', 38 *Journal of Strategic Studies* (2015) p. 4, 32.

15 Norway's statement, *supra* note 3.

16 *Ibid.*

these steps involve interfering with legally protected interests of another state, for instance its right to territorial sovereignty,[17] then invoking necessity might remain the only viable option in some circumstances.

In light of the above, the plea of necessity can be expected to remain particularly relevant for smaller states, including the Nordics, or those that lack the capacity or the political will to maintain surveillance infrastructures capable of monitoring activity in adversarial networks with the purpose of facilitating quick identification and attribution in case of an incident.[18]

Irrespective of the seemingly growing acknowledgment of the utility and applicability of the doctrine in the cyber context, necessity is yet to receive a relevant degree of attention in the literature. Some of this neglect may be explained with a view to its rather uncertain and still not consistently undisputed nature under customary international law. Connected to this, as a defence inscribing the exception, by definition the state of necessity involves some crucial yet uncomfortable implications regarding the international rule of law.[19] Yet aside from such more fundamental concerns, a string of largely unaddressed doctrinal questions remains, namely regarding the "only way" requirement, the imperilled state's contribution to the emergency situation, and the issue of a third state's assistance to measures taken under the plea of necessity. After briefly outlining the elements of necessity as a circumstance precluding wrongfulness under the customary law of state responsibility, this chapter addresses these three doctrinal aspects in turn. As indicated by the scenario introduced at the outset as well as in Norway's official statement, the analytical focus will be on "active defensive cyber measures"[20] that a state might resort to in order to disrupt an adversarial cyber operation.

17 Whether (territorial) sovereignty has the status of a rule or merely a principle under customary international law remains contested; see for the different state positions on this question Cyber Law Toolkit, 'Sovereignty', last edit 17 March 2023, <https://cyberlaw.ccdcoe.org/wiki/Sovereignty>.

18 See E.D. Lonergan, 'Operationalizing Defend Forward: How the Concept Works to Change Adversary Behavior', *Lawfare*, 12 March 2020, <www.lawfareblog.com/operationalizing-defend-forward-how-concept-works-change-adversary-behavior>.

19 See H. Lahmann, '"Hacking Back" by States and the Uneasy Place of Necessity within the Rule of Law', 80 *Zeitschrift für ausländisches öffentliches Recht und Völkerrecht* (2020) p. 453.

20 S. Herpig, *Active Cyber Defense Operations: Assessment and Safeguards* (Stiftung Neue Verantwortung, Berlin 2021), < www.stiftung-nv.de/sites/default/files/active_cyber_defense_operations.pdf>.

2 Necessity under Customary International Law

Although it had a quite extensive history of recognition and contestation in state practice,[21] when the International Law Commission (ILC) sought to include the notion of necessity during the drafting process of what would become the ASR, a number of scholars as well as states raised considerable doubts as to the wisdom of attempting to codify the concept.[22] Up until the publication of the Draft Articles in 2001, necessity remained one of the most contentious provisions, with one state objecting that it "would be open to very serious abuse across the whole range of international relations".[23] Similarly, scholars commenting on the proceedings objected that practice and expressions of *opinio juris* were insufficient to consider the defence part of custom, and that such an exceptional concept ran counter to the general structure of international law, inherently favouring more powerful states at the expense of the rule of law in the international order.[24] Such express reservations have continued to pop up on occasion.[25] At the same time, courts and tribunals had started to explicitly refer to the defence of necessity as a circumstance precluding wrongfulness under customary international law even before the conclusion of the ILC drafting process,[26] and since the publication of the text of the ASR, the doctrine has gained further traction. Its general acceptance is not least reflected in the above cited official legal positions on the application of international law in cyberspace.

The version of necessity as supposedly being expressive of existing custom is laid down in Article 25 ASR:

1. Necessity may not be invoked by a State as a ground for precluding the wrongfulness of an act not in conformity with an international obligation of that State unless the act:
   (a) is the only way for the State to safeguard an essential interest against a grave and imminent peril; and

21 For an historical overview see F. Paddeu, *Justification and Excuse in International Law: Concept and Theory of General Defences* (Cambridge University Press, Cambridge, 2018), pp. 339–386.

22 *Ibid.*, pp. 398–401.

23 UN Doc. A/CN4/488 (25 March 1998), at 88 (United Kingdom).

24 See Paddeu, *supra* note 20, p. 375.

25 See most succinctly R.D. Sloane, 'On the Use and Abuse of Necessity in the Law of State Responsibility', 106 *American Journal of International Law* (2012) pp. 447, 450ff.

26 See *Gabčíkovo-Nagymaros Project* (*Hungary v. Slovakia*), 25 September 1997, ICJ, Judgment; *M/V Saiga* (*No 2*) (*Saint Vincent and the Grenadines v. Guinea*), 1 July 1999, paras. 133–134.

(b) does not seriously impair an essential interest of the State or States towards which the obligation exists, or of the international community as a whole.

2. In any case, necessity may not be invoked by a State as a ground for precluding wrongfulness if:
   (a) the international obligation in question excludes the possibility of invoking necessity; or
   (b) the State has contributed to the situation of necessity.

The exceptional character of the defence is made clear by the provision's negative phrasing (" ... may *not* be invoked ... unless ... "). Moreover, the doctrinal design in its entirety unambiguously strives to ensure that necessity will not turn into a readily abused tool for purely political pretexts by laying out a number of very strict and narrowly circumscribed cumulative preconditions for successful invocation.[27] Despite not being dependent on any prior conduct of the injured state, be it consent or an unlawful act, as mentioned, necessity is supposed to only be available in situations in which there exists an "irreconcilable conflict" between the invoking state's international obligation and one of its "essential" interests due to a "grave and imminent peril", which should only very rarely be the case to begin with.[28]

2.1 *Critical Infrastructures as Essential Interest*

As for the condition of an "essential interest" that must be endangered, after initial debates that this should, in light of the history of the doctrine, be limited to the very existence of the state,[29] more recent state practice demonstrates that the scope of possible interests that may legitimately be sought to be protected by way of invoking the defences is much broader. As Crawford explained, "[t]he extent to which an interest is 'essential' depends on all the circumstances";[30] the safety of the civilian population or safeguarding the environment have previously been referred to as essential interests by states.[31] Even if a natural gas leak has less immediate environmental consequences than an oil spill, as evidenced by the 2022 Nord Stream incident in the Baltic Sea,[32] considering the state of greenhouse gas emissions and the gravity of the

27 J. Crawford, *State Responsibility: The General Part* (Cambridge University Press, Cambridge, 2013), p. 306.
28 International Law Commission, *Draft Articles on Responsibility of States for Internationally Wrongful Acts, with Commentaries* (United Nations, 2001), Art. 25, para. 2.
29 Paddeu, *supra* note 20, p. 391.
30 Crawford, *supra* note 26, p. 308.
31 Paddeu, *supra* note 20, p. 397.
32 McVeigh and Oltermann, *supra* note 2.

threat of climate change, Norway might reasonably invoke safeguarding the environment as a sufficiently essential interest in the scenario introduced at the outset in addition to protecting the wellbeing of its civilian population.

In the cyber context, there is moreover growing consensus as to the recognition of secure and functioning "critical infrastructures" as essential to a society's welfare.[33] This development was explicitly taken up by Germany in its statement on international law in cyberspace, holding that "the affectedness of an 'essential interest' may *inter alia* be explained by reference to the type of infrastructure actually or potentially targeted by a malicious cyber operation and an analysis of that infrastructure's relevance for the State as a whole. For example, the protection of certain critical infrastructures may constitute an 'essential interest'".[34] Despite continuing differences between states as to the precise definition of "critical infrastructures" and what list of assets to include, given their crucial position for the functioning of modern societies, generally considering them "essential" for the purpose of the necessity defence does not seem all that controversial.

2.2 *Grave and Imminent Peril*

Concerning the requirement that the state's essential interest must be threatened by a "grave and imminent peril", Crawford has clarified that the latter is to be established "objectively", which implies that the question whether this has been the case is subject to outside assessment, for example by way of adjudication by a court or tribunal. At the same time, a state cannot be asked to have complete certainty as to the probability and gravity of the risk of severe consequences from the peril materialising, so it must be allowed some margin of appreciation.[35] Where a cybersecurity incident endangers the continuous functioning of critical infrastructures, imperilling the wellbeing of the civilian population, or involves likely threats to the environment,[36] the precondition is met. The inherent uncertainty in evaluating the situation and predicting different outcomes plays perhaps an even larger role when it comes to the "only way" criterion, to which we turn in the next section.

---

33 See generally T. Kouloufakos, 'The Cyber Norm to Protect Critical Infrastructures', SSRN, 2022 <papers.ssrn.com/abstract=4268660>.

34 Federal Government of Germany, supra note 8, p. 14.

35 Crawford, *supra* note 26, p. 311.

36 See on this C. Foster, 'Necessity and Precaution in International Law: Responding to Oblique Forms of Urgency', 23 *New Zealand Universities Law Review* (2008), p. 265.

3 The "Only Way"

As made clear by Article 25 ASR, any measure that a state undertakes in response to the imminent and grave peril to its essential interest, including, in the cyber context, active defensive measures to shut down information and communications infrastructures on the territory of another state – thus *prima facie* violating the latter's territorial integrity – must be the "only way" to safeguard the interest in order for the conduct's wrongfulness to be precluded. In its commentary to the ASR, the ILC explained that a state cannot rely on the plea of necessity if "there are other (otherwise lawful) means available, even if they may be more costly or less convenient".[37] This requirement furthermore implies that "any conduct going beyond what is strictly necessary for the purpose will not be covered" by the circumstance precluding wrongfulness.[38]

As Crawford memorably made clear, "[h]ere 'only' means 'only'".[39] Following the phrasing of the provision and its rationale to make the plea available in as few situations as possible, this means that the state's options must effectively have been reduced to two: either to allow harm to its essential interest to occur or to protect it by pursuing a path of action that will lead to a breach of one of its international obligations.[40]

3.1 *The "Only Way" Requirement in International Jurisprudence*

Unsurprisingly, it is in the context of this deliberately very strict precondition that most invocations of necessity have failed when scrutinized by international courts and tribunals after the fact. In its Gabčíkovo-Nagymaros Project decision, the International Court of Justice (ICJ) could not be persuaded by the argument that unilaterally suspending and abandoning the bilaterally agreed undertaking was the only means available in view of the circumstances.[41] A couple of years later, when issuing its Advisory Opinion on Israel's construction of a security barrier in the Occupied Palestinian Territory, the Court observed curtly that it could not be "convinced that the construction of the wall along the route chosen was the only means to safeguard the interests of Israel against the peril which it has invoked as justification for that construction".[42] Similarly, in *M/V Saiga (No 2)*, the International Tribunal for the Law of the Sea (ITLOS) held

37 International Law Commission, *supra* note 27, Article 25, para. 15.

38 *Ibid.*

39 Crawford, *supra* note 26, p. 311.

40 Paddeu, *supra* note 20, p. 427.

41 *Gabčíkovo-Nagymaros Project, supra* note 25, para. 54.

42 *Legal Consequences of the Construction of a Wall in the Occupied Palestinian Territory*, 9 July 2004, ICJ Advisory Opinion, para. 140.

that "however essential Guinea's interest in maximizing its tax revenue from the sale of gas oil to fishing vessels, it cannot be suggested that the only means of safeguarding that interest was to extend its customs laws to parts of the exclusive economic zone".[43] The general dismissiveness towards the condition has probably been most pronounced in state-investor disputes before ICSID tribunals, which have by now compiled the most extensive jurisprudence on the necessity defence. The overall attitude can be exemplified with a quote from *Sempra Energy International v. Argentine Republic*: "A rather sad global comparison of experiences in the handling of economic crises shows that there are always many approaches to addressing and resolving such critical events. It is therefore difficult to justify the position that only one of them was available in the Argentine case".[44] Most recently, an ICSID tribunal found it "sufficient to articulate the hypothesis [that the inaction of Malagasy law enforcement on the ground was the 'only way' in the given situation] to see that it has no basis".[45]

As all these cases uniformly demonstrate, the "only way" condition has been interpreted as a requirement so strict as to render it virtually impossible for a state to successfully invoke the necessity defence, which is of course intentional in light of potential abuse. However, this operationalisation of the condition in international jurisprudence has become subject to persistent critique in the literature. Most prominently, Paddeu and Waibel have recently suggested that the described practice shows that it is here where the plea of necessity in its current manifestation falls short conceptually.[46] They base their argument on two main observations concerning how judges and arbitrators have dealt with the question whether a certain measure undertaken by the state could be considered the "only way" to avert the peril: the problem of the complexity of macro-crises and the related but separate issue of hindsight bias.

First, the authors observed, especially with a view to the investor-state disputes in the context of the Argentine crisis from 1998 to 2002, that any such complex economic situation will invariably require a combination of different types of measures. However, the approach the ICSID tribunals took to interpret

---

43 *M/V 'SAIGA' (No 2)*, *supra* note 26, para. 134.

44 *Sempra Energy International v. Argentine Republic*, 28 September 2007, ICSID Case No ARB/02/16, para. 350.

45 *(DS)2, S.A., Peter de Sutter and Kristof de Sutter v. Republic of Madagascar*, 17 April 2020, ICSID Case No ARB/17/18, para. 347 (translated from the French in *Responsibility of States for internationally wrongful acts, Compilation of decisions of international courts, tribunals and other bodies*, UN Doc. A/77/74, 29 April 2022, p. 21).

46 F. Paddeu and M. Waibel, 'Necessity 20 Years On: The Limits of Article 25', 37 *ICSID Review* (2022), p. 160.

the customary rule was to expect the respondent state to accurately predict the one measure that will work to avert or alleviate further economic harm to its society. But this is almost by definition virtually impossible in a multi-faceted crisis that can only, if at all, be tackled with a mix of different steps of which each individually will not be the "only way". Thus, if an adjudicator zooms in *ex post facto* and assesses singular courses of action while missing the broader picture of state measures, the outcome is predetermined. As "macro-crises require multipronged responses", to "assess a single measure of this package alone is artificial".[47]

Furthermore, relevant for the legal analysis can only be the instruments that were available to the state at the time the peril materialised and not those that *would* have been available had the state acted with more prescience.[48] Paddeu and Waibel point out that a few tribunals have acknowledged the complexities such situations inherently involve and thus appraised the condition in a more balanced manner. They note that investment tribunals only more recently have begun to show more sensitivity toward the question of whether there in fact were actual alternatives available to the state when it embarked on its course of action.[49]

Closely connected to the issue of alternative measures is the problem of hindsight bias. As the available case law shows, adjudicators have been displaying a clear tendency to look at the situation at hand purely from the perspective of someone with the knowledge of the entire course of events. With that advantage, it is almost inevitable that a different option would in fact have been at the state's disposal in order to avert the peril. But as the authors point out, this cannot possibly be the correct interpretation of the law. The decisive point in time for the legal assessment is the moment at which the state had to make a decision as to what measure to take, and the applicable standard must be what it could reasonably know at the time. The benefit of hindsight cannot be allowed to play a role in the judicial decision afterwards.[50] Of course, given that hindsight bias is a known cognitive tendency, even adjudicators consciously attempting to avoid making assessments based on knowledge only available after the fact easily fall prey to this propensity. Nevertheless, for obvious reasons it amounts to a standard that states simply cannot meet.[51] Naturally, the issue affects states faced with macro-crises to an even greater

---

47 *Ibid.*, p. 175.

48 *Ibid.*, p. 177.

49 *Ibid.*, p. 176, with reference to *Unión Fenosa Gas SA v. Arab Republic of Egypt*, 31 August 2018, ICSID Case No. ARB/14/4, paras. 8.41–8.46.

50 *Ibid.*, pp. 164–165.

51 *Ibid.*, p. 166.

degree due to the complexity of the task at hand and the corresponding need to make decisions on the basis of intricate probabilities regarding the potential to avert future harms. In macro-crises, these probabilities are often not even measurable, which turns them into situations of uncertainty rather than risk.[52]

For the above reasons, the Paddeu and Waibel consider the "only way" requirement as currently predominantly understood unduly strict and thus inadequate at least as far as the situation under scrutiny concerns a multi-dimensional emergency situation. In light of this difficulty, Paparinskis recently suggested that future state practice might gradually move towards reconfiguring the necessity defence as demanding the state to adopt "reasonable means" when acting to counter a peril instead of the only one available.[53] While this does not sound like a far-fetched prediction per se particularly in view of the troubles many states experienced with trying to get a handle on the Covid-19 pandemic especially in its early stages of overwhelming uncertainty, so far the international community does not appear to have initiated steps in that direction. Considering the fundamental rule-of-law concerns that inevitably accompany any invocation of the plea of necessity, it is furthermore questionable whether such a development would be advisable.

3.2 *Cybersecurity Incidents and Emergency Protocols*

As illustrated, the main points of critique originate with the failure to meaningfully apply the customary necessity defence to macro-crises stemming from economic or financial perils; examples of other such multi-faceted situations are quickly at hand, above all climate change. At the same time, the arguments do not easily map onto cybersecurity incidents as these will usually involve a singular source that is identifiable at least in principle. The options available to avert the peril or to mitigate the consequences will by default be equally limited. What will nonetheless be relevant, however, is the problem of hindsight bias. The principal reason for this is the consideration that incidents caused by a malicious cyber operation will most often call for a quick response that will not allow for extensive planning and strategizing as to the measure that will predictably be most effective. Thus, when it comes to legally assessing the course of action that the state seeks to justify by invoking necessity, it will be crucial to carefully adopt its point of view and assess the information reasonably available to it at the time the incident occurred.

52 *Ibid.*, p. 163.

53 M. Paparinskis, 'The Once and Future Law of State Responsibility', 114 *American Journal of International Law* (2020), p. 618, 625.

At the same time, to prevent abuse by allowing states too much leeway to launch highly intrusive and potentially hazardous counter-operations on the active defence spectrum, the overall rationale of the necessity defence advocates requiring states to adequately prepare for such emergency situations in order to have at the ready a toolbox of escalating defensive measures that can be implemented step by step. To operationalise necessity in the cyber context without compromising the international rule of law, states should generally have implemented a multi-stage emergency plan that enables them to move from less to more intrusive measures quickly but in a controlled manner. As long as purely defensive procedures – for instance disconnecting or shutting down affected parts of a network, patching software vulnerabilities, or installing backups – prove sufficient to repel the threat, the state must employ those first. This is precisely what the "only way" condition demands: if non-intrusive means are available that are able to thwart the incident without the need to infringe on the legally protected interests of the state of origin, then those means must be chosen even in the case that they are more costly or less convenient.[54]

If a state established an appropriate cyber emergency response plan involving clear risk assessments for every conceivable measure prior to the occurrence of a security incident, then an *ex post facto* legal assessment may reasonably start with the assumption that an ultimately taken active defensive cyber measure – such as the disruption of information and communications infrastructures on the territory of another state – was genuinely the imperilled state's last resort in the case at hand. Likewise, if the state transparently followed its emergency protocol of gradual escalation, it should be given the benefit of the doubt even if a subsequent comprehensive analysis concludes that a less intrusive defensive measure would ultimately have averted the peril as well. Such an approach would be able to at least reduce the risk of unfair hindsight bias while also decreasing the risk of abuse of the necessity defence.

Under normal circumstances, overall considerations should require one of the steps that a state must take before resorting to intrusive measures to be the notification of the state from whose territory the malicious activity is emanating, unless there are strong indications that justify the assumption that such a call for assistance would be futile or even counterproductive. Such a general obligation, albeit not directly in the context of necessity, has been

54 See H. Lahmann, *Unilateral Remedies to Cyber Operations: Self-Defence, Countermeasures, Necessity, and the Question of Attribution* (Cambridge University Press, Cambridge, 2020), p. 218.

acknowledged by the GGE.[55] Finally, the fact that the situation of necessity would likely have been avoided had the state observed better cyber hygiene (e.g., the cybersecurity incident would not have occurred if the affected systems had been provided with the latest software updates) does not affect the assessment of the "only way" requirement. This is because the decisive point in time is the moment when the grave peril materialises and becomes imminent, as explained above. However, the affected state's security practices vis-à-vis its own critical cyber infrastructures may be consequential when it comes to examining the so-called "non-contribution" requirement, to which we turn in the subsequent section.

4 "Non-Contribution"

Article 25(2)(b) ASR provides that "necessity may not be invoked by a State as a ground for precluding wrongfulness if (…) the State has contributed to the situation of necessity". During the drafting process of the ASR, the inclusion of this non-contribution requirement by the ILC caused some controversy and pushback from states, as general consensus went that it had not been part of custom and constituted a questionable progressive development of international law. Nonetheless, the drafters ultimately prevailed, again with regard to general considerations that the necessity defence must be available as rarely as possible. The precondition aims at preventing "moral hazard" by strongly incentivising states to act with prudence.[56] Already in 1997, the ICJ had accepted this doctrinal construction, denying Hungary the plea of necessity on the grounds that it had "helped, by act or omission to bring about" the perilous situation.[57] And although some states had noted critically that in the majority of conceivable cases, it is highly likely that there will be, to at least some extent, a causal link between a state's decisions and actions prior to the occurrence of a situation of emergency, the precondition now seems firmly entrenched. For one, however, the issue is somewhat abated by the fact that the contribution "must be sufficiently substantial and not merely

55 GGE Report 2021, Norm 13(c), para. 30(c): "An affected State should notify the State from which the activity is emanating. The notified State should acknowledge receipt of the notification to facilitate cooperation and clarification and make every reasonable effort to assist in establishing whether an internationally wrongful act has been committed. Acknowledging the receipt of this notice does not indicate concurrence with the information contained therein."

56 Paddeu and Waibel, *supra* note 45, p. 178.

57 *Gabčíkovo-Nagymaros Project*, *supra* note 25, para. 57.

incidental or peripheral".[58] Furthermore, Paddeu and Waibel have suggested that in addition to a causal relationship between the state's behaviour and the perilous situation, the requirement should be interpreted as demanding some degree of fault on part of the state, for instance negligence.[59] It should be noted that the ILC Commentary to the ASR does not mention fault as a factor,[60] even though earlier iterations of the ASR during the long drafting phase did.[61] The available case law from investment arbitrations is divided on this question.

In the cybersecurity context, these considerations specifically raise the question whether the lack of implementation of adequate cybersecurity policies and architectures may be qualified as such a substantial contribution if the peril to the state's essential interest caused by a cybersecurity incident and the omission are causally related. The Tallinn Manual 2.0 suggests not, asserting that "mere failure to take preventive measures to protect a State's cyber infrastructure from harmful cyber operations amounting to 'grave and imminent peril' does not bar measures based on necessity."[62] However, the reasons for how the International Group of Experts arrived at this conclusion are unclear. In any case, by now it has been firmly established, and repeatedly confirmed, that the implementation of basic cybersecurity policies, legislation, infrastructures, and measures is an essential component of what the international community considers "responsible state behaviour in cyberspace". As early as 2004, UN General Assembly resolution 58/199 stressed the need for states to engage in comprehensive cybersecurity practices and laid down a catalogue of "Elements for protecting critical information infrastructures".[63] Recognizing that cybersecurity incidents affecting critical communications infrastructures may not only endanger a state's national security but perhaps even threaten international peace and security, the General Assembly laid down eleven components for an improved cyber hygiene and called on member states to implement them, including "emergency warning networks", "crisis communication networks", the facilitation of "the tracing of attacks on critical information infrastructures", and "training and exercises to enhance response capabilities" as well as "continuity and contingency plans in the event of an information infrastructure attack".

58 International Law Commission, *supra* note 27, Article 25, para. 20.
59 See Paddeu and Waibel, *supra* note 45, p. 180.
60 International Law Commission, *supra* note 27, para. 20.
61 See Paddeu and Waibel, *supra* note 45, p. 180.
62 Schmitt, *supra* note 12, Rule 26, at para. 19.
63 *Creation of a global culture of cybersecurity and the protection of critical information infrastructures*, UN Doc. A/RES/58/199, 30 January 2004.

In its 2015 Report, the UN GGE formulated (voluntary) Norm 13(g) to the same effect, calling on states to "take appropriate measures to protect their critical infrastructure from ICT threats".[64] In 2021, the UN OEWG likewise emphasised "the primary responsibility of States for maintaining a secure, safe and trusted ICT environment".[65] Such an obligation follows not least from a state's territorial sovereignty, given that only a properly maintained domestic cyber infrastructure can ensure that the networks are not utilised by private actors or third states for nefarious ends to the detriment of other states. In this way, cyber hygiene is part of a state's due diligence obligation to prevent adversarial cyber operations emanating from its territory.[66] But to the extent that the norm expresses a more general duty to set up at least "minimum levels of national ICT risk management protocols and programs to protect critical infrastructures",[67] there is no apparent reason not to consider a state's compliance at least one factor in the assessment of whether it has substantially contributed to a situation of necessity caused by a cybersecurity incident. Taking the existence or lack of protective measures into account in the overall evaluation in such a way, it should be noted, is without prejudice to the larger doctrinal question of the precise legal status of the UN GGE's voluntary cyber norms.[68] As a factual concern, widespread carelessness as to the simplest ICT security measures continues to present one of the most prevalent attack vectors for malicious cyber actors, as exemplified by the devastating 2017 WannaCry global ransomware attack.[69] The above consideration may serve as yet another argument for a requirement of fault in addition to causality; without it, states with fewer resources and capacities would end up in a legally worse position as compared to wealthier states.

---

64 *Group of Governmental Expert on Developments in the Field of Information and Telecommunications in the Context of International Security*, UN Doc. A/70/174, 22 July 2015, para. 13(g).

65 *Developments in the field of information and telecommunications in the context of international security*, UN Doc. A/75/816, 18 March 2021, para. 36.

66 See generally Coco and de Souza Dias, *supra* note 5.

67 M. Berk, 'Recommendations 13(g) and (h)', in E. Tikk (ed.), *Voluntary, Non-Binding Norms for Responsible State Behaviour in the Use of Information and Communications Technology: A Commentary* (United Nations Office for Disarmament Affairs, 2017), p. 204.

68 See L. Adamson, 'International Law and International Cyber Norms: A Continuum?', in D. Broeders and B. van den Berg (eds.), *Governing Cyberspace: Behavior, Power, and Diplomacy*, Rowman & Littlefield, Lanham, 2020), p. 19; S. Haataja, 'Cyber Operations Against Critical Infrastructure Under Norms of Responsible State Behaviour and International Law', 30 *International Journal of Law and Information Technology* (2022), p. 423, 429–433.

69 L. Eadicicco, 'The Latest Ransomware Proves Delaying Updates Is a Bad Idea, *Time*, 15 May 2017, <time.com/4779750/wannacry-ransomware-patch-windows-cybersecurity/>.

To be sure, it should be up to states to decide on their own what measures to take and how to implement them. In line with the principle of due diligence, differences in capacity between states should be taken into account, acknowledging the more general idea that "states have common but differentiated responsibilities in international law".[70] This does not mean that the state is at liberty to refrain from initiating steps altogether; a minimum degree of establishing legislative, judicial, and executive infrastructures to deal with cyber threats is required.[71] The number of states that have adopted respective legislative, strategic, and technical frameworks to increase security levels in line with international standards has been rising steadily over the past years.[72] Bearing in mind that "the state of perfect security is not attainable",[73] the requirement can never be the complete prevention of a perilous cybersecurity incident, but complete negligence in this regard should preclude reliance on the plea of necessity if there is a causal nexus between the state's omission and the grave and imminent peril to the essential interest, as the state then has substantially contributed to the situation.

5 "Collective" Necessity?

Coming back to our fictitious scenario, having been able to trace the malicious cyber operation that is threatening to blow up the natural gas pipeline to Kollsnes back to the command-and-control server on Russian territory, the Norwegian cybersecurity specialists hit a roadblock: While they could principally figure out how to disable the server by injecting malware, they did not have the needed piece of code to gain access to the system at their disposal. Developing it themselves would never be possible within the short timeframe available before the pipeline's hull would start caving in. However, they were aware that as part of their strategies of "Persistent Engagement" and "Defend Forward",[74] Norway's NATO allies in Washington, D.C. had been "preparing the battlefield" in cyberspace for precisely this type of situation, continuously engaging in "[i]ntrusions into the systems of potential adversaries in order to secure access of a kind that can be exploited for disruptive or destructive effect

70 Coco and de Souza Dias 2021, *supra* note 5, p. 804.

71 *Ibid.*

72 Berk, *supra* note 66, p. 202.

73 *Ibid.*, p. 206.

74 M.P. Fischerkeller and R.J. Harknett, 'Persistent Engagement, Agreed Competition, and Cyberspace Interaction Dynamics and Escalation', *Cyber Defense Review* (2019), p. 267.

if and when the need later arises".[75] If asked to do so by the authorities in Oslo, would the U.S. be permitted to carry out the operation to destroy the server on Russian territory on behalf of Norway?

5.1 *An Ongoing Debate: The Right to Collective Countermeasures*

That the right to self-defence allows for collective action in the case of an armed attack is beyond dispute, as Article 51 UN Charter unambiguously speaks of "the inherent right of individual *or collective* self-defence". More controversially, the growing threat of malicious inter-state cyber activity has sparked a debate concerning the lawfulness of collective countermeasures. The first to come out in favour of such a right, then-president of Estonia Kersti Kaljulaid argued at the 11th International Conference on Cyber Conflict in Tallinn in 2019 that "states which are not directly injured may apply countermeasures to support the state directly affected by the malicious cyber operation".[76] The main rationale she offered for this position was that "[i]nternational security and the rules-based international order have long benefited from collective efforts to stop the violators",[77] but it seems clear that at least part of the underlying, if tacit, consideration is that such a doctrinal construction would benefit states that lack the resources to counter adversarial cyber conduct on their own.

The debate surrounding collective responses through the concept of countermeasures is of course neither new nor limited to the context of transnational cybersecurity. To the contrary, already during the drafting process of the ASR this question was controversial, resulting in the slightly awkward solution of Article 54 ASR merely stating that the Draft Articles do not "prejudice the right of any State [that is entitled to invoke the responsibility of another State for the violation of an obligation *erga omnes* pursuant to Article 48] to take lawful measures against that State to ensure cessation of the breach and reparation in the interest of the injured State or of the beneficiaries of the obligation breached". As Brunner has pointed out, advocating a more general right to collective countermeasures in the cyber context would go beyond *erga omnes* violations and thus be much broader in scope than even

75 R. Chesney, 'The 2018 DOD Cyber Strategy: Understanding "Defense Forward" in Light of the NDAA and PPD-20 Changes', *Lawfare*, 25 September 2018, <www.lawfareblog.com/2018-dod-cyber-strategy-understanding-defense-forward-light-ndaa-and-ppd-20-changes>.

76 *ERR News*, 'President Kaljulaid at CyCon 2019: Cyber Attacks Should not Be Easy Weapon', 29 May 2019, <news.err.ee/946827/president-kaljulaid-at-cycon-2019-cyber-attacks-should-not-be-easy-weapon>.

77 *Ibid.*

tacitly acknowledged by the ILC.[78] Accordingly, France has come out explicitly against such a right,[79] and the literature has so far been divided.[80] A majority of the International Group of Experts that drafted the Tallinn Manual 2.0 was opposed to the idea of collective countermeasures.[81]

5.2 *The Doctrinal Status of Necessity and Article 16 ASR*

Irrespective of the question whose arguments are considered more persuasive, the rationale for permitting collective responses under the doctrine of countermeasures cannot simply be applied to necessity. For one, note how Estonia's president reasoned that the global community has "long benefited from collective efforts to stop the violations":[82] Strictly speaking, in an emergency situation as described at the outset, there exists no violation due to the lack of a violator – because timely attribution of the malicious cyber conduct failed or was at least impossible to carry out in time, there is only a cybersecurity incident imperilling the state's essential interest, but not an internationally wrongful act that the state is responding to. More fundamentally, as Crawford observed during the ASR drafting process, necessity stands "at the outer edge of the tolerance of international law for otherwise wrongful conduct".[83] In light of this argument, and not least given the risk of abuse as the most critical consideration underlying the very strict preconditions and narrow scope of application of the customary necessity defence, the plea should only ever be available to a state that itself is in an emergency situation.

The issue of genuinely "collective" necessity must be distinguished from the question whether a third state may assist the imperilled state in order to enable the latter to successfully handle the emergency situation by way of *prima facie* violating one of its international obligations. If not permitted to carry out the cyber operation to destroy the server on Russian territory on

78 I. Brunner, '1998 – UNGA Resolution 53/70 "Developments in the Field of Information and Telecommunications in the Context of International Security" and Its Influence on the International Rule of Law in Cyberspace', *SSRN*, 2020, p. 11, <papers.ssrn.com/abstract=3856900>.

79 Ministère des Armées, *Droit International Appliqué aux Opérations dans le Cyberespace*, p. 8: "Les contre-mesures collectives ne sont ainsi pas autorisées, ce qui exclut la possibilité pour la France d'adopter de telles mesures en réponse à une atteinte aux droits d'un État tiers."

80 In favour see M.N. Schmitt and S. Watts, 'Collective Cyber Countermeasures?', 12 *Harvard National Security Journal* (2021) p. 176; sceptically J. Kosseff, 'Collective Countermeasures in Cyberspace', 10 *Notre Dame Journal of International & Comparative Law* (2020), p. 18.

81 Schmitt, *supra* note 12, Rule 24, para. 8.

82 ERR News, *supra* note 74.

83 Report of the International Law Commission on the Work of its Fifty Fourth Session, Supplement No. 10, UN Doc. A/54/10, p. 378.

behalf of Norway, could the U.S. instead lawfully transfer the needed code to the Norwegian authorities for them to pursue the operation, or share crucial information about vulnerabilities in the Russian system? The International Group of Experts tackled the question of lawful assistance in the context of countermeasures, with divided views.[84]

The answer to the question in relation to necessity can arguably be found by properly analysing Article 16 ASR. The rule provides:

> A State which aids or assists another State in the commission of an internationally wrongful act by the latter is internationally responsible for doing so if:

(a) that State does so with knowledge of the circumstances of the internationally wrongful act; and
(b) the act would be internationally wrongful if committed by that State.

As is clear from the wording, a state incurs responsibility if and only if it aids or assists another state *in the commission of an internationally wrongful act*. Consequently, if the latter state's conduct is lawful, then the former state is at liberty to come to its help. This raises the question whether a successful invocation of the necessity defence renders the act that *prima facie* was in violation of the state's international obligation lawful or not. If it does, then at least from a doctrinal perspective there is no reason why an assisting state should not benefit from the circumstance precluding wrongfulness that the acting state relies on.[85] The issue haunted the ASR drafting process since its inception. Some assertions coming out of the ILC were ambiguous at best; for instance, in 1999 then-Special Rapporteur Crawford held that "the conduct does not conform, but if the circumstance precludes the wrongfulness of the conduct, neither is there a breach",[86] which leaves somewhat open the question of the exact legal nature of such an act. This leads back to long-running debates within the ILC and among scholars whether all the defences listed in Chapter V of the ASR should be understood in the same way, as properly *circumstances precluding wrongfulness*, which implies that they *justify* the state's act; or rather some of them as merely *precluding responsibility* for the conduct, meaning the

84 Schmitt, *supra* note 12, Rule 24, para. 9.
85 See generally K. Greenawalt, 'The Perplexing Borders of Justification and Excuse', 84 *Columbia Law Review* (1984), p. 1897, 1900.
86 J. Crawford, *Second Report on State Responsibility – Addendum 2*, International Law Commission, 1999, UN Doc. A/CN4/498/Add2, at 226.

state would be *excused* for having acted unlawfully without altering the fact that the act itself remains a breach of an international obligation.[87]

As Aust has argued persuasively, a consistent differentiation between circumstances precluding wrongfulness – consent, self-defence, countermeasures – on the one hand, and circumstances merely precluding responsibility – force majeure, distress, necessity – on the other "might have helped to clarify this matter".[88] The distinguishing factor between the two groups is, of course, that the former three necessarily involve some activity of the state whose rights are infringed on, while the latter three do not.[89] During the drafting process, a number of states strongly favoured this bifurcated approach.[90] Most discomfort was voiced in light of the consideration that a circumstance precluding *wrongfulness*, that is one that renders the conduct lawful, would necessarily imply that the invoking state would be under no duty to pay compensation.[91] Upholding the distinction has received much support in the literature,[92] despite the fact that at least the question of compensation has been dealt with in Article 27(b) ASR, which clarifies that "[t]he invocation of a circumstance precluding wrongfulness in accordance with this chapter is without prejudice to the question of compensation for any material loss caused by the act in question".

If we assume the existence of a conceptual distinction, then it would make sense to contend that only those circumstances actually *justifying* the conduct have an impact on states that came to aid or assist. Aust further rationalises such a legal evaluation by pointing out that self-defence and countermeasures in particular serve the function to preserve or restore the rule of law in the decentralised international legal order, whereas the state of necessity merely responds to purely extrinsic factors without any inherent connection to a breach of an international obligation. For this reason, he concludes, it is not "warranted to expand the group of actors who can rely on these ad hoc

87 See only V. Lowe, 'Precluding Wrongfulness or Responsibility: A Plea for Excuses', 10 *European Journal of International Law* (1999), p. 405.

88 H. Aust, 'Circumstances Precluding Wrongfulness', in A. Nollkaemper and I. Plakokefalos (eds.), *Principles of Shared Responsibility in International Law: An Appraisal of the State of the Art* (Cambridge University Press, Cambridge, 2014), p. 169, 202.

89 *Ibid.*, p. 204.

90 UN Doc. A/CN4/488, 25 March 1998, p. 79 (France, United Kingdom); UN Doc. A/CN4/492, 10 February 1999, p. 11 (Japan).

91 *Ibid.* (United Kingdom).

92 See only Sloane, *supra* note 24, pp. 483ff.; B. Simma, 'Grundfragen der Staatenverantwortlichkeit in der Arbeit der International Law Commission', 24 *Archiv des Völkerrechts* (1986) pp. 357, 381ff.; O. Schachter, 'The Lawful Use of Force by a State against Terrorists in Another Country', 19 *Israel Yearbook on Human Rights* (1989) p. 209, 230.

mechanisms" such as necessity. Concerning those circumstances that merely preclude responsibility, assistance would incur responsibility of the third state unless the preconditions of necessity apply to the latter as well in the situation at hand.[93]

Be that as it may, it bears noting that the ILC ultimately and consciously decided against inscribing any formal distinction between the circumstances in Chapter V, with the result that all of them possess the same legal status within the ASR. Crawford sought to justify this construction by claiming that "a clear example of distress or even necessity may be more convincing as a circumstance precluding wrongfulness than a marginal case of self-defence",[94] which has been criticised as failing to distinguish between questions of fact and principle.[95] That aside, however, Paddeu has observed that "states invoking the plea of necessity maintain that their conduct was lawful and not that they are excused despite their conduct being unlawful".[96] Ultimately, although descriptors such as "non-wrongful" instead of "lawful" for the necessity defence may accurately give expression to a general undesirability on a moral or political level, this "has no bearing on the legal characterisation of [necessity] as permissible and, as such, lawful".[97]

Although there are convincing arguments in favour of either position, at least textually it is difficult to ignore the doctrinal construction that a successful invocation of the necessity defence precludes the conduct's wrongfulness, while the wrongfulness of aid or assistance depends entirely on the wrongfulness of the assisted act. From a political perspective, one may take up Estonia's implicit rationale in the context of countermeasures and add that if assistance to active cyber defensive measures were not permitted under a state of necessity, then states with superior intelligence and cyber capacities that allow them to deal with such incidents on their own would be inherently privileged. Then again, this is of course rather the rule than the exception in international relations under any circumstances. Either way, even if we assume that assistance is permissible, it will often be difficult to draw a clear line between mere assistance and conduct that in fact amounts to an act on behalf of the imperilled state, in which case the "assisting" state would have to invoke

93 Aust, *supra* note 86, pp. 204–206.

94 Crawford, *supra* note 84, p. 353.

95 Sloane, *supra* note 24, p. 483.

96 Paddeu, *supra* note 20, p. 419.

97 F. Paddeu, 'Clarifying the Concept of Circumstances Precluding Wrongfulness (Justifications) in International Law', in L. Bartels and F. Paddeu (eds.), *Exceptions in International Law* (Oxford University Press, Oxford, 2020), p. 203, 223.

its own circumstance precluding wrongfulness lest it incur responsibility vis-à-vis the third state.[98]

Finally, according to Article 16(a) ASR, if the assisting state is not aware of the concrete circumstances that render the conduct of the assisted state unlawful, then it bears no international responsibility. Thus, if the U.S. provides Norway with the malicious code without any further information about the situation and Norway fails to successfully invoke the necessity defence, for example because it contributed to the situation of necessity in some way, then the U.S. is not responsible pursuant to Article 16. According to the ILC, in normal international affairs, a "State providing material or financial assistance or aid to another State does not normally assume the risk that its assistance or aid may be used to carry out an internationally wrongful act".[99] Crawford clarified that the provision requires actual knowledge of the facts, constructive knowledge ("should have known") is not sufficient to trigger application of Article 16.[100] In light of this requirement, given the somewhat uncertain legal status of the necessity defence, among allies one might thus suggest that it might be advisable to only confer the absolutely necessary amount of information when asking for aid or assistance so as to avoid legal complicity. At the same time, however, it should be noted that "wilful blindness", that is "a deliberate effort by the assisting State to avoid knowledge of illegality on the part of the State being assisted, in the face of credible evidence of present or future illegality",[101] will prevent the possibility to evade responsibility pursuant to Article 16 ASR.[102]

6 Conclusion

The engagement with the plea of necessity in their official statements may be taken as evidence that an increasing number of states takes seriously the possibility that they might have to rely on the defence in a future cybersecurity incident that is obviously caused by a malicious actor located on foreign territory yet where timely attribution is difficult or impossible. That the states have started to make this explicit is commendable within the larger context of the various legal processes to clarify the law applicable to state behaviour

98 See Schmitt, *supra* note 12, Rule 18, para. 7.

99 International Law Commission, *supra* note 27, Article 16, para. 4.

100 Crawford, *supra* note 26, p. 406.

101 H. Moynihan, 'Aiding and Assisting: The Mental Element Under Article 16 of the International Law Commission's Articles on State Responsibility', 67 *International and Comparative Law Quarterly* (2018), p. 455, 461.

102 *Ibid.*, p. 462.

in cyberspace and thus to strengthen the international rule of law. Norway, in particular, has laid out a clear position that even hints at concrete circumstances that its decision-makers had in mind while drafting the document.

At the same time, the necessity defence continues to pose some intricate doctrinal puzzles that so far have only insufficiently been addressed in the literature especially in the context of transnational cybersecurity. While actual practice remains few and far between and mostly concerns matters of international economic law, the official expressions of legal interpretation remain general and vague when it comes to the actual application of necessity in situations of cyber emergency. Raising no claim to completeness, this chapter has attempted to shed light on some of the most contentious issues: the "only way" requirement, the condition of non-contribution, and the question of assistance. Whether Norway could in fact rely on necessity to preclude the wrongfulness of infringing on the territorial sovereignty of Russia, as discussed throughout the piece, will not only depend on the particular factual circumstances of the scenario, but also on the understanding of necessity within the larger nexus of the rules on state responsibility. Ultimately, it would be preferable if the states themselves strove for further legal clarity in the future.

CHAPTER 11

Disinformation, Strategic Corruption, and International Law: An Opportunity for Nordic Leadership

Kimberly Breedon[1] *and A. Christopher Bryant*[2]

1 Introduction

Authoritarianism is ascendant. Democracy is in decline. Such is the present state of the world, according to the 2022 Freedom House Report, *Freedom in the World 2022: The Global Expansion of Authoritarian Rule*.[3] As illiberal regimes establish a growing global footprint, and as they seek to weaken democratic states, they have discovered an effective handmaiden in two distinct but related forms of hybrid interference: strategic corruption efforts that compromise or coopt government officials in democratic societies to adopt rhetorical or policy positions favorable to the autocratic regimes, and cyber-based disinformation campaigns that target the voting behavior and political opinion-making of the citizenry in those societies.[4]

This chapter examines the implications of strategic corruption and cyber-based disinformation campaigns for the development of customary international law and argues that the Nordic countries are particularly well equipped to lead the global task of anticipating and preparing responses to issues arising at the corruption–disinformation nexus because that bloc of States are global exemplars in combating the sort of governmental corruption that might be at the root of target State officials' complicity in digital disinformation campaigns designed to manipulate democratic opinion-making, because Nordic countries have been at the forefront in adopting effective strategies to combat

1 Associate Professor of Law, Ohio Northern University College of Law.

2 Rufus King Professor of Constitutional Law, University of Cincinnati College of Law.

3 S. Repucci and A. Slipowitz, Freedom House, *Freedom in the World 2022: The Global Expansion of Authoritarian Rule*, <freedomhouse.org/sites/default/files/2022-02/FIW_2022_PDF_Booklet_Digital_Final_Web.pdf>, visited on 12 January 2023.

4 *See, e.g.*, C. A. Theohary, Congressional Research Service, *Information Warfare: Issues for Congress*, March 2018 <sgp.fas.org/crs/natsec/R45142.pdf>, visited on 12 January 2023.

 | DOI:10.1163/9789004703933_012

disinformation, and because Nordic countries have a proven track record of success as leaders in other areas of major global concern.

1.1 *Relevant Terms*

Strategic corruption is a particular form of corruption that serves "as an instrument of national strategy".[5] Its hallmark is the use of "corrupt inducements ... wielded against a target country by foreigners as a part of their own country's national strategy".[6] Manifestations of strategic corruption fall on a spectrum from indirect and chronic to direct and acute. Indirect and chronic strategic corruption includes, for example, the investment of 'corrosive capital' by authoritarian, kleptocratic governments in projects located in other countries, with a view toward exporting their kleptocratic model of illiberal governance through the use of corrupt patronage networks and opaque business transactions and structures. At the other end of the spectrum, direct and acute instances of strategic corruption include election interference through covert political financing. In between these two extremes fall malign influence campaigns, which may include bribes or other corrupt inducements to domestic government officials to coopt them into delivering policy decisions that subvert the public interest to the interests of the foreign government.[7] Corruptly obtained political messaging and disinformation campaigns would appear to fall within the in-between zone, as well. In addition, various forms of strategic corruption are susceptible to combination with other forms. For example, disinformation campaigns may be combined with covert political financing.

Disinformation in this context involves the digital dissemination of deliberately false messaging to advance a particular narrative favorable to the source of the disinformation, be it a State, a political party or candidate, or a government official. Digital propagation of disinformation that seeks to manipulate democratic opinion-making may be called 'de-democratising digital disinformation' (hereinafter, when abbreviated, 'DDD'). The broader, long-term goal of foreign governments in conducting such disinformation campaigns is to weaken and ultimately dismantle liberal western democracies.[8] Some of the

5 *See* P. Zelikow, *et al.*, 'The Rise of Strategic Corruption: How States Weaponize Graft', *Foreign Affairs*, July/August 2020.

6 *Ibid.*

7 J. Rudolph, Alliance for Securing Democracy, *The Development Response to Kleptocracy and Strategic Corruption*, 19 January 2022, pp. 2–4 <securingdemocracy.gmfus.org/wp-content/uploads/2022/01/the-development-response-to-kleptocracy.pdf>, visited on 8 January 2023.

8 "Today, actors such as Russia are using information tools in an attempt to undermine the legitimacy of democracies. Adversaries target media, political processes, financial networks, and personal data." *National Security Strategy of the United States of America*,

specific objectives used to achieve this goal are illustrated by Russia's information warfare against the United States and include the following: undermining the position of the United States as a global leader, sowing internal discord, influencing American voters, and shaping decision-making by the U.S. government.[9] In addition, such operations aim to create doubt about the legitimacy of electoral outcomes,[10] and to erode the stability and security of western democratic alliances.[11] These objectives do not uniquely target the U.S., but rather attack liberal democracies worldwide, and the particulars of information warfare campaigns tend to be tailored to the specific circumstances of the State where they are employed.[12]

1.2 *Unresolved Questions Implicated by the Intersection of Strategic Corruption and De-democratising Disinformation*

At the intersection of strategic corruption and DDD arise a number of unresolved questions under international law. A consensus has formed among international law experts that customary international law applies generally to cyberspace, but beyond that threshold understanding lies much uncertainty.[13] Much of the uncertainty involves three categories of unresolved questions

---

December 2017, p.14, <trumpwhitehouse.archives.gov/wp-content/uploads/2017/12/NSS-Final-12-18-2017-0905.pdf>, visited on 14 January 2023.

9 Office of the Director of National Intelligence, *Annual Threat Assessment of U.S. Intelligence Community*, 9 April 2021, <www.dni.gov/index.php/newsroom/reports-publications/reports-publications-2021/item/2204-2021-annual-threat-assessment-of-the-u-s-intelligence-community>, visited on 12 January 2023. *See also* S. J. Barela, 'Cross-Border Cyber Ops to Erode Legitimacy: An Act of Coercion', *Just Security*, 12 January 2017, <www.justsecurity.org/36212/cross-border-cyber-ops-erode-legitimacy-act-coercion>, visited on 12 January 2023.

10 Barela, *supra* note 9.

11 B. Connable, *et al.*, RAND Corp., *Russia's Hostile Measures: Combating Russian Gray Zone Aggression Against NATO in the Contact, Blunt, and Surge Layers of Competition*, p. iii, 2020 <www.rand.org/pubs/research_reports/RR2539.html>, visited on 12 January 2023.

12 M. Endicott, 'Propaganda's New Goals: Create Confusion, Sow Doubt', *US News and World Report*, 31 January 2017 <www.usnews.com/news/national-news/articles/2017-01-31/russian-propagandas-new-goals-create-confusion-sow-doubt>, visited on 12 January 2023.

13 M. N. Schmitt and L. Vihul, 'Respect for Sovereignty in Cyberspace', 95:7 *Texas Law Review* (2017) p. 1639 n. 3. *See also, e.g.*, UNGA, Report of the Group of Governmental Experts on Developments in the Field of Information and Telecommunications in the Context of International Security, UN Doc A/68/98 (24 June 2013) para 20; UNGA, Report of the Group of Governmental Experts on Developments in the Field of Information and Telecommunications in the Context of International Security, A/70/174 (22 July 2015) paras 27, 28(b); UNGA, Report of the Group of Governmental Experts on Advancing Responsible State Behaviour in Cyberspace in the Context of International Security, A/76/135 (14 July 2021) paras 70, 71(b).

relating to the principles of sovereignty and non-intervention: the first category includes questions that, though not new, have taken on greater urgency; the second includes questions that have emerged in response to technological evolution and innovations; and the third involves questions that currently remain at the periphery of State and scholarly attention, but that nevertheless warrant treatment to minimise the potential damage that, if ignored, they could inflict upon democratic societies. Within the first category fall questions such as whether sovereignty is a standalone rule or merely a guiding principle (or both), and when State conduct below the use of force qualifies as coercion under the non-intervention principle. The second category includes questions about which, if any, customary international law rules apply to specific types of cyber-based conduct. The final category consists, in part, of questions which incorporate ambiguities from the other two categories, with the added complication of strategic corruption.

2 Unresolved Questions under International Law Relating to Strategic Corruption and Disinformation

As States have determined in recent years how international law should apply to cyberspace, they have faced an array of difficult questions. The primary considerations to date have involved cyber activities conducted by a foreign State that physically intrude upon another State's territorial sovereignty or that interfere with another State's inherently governmental functions. More recently, attention has expanded to include activities involving disinformation, especially disinformation that targets the democratic opinion-making of the polity of another State. This section addresses the role that strategic corruption might play in securing the cooperation or complicity of the target State's government officials to withhold response to such disinformation, and it identifies some unresolved questions under relevant international law principles.

2.1 *Relevant International Law Principles*

The most commonly invoked international law principles giving rise to a right of response if violated by cyber-based conduct are sovereignty and non-intervention.[14] Sovereignty is a principle of international law giving rise both

14 Although the right of self-determination has been subject to recent scholarly attention as a potential rule of international law to be invoked in the context of digital disinformation targeting democratic opinion-making, this chapter limits discussion to the more frequently invoked principles of sovereignty and non-intervention.

to rights that a State enjoys in relation to other States and to duties that a State must fulfill in relation to other States.[15] Under this principle, a State possesses "the supreme authority … to territorial integrity, sovereign equality and political independence within its territory to the exclusion of all other [S]tates".[16] Major cases decided by international tribunals affirm these aspects of sovereignty. For example, in the *Corfu Channel* case, in which the International Court of Justice (ICJ) concluded, *inter alia,* that the United Kingdom had violated the sovereignty of the Republic of Albania by conducting minesweeping operations in Albanian territorial waters without the consent of the Albanian government, the majority opinion stated: "Between independent States, respect for territorial sovereignty is an essential foundation of international relations".[17] In a concurring opinion, Judge Alvarez explained further: "By [sovereignty], we understand the whole body of rights and attributes which a State possesses in its territory, to the exclusion of all other States, and also in its relations with other States".[18]

A different tribunal, the Permanent Court of Arbitration, decided a case in which the United States and The Netherlands laid conflicting claims to the Island of Palmas (or Miangas). There, the Court observed: "[T]erritorial sovereignty belongs always to one, or in exceptional circumstances to several States, to the exclusion of all others".[19] The right to exclude others is related to, but distinct from, the sovereign right of political independence, which recognizes a State's sole authority to exercise "the functions of a State" within its territory.[20] Stated differently, "[t]erritorial sovereignty . . . involves the exclusive right to display the activities of a State".[21] Sovereignty, then, protects a State from territorial intrusions by another State,[22] and, distilled to its core, sovereignty

15 *Corfu Channel* case (*United Kingdom* v. *Albania*), Separate Opinion by Judge Alvarez, 9 April 1949, ICJ Rep., p. 43 ("Sovereignty confers rights upon States and imposes obligations on them.").

16 H. Moynihan, Chatham House, The Royal Institute of International Affairs, *The Application of International Law to State Cyberattacks: Sovereignty and Non-Intervention,* December 2019, pp. 8, <www.chathamhouse.org/2019/12/application-international-law-state-cyber attacks>, visited on 13 January 2023.

17 *Corfu Channel* case, *supra* note 15, p. 35.

18 *Corfu Channel* case, Separate Opinion by Judge Alvarez, *supra* note 15, p. 43.

19 *Island of Palmas* case (*USA* v. *Netherlands*), PCA 4 April 1928, pg. 838.

20 *Ibid.*, pg. 838.

21 *Ibid.*, pg. 839.

22 *See S.S. Lotus* (*France* v. *Turkey*), Judgment, 7 September 1927, PCIJ (series A) No. 1, p. 18 (stating that the "first and foremost restriction imposed by international law upon a State is that—failing a permissive rule to the contrary—it may not exercise power in any form in the territory of another State").

means that a State may make freely its "choice of a political, economic, social and cultural system, and the formulation of foreign policy".[23] A State which engages in conduct resulting in territorial manifestation in the target State or interference with inherently governmental functions of the target State breaches the principle of sovereignty.[24] A target State, however, may consent to such activities by another State, thereby nullifying what would otherwise constitute a violation of sovereignty.[25] Such consent may be explicitly granted, but it may, under some, as yet undefined, circumstances be deemed granted by silence.[26] The consent exception under the principle of sovereignty raises the question of whether a target State's silence or passivity in the face of otherwise sovereignty-violating conduct by another State can or does operate as implied consent to, or ratification of, the otherwise internationally wrongful activity.[27] Contextualizing the issue more discretely, given the limited scope of this discussion, the question becomes whether a target State's silence or failure to respond to a foreign State's use of cyberspace to wage a disinformation campaign for the purpose of affecting voter behavior in the target State effectively constitutes consent.

The non-intervention principle prohibits a State from intervening in another State's internal affairs, even when such intervention does not involve the use of force.[28] More precisely, it prohibits coercive conduct by one State "in relation to the inherently sovereign powers of another state".[29] Like the principle

23 Case *Concerning the Military and Paramilitary Activities in and Against Nicaragua* (*Nicaragua* v. *United States of America*), Merits, 27 June 1986, ICJ 14, para. 205.

24 Inherently governmental functions "are understood as activity at the very core of state authority, including the activities of the authorities responsible for foreign and military affairs; legislation and the exercise of the police power; and the administration of justice." Moynihan, *supra* note 16, p. 15.

25 Moynihan, *supra* note 16, p. 19.

26 *Sovereignty over Pedra Branca/Pulau Batu Puteh, Middle Rocks and South Ledge* (*Malaysia/Singapore*), 2008 ICJ Rep. 14, para. 121 (noting, in the context of passing title of sovereignty to another States, that, "[T]he absence of a reaction may well amount to acquiescence.").

27 For discussion of the role that silence plays in the international legal framework, *see* H. Quane, 'Silence in International Law', 84 *British Yearbook of International Law* (2014) p. 240.

28 D. B. Hollis, 'Russia and the DNC Hack: What Future for a Duty of Non-Intervention?', *Opinio Juris*, 25 July 2016 (noting that "[c]ustomary international law has long recognized a 'duty of nonintervention' that applied to state behavior falling short of the use of force"); M. Schmitt, 'The Netherlands Releases a Tour de Force on International Law in Cyberspace: An Analysis', *Just Security*, 14 Oct. 14 2019 (observing that non-intervention prohibits a foreign State from using coercion to effect an activity that falls within the target state's *domaine reservé* including, for example, elections).

29 Moynihan, *supra* note 16, p. 8.

of sovereignty, the non-intervention principle has been affirmed in multiple decisions by international tribunals. In 1986, the ICJ, for example, observed in the Case *Concerning the Military and Paramilitary Activities in and Against Nicaragua* (*Nicaragua* v. *United States of America*) that "[t]he principle of non-intervention involves the right of every sovereign State to conduct its affairs without outside interference[,] [and] the Court considers that it is part and parcei of customary international law".[30] Elaborating, the Court continues:

> A prohibited intervention must accordingly be one bearing on matters in which each State is permitted, by the principle of State sovereignty, to decide freely. One of these is the choice of a political, economic, social and cultural system, and the formulation of foreign policy. Intervention is wrongful when it uses methods of coercion in regard to such choices, which must remain free ones.[31]

To qualify as coercion for purposes of violating the non-intervention principle, conduct below the level of force must be something more than mere influence or persuasion. Rather, it must compel a State to take action that it otherwise would not take or, on some views, it must deprive the target State of its ability to control or govern matters that are reserved to it under international law.

2.2 *Insights from Formal State Positions on the Application of International Law to Cyberspace*

Several States have issued position statements on the application of international law to cyber activities, and the number of such States has continued to grow, but only a handful of the published formal statements specifically address the application of international law to cyber operations involving DDD.[32] Nevertheless, several insights may be gleaned in this regard.

First, among the most pressing concerns appearing in States' positions on sovereignty are those cyber operations which cause physical damage, impair

---

30 Case *Concerning the Military and Paramilitary Activities in and Against Nicaragua*, *supra* note 23, para. 202.

31 Case *Concerning the Military and Paramilitary Activities in and Against Nicaragua*, *supra* note 23, para. 205.

32 *See* Cyber Law Toolkit 2024, *Legal Concepts, General International Law, Sovereignty*, p. 3 (citing the Tallinn Manual 2.0 and listing State positions as of March 2024), <cyberlaw.ccdcoe.org/wiki/Sovereignty>, visited on 25 March 2024 (hereinafter 'Cyber Toolkit, Sovereignty'); Moynihan, *supra* note 16, pp. 9–10 (citing the Tallinn Manual 2.0 and discussing State practice as of December 2019).

the functionality of the domestic State's cyber infrastructure, interfere with data or services required for performing inherently governmental functions, or usurp inherently governmental functions.[33] Disinformation as a concern appears far less frequently.

Second, when disinformation does appear, the consensus seems to be that a foreign State's dissemination of disinformation inside a target State, without more, does not violate sovereignty, and, moreover, is likely a protected right to freedom of opinion and expression under international human rights law.[34] Switzerland's official statement, however, contains a clear carve-out for the need to resolve an open debate concerning whether certain cases "violate the[S]tate's territorial integrity and ... constitute an interference with or usurpation of an inherently governmental function", including, *inter alia*, "situations in which a [S]tate has sought to influence, disrupt or delay democratic decision-making processes in another [S]tate through the coordinated use of legal and illegal methods in cyberspace[,] e.g., propaganda, disinformation[,] and covert action by intelligence services".[35]

Relatedly, the third insight that may be drawn is that influence operations employing disinformation and targeting the voting population in another State, without more, are "unlikely" to violate the principle of non-intervention because they are not coercive in nature.[36] Nevertheless, a number of States have indicated that additional circumstances accompanying or resulting from DDD may shift DDD itself over the line into a violation of sovereignty or may supply the necessary ingredient of coercion to meet the requirement for a violation of the non-intervention principle. Norway, for example, has taken the position that, "carrying out cyber operations with the intent of altering election results in another State ... by ... unduly influencing public opinion through the dissemination of confidential information obtained through cyber operations ('hack and leak') [] would be in violation of the prohibition of intervention".[37]

---

33 Cyber Toolkit 2024, *List of Articles, Scenarios, "Scenario 01: Election Interference"*, pp. 6–7, <cyberlaw.ccdcoe.org/wiki/Scenario_01:_Election_interference>, visited on 25 March 2024 (hereinafter 'Cyber Toolkit, Election Interference').

34 *Ibid.*, pp. 8–9.

35 Cyber Law Toolkit, Sovereignty, *supra* note 32, p. 30.

36 Cyber Toolkit, Election Interference, *supra* note 33, p. 11) ("merely influencing the target State by persuasion or propaganda or causing a nuisance without any particular goal is insufficient to qualify as coercion").

37 UNGA Official Compendium of Voluntary National Contributions on the Subject of How International Law Applies to the Use of Information and Communications Technologies by States Submitted by Participating Governmental Experts in the Group of Governmental Experts on Advancing Responsible State Behaviour in Cyberspace in the Context of

Germany's statement provides other potential circumstances involving DDD that could implicate the violation of the non-intervention principle, noting that "a State, by spreading disinformation via the internet, may deliberately incite violent political upheaval, riots and/or civil strife in a foreign country, thereby significantly impeding the orderly conduct of an election and the casting of ballots" and opining that "[s]uch activities may be comparable in scale and effect to the support of insurgents and may hence be akin to coercion" in the context of the non-intervention analysis.[38] Germany also cites the following example as potentially coercive:

> [C]yber activities targeting elections may be comparable in scale and effect to coercion if they aim at and result in a substantial disturbance or even permanent change of the political system of the targeted State, i.e., by significantly eroding public trust in a State's political organs and processes, by seriously impeding important State organs in the fulfillment of their functions or by dissuading significant groups of citizens from voting, thereby undermining the meaningfulness of an election.[39]

Although this situation, unlike the previous example cited, does not specifically mention disinformation, the role that DDD can and does play in the described conduct is significant. More generally worded statements from, among other States, Estonia, Denmark, and Sweden also suggest that cyber activities which target "national democratic processes such as elections"[40] also leave open the possibility that DDD in combination with some additional—though unspecified—conduct (e.g., "hack and leak" operations) or outcome (e.g., voter suppression) could violate the principle of sovereignty or non-intervention.[41]

A commonly repeated refrain in States' formal statements is the need for case-by-case assessments and ongoing discussions to address these and other issues. Germany's statement, in this respect, also contains the following important disclaimer: "The choice of rules and principles discussed [in its statement] is necessarily selective and no conclusions regarding Germany's legal positions

---

International Security Established Pursuant to General Assembly Resolution 73/266, A/76/136, p. 69, 13 July 2021 (hereinafter "UN Compendium").

38 *Ibid.*, p. 34–35.

39 *Ibid.*, p. 35, 13.

40 *Ibid.* p. 25 (Statement of Estonia).

41 Cyber Law Toolkit, Sovereignty, *supra* note 32; Cyber Law Toolkit 2024, *Legal Concepts, General International Law, Prohibition of Intervention*, <cyberlaw.ccdcoe.org/wiki/Prohibition_of_intervention>, visited on March 23, 2024 (hereinafter 'Cyber Law Toolkit, Intervention'); UN Compendium, *supra* note 37, p. 25 (Statement of Estonia).

can be drawn from any actual or perceived omission to mention certain rules, principles, criteria, or legal considerations".[42] This disclaimer operates as a prophylactic against an interpretation of silence as a substantive contribution to the development of international law's application to cyber activities.

For purposes of this discussion, a final insight merits mention, and that is that no State has yet officially addressed the role that strategic corruption might play in the analysis of coercion under the non-intervention principle, or the role it might play in the analysis of the consent exception under the sovereignty principle. These omissions are unsurprising, and they are concededly not without warrant. Matters that are both more obvious and more pressing understandably absorb most of the energy and attention of government officials, as well as practitioners and scholars with expertise in international law or cyber operations. Moreover, corruption, especially strategic corruption, may be hard to discern. Nevertheless, as autocratic governments increasingly rely on both strategic corruption and DDD to achieve their goals, the question of whether strategic corruption operates as a potentially coercive weapon for disseminating DDD that targets another country's democratic processes is one that should not be lightly disregarded.

2.3 *Sources of Uncertainty*

Whether State-sponsored, cyber-based disinformation campaigns designed to manipulate democratic opinion-making in a target State violate international law, and if so, how, remains an open question regarding which rule or rules may have been violated and what conditions must obtain to constitute a violation. The uncertainty in this regard derives in part from disagreement among States on basic questions of international law, such as whether the prohibition against violating another State's sovereignty constitutes a standalone primary rule that itself may be violated, or merely a guiding principle that channels the development of binding rules, but rather is itself not a rule that can be breached.[43]

When a State engages in cyber activities that do not involve the use of force,[44] the standard against which to measure whether such activities violate

42 UN Compendium, *supra* note 37, p. 31, n. 53.

43 Schmitt, *supra* note 28 (describing disagreement among international law experts and divergence in State practice on the question of whether sovereignty is a standalone rule or a guiding principle).

44 Article 2 of the United Nations Charter "prohibits the threat or use of force and calls on all Members to respect the sovereignty, territorial integrity and political independence of other States." U.N. Charter, art. 2, para 4.

international law—thereby triggering a right of response—is unclear, but two broad approaches have emerged in the relevant legal commentary.[45] Some commentators have taken the position that a State's cyber activity below the use of force violates international law and gives rise to a right of response only if the intrusion runs afoul of the non-intervention principle.[46] Those adhering to this philosophy view sovereignty in the cyber context as a guiding principle that may inform States in their conduct relating to cyberspace rather than as "a standalone rule" which itself may be violated. In other words, if the requirements for a violation of the non-intervention principle—including the requirement of coercion—are not met, then the cyber activity in question does not violate international law.[47] Other commentators have taken the position that a state's cyber intrusions need not meet the non-intervention threshold to constitute an unlawful violation of the target state's sovereignty. On this view, sovereignty is a standalone primary rule, the breach of which authorizes response by the target state under international law.[48]

State practice regarding these two approaches remains somewhat in a state of flux.[49] The United States, for example, at one time appeared to adopt (or at least to be open to adopting) the 'sovereignty-as-rule' approach when the Department of Defense opined in 1999 that at least some cyber activities undertaken by a State against another State could violate the target State's sovereignty, thereby constituting an "internationally wrongful act".[50] More recently, the United States appears to have drifted toward the school of thought that conceives of sovereignty in the cyber context as an underlying principle to guide the establishment of binding norms rather than a rule of international law that itself can be breached and thereby result in an international obligation.[51] The

45 Schmitt, *supra* note 28 (describing disagreement among international law experts and divergence in State practice on the question of whether sovereignty is itself "a rule of law that … may be violated.").

46 Schmitt, *supra* note 28.

47 For discussion of the coercion element of the non-intervention principle, *see infra* notes 58–69 and accompanying text.

48 *See, e.g.*, Schmitt and Vihul, *supra* note 13, p. 1650 (arguing that "overwhelming evidence of State practice and *opinio juris*—the foundational elements of customary international law—supports the assertion" that sovereignty operates as a primary rule rather than a guiding principle").

49 Moynihan, *supra* note 16, pp. 8–9 (explaining that States have opted for a "'policy of ambiguity and silence'" on this question). Moreover, no treaties are in place to fill the gap left by the decision of most States not to "put on the record how they think these principles apply in practice." (*ibid.*, p. 10) (noting the exception of the Council of Europe's Budapest Convention, which covers cybercrimes).

50 Schmitt and Vihul, *supra* note 13, p. 1640.

51 Schmitt and Vihul, *supra* note 13, p. 1640–42.

United Kingdom also tacks in the same direction.[52] The United States and the United Kingdom are outliers, however, as the sovereignty-as-principle-only position runs counter to the unanimous position of the international group of experts reported by the Tallinn Manual 2.0, which adopted the 'sovereignty-as-rule' approach to cyber operations.[53] The U.S. and U.K. position also runs counter to every other nation which has taken a public stance on the question, including, for example, Austria, Brazil, Canada, the Czech Republic, Denmark, Estonia, Finland, France, Germany, Iran, Italy, Japan, the Netherlands, New Zealand, Norway, Romania, and Sweden.[54] Nevertheless, because the U.S. and the U.K. continue to wield significant global influence, any discussion of sovereignty under international law must account for their position.

The difference between these two approaches to sovereignty has implications for how international law is to treat a foreign State's cyber operations that involve propagating disinformation campaigns in a target State in an attempt to manipulate the target State's democratic decision-making. If sovereignty is a primary rule of international law, then a remote cyber operation may violate sovereignty if the operation either manifests on the territory of the target state or if it "interferes with or usurps inherently governmental functions of [the target] state".[55] An example of a territorial manifestation of a remotely conducted cyber operation constituting a violation of sovereignty is physical damage to the target state's infrastructure.[56] An example of an inherently government function—that is, a function that only States may undertake (or authorize other entities to undertake)—is conducting elections.[57] If sovereignty is a only a guiding principle, then violation of international law for conducting remote

52 Moynihan, *supra* note 16, p. 8 and n. 28.

53 Schmitt and Vihul, *supra* note 13, p. 1640–42 ("Tallinn Manual 2.0 accordingly provides that '[a] State must not conduct cyber operations that violate the sovereignty of another State.'" *Ibid.* at 1642); *see also* M. N. Schmitt, 'Grey Zones in the International Law of Cyberspace', 42:2 *Yale Journal of International Law Online* (2017) p. 5 (The U.K.'s "'sovereignty as principal, but not rule' approach contradicts extensive State practice and *opinio juris* in the non-cyber context, which treat the prohibition as a primary rule, such that a violation of sovereignty would constitute an internationally wrongful act.").

54 Cyber Law Toolkit, Sovereignty, *supra* note 32.

55 Schmitt, *supra* note 28; Schmitt and Vihul, *supra* note 13, p. 1649 (arguing that cyber operations which "interfere with or usurp a State's inherently governmental functions" constitute a violation of sovereignty, regardless of whether such operations cause damage or injury within the target State, and regardless of the infringing State's use of coercion). Elections are considered an inherently governmental function. *See e.g.,* Schmitt, *supra* note 28.

56 Schmitt, *supra* note 28.

57 Schmitt, *supra* note 28.

cyber operations must be based upon some other principle that does constitute a binding rule, such as the non-intervention principle.

Another reason for uncertainty rests on the absence of an accepted international law definition of coercion—a required element for the violation of the principle of non-intervention. Despite widespread consensus that customary international law imposes a duty of non-intervention, "the scope and substance of the duty remain unclear".[58] This lack of clarity exists partly because coercion, while an essential element of a violation of the non-intervention principle, does not enjoy an accepted international law definition.[59] The use of force clearly constitutes coercive intervention, but measures that do not reach the level of force generate disagreement about where, and how, to demarcate permissible, noncoercive conduct from impermissible, coercive conduct.[60]

Two general approaches to this question have emerged. Under a narrow approach, coercion is understood as "compelling a state to take a course of action (whether an act or omission) that it would not otherwise pursue" within its *domaine reservé*.[61] This understanding differentiates the use of cyber operations to *influence* the target State from the use of cyber operations to *coerce* the target State.[62] A broad approach to the conception of coercion has its roots in the following provision of the 1970 U.N. General Assembly Declaration on Friendly Relations Among States regarding the duty of non-intervention: "Every State has an inalienable right to choose its political, economic, social, and cultural systems, without interference *in any form* from another State".[63] Some commentators have argued that a State's "interference in any form" with another State's right to choose its political system implicates the non-intervention principle, and, accordingly, that the broad language used in the Declaration on Friendly Relations would allow the element of coercion

58 Hollis, *supra* note 28.

59 Schmitt, *supra* note 28.

60 Hollis, *supra* note 28 ("[M]uch of the debate over the duty of nonintervention has focused on identifying which coercive measures below the use of force threshold are covered by the prohibition.").

61 Schmitt, *supra* note 28. States adopting this approach include Estonia, Germany, Italy, the Netherlands, Norway, Romania, and Switzerland. Cyber Law Toolkit, Intervention, supra note 41. In addition, the majority of experts who produced the Tallinn Manual 2.0 took "the view that the coercive effort must be designed to influence outcomes in, or conduct with respect to, a matter reserved to a target State." Tallinn Manual 2.0, commentary to rule 66, para 19.

62 Schmitt, *supra* note 28.

63 Declaration on Principles of International Law Concerning Friendly Relations and Cooperation among States, G.A. Re. 2625 (XXV), Annex, U.N. Doc. A/RES/25/2625 (Oct. 24, 1970) (emphasis added).

in the non-intervention principle to be more readily satisfied by influence operations.[64] On this view, a target State need only be deprived of its control over a matter within its *domaine reservé* by the intentional conduct of the foreign State. The foreign State need not actually or potentially compel the target State to change its behaviour for the foreign State's conduct to constitute intervention.[65] Of course, how coercion is defined will determine not only whether any given cyber operation violates the non-intervention principle, but also, by extension, whether the target State enjoys a right of response under international law.[66]

A related area of uncertainty concerning the coercion element in the context of DDD is a two-pronged issue: (1) whether the information digitally disseminated is factually accurate or deliberately false; and (2) whether the foreign State is conducting its operations covertly or overtly in relation to the targeted public. A cyber operation which is covertly promoted by a foreign State and which disseminates disinformation and to affect the voting behavior of another State's polity qualifies as an "attempt to manipulate the will of the people" and could constitute intervention because it "undermine[s] the target state's sovereign will over its choice of political system" by impeding the target state's from holding free and fair elections.[67] On this view, the twin deceptions of disinformation and covert action are critical to a showing of coercion in a cyber-based influence operation because they distort the electoral discourse and deprive the voting population of the "open democratic space in which to conduct free and fair elections" and, by extension, to decide its political system freely.[68] Unless the cyber activity encompasses these deceptions, the foreign State's conduct may be categorised as nothing more than an influence

---

64 *See, e.g.*, N. Tsagourias, 'Electoral Cyber Interference, Self-Determination and The Principle of Non-Intervention in Cyberspace', April 2020 <eprints.whiterose.ac.uk/159652/>, visited on 13 January 2023; Hollis, *supra* note 28.

65 Australia, New Zealand, and the United Kingdom have adopted this view of coercion in the cyber context. Cyber Law Toolkit, Intervention, *supra* note 41.

66 For discussion of the right of response options that a State may employ, *see* Schmitt, *supra* note 28.

67 Moynihan, *supra* note 16, pp. 41–42; *see also* K. Jones, Chatham House, The Royal Institute of International Affairs, *Research Paper, Online Disinformation and Political Discourse: Applying a Human Rights Framework*, pp. 32–37, 9 November 2019, <www.chathamhouse.org/2019/11/online-disinformation-and-political-discourse-applying-human-rights-framework>, visited on 13 January 2023 (using a human rights framework to argue that "rights to freedom of thought and opinion are critical to delimiting the appropriate boundary between legitimate influence and illegitimate manipulation").

68 Moynihan, *supra* note 16, p. 42.

campaign.[69] Although international law commentators have opined on the need for such operations to involve both the deliberately false information and the impersonation by foreign actors of domestic citizens, no State has, as of this writing, addressed this specific point.

The questions currently at the periphery concerning the relationship between strategic corruption and digital disinformation campaigns may be less urgent than those which States and scholars presently have under greater scrutiny, but they are no less important, and by the time they become urgent, irreparable damage may have been inflicted upon multiple democratic societies. Accordingly, how international law applies to specific instances of malign cyber operations when digital disinformation seeking to manipulate democratic opinion-making finds amplification or dissemination by target State government officials as a result of strategic corruption raises questions that States may need to address sooner rather than later.

In addition to the unsettled international law questions that commentators have identified in the context of cyberspace more generally, the silence or inaction of government heads corruptly obtained also raises a number of distinct, but related, issues concerning some of the more granular details of international law's application. Specifically, issues arise pertaining to the specific elements of consent (in relation to the sovereignty principle) and coercion (in relation to the non-intervention principle), which, to date, have not been addressed. More particularly, missing from the scholarly and State treatment is the role that corruption, and relatedly, the role of silence, could play in securing consent under the sovereignty principle or in functioning as coercion under the non-intervention principle.

These questions have become salient in recent years because, in a remarkable development, government officials in and candidates for public office in several Western democracies have proven willing to propagate disinformation among their own citizens. Although some such willingness no doubt derives from common beliefs and shared ideologies, some of it also results from illicit funding funneled into political parties, election campaigns, or the personal

69 Moynihan, *supra* note 16, p. 42 ("[O]fficial statements that seek to steer another government's population on a matter may be perceived as propaganda, but if they are open and factually correct, then they would be less likely to violate the principle of non-intervention because the target state would still have the free will to respond."); M. N. Schmitt, 'Grey Zones in the International Law of Cyberspace', 42:2 *Yale Journal of International Law Online* (2017) p. 8, ("Coercion is accordingly more than mere influence. It involves undertaking measures that deprive the target State of choice."), <www.yilj.yale.edu/grey-zones-in-the-international-law-of-cyberspace/>, visited 14 January 2023.

pockets of the 'dis-informers' themselves. Regardless of the motives, the assistance that domestic officials afford a foreign state's disinformation campaign presents many challenges under international law. Among such challenges is how to situate the role of a domestic head of government, or a critical mass of other policymakers, who, perhaps as a result of strategic corruption, fail to respond to cyber-based disinformation campaigns conducted by a foreign state and aimed at the domestic state's democratic opinion-making.

Under what circumstances silence acts as a (perhaps unintentional) norm-creating force in international law development poses an important question. Also significant is the question of when silence can operate as consent to conduct that would otherwise constitute a breach of sovereignty. More concretely, the consent exception implicates the issue of whether a target State's silence or passivity in the face of otherwise sovereignty-violating conduct by another State functionally operates as implied consent to, or ratification of, the otherwise internationally wrongful activity.[70] In the context of a foreign state's use of DDD, the question becomes whether a target State's silence or failure to respond may be deemed to constitute consent.

The dividing line between activities that breach the non-intervention principle and those that violate sovereignty will generally not, a practical matter, make a difference in terms of outcome.[71] Accordingly, the absence of consent and the presence of coercion will also, at times, intersect if not overlap. For this reason, as autocratic governments increasingly employ strategic corruption as a weapon against democratic societies, a related, if separate, question is what, if any, implications for international law development may flow from a situation in which a State's silence is deemed to be consent, but that silence has been coerced or corruptly obtained by the infringing State. The question might be stated thusly: If silence-as-consent has been coerced or corruptly obtained, does the principle of non-intervention become applicable? A related question is whether silence obtained by corruption might operate as coerced consent, and if so, does the coercive nature of the corruption both violate the non-intervention principle and nullify the consent ostensibly granted, thereby also breaching sovereignty?[72]

---

70 For analysis of silence in other international law contexts, *see* H. Quane, *supra* note 27.

71 Moynihan, *supra* note 16, p. 48; Schmitt and Vihul, *supra* note 13, p. 1653 (describing State sovereignty and coercive intervention as related but distinct "prescriptive norms").

72 This question—though posed here in the specific context of disinformation targeting another State—is widely applicable to the questions of consent and coercion in various contexts involving the international legal system more generally.

One inference to be drawn from preceding questions is that the principles of sovereignty and non-invention are closely related. Consequently, conduct that violates one is likely, in many instances, to violate the other. They are distinct, however, and a key difference between them is that a violation of the non-intervention principle requires coercive behavior by the infringing State, whereas the sovereignty principle has no such requirement.[73] For this reason, the extent to which the two principles overlap will depend partly upon how broadly or narrowly coercion is defined for purposes of the analysis.[74] Assuming that a broad conception of coercion may potentially crystallise, the following articulation provides an instructive baseline: "pressure on the victim state to deprive the target of its free will in relation to the exercise of its sovereign powers in order to compel conduct or an outcome with respect to a matter reserved to the target state".[75] This definition of coercion results in significant overlap between the principles of sovereignty and non-intervention in relation to the coercive conduct because the definition could include activity that merely "hamper[s] the target state in ... the exercise of its sovereign functions in some way[,]" reflecting a close similarity "to the conception of violation of sovereignty as one state's exercise of unauthorised power that usurps the target state's own independent authority".[76]

According to the Tallinn Manual 2.0, the international consensus holds that, "[c]yber operations that prevent or disregard another State's exercise of its sovereign prerogatives constitute a violation of such sovereignty and are prohibited by international law".[77] Given the ICJ's recognition that the principle of sovereignty includes a State's authority to decide freely its "choice of a political ... system",[78] international law experts agree that one of the "inherently sovereign functions" of a democratic state is the administration of free and fair elections.[79] If sovereignty is treated as merely a guiding principle, however,

---

73 Moynihan, *supra* note 16, p. 48 (citing Tallinn 2.0 Manual, para 84 or commentary to Rule 4).

74 Moynihan, *supra* note 16, p. 48; J. D. Ohlin, 'Did Russian Cyber Interference in the 2016 Election Violate International Law?', 95:7 *Texas Law Review* (2017) p. 1518 ("The concept of coercion can be defined narrowly or broadly, with huge consequences for the outcome of the analysis in this case.").

75 Moynihan, *supra* note 16, p. 48.

76 Moynihan, *supra* note 14, p. 48.

77 *Tallinn Manual 2.0, Commentary to Rule 4* (quoted in Schmitt and Vihul, *supra* note 13, p. 1647).

78 Case *Concerning the Military and Paramilitary Activities in and Against Nicaragua*, supra note 23, para. 205.

79 Moynihan, *supra* note 16, p. 40.

then the conduct can be a violation only if breaches another, primary rule, such as the non-intervention principle. Accordingly, to the extent that a State's cyber operations interfere with the elections of another state—an inherently governmental function which a state is permitted to decide freely—the specific question becomes, for the limited purpose of this discussion, whether cyber-based disinformation to manipulate democratic opinion-making in the target State qualifies as coercion under the non-intervention principle. At least some experts suggest that the answer is yes.[80] As one commentator observes, disinformation that targets voting behavior violates the non-intervention principle by "nullif[ying] the genuine expression of authority and will by the people," and by "taint[ing] the internal or external manifestation or expression of authority and will by the government that emerges" from the electoral process.[81] A growing consensus, however, points the other way—at least to the extent that no additional circumstances or outcomes are present.[82]

One wrinkle in the prevailing analyses, however, is that they presuppose a public response by the target State that seeks to diffuse the effects of DDD on the target population, either before a given election or afterward. For example, in response to Russia's hack and release of Democratic National Committee emails during the 2016 election period, Department of State Legal Adviser Brian Egan, speaking on behalf of the Obama Administration, provided the following public legal interpretation: "[A] cyber operation by a State that interferes with another country's ability to hold an election or that manipulates another country's election results would be a clear violation of the rule of non-intervention".[83] One would expect the same type of forceful public pushback against a foreign State's DDD campaigns. If, however, instead of mounting such pushback—instead of attempting to strengthen the public's resilience to the

80 *See, e.g.*, H. H. Koh, 'The Trump Administration and International Law', 56:3 *Washburn Law Journal* (2017) p. 450 (taking the position that "coercive interference in another country's electoral politics—including the deliberate spreading of false news—constitutes a blatant intervention in violation of international law"); Barela, *supra* note 9 (arguing that a foreign power weakening confidence in the legitimacy of a democratic election should be interpreted as an act of coercion); Moynihan, *supra* note 16, p. 42 (stating that "[c]oercive efforts to manipulate voting behavior could also amount to intervention in another state's affairs").

81 Tsagourias, *supra* note 64, pp. 13–14 (explaining that "the principle of non-intervention protects against external interference the expression of authority and will by the people and also protects the conditions that enable the people to form authority and will freely and make free choices").

82 *See* discussion *supra* notes 37–41 and accompanying text.

83 B. J. Egan, *Remarks on International Law and Stability in Cyberspace,* 10 November 2016, <2009-2017.state.gov/s/l/releases/remarks/264303.htm>, visited on 13 January 2023.

DDD campaign—the target State were to remain silent and passive, that lack of response at least raises the possibility that the State's silence may be deemed to operate as consent under the principle of sovereignty, which, in turn, could potentially cast the coercion inquiry under the non-intervention principle in a different light: If the target State, for some reason, acting in its own best interest, were to adopt silence strategically as an indication of voluntary consent, then the perpetrating State has not acted coercively, but if the perpetrating State obtains the target State's silence by corrupt means, for example by bribery or extortion, and the target State consequently fails to expose to its own population the foreign State's interference in the electoral discourse, then perhaps the coercion element should be deemed met.[84]

3 State Silence

Three major concerns relating to State silence warrant brief attention at this juncture: possible reasons explaining State silence in various situations; why clarity is important; and the problems that may result from State silence. This section considers each concern in turn.

3.1 *Possible Explanations for State Silence*

In this and other contexts, States may choose to remain silent from a range of motives—legal, strategic, political, diplomatic, or military, for example—that suggest State silence, standing alone, should not be deemed as consent to a foreign State's cyber operations targeting another State's democratic opinion-making. A State may opt for silence under circumstances in which the State concludes that a binding international rule has not yet crystallised. Silence may, at times, be essential to protect a target State's own military operations or national security. State silence may also reflect strategic ambiguity so as to

84 Of course, one of the difficulties for international law development in this regard is the public disclosure or exposure of the corruption that would be necessary to apply international law principles to this scenario. Moreover, the questions of what constitutes corruption and how international law treats transnational corruption fall beyond the scope of this chapter, but they merit further scholarly attention in the context of malign cyber operations, including information warfare. For a history of anti-corruption features in the international legal system through the Twentieth Century, *see* Alejandro Posadas, 'Combating Corruption under International Law', 10:2 *Duke Journal of Comparative & International Law* (2000) p. 345. For treatment of the more recent problem of strategic corruption, that is, corruption as national strategy employed against a target State, *see* Zelikow, *et al.*, *supra* note 5.

keep open its own options while the law develops, or it may imply internal disagreement over the rights and obligations currently imposed by international law.[85]

3.2 *Functions Served by Clarity*

Despite these, and other, valid reasons for State silence, the proliferation of hostile disinformation campaigns in cyberspace suggests a pressing need for clarity in the governing rules under international law to establish the standards for the cyber activities that a State may lawfully initiate, which in turn will promote stability, predictability, and consistency by more concretely delineating permissible cyber activities from impermissible ones.[86] In this way, clear standards serve to deter impermissible activities, lower the risk of unintended escalation, and enable robust responses to hostile cyber operations.[87] In addition, adherents to a rules-based world order should both expect and demand unambiguous legal standards to govern circumstances under a state may lawfully invoke a right to respond to a cyber operation.[88] In this regard, clarity concerning both the consent exception under the principle of sovereignty and the coercion element under the non-intervention principle is important because these elements form part of the predicate for a targeted state's permissible response options under international law.[89] This is so because the determination of whether cyber operations by a State employing disinformation to manipulate democratic opinion-making in another State violate international law may depend, for example, on whether such operations are analyzed under the principle of sovereignty, the principle of non-intervention, or potentially some other principle of international law, or on whether the conduct is undertaken covertly or overtly, or, for purposes of a non-intervention analysis, how the element of coercion is defined. Nevertheless, most States have not taken public positions on how international law applies specifically to cyber-based disinformation campaigns or even to cyber operations more generally.[90]

---

85 R. Alcala, United States Military Academy, *Opinio Juris and the Essential Role of States, Articles of War*, 11 February 2021; Moynihan, *supra* note 16, pp. 9–10; D. Efrony and Y. Shany, 'A Rule Book on the Shelf? Tallinn Manual 2.0 on Cyber Operations and Subsequent State Practice', 112:4 *The American Journal of International Law* (2018) p. 583.

86 M. Schmitt, 'Tallinn Manual 2.0 on the International Law of Cyber Operations: What It Is and Isn't', *Just Security*, 9 February 2017.

87 Schmitt, *supra* note 28.

88 Moynihan, *supra* note 16, p. 4.

89 Schmitt, *supra* note 28.

90 Moynihan, *supra* note 16, pp. 9–10.

3.3 *Potential Problems Caused by State Silence*

States' silence on their views concerning how international law applies to cyberspace creates several potential problems beyond the failure to provide the necessary clarity for correctly drawing the line between permissible and impermissible cyber activities. First, State silence may retard the development of international law if the State fails to acknowledge that it has initiated what it believes to be an internationally lawful cyber operation or to react openly to what it believes to be an internationally wrongful cyber operation.[91] State silence is particularly noteworthy when a State remains silent after becoming the victim of a publicly known cyber operation by an infringing State. Although the target State may in fact launch a response (cyber or otherwise) in this situation, it may do so out of public view and without acknowledging it.[92] In other words, merely because the public is unaware of a response does not necessarily mean the absence of one. Nevertheless, as some commentators have argued, a State's conduct pursued in secret does not constitute State practice for customary international law development.[93] Accordingly, silence may hamper the formation and crystallisation of customary international law concerning cyber activities.

Second, and relatedly, a State's failure to respond publicly may create a potentially false impression that the international community has reached consensus that particular cyber operations, including practices of information warfare, are internationally lawful. Such a false impression threatens to prematurely crystallise limitations on permissible actions that target states may undertake in response under customary international law.[94] In other words, because silence may function as a norm-creating force in the development of customary international law, States may unintentionally contribute to new norms involving cyber behaviors merely by choosing silence or inaction in

91 Barela, *supra* note 9 ("Along with jurisprudence, how States react and speak publicly about such activity matters for determining what the law is."); Schmitt and Vihul, supra note 13 ("[I]t is essential to be sensitive to customary law's formal components of State practice and *opinio juris* when examining what States do, how they react to actions by other States, and what their officials say publicly.").

92 Moynihan, *supra* note 16, p. 6.

93 I. Navarrete and R. Buchan, 'Out of the Legal Wilderness: Peacetime Espionage, International Law and the Existence of Customary Exceptions', 51:4 *Cornell International Law Journal* (2019) pp. 912–14.

94 Schmitt and Vihul, *supra* note 13, p. 1647 (noting that, absent treaty agreements, cyber operations which might currently be impermissible under international law by violating another State's territorial sovereignty could become permissible only if *lex specialis* emerges later through the crystallisation of customary international law).

response to such behaviors.[95] The role of state practice in the development of customary international law, which has a long history as a primary source of international law, is of paramount importance.[96]

Finally, silence or failure to respond publicly poses the risk that corrupt actors will be able to establish the contours of customary international law in the emerging application of international rules to cyberspace, or at the very least to delay its development.[97] In light of the ongoing discussions on the emerging issues in this area, the opportunity is ripe for States with robust anti-corruption cultures and strong disinformation defences to lead the way in filling at least some of the silences.

3.4 *Factors Influencing States' Analyses of Issues Arising from Strategic Corruption and DDD*

The arguments that such States might employ to address issues arising out of the DDD-strategic corruption nexus are likely to vary, depending on a number of factors. The first is whether sovereignty is viewed as a standalone rule or merely as a guiding principle. If it is a standalone rule, then a relevant consideration is whether corruptly obtained consent (implied or express) from a

---

95 Hollis, *supra* note 28 (posing the following questions relating to Russia's exfiltration and release of DNC emails through Wikileaks: "[W]hat happens if international law is not invoked and applied to this case? To the extent state practice can involve acts and omissions, might silence suggest that this sort of behavior (hacking and releasing political parties' internal communications) is perceived as lawful (or at least as not internationally wrongful)? In other words, how States react to this case will have follow-on effects on future expectations of responsible State behavior, leading to new norms of behavior in cybersecurity.").

96 A. M. Weisburd, 'The International Court of Justice and the Concept of State Practice', 31:2 *University of Pennsylvania Journal of International Law* (2009) p. 299 ("The significance of state practice in international law is difficult to overstate.").

97 Some scholars have observed that malign actors can exploit the legal ambiguities created by States' inconsistencies in response to cyber operations. *See, e.g.*, Schmitt, *supra* note 53, pp. 1–2. This observation has led at least one scholar to question whether the growing number of formal State statements concerning the application of international law to cyberspace is creating more, rather than less, ambiguity. The more States that announce formal positions on the application of international law to foreign disinformation campaigns, the argument goes, the greater the discontinuity, and the greater the opportunity for malign actors to defend their conduct by arguing that no binding international law rule has coalesced around the particular activity in question. *See* P. Pijpers, 'Towards a Legal Framework for Influence Operations in Cyberspace' [paper presentation], Democracy and Information Warfare 2.0—An International Law Perspective, Trier, Germany, *Amsterdam Law School Research Paper No. 2022–11, Amsterdam Center for International Law No. 2022–06*, <dx.doi.org/10.2139/ssrn.4112370>, visited on 14 January 2023.

target State's government to disseminate DDD on behalf of a foreign government or to refrain from reacting to the dissemination of DDD by the foreign government, or its proxies, is valid consent, and if not, whether the presence of strategic corruption, along with DDD, in situations involving electoral systems or processes constitutes interference with inherently governmental functions. In short, an argument could be made that certain manifestations of strategic corruption, such as direct bribery or indirect bribery through political financing, as an inducement to propagate DDD (or to refrain from responding to DDD) which aims to disrupt or delay the electoral processes of the target State, violate the target State's sovereignty, both on the basis that it interferes with an inherently governmental function and that corrupt inducements nullify any purported consent.

By contrast, if sovereignty is a guiding principle, then a relevant question is whether DDD counts as intervention in situations in which it is accompanied by other cyber-related activity or it produces an outcome that affects the target State's *domaine reservé*, and if so, what circumstances accompanying DDD (e.g., hack and leak operations; covert or deceptive conduct) or what results flowing from it (e.g., voter suppression; civil unrest; delay in or prevention of the counting of votes) will tip the scale in favor of finding that the foreign conduct qualifies intervention as opposed to mere influence. Here, an argument could be made that the 'extra ingredient' found in the presence of certain manifestations of strategic corruption, such as (again) direct bribery or indirect bribery through political financing, as an inducement to propagate DDD (or to refrain from responding to DDD) which aims to disrupt or delay the electoral processes of the target State, shifts the disinformation campaign across the line from a permissive influence operation to a prohibited interference with the target State's *domaine reservé* in conducting elections.

Another factor to be considered is whether coercion is to be defined narrowly, to include only conduct specifically designed to compel the victim State to change its behaviour, by either taking action that it would not otherwise take or by refraining from taking action that it would otherwise take, with respect to a matter within its *domaine reservé*, or defined broadly, to include conduct that merely deprives the target State of control over a protected matter, without actually or potentially compelling that State to change its behaviour. If the narrow conception of coercion is adopted, then the corollary consideration is whether any manifestations of strategic corruption operate to compel the victim State to disseminate DDD that it would not otherwise disseminate or to refrain from responding a foreign State's dissemination of DDD targeting the target State's voters or policymakers. An argument under the narrow definition of coercion would be difficult to make, unless the form of inducement falls into the category of extortion. The acceptance of bribes or political campaign financing is typically made by choice, not compulsion. If the broader understanding of coercion is adopted, however, then the relevant consideration is whether any manifestations of strategic corruption operate to deprive the target State of control over it electoral and political processes by the dissemination of DDD or the lack of response thereto. In this regard, the broader conception of coercion is more likely to support a determination of coercion for purposes of the non-intervention analysis. The argument here would be that the perpetrating State has corruptly taken control of at least part of the information space necessary for transparent and fact-based democratic deliberation and opinion-making in the victim State, with the intent to substantively disturb the political system of or significantly impede the orderly conduct of elections in the victim State. Such a combination of DDD and strategic corruption could qualify as coercion under the broader definition sufficient to constitute intervention.

Of course, States taking the lead on these questions may well determine that most, or even all, issues arising at the intersection of DDD and strategic corruption are domestic matters that do not implicate international law at all. Regardless of any final determination made on such issues, they deserve considered attention, preferably first by those States which are committed to corruption-free government, embody healthy democracies, and promote societal resistance to disinformation campaigns. In all of these respects, the Nordic countries earn high marks. They are among the best candidates, therefore, to act as norm entrepreneurs and to guide agenda-setting in this area. Moreover, the role of norm-entrepreneur and agenda-setter in global affairs is not new to the Nordic States.[98] Independently and collectively, they have successfully influenced other, more politically, militarily, and economically powerful States in the international community.[99]

4 Leadership from Nordic Countries

As more States take public positions on emerging international issues relating to cyberspace, the Nordic nations have an invaluable role to play in guiding the contours of international law responses to issues in the intersecting space of strategic corruption and cyber-based disinformation, and they have

98 C. Ingebritsen, 'Norm Entrepreneurs: Scandinavia's Role in World Politics', 37:1 *Cooperation and Conflict: Journal of the Nordic International Studies Association* (2002) p. 11.

99 *Ibid.*

an opportunity to help shape the international law response in a way that will not only protect their own interests and values concerning corruption-free and democratic governance, but also defend against government corruption and democratic decline worldwide. This section offers several reasons why the Nordic States are especially well equipped to anticipate and prepare international law responses relating to the questions identified in this chapter. These reasons include the commonality of positions taken by the Nordic countries regarding the application of international law to cyberspace, and the domestic conditions within the Nordic States that facilitate effective international law development on corruption-disinformation issues.

4.1 *Nordic States' Common Positions on Application of International Law to Cyberspace*

Among the Nordic countries, Finland was the first to publish its official position on key questions concerning the application of international law to cyberspace, which it did in the fall of 2020.[100] Several months later, in the spring of 2021, Norway followed suit.[101] Sweden then published its national position in July 2022.[102] Denmark finalized and published its report the following year.[103] At the macro level, the positions of the Nordic nations closely align with one another on the core issues. Specifically, as a relevant to this chapter, they agree that the existing international law framework applies to cyberspace; that sovereignty constitutes a primary, standalone rule, which applies to cyber operations; and that the principle of non-intervention also applies to cyber operations that compel or coerce conduct by a target State in relation its internal affairs.

These statements also reflect a common approach to the application of the sovereignty rule to specific instances of cyber activities: assessments of

100 Finland Ministry for Foreign Affairs, *Finland Published Its Position on Public International Law in Cyberspace*, 15 October 2020, <valtioneuvosto.fi/en/-/finland-published-its-positions-on-public-international-law-in-cyberspace>, visited on 12 January 2023.

101 Norwegian Positions on Selected Questions of International Law and Cyberspace, May 2021 <www.regjeringen.no/contentassets/a8911fc020c94eb386a1ec7917bf0d03/norwegian_positions.pdf>, visited on 12 January 2023.

102 Government Offices of Sweden, *Position Paper on the Application of International Law in Cyberspace*, July 2022. Sweden's position paper has been reprinted with an introductory note by Ola Engdahl, 'Sweden's Position Paper on the Application of International Law in Cyberspace', 92:3 *Nordic Journal of International Law* (2023) p. 489.

103 Denmark's *Position Paper on the Application of International Law in Cyberspace*, May 2023. Denmark's position paper has been reprinted with an introductory note by Jeppe Mejer Kjelgaard and Ulf Melgaard, 'Denmark's Position Paper on the Application of International Law in Cyberspace', 92:3 *Nordic Journal of International Law* (2023) p. 446.

whether a particular cyber activity violates a State's sovereignty should be made on a case-by-case basis. This 'wait-and-see' approach may enable the Nordic countries to respond effectively (and perhaps quickly) with a relevant statement or action as emerging circumstances warrant, while simultaneously preventing malign actors from disrupting or preventing the development of customary international law rules applicable to the cyber realm. If the Nordic nations continue to row in the same direction, so to speak, on how international law applies to specific cyber activities, then, in light of the domestic conditions in each one pertaining to corruption and disinformation, they will be especially well suited to address emerging issues involving strategic corruption and DDD.

4.2 *Domestic Conditions Facilitating Effective International Law Development*

Countries which are best positioned to anticipate and prepare responses under international law to potentially emerging threats that arise at the intersection of strategic corruption and digital disinformation are likely to be those which enjoy the following domestic conditions: (1) an unwavering commitment to the rule of law; (2) healthy and strong democratic institutions; (3) robust defences against public corruption; and (4) a high degree of resilience to disinformation. To the extent that these standards can be reduced to numeric metrics, the Nordic countries consistently earn the highest scores on each of these criteria, thereby positioning them as the most well equipped to lead the task of anticipating and modeling State statements in response to the emerging but not-yet urgent problem of strategic corruption as a contributing factor to the growth of digital disinformation designed to disrupt democratic processes.

4.2.1 Rule of Law, Democratic Governance, and Absence of Corruption

According to the World Justice Project's Rule of Law Index 2022, which uses several factors to measure adherence to the rule of law, the Nordic countries placed in the top four positions worldwide, with Denmark earning a score of 90 out of 100, Norway earning a score of 88, Finland earning a score of 87, and Sweden earning a score of 86.[104] Similarly, the Nordic bloc earns the highest

---

104 The measuring factors include constraints on government powers, absence of corruption, open government, fundamental rights, order and security, regulatory enforcement, civil justice and criminal justice. For additional breakdown of the components of the measuring factors and a description of the methodology used to compile the index, *see* World Justice Project, *World Justice Project Rule of Law Index 2022*, <worldjusticeproject.org/rule-of-law-index/global/2022/>, visited on 11 January 2023.

scores from the 2021 Freedom House Report on democratic governance, which provides aggregate ratings for each country based on separate scores for national and local governance, electoral process, independent media, civil society, judicial framework and independence, and corruption.[105] On these factors, Finland, Norway, and Sweden each scored an aggregate of 100, and Denmark scored an aggregate of 97.[106] Specific scores for corruption-free governance are equally strong. On the "absence of corruption" factor used to rate adherence to the rule of law, the World Justice Project Index in 2022, ranked Nordic countries in the top five places globally, giving Denmark a score of 96 out of 100, Norway a score of 93, Sweden a score of 90, and Finland a score of 89.[107] According to Transparency International's Corruption Perceptions Index of 2021, Denmark and Finland, which, along with New Zealand, scored 88 out of 100, in a three-way tie for the top rank, and Norway and Sweden, along with Singapore, tied for fourth place, with a score of 85.[108]

Nations such as the U.S. and the U.K., which in the past might have been expected to join the Nordic bloc as partners in anticipating and responding quickly to emerging issues relating to strategic corruption and de-democratising influence campaigns, have dropped precipitously in the rankings on each metric. The U.S. now scores a mere 71, with a rank of 26, on the World Justice Project's Rule of Law Index, while the U.K. fares slightly better with a still-anemic score of 79 and a rank of 15.[109] The two nations' democratic governance assessments from Freedom House place the U.K., which earned a respectable if less than ideal score of 93, somewhat closer to the scores of the Nordic States, while the U.S. obtained a meagre score of only 83.[110] On the World Justice Project's Rule of Index measurement of "absence of corruption", the U.K., though still ranked among the top ten worldwide, receives a score of only 83, while the U.S. drops to a global ranking of 22, with a score of 73.[111] The Corruption Perceptions Index published by Transparency International in 2021

105 For additional details regarding the methodology used to assess scores, *see* Freedom House, *Freedom in the World Research Methodology* <freedomhouse.org/reports/freedom-world/freedom-world-research-methodology>, visited on 11 January 2023.

106 Repucci and Slipowitz, *supra* note 3.

107 World Justice Project, *World Justice Project Rule of Law Index 2022, Absence of Corruption*, <worldjusticeproject.org/rule-of-law-index/global/2022/Absence%20of%20 Corruption/>, visited on 11 January 2023.

108 Transparency International, *Transparency International Corruption Perceptions Index*, <www.transparency.org/en/cpi/2021>, visited on 11 January 2023.

109 World Justice Project Rule of Law Index 2022, *supra* note 107.

110 Repucci and Slipowitz, *supra* note 3.

111 World Justice Project Rule of Law Index 2022, Absence of Corruption, *supra* note 107.

reflects a similar disparity: The U.K., with a score of 78, rates significantly lower than the Nordic nations, and the U.S. rates lower still, with a score of 67.[112]

Such declines are perhaps unsurprising given reports in recent years of successful political financing in the U.K. and the U.S. by foreign government proxies. For example, in the U.K., among the top donors to one of that nation's major political parties are foreign nationals with alleged ties to the various arms of the Russian State.[113] In the U.S., the Campaign Legal Center (CLC), a non-partisan domestic organisation which advocates for meaningful access of all citizens to the democratic process, reported in November 2022 that the Federal Election Commission, the administrative agency responsible for administering and enforcing federal campaign finance laws, has failed to enforce prohibitions against political campaign financing by foreign nationals. The report specifically cites a case involving funding from Russian oligarchs,[114] a class of donors widely believed to operate on behalf of the Kremlin's interests.[115] The CLC also points to significant loopholes under U.S. law that allow foreign governments and foreign nationals—and proxies operating on their behalf—to evade the ban on foreign-sourced campaign financing. In this regard, the CLC observes that U.S. law currently permits foreign actors to evade detection as the source of campaign funds by hiding their identity through other, legitimate donors, including political action committees. Likewise, what the CLC calls foreign-influenced corporations are allowed to engage in political spending in U.S. elections, and foreign nationals may legally spend funds on ballot measures at the state and local levels.[116] Each of these vectors for political funding leaves the U.S. vulnerable to the strategic corruption efforts employed by foreign autocratic regimes, and arguably, provides incentive or leverage for the foreign governments' de-democratising digital disinformation campaigns.

4.2.2 Societal Resistance to Disinformation

In addition to the Nordic States' uncontested position as leaders of democratic and corruption-free governance, they are also masters of resistance to malign,

112 Transparency International, Corruption Perceptions Index, *supra* note 108.

113 Rudolph, *supra* note 7, p. 4.

114 S. Ghosh, Campaign Legal Center, *The FEC is Allowing Foreign Money to Influence Our Elections,* 10 November 2022 <campaignlegal.org/update/fec-allowing-foreign-money-influence-our-elections>, visited on 11 January 2023.

115 Rudolph, *supra* note 7, p. 4.

116 Campaign Legal Center, *Foreign Interference in U.S. Elections* <campaignlegal.org/sites/default/files/2020-12/Foreign%20Interference%20One-Pager.pdf>, visited on 12 January 2023.

cyber-based influence operations. The strength of their resistance is not accidental. Each country has, individually and collectively, committed itself to combatting disinformation, focusing heavily on media literacy and inculcating among its population critical thinking skills, as well as promoting a sense of shared responsibility for fighting the spread of false information. In this regard, the Nordic nations have adopted an all-of-country approach.[117] In Sweden, for example, Bamse, a cartoon bear teaches young children how to think critically about information they see on the internet.[118] In Finland, the government sponsors media literacy programs for all ages, from primary school children through adult education.[119] In 2016, Finland introduced a national secondary-school curriculum to teach media literacy and critical thinking skills across core subjects.[120] In Denmark, Aarhus University is leading a consortium of researchers and fact-checkers from Denmark, Finland, Norway, and Sweden to study and counter disinformation (and misinformation).[121] In Norway, the four largest news outlets have joined forces to develop a fact-checking cooperative, Faktisk.no, to work collaboratively to debunk disinformation.[122]

Due in part to these and other, similar efforts, such as the Swedish government's formation of the Swedish Psychological Defence Agency, created, in the words of Sweden's Minister for Foreign Affairs Tobias Billström, as a mechanism for "reinforcing [Sweden's] national capabilities to respond to disinformation campaigns, cyber attacks and hybrid influence",[123] the Nordic States have

---

117 *See, e.g.*, 'Denmark's Defence Against Disinformation', *EUvsDisinfo*, 10 September 2018, <euvsdisinfo.eu/denmarks-defence-against-disinformation>, visited on 12 January 2023.

118 J. Lytvynenko, 'This Comic Book Wants to Teach Kids about Online Disinformation: Does Bamse the Swedish Cartoon Bear Brush His Teeth?', *Buzzfeed News*, 23 January 2017 <www.buzzfeednews.com/article/janelytvynenko/bamse-the-bear>, visited on 12 January 2023.

119 E. Mackintosh, 'Finland Is Winning the War on Fake News: What It's Learned May Be Crucial to Democracy', *CNN Special Report*, May 2019, <edition.cnn.com/interactive/2019/05/europe/finland-fake-news-intl/>, visited on 12 January 2023.

120 J. Henley, 'How Finland Starts Its Fights Against Fake News in Primary Schools', *The Guardian*, 29 January 2020, <www.theguardian.com/world/2020/jan/28/fact-from-fiction-finlands-new-lessons-in-combating-fake-news>, visited on 10 January 2023.

121 J. K. Revsbech, Aarhus University Faculty of Arts News Release, 'A Nordic Collective Effort to Combat Misinformation', 11 August 2021, <arts.au.dk/en/news-and-events/news/show/artikel/nyt-nordisk-samarbejde-vil-bekaempe-misinformation-og-fake-news-1#:~:text=A%20Nordic%20collective%20effort%20to%20combat%20misinformation%20Funded,NORDIS%2C%20is%20led%20by%20DATALAB%20at%20Aarhus%20University>, visited on 12 January 2023.

122 K. Egeberg, 'The Age of Disinformation, Faktisk: Norway's Fact-checking Cooperative', *Magazines Canada*, 2 March 2020, <magazinescanada.ca.wp-content/uploads/2020/03/DCI-CaseStudy-Faktisk.pdf>, visited on 11 January 2023.

123 *Opportunities and Challenges for Swedish Foreign Policy*, Speech by Minister for Foreign Affairs Tobias Billström, held at the Swedish Institute of International Affairs 21 December

earned top scores in media literacy from the Open Society Institute's European Policies Initiative, which assesses a society's resilience to disinformation based on several metrics.[124] Finland ranks first in the world, with a composite score of 75 out of 100, followed immediately by Norway and Denmark, each with a composite score of 73. Sweden earns a sixth-place world ranking, with a score of 70. By contrast, the UK and the US earn significantly lower media literacy scores; the U.K. scores 61, and the U.S. scores 60, placing these nations in thirteenth and eighteenth places, respectively.[125]

4.2.3 Summary of Scores and Rankings

The table below summarises the scores and rankings of Denmark, Finland, Norway, Sweden, the United Kingdom, and the United States on the rule of law, democratic health, absence of corruption, and resistance to disinformation.

A thorough exploration of the political and policy considerations that explain how and why, as mature democracies, the U.S. and the U.K. have reached this point would be as interesting as it would be invaluable, but it is also beyond the scope of this chapter. Nevertheless, whatever its causes, the passivity of these States suggests that, for the foreseeable future, they are likely to prove less-than-reliable partners in efforts to address questions involving strategic corruption and DDD under international law. Accordingly, the Nordic countries' leadership assumes even greater importance. Their past leadership efforts to promote the norms and values they hold in common and to strengthen those norms and values within the international community have earned them a global reputation for trustworthiness and effectiveness as partners in influencing "internationally accepted codes of conduct in world politics."[126] They have proven particularly effective in integrating sustainable development norms in global development policy, in part because of their domestic circumstances and commitment to environmental protection.[127] The Nordic States have also played a key agenda-setting role in peaceful conflict resolution and have served as models for global aid and welfare.[128] By drawing on their shared democratic commitments and values, as well as their track

---

2022, published 30 December 2022, <https://www.government.se/speeches/2022/12/opportunities-and-challenges-for-swedish-foreign-policy/>, visited 14 January 2023.

124 For details on the methodology used, *see* Open Society Institute, *European Policies Initiative Media Literacy Index 2022*, <osis.bg/wp-content/uploads/2022/10/HowItStarted_MediaLiteracyIndex2022_ENG_.pdf>, visited on 12 January 2023.

125 *Ibid.*

126 Ingebritsen, *supra* note 98, at 13–14.

127 Ingebritsen, *supra* note 98, at 14–16.

128 Ingebritsen, *supra* note 98, at 16–20.

TABLE 11.1 Scores and Global rankings from World Justice Project (WJP)[(1)], Freedom House (FH)[(2)], Transparency International (TI)[(3)], and the Open Society Institute's European Policies Initiative (EPI)[(4)]

Country	Rule of law	Democratic health	Absence of corruption	Resistance to disinformation
	Nordics			
Denmark	WJP: 90 Rank: 1	FH: 97 No ranking provided	WJP: 96; TI:88 Rank (WJP): 1; (TI): 1	EPI: 73 Rank: 3
Finland	WJP: 87 Rank: 3	FH: 100 No ranking provided	WJP: 89; TI:88 Rank (WJP): 4; (TI): 1	EPI: 75 Rank: 1
Norway	WJP: 88 Rank: 2	FH: 100 No ranking provided	WJP: 93; TI:85 Rank (WJP): 2; (TI): 4	EIP: 73 Rank: 2
Sweden	WJP: 86 Rank: 4	FH: 100 No ranking provided	WJP: 90; TI:85 Rank (WJP): 3; (TI): 4	EPI: 70 Rank: 6
	UK/US			
United Kingdom	WJP: 79 Rank: 16	FH: 93 No ranking provided	WJP: 83; TI:78 Rank (WJP): 10; (TI): 11	EPI: 61 Rank: 13
United States	WJP: 71 Rank: 26	FH: 83 No ranking provided	WJP: 73; TI:67 Rank (WJP): 22; (TI): 27	EPI: 60 Rank: 18

Sources:

(1) World Justice Project Rule of Law Index 2022, https://worldjusticeproject.org/rule-of-law-index/global/2022/.

(2) Freedom House Global Freedom Report 2021, https://freedomhouse.org/countries/freedom-world/scores.

(3) Transparency International Corruption Perceptions Index 2021, https://www.transparency.org/en/cpi/2021.

(4) Open Society Institute's European Policies Initiative Media Literacy Index 2022, https://osis.bg/wp-content/uploads/2022/10/HowItStarted_MediaLiteracyIndex2022_ENG_.pdf.

record as reliable partners in the international community, the Nordic nations have every reason to assume a leadership role in addressing international law issues that arise at the intersection of DDD and strategic corruption.

5 Conclusion

The Nordic nations are ideally positioned to anticipate and prepare appropriate international law responses to the unique intersection of threats to democracy posed by autocratic regimes' combined tactic of strategic corruption and de-democratising digital disinformation. Individually and collectively, the Nordic States have led the world in establishing governmental and societal structures, institutions, and norms that operate effectively to blunt public corruption and to combat disinformation within their respective borders. Nordic countries' global leadership in these areas is now needed to fight on a different but related front: developing an effective response to these threats under an international law framework, as states wrestle with the application of customary international law to hostile cyber activities and continue to articulate formal statements addressing various aspects of that question. Many fundamental questions have reached consensus;[129] others remain in flux;[130] and still others have yet to draw widespread attention.[131] Within this last category is the question this chapter raises, that is, whether corruptly obtained consent to interfere in another nation's internal affairs can constitute coercion under the non-intervention principle when such interference occurs as a cyber-based disinformation campaign, and, relatedly, whether consent obtained corruptly is valid consent under the principle of sovereignty.

The Nordic states' leadership has particular relevance for this question because States targeted with disinformation campaigns may remain silent on their view of whether the interference violates international law, and such silence, especially if corruptly obtained, may depress the development of international law. More specifically, by failing to respond timely, publicly, and forcefully to a foreign-state's disinformation attack, the target State may hamper

129 Schmitt and Vihul, *supra* note 13, p. 1639 n. 3 ("There appears to be near-universal consensus that the extant international law governs cyber activities.").

130 One example is whether sovereignty is a standalone rule, the breach of which constitutes a wrongful act under international law, or merely a guiding principle, which requires the breach of a corollary rule to constitute a wrongful act.

131 The question that is the focus of this chapter is one such concern, that is, whether corruptly obtained consent to interfere in another nation's internal affairs can constitute coercion under the non-intervention principle.

the formation and crystallisation of customary international law concerning cyber activities. Because Nordic nations have earned a sterling reputation for corruption-free governance and have also been at the forefront in adopting effective strategies to combat disinformation, they are especially well prepared to lead efforts to address these issues.

Absent treaties or other international agreements governing cyber-based campaigns involving de-democratising disinformation, customary international law will, over time, likely coalesce and provide answers to at least some of the questions raised.[132] To crystallise into binding rules, customary international law requires State practice and *opinio juris*, but a target State's silence or inaction in response to another State's hostile activities can also potentially operate as a norm-creating force in international law, leaving greater leeway for an infringing State to ratchet up the standard for what conduct is sufficiently egregious to warrant a right of response by the target State under international law. To the extent that this is so, international law experts' calls for clarity from States regarding cyber operations should be heeded. In addition to providing clarity on these questions, however, States—and international law experts—would also do well to engage deliberately and prophylactically with a number of peripheral questions concerning the international law implications of State silence, particularly concerning consent and coercion. To protect domestic democratic, corruption-free governance, Nordic countries would serve not only their own interests, but also those of the world's other democracies by ensuring that these inquiries considering the application of international law to cyberspace also address what effect, if any, on international law principles may obtain from a target State's corruptly obtained silence or passivity in response to the weaponised use of cyber operations to manipulate democratic opinion-making. Indeed, their leadership in this regard may well be indispensable.

132 Whether formal agreements or customary international law offers a more effective and practicable framework for addressing these questions is an issue left for further analysis elsewhere, as is discussion of impediments that domestic legal frameworks may pose to implementing possible approaches that may be proposed.

CHAPTER 12

The Human Rights Challenges of Private Military and Security Companies and Mercenaries in Cyberspace

Sorcha MacLeod[1] *and Daniel Wand*[2]

1 Introduction and Context

Private actors such as private military and security companies (PMSC) and mercenaries are increasingly being contracted to provide both defensive and offensive military and security services in the cybersphere.[3] They are hired by States, and non-State actors to provide a wide variety of services in peacetime, as well as in situations of armed conflict. Such services include the maintenance of security, domestic law enforcement, data-collection, intelligence-gathering, espionage, and the provision of cyber products. In some cases they are used by third-party States as proxy actors.[4] Disinformation campaigns are also often undertaken on behalf of clients, and were recently highlighted by the UN Secretary-General at a Security Council high-level open debate, who noted with great concern that '[m]alicious activity that undermines public institutions, electoral processes and online integrity erodes trust, fuels tensions, and even sows the seeds of violence and conflict.'[5]

In addition, by engaging in sabotage via the deployment of malware or ransomware, important infrastructure such as 'electricity and water supplies,

1 University of Copenhagen: sorcha.macleod@jur.ku.dk and member of the UN Working Group on mercenaries 2018–2024.

2 Barrister, 4 Kings Bench Walk: djw@4kbw.co.uk.

3 Report of the Working Group on the use of mercenaries as a means of violating human rights and impeding the exercise of the right of peoples to self-determination, 'The human rights impacts of mercenaries, mercenary-related actors, and private military and security companies engaging in cyberactivities' (2021) A/76/151. This chapter builds on earlier research undertaken by the authors for that report.

4 Ibid, note 3 at paragraphs 15–21.

5 UN Secretary-General's remarks to the Security Council's High-Level Debate on "Maintenance of International Peace and Security: Addressing Evolving Threats in Cyberspace, 20 June 2024: <https://www.un.org/sg/en/content/sg/statement/2024-06-20/secretary-generals-remarks-the-security-council%E2%80%99s-high-level-debate-%E2%80%9Cmaintenance-of-international-peace-and-security-addressing-evolving-threats-cyberspace%E2%80%9D>.

 | DOI:10.1163/9789004703933_013

hospitals, surveillance services and communication facilities' can be damaged by PMSC and mercenaries, and they can also 'facilitate the targeting or incapacitation of military defence and other systems.'[6] The UN Secretary-General also highlighted the dangers of such activities stating that '[e]ssential public services such as healthcare, banking and telecommunications are frequently breached,' and that various actors including "cyber mercenaries" are engaging in 'relentless illicit activities.'[7]

While in some cases PMSC and mercenaries are utilised to protect networks and infrastructure, in other cases they participate in hostilities and can seek to weaken the military capabilities of enemy armed forces by infiltrating, disrupting, damaging, and destroying military objects.[8] They also target civilian objects, and the ICRC and the UN Working Group on the use of mercenaries have recognised that this type of cyberwarfare has the capacity to cause serious human harm.[9]

It is beyond dispute that human rights norms apply and that they offer protection to persons in all situations of armed conflict subject to permitted (and contentious) derogations.[10] It therefore follows that cyber activities carried out by mercenaries or PMSC are subject to human rights norms and this position has been adopted by the UN Working Group on mercenaries and will be discussed further later in the chapter.[11]

Grave human rights impacts on civilian populations, both direct and indirect, as well as violations of international humanitarian law caused by cyber activities are of serious concern.[12] Four types of cyber activities linked to

6 Working Group on mercenaries note 3 at paragraph 17.

7 UN Secretary-General note 5; UN chief warns of 'cyber mercenaries' amid spike in weaponising digital tools <https://news.un.org/en/story/2024/06/1151266>.

8 Note 3 at paragraph 21.

9 See e.g. ICRC, 'International humanitarian law and cyber operations during armed conflicts,' ICRC position paper submitted to the Open-Ended Working Group on Developments in the Field of Information and Telecommunications in the Context of International Security and the Group of Governmental Experts on Advancing Responsible State Behaviour in Cyberspace in the Context of International Security, November 2019 International Review of the Red Cross (2020), 102 (913), 481–492. Digital technologies and war doi:10.1017/S1816383120000478; UN Working Group on mercenaries, note 3.

10 https://casebook.icrc.org/law/ihl-and-human-rights. See also: See e.g. Noam Lubell, Challenges in applying human rights law to armed conflict. International Review of the Red Cross. 2005;87(860):737–754. doi:10.1017/S1816383100184541; OHCHR, International Legal Protection of Human Rights in Armed Conflict (2011) HR/PUB/11/01; Daragh Murray, Elizabeth Wilmshurst, Françoise Hampson, Charles Garraway, Noam Lubell, Dapo Akande (eds), Practitioners' Guide to Human Rights Law in Armed Conflict (2016, CUP).

11 UN Working Group on mercenaries, note 3 at paragraph 11.

12 See ICRC note 9.

mercenaries and PMSC violate particular human rights protected by international and regional human rights instruments and are addressed in this chapter: (1) Targeting of infrastructure; (2) Destruction, Disruption or Theft of Data; (3) Surveillance; and (4) Disinformation / Interference with Elections. Human rights impacted include physical integrity rights such as the right to life, and the right to be free from torture and inhuman and degrading treatment. Furthermore, by targeting important State infrastructure, these actors cause indirect impacts by undermining healthcare, utilities, communications, and the security environment, which impact the right to adequate healthcare, the right to privacy, and the right to freedom of expression, among others. In addition, in both peacetime and armed conflicts, certain groups may be differently and disproportionately impacted, such as persons with disabilities, elder persons, the LGBTQI+ community, migrants, human rights defenders, opposition leaders, and journalists.

This purpose of this chapter is to: (1) examine the use and role of private military and security contractors and mercenaries in cyber operations in situations of armed conflict, including those above and below the threshold of war, given the variegated situations in which such operations may be deployed; (2) assess how human rights protections may be engaged in relation to cyber operations and how particular international and regional human rights norms may be violated as a consequence of specific identified cyber operations; and (3) to examine some of the challenges in ensuring compliance with human rights standards and confronting violations given the particular peculiarities which arise in the context of policing cyber operations, as compared to traditional kinetic methods of warfare, and of the activities of PMSC and mercenaries.

The importance of this chapter lies in the confluence of two relatively new phenomena; the rise of PMSC and mercenaries acting on behalf of states in warfare and other operations below the threshold of war, and the increasing deployment of cyber operations by states in the context of military operations in warfare or otherwise, and the particular relationship between the two in light of the particular and growing involvement of PMSC and mercenaries in the deployment of offensive cyber operations.[13] Moreover, whilst there has been a considerable focus within the literature on the regulation of cyber

13 See e.g. José da Cruz and Stephanie Pedron, 'Cyber Mercenaries: A New Threat to National Security' (2020) 96 International Social Science Review <https://www.jstor.org/stable/27071316?seq=3>; Aleksi Kajander, Agnes Kasper, Evhen Tsybulenko, 'Making the Cyber Mercenary – Autonomous Weapons Systems and Common Article 1 of the Geneva Conventions', 2020 12th International Conference on Cyber Conflict (CyCon) (2020); Tim Maurer, 'Cyber Proxies and Their Implications for Liberal Democracies' (2018) 41 The Washington Quarterly 171 <https://doi.org/10.1080/0163660X.2018.1485332>; Jesse Jacob

operations under international humanitarian law, there has been much less consideration of the human rights aspects of cyber operations, and this chapter seeks to contribute to addressing that deficiency.[14]

This issue has been identified as a significant matter of concern by the United Nations Working Group on the use of mercenaries as a means of violating human rights and impeding the exercise of rights of peoples to self-determination in its 2021 report to the UN General Assembly, entitled 'The human rights impacts of mercenaries, mercenary-related actors and private military and security companies engaging in cyber activities'.[15] This chapter builds on and advances the discussion as set out in that report.

2 Definitions

2.1 *Mercenaries*

This chapter refers to both 'mercenaries' and 'private military and security companies' as both types of actor are involved in the problematic cyber activities highlighted above. While the term 'mercenary' is legally defined under international law, PMSC is not.

Article 47 (2) of Additional Protocol I to the Geneva Conventions defines a mercenary in accordance with six cumulative criteria.[16] It is a difficult

---

McMurdo, 'Cybersecurity Firms – Cyber Mercenaries' (2016) 4 Homeland & National Security Law Review 35 <https://heinonline.org/HOL/P?h=hein.journals/hnslr4&i=41>.

14 See e.g. Laurent Gisel, Tilman Rodenhäuser and Knut Dörmann, 'Twenty Years on: International Humanitarian Law and the Protection of Civilians against the Effects of Cyber Operations during Armed Conflicts' (2020) 102 International Review of the Red Cross 287 <https://www.cambridge.org/core/journals/international-review-of-the-red-cross/article/twenty-years-on-international-humanitarian-law-and-the-protection-of-civilians-against-the-effects-of-cyber-operations-during-armed-conflicts/BE68981904487F07B9919836B78B6DAD> accessed 11 July 2024; Jonathan Horowitz, 'Cyber Operations under International Humanitarian Law: Perspectives from the ICRC' (2020) 24 ASIL Insights <https://www.asil.org/insights/volume/24/issue/11/cyber-operations-under-international-humanitarian-law-perspectives-icrc> accessed 11 July 2024; Michael N Schmitt and Sean Watts, 'The Decline of International Humanitarian Law Opinio Juris and the Law of Cyber Warfare' (2015) 50 Texas International Law Journal 189 <https://heinonline.org/HOL/P?h=hein.journals/tilj50&i=220> accessed 11 July 2024.

15 Working Group on mercenaries, note 3.

16 Protocol Additional to the Geneva Conventions of 12 August 1949, and relating to the Protection of Victims of International Armed Conflicts (Protocol I), 8 June 1977: <https://ihl-databases.icrc.org/en/ihl-treaties/api-1977>.

definition to satisfy as all six criteria must be met for a person to be classified as a mercenary.[17] Thus, under Article 47(2) a mercenary is an individual who:

a) Is specially recruited locally or abroad in order to fight in an armed conflict;
b) Does, in fact, take a direct part in the hostilities;
c) Is motivated to take part in the hostilities essentially by the desire for private gain and, in fact, is promised, by or on behalf of a Party to the conflict, material compensation substantially in excess of that promised or paid to combatants of similar ranks and functions in the armed forces of that Party;
d) Is neither a national of a Party to the conflict nor a resident of territory controlled by a Party to the conflict;
e) Is not a member of the armed forces of a Party to the conflict; and
f) Has not been sent by a State which is not a Party to the conflict on official duty as a member of its armed forces.

This definition of mercenary does not refer directly to cyber activities or actors but the Working Group on mercenaries considers that 'some actions in the cybersphere may rise to the level of mercenarism or may be considered mercenary-related activities and also impact human rights both in armed conflict and in peacetime.'[18]

2.2 *Private Military and Security Companies (PMSC)*

The term 'private military and security company' (PMSC) is more definitionally amorphous, controversial, and lacking universality but is used in some important regulatory contexts, most notably the Montreux Document and a UN Open-ended Intergovernmental Working Group developing a regulatory instrument on PMSC.[19] Another oft-used term 'private military company'

17 Report of the Working Group on the use of mercenaries as a means of violating human rights and impeding the exercise of the right of peoples to self-determination, 'Regulatory environment for mercenaries, mercenary-related actors, and private military and security companies: a call to action' (2023) A/78/535 paragraph 12.

18 Working Group on mercenaries, note 3 at paragraph 9.

19 See e.g. 'The Montreux Document on Pertinent International Legal Obligations and Good Practices for States Related to Operations of Private Military and Security Companies during Armed Conflict' (Montreux Document Forum, 2008) <https://www.montreuxdocument.org/about/montreux-document.html>; UN Open-ended Intergovernmental Working Group to elaborate the content of an international regulatory framework, without prejudging the nature thereof, relating to the activities of private military and security companies <https://www.ohchr.org/en/hr-bodies/hrc/pms-cs/igwg-index/5th-session-igwg-military>.

(PMC) is not legally defined, nor used in regulatory contexts.[20] For the purposes of this chapter, therefore, the long-standing definition of PMSC set out by the UN Working Group on mercenaries is used which notes that:

> there is no universally accepted, legally binding, standard definition of a "military company" or a "security company", the Working Group on the use of mercenaries uses the term "private military and security companies" to refer to corporate entities providing, on a compensatory basis, military and/or security services by physical persons and/or legal entities. That definition focuses on the activities performed by corporate entities rather than the way a company or entity may self-identify.[21]

Consequently, this definition encompasses a wide variety of services:

> Services include, for example: knowledge transfer with security, policing and military applications; development and implementation of informational security measures; land, sea or air reconnaissance; satellite surveillance; and crewed or uncrewed flight operations of any type. In line with this definition, the present thematic report focuses on companies that provide private military and security services, including not only private military and security companies, but also defence companies, corporations specialized in information and advanced technologies, and airlines that provide such services.[22]

While this definition makes no direct reference to cyber activities, it is not an exhaustive list and the UN Working Group on mercenaries considers such activities to be included within its definition of PMSC and the services they offer.[23] The Working Group has also noted that the 'market for offensive cyber capabilities is growing rapidly' and that many PMSC are 'developing cybersecurity divisions.'[24] It therefore follows that the Working Group recognises that PMSCs can be involved in the provision of both offensive and defensive cyber services which impact negatively on civilians.

---

20 UN Working Group on mercenaries, note 17 at paragraph 39.

21 Report of the Working Group on the use of mercenaries as a means of violating human rights and impeding the exercise of the right of peoples to self-determination (2010) A/HRC/15/25, annex, part I, art. 2.

22 UN Working Group on mercenaries, note 17 at paragraph 40.

23 UN Working Group on mercenaries, note 3 paragraphs 15–21.

24 UN Working Group on mercenaries, note 3 at paragraph 20.

2.3 *Cyber Operations*

In this chapter the term 'cyber operations' is used. It describes the multiplicity of activities which can be carried out in cyberspace by various private and quasi-private actors that fall within the definitions of PMSC or mercenary and which have the intention to protect, secure, obtain or destroy computer networks and infrastructure, and digitally held information. As has been noted above, these cyber operations may be offensive or defensive in their nature and purpose, and these operations can take a variety of forms. 'Cyber activities' is employed as a collective term for the specific methods that are used to carry out cyber operations.

3 Cyber Operations in Situations of Armed Conflict

It is well understood that there is currently ongoing a seismic and likely permanent shift in the way in which inter-state hostilities, including attacks and warfare, are being carried out.[25] While traditionally warfare and armed attacks would be conducted openly by kinetic means and on a physical battlefield, attacks are now increasingly being perpetrated at a distance, surreptitiously by means of cyber operations using a range of technology and methods.[26]

These types of operations can be directed towards military targets, either in peacetime or during armed conflicts, such as to disable or to interfere with the use of particular weapons systems, other military hardware and installations, or communications systems.[27] Cyber operations can, however, also be used to target the civilian population or civilian infrastructure directly including so as to bring about immediate and substantial consequences or, alternatively, more subtle and long terms affects which are aimed at destabilising a state and its society, and undermining trust and confidence between a government and its population.[28] The wide ranging and developing means by which cyber

25 UN Working Group on mercenaries, note 3 at paragraphs 11 and 12.

26 ICRC note 9 at p.483.

27 ICRC, 'International humanitarian law and cyber operations during armed conflict', (2020) 102 (913) International Review of the Red Cross, ICRC, note 9 at p. 418–492.

28 Ibid.

hostilities are conducted, and the variety of impacts that such operations can have, make understanding the landscape and responding with legal frameworks very difficult.

The types of cyber activities that may be utilised by states include, but are not limited to: sabotage by way of the use of malware to disrupt, degrade, and/or destroy computer systems or networks; intelligence gathering by way of hacking to obtain information and data, or the use of spyware to gather information and data surreptitiously; surveillance through closed circuit television and other more sophisticated means including the use of facial recognition software, 'silhouette recognition', or satellite location tracking; the spreading of misinformation and disinformation online, either in a general or a more targeted way, including through the use of social media; and the gathering and analysis of big data.[29]

Cyber activities and operations are of immense benefit to states for a variety of reasons. First, the source of and perpetrators of operations are difficult, or perhaps even impossible, to identify. Second, they are less resource intensive than traditional military operations which are often conducted with vast numbers of people and military hardware at great resource and financial expense. Third, they can have substantial and widespread impacts with relatively minimal input, or alternatively, they can be used discreetly and in a targeted manner. Fourth, they will cause damage and impose a cost to opponents but are perhaps more likely to avoid a violent response than would a traditional use of armed force. Finally, they provide new avenues for the conduct of hostilities such as spreading of disinformation online or the disruption of civil engagement which seeks to spread discontent within society.

4 Cyber Operations by PMSC and Mercenaries in Situations of Armed Conflict

Traditionally PMSC and mercenaries have been engaged by states in traditional, kinetic uses of force including in the context of warfare. However, as a direct corollary to the development and use of cyber operations by States, PMSC and mercenaries have become active in this area and they are increasingly being

29 United Kingdom Ministry of Defence, Cyber Primer (2022) <https://assets.publishing.service.gov.uk/media/63623df5d3bf7f04e12196d0/Cyber_Primer_Edition_3.pdf> (last accessed 17 August 2024).

engaged by states including for the purposes of providing States with the necessary technology and capabilities to carry out cyber operations, to assist States in developing and implementing cyber operations, and/or to carry out activities for and on behalf of states, including both offensive and defensive operations.[30]

One of the reasons states use PMSC and mercenaries in cyberspace is that such entities can offer governments a wide range of cyber services and products. States may not have the necessary or sufficient technological capabilities to engage in defensive or offensive cyber operations, and engaging external entities to provide capabilities may be a necessary or simply a more time- and/or cost-efficient means of delivery, and it can put them at the forefront of such activities and give them a significant military and/or strategic advantage over other states or non-state entities. PMSC and other entities are continuously developing specialist cyber products that are at the cutting edge of technological development and which will be of great use to states.[31]

Further and in addition, the engaging of PMSC and mercenaries to carry out cyber operations is a useful means by which States can distance themselves from such operations and the consequences thereof, and preventing attribution, or at least making it incredibly difficult to establish. It is, of course, an initial challenge in identifying the source of a cyber operation but if the source of the operation is traced back to a private entity, a state can plausibly deny its involvement. It may even be a complete impossibility to determine whether the entity was acting for or on behalf of the state.

Considering the increasing prevalence of cyber activities, both defensive and offensive, both in the context of warfare and otherwise, and given the benefits for states of utilisation the capacity and skills that can be provided by PMSC and mercenaries, the market for relevant technology, skills and the carrying out of cyber operations is growing and it is likely to continuing growing significantly into the future. This growth has been highlighted as a concern by

30 Report of the UN Working Group on mercenaries as a means of violating human rights and impeding the exercise of the right of peoples to self-determination, 'The human rights impacts of mercenaries, mercenary-related actors, and private military and security companies engaging in cyber activities' (2021) A/76/151 (ref 3), pp.6–7; Tim Maurer and Wyatt Hoffman, The Privatization of Security and the Market for Cyber Tools and Services' (2019) <https://www.dcaf.ch/sites/default/files/publications/documents/Carnegie_MaurerHoffmann_July2019.pdf> (last accessed 17 August 2024).

31 Report of the UN Working Group on mercenaries as a means of violating human rights and impeding the exercise of the right of peoples to self-determination, 'The human rights impacts of mercenaries, mercenary-related actors, and private military and security companies engaging in cyber activities' (2021) A/76/151 (ref 3), pp 10–12.

both the ICRC and the UN Working Group on mercenaries, with the ICRC noting that cyber attacks 'are reportedly becoming more frequent and their severity is increasing more rapidly than experts had anticipated.'[32] Research into this area is therefore of particular importance as there is an increasing need for greater appreciation and understanding of the issue, and development of effective regulation.

5 Human Rights and Cyberspace

Much has been written in the academic literature about the deployment of cyber operations in the context of armed conflicts, and the consequent engagement and violations of international humanitarian law, but comparatively little is said about the human rights aspects.[33]

There is now a widespread consensus that human rights norms and standards shall and do apply to operations that are carried out by and on behalf of states in cyberspace just as they would in respect of traditional uses of force and kinetic warfare any cyber operation adversely affecting human rights, would therefore be within the ambit of humanrights treaties.[34] Furthermore, as has been explained by the UN Working Group on mercenaries: '[i]t is undeniable that cyber activities engage human rights norms and rules and have the ability to cause violations both in armed conflicts and in peacetime, and thus that a whole variety of rights are engaged'.[35] It is accepted law that human rights obligations continue to apply in times of armed conflict, even if the practicalities of doing so are challenging.[36]

Given the wide breadth and scope of cyber activities and operations, and particularly given the reality of currently unimaginable technological

---

32 ICRC note 9 at p 484; UN Working Group on mercenaries, note 3 paragraphs 20,25, and 35.

33 Notes 14 and 28.

34 M. Milanovic, 'Surveillance and cyber operations' in M. Gibney et al, The Routledge Handbook on Extraterritorial Human Rights Obligations' (Routledge, Oxford, 2022) at p. 369.

35 UN Working Group on mercenaries, note 3 at paragraph 60–68.

36 See e.g. Noam Lubell, Challenges in applying human rights law to armed conflict. International Review of the Red Cross. 2005; 87(860): 737–754. doi:10.1017/S1816383100184541; OHCHR, International Legal Protection of Human Rights in Armed Conflict (2011) HR/PUB/11/01; <https://opil.ouplaw.com/view/10.1093/law/9780198791393.001.0001/law-9780198791393> Daragh Murray, Elizabeth Wilmshurst, Françoise Hampson, Charles Garraway, Noam Lubell, Dapo Akande (eds), Practitioners' Guide to Human Rights Law in Armed Conflict (2016, CUP).

developments in the cyber sphere, as well as how, in what circumstances and to what end they are deployed, and in light of the fact that cyber operations can easily be deployed against, or have ramifications for, civilian populations, cyber operations are likely to engage the whole spectrum of human rights. The international human rights framework can therefore potentially provide a valuable means of regulating cyber activities. However, in order for this to take place, there is a need for a better understanding of the relationship as between cyber operations and human rights.

In the next section of this chapter, we identify examples of offensive cyber operations which can, and have been, deployed by PMSCs and mercenaries, and the human rights norms which may be engaged and violated as a consequence of those cyber operations. Given that this is an underexamined topic, this initial scoping is limited and the focus is on four types of focus cyber activities that can be linked to mercenaries and PMSC: (1) Targeting of infrastructure; (2) Destruction, Disruption or Theft of Data; (3) Surveillance; and (4) Disinformation / Interference with Elections. The depth of the examination is also necessarily limited but the primary purpose of this work is to begin a process of identifying when and how particular human rights may be engaged and violated in the course of cyber operations by these actors with more substantive research to be undertaken moving forward

6 Cyber Operations and Their Human Rights Implications

6.1 *Targeting of Infrastructure*

One of the most significant ways in which offensive cyber operations can be deployed is against state infrastructure, and while the occurrence of such events remains rare, it is increasing.[37] Malware can be used in order to disrupt or disable computer systems necessary for operating civilian infrastructure such as, for example, electricity generation plants or supply networks; the internet and communications systems including networks for mobile phone communications; the treatment and supply of water; and government operating systems which ensure general administration of state infrastructure, including healthcare, welfare, and social care.

These types of attacks, if successful, can have immediate, significant detrimental impacts upon the civilian population such as, for example, the disabling of electricity generation could result in hospitals being left without

37 UN Secretary General, note 5.

any or sufficient power which may prevent critical life sustaining care being provided to patients which could result in death and serious injury. Any interference with the internet or communications systems could interfere with trade and commerce and may create an economic shock with a lasting impact upon the civilian population. In addition, these types of cyber operations can have more subtle and long-term impacts, particularly if the issues created by the operation are difficult to rectify or attacks are repeated. For example, disruption of a system for the treatment and supply of water could result, over an extended period of time, in unsafe water being distributed to the civilian population which could have very serious long term health consequences. Similarly, the disruption of systems for the administration of state functions such as the assessment and collection of tax revenues, or the distribution of welfare benefits may have immediate and critical impact because people are left without money but they can also facilitate a longer-term break down in the relationship between the state and the civilian population if the public comes to believe the state is not in a position to execute public functions adequately.

The human rights consequences of such cyber operations are varied and multifaceted given the almost unlimited extent of operations that could be undertaken and the consequences thereof. Multiple human rights protected under international and regional human rights instruments are at serious risk, and the potential harms cut across the spectrum of human rights, including civil and political rights, and economic, social, and cultural rights. Applicable instruments include the International Covenant on Civil and Political Rights (ICCPR), International Covenant on Economic, Social, and Cultural Rights (ICESCR), European Convention on Human Rights (ECHR), African Charter on Human and Peoples' Rights (African Charter), and the Inter-American Convention on Human Rights (IACHR), among others.[38]

The right to life as guaranteed under Article 6 ICCPR, as well as Article 2 ECHR, Article 4 African Charter, and Article 4 IACHR would almost certainly be engaged given the possibility of serious consequences as a result of cyber operations directed in infrastructure critical for the maintenance of the civilian population and this right may be violated if death or serious injury resulting

38 International Covenant on Civil and Political Rights (Adopted 16 December 1966, Entered into Force 23 March 1976), 999 UNTS 171; .International Covenant on Economic, Social and Cultural Rights (Adopted: 16 December 1966, Entry into Force: 3 January 1976) 993 UNTS 3; European Convention on Human Rights and Fundamental Freedoms as amended by Protocols 11, 14, and 15, Council of Europe Treaty Series, No. 5 (1950); African Convention on Human and Peoples' Rights 1520 UNTS 217 (1981); Inter-American Convention on Human Rights OAS Treaty Series, N° 36 (1969).

in death is inflicted upon persons as a result of the operation. As has been argued: [i]t is easy to see why cyber operations against the healthcare sector directly implicate the right to life … those already undergoing medical treatment … may suffer life threatening harm or face the risk of such harm from disruptive cyber operations against hospital systems and equipment'.[39] In the context of armed conflict specifically, the Human Rights Committee has identified in General Comment 36 that: 'practices inconsistent with international humanitarian law, entailing a risk to the lives of civilian and other persons protected by international humanitarian law, including the targeting of civilians, civilian objects and object indispensable to the survival of the civilian population … would also violate Article 6 of the [ICCPR]Covenant'.

Further, the freedom of movement as articulated under Article 12 ICCPR may be violated if a cyber operation disrupts transport networks to such extent that people are unable to freely move around a country. Article 11 ICESCR, which recognises a right to an adequate standard of living including food, clothing and housing, may be violated if a state is Unable to administer a welfare system, and similarly, the Article 12 ICESCR right to the highest attainable standard of physical and mental health may be violated by the disruption or destruction of healthcare provision.

6.2 *Destruction, Disruption or Theft of Data*

A potentially more subtle cyber operation in terms of its immediate visible impact but one that is likely to be highly disruptive, and also pose a very significant threat to a civilian population, is the interference with data stored by a state or private entities. As is well known, in the age of the internet and electronic communications, vast amounts of personal data are collected and stored in relation to the civilian population; this includes health data, financial information; and other intimate, sensitive, and confidential details about peoples' lives.

Cyber operations can be directed at such data in various ways including the outright extraction and theft of data; the manipulation of data; the destruction of data with or without its extraction; the taking hostage of data by the use of ransomware; or by disrupting access to the data. The purpose of such activities can be to obtain valuable information which could be used to identify vulnerabilities within the civilian population that could be exploited by other means at a later date; to disrupt the delivery of public functions such as healthcare by way of data being lost or otherwise unavailable to be used or, even more

39 Priya Urs and others, 'The International Law Protections against Cyber Operations Targeting the Healthcare Sector' (Oxford Institute for Ethics, Law and Armed Conflict (ELAC) 2023) <https://www.elac.ox.ac.uk/new-research-report-the-international-law-protections-against-cyber-operations-targeting-the-healthcare-sector/> accessed 11 July 2024 p. 175

sinister, healthcare data being manipulated so that incorrect treatments are administered; and/or to induce frustration and fear among the public. The targeting may also have the consequence of people being unable to gain access to their money or use electronic payments which can be incredibly disruptive to daily life but also have serious long-term economic impacts.

The interference with personal data in the various ways described will certainly engage and likely amount to a violation of the right to privacy as guaranteed under Article 17 ICCPR as well as Article 8 ECHR and Article 11 IACHR. It can also be said that the interference or theft of data could constitute a violation of the right of property as protected under e.g. Article 1 of Protocol 1 to the European Convention on Human Rights.[40] The European Court of Human Rights has recognised that the protection of personal data is of fundamental importance to a person's enjoyment of their right to private and family life as guaranteed under Article 8 ECHR[41] and therefore, albeit in the purely domestic context, the Court has determined that the release of information may fall within the scope of Article 8[42] as does the taking of personal data in circumstances where there was no lawful authority to do so.[43]

6.3 *Surveillance*

The surveillance of a civilian population or particular parts of the population is another cyber operation which can be carried out on behalf of a state. The purpose of and ways in which such operations can be conducted are multifarious. These operations may be conducted by spyware being placed in a computer system allowing the monitoring and gathering of data; the interception and monitoring of electronic communications; the infiltration of closed-circuit television system; and the use of facial and body recognition software as a means of identifying particular persons. The purpose of such surveillance may be to monitor particular persons; to obtain private and confidential information; as a means of identifying trends and habits which could be exploited for future purposes, and which would constitute planning for future operations; or for profiling the general population.

These types of activities when conducted as part of cyber operations will squarely engage the right to privacy. It could also violate the right to freedom of movement if surveillance activity is preventing or hindering persons for moving

40 European Convention on Human Rights, Council of Europe Treaty Series, No. 5.

41 Satakunnan Markkinapörssi Oy v Satamedia Oy v Finland (Application No. 931/13, 27 June 2017), paragraph 137.

42 Rotaru v Romania (Application No. 28341/95, 4 May 2000), paragraph 43.

43 Modestu v Greece (Application No, 51693/13, 16 March 2017), paragraph 29.

about as they would otherwise do (Article 12 ICCPR, Article 2 of Protocol 4 ECHR, Article 12 African Charter, Article 22 IACHR). It could also violate the right to freedom of thought as guaranteed under Article 18 ICCPR, Article 9 ECHR, Article 8 African Charter and Article 13 IACHR; the right to freedom of expression under Article 19 ICCPR, Article 10 ECHR Article 9 African Charter, and Article 13 IACHR; and the right to freedom of association under Article 22 ICCPR, Article 11 ECHR, Article 10 African Charter, and Article 16 IACHR if persons are deterred or inhibited from enjoying such rights as a consequence of their knowledge or belief that they are being surveiled and monitored.[44] In a thematic report on 'Surveillance and human rights,' the UN Special Rapporteur on freedom of opinion and expression explained that: '[t]argets of surveillance suffer interference with their rights to privacy and freedom of opinion and expression whether the effort to monitor is successful or not'.[45] While not in the context of cyber operations, the European Court of Human Rights has determined that mass surveillance,[46] as well as covert surveillance,[47] can interfere with the right to privacy.

6.4 *Disinformation/Interference with Elections*

Cyber operations may also take the form of spreading of disinformation which can occur in the context of state elections, including through the use of social media. This type of operation can be carried out by circulating false information which is designed to undermine a specific person or position; the creation of false support for a particular person or position, and/or the censuring of an another person or position, which is designed to influence group-think; and the use of AI-generated videos in order to, for example, present a false impression of a person or to encourage viewers to believe they have said or done something, or adopted a position on an issue, which is untrue or misleading. Other methods which may be deployed include direct interference with electronic voting systems and the collating of votes.

The purpose of the operation may be to directly influence an election in a particular way or in favour of a certain candidate, which directly undermines the electoral and democratic process. It can also be deployed, however, – in perhaps an even more nefarious and malign way – as a means of casting doubt

44 See also e.g. Article 9 ECHR, Article 10 ECHR, Article 11 ECHR.

45 Report of the Special Rapporteur on the promotion and protection of the right to freedom of opinion and expression, 'Surveillance and human rights' A/HRC/41/35, paragraph 21.

46 The Association for European Integration and Human Rights and Ekimdzhiev v Bulgaria (Application No. 62540/00, 28 June 2007), paragraph 71.

47 PG and JH v United Kingdom (Application No. 44787/98, 25 September 2001), paragraph 59.

on the security and integrity of the democratic process, without having any direct effect, which undermines and damages public confidence in the government and society, and serves to precipitate disharmony and instability that weakens social fabric and undermines national unity.

This type of cyber operation will engage and violate various human rights norms and standards. The interference with discourse in the context of an election by the means identified above is likley to constitute a violation the right to free elections as protected under Article 25 ICCPR, Article 3 of Protocol 1 of the ECHR, Article 13 African Charter, and Article 23 IACHR. If the cyber operation is conducted by means which prevents or hinders people from freely participating in election campaigning, expressly their views, and/or engaging with other people in pursuit of a specific objective, the cyber operation is likely to violation rights in respect of freedom of expression, freedom of assembly, freedom of thought and conscience, as outlined above in Section 3, as well as the right to hold opinions without interference as guaranteed under Article 19 ICCPR.

6.4.1 Human Rights Impacts on Persons in Vulnerable Situations

It is also important to take note of the fact that offensive cyber operations are likely to be targeted at certain sections of the population and to have disproportionate impacts on particular persons or groups, most likely, the most marginalised and vulnerable people in society. It should be recalled that Article 1 of the Universal Declaration on Human Rights sets forth that '[a]*ll human beings are born free and equal in dignity and in rights*' and Article 2 provides that: '[e]veryone is entitled to all the rights and freedoms set forth in this Declaration without distinction of any kind such as race, colour, sex, language, religion, political or other opinion, national or social origin, property birth or other status', and that such protections and similar non-exhaustive prohibitions on discrimination are also included in Article 26 ICCPR, Article 2(2) ICESCR, Article 14 ECHR, Article 2 African Charter, and Article 1 IACHR.

While all civilians are at an increased risk of harm during armed conflicts, it is often persons in the most vulnerable situations such as children, older persons, persons with disabilities, and displaced persons, and the LGBTI+ community who experience the most severe impacts. Cyber operations during armed conflict are no different. The targeting of infrastructure, surveillance, and data theft results in clearly different and differentiated impacts for individuals and groups in vulnerable situations.

For example, with 20% of the world's children living in conflicted affected zones, human rights risks and impacts in armed conflicts are of real and urgent concern.[48] UNICEF in its 2022 report Protecting Children in Cyberconflicts identified a myriad of direct and indirect risks to children resulting from cyber operations, stating that '[h]arms range from direct targeting for influence and recruitment into armed forces and armed groups, to personal data manipulation and theft, to cyber attacks on infrastructure across sectors critical to child well-being such as education and health facilities.'[49] Such risks limit severely the rights of children to healthcare, education, privacy, protection from sexual exploitation, and liberty, among others.[50]

Similarly, cyber operations that result in damage to critical infrastructure, such as hospitals and schools, and displacement of populations results in particular harms for persons with disabilities. The UN Special Rapporteur on rights of persons with disabilities emphasises the 'invisibility' of persons with disabilities in armed conflicts and laments the 'data gap' that 'undermines the ability to fully comprehend the actual harm an attack might cause.'[51] The Committee on the Rights of Persons with Disabilities has highlighted that in situations of armed conflict persons with disabilities are 'disproportionately at risk of being neglected, excluded or even abused because of their impairments and traumas, particularly the most vulnerable women and children with disabilities.'[52] In addition, the Committee in its General Comment 6 has stressed the additional and specific challenges faced by persons with disabilities in situations of armed conflicts. It cites displaced persons with disabilities being denied 'equal access to basic necessities, such as water, sanitation, food and shelter', women with disabilities having a 'particularly increased risk of violence, including sexual violence, exploitation or abuse', and children with disabilities facing additional barriers to education.[53]

---

48 UN Committee on the rights of the child, 'End the killing of children in armed conflict, UN committee urges,' 20 November 2023: International Convention against the Recruitment, Use, Financing and Training of Mercenaries UNGA Res. 44/34 New York, 4 December 1989.

49 UNICEF, Office of Global Insight and Policy (July 2022) <https://www.unicef.org/innocenti/reports/protecting-children-cyberconflicts> at p.3.

50 UN Convention on the Rights of the Child, (1989) General Assembly resolution 44/25, Article 24 health, Article 28 education, Article 16 privacy, Article 34 sexual exploitation, Article 37 torture and liberty.

51 Report of the Special Rapporteur on the rights of persons with disabilities, Gerard Quinn, (2022) paragraph 25.

52 Press Release, 'Persons with disabilities 'forgotten victims' of Syria's conflict – UN committee' September 2013 <https://www.ohchr.org/en/press-releases/2013/09/persons-disabilities-forgotten-victims-syrias-conflict-un-committee>.

53 Committee on the Rights of Persons with Disabilities, General comment No.6 on equality and non-discrimination, 26 April 2018, CRPD/C/GC/6 <https://www.ohchr.org/en/documents/general-comments-and-recommendations/general-comment-no6-equality-and-non-discrimination> paragraphs 44–45.

which will need to be confronted in the development of an effective regulatory framework.

7.1 *Limitations in Regulatory Frameworks*

One of the principal issues that will need to be confronted in the development of measures and frameworks for protecting human rights in the context of offensive cyber operations is the refinement of our understanding of the nature and the implementation of cyber operations, and their effects on civilian populations, both in the immediate and longer term. Without such an understanding it is difficult to establish exactly how particular human rights can be violated. There will also need to be some conceptual work undertaken, both in the context of particular actions and litigation, but also extra-judicially, in mapping cyber operations and the effects on our existing understanding and application of human rights norms and standards.

7.2 *Attribution*

A particular issue that will arise in the context of establishing human rights violations and in bringing actions against perpetrators, either in court or through other mechanisms, is the issue of attribution. As identified above, one of the particular benefits of cyber operations for states, and particularly those carried out on behalf of states by PMSC and mercenaries, is the difficulty or even the impossibility of such operations being attributed to the state. This is a consequence of the fact that such operations are conducted remotely from a distance and by means that are often deliberately concealed from tracing. The use of third parties such as PMSC and mercenaries also creates a further degree of separation, and one that is potentially unbridgeable from the originator of the cyber operation. As one report frames it:

> attribution of cyber operations to states is notoriously difficult. On the one hand, despite advances in cyber forensics, it is often impossible to trace with confidence the factual origin of certain operations, given the Internet's decentralized nature, user anonymity and the use of spoofing techniques. On the other hand, the legal standard for attributing the conduct of private groups or individuals to states is exacting.[57]

---

57 Priya Urs and others, 'The International Law Protections against Cyber Operations Targeting the Healthcare Sector' (Oxford Institute for Ethics, Law and Armed Conflict (ELAC) 2023) <https://www.elac.ox.ac.uk/new-research-report-the-international-law-protections-against-cyber-operations-targeting-the-healthcare-sector/> accessed 11 July 2024 note 39, pp. 170–171.

In a final example, the LGBTI+ community is at particular risk from both data theft and surveillance. In a 2019 report to the Human Rights Council, the Independent Expert on Sexual Orientation and Gender Identity highlighted that there are often particular risks around data collection and management for LGBTI+ persons noting that 'the risks are exacerbated owing to the associated stigmatization in certain social contexts, which might create a motivation to hack or steal the data or otherwise unlawfully access it.'[54] It follows, therefore, that data theft by PMSC or mercenaries in cyber operations render LGBTI+ persons particularly vulnerable as it is already well known that such data may be used 'as the basis for surveillance, harassment, entrapment, arrest and persecution by government officials.'[55] In addition, civilian displacement caused by cyber operations that damage State infrastructure can result in heightened human rights risks for LGBTI+ persons such as 'stigmatization, sexual and gender-based violence, abuse by or lack of protection from security forces, arbitrary detention and exclusion from access to essential basic services.'[56]

7 Regulatory and Accountability Challenges

The chapter so far has considered the evolution of cyber operations as an addition or alternative to traditional kinetic means of conducting hostilities, attacks and warfare, the role of PMSC and mercenaries in cyber operations, the nature and impact of various operations, and the impact on human rights protections. This final section briefly identifies and considers some of the challenges which exist in relation to the regulation of cyber operations by PMSC and mercenaries and the enforcement of human rights norms and standards. Once again, the matters identified are not intended to be exhaustive but rather considers some of the key limitations of protective mechanisms, which will need to be subjected to more detailed analysis elsewhere, and the issues

54 Report of the Independent Expert on protection against violence and discrimination based on sexual orientation and gender identity Victor Madrigal-Borloz, 'Data collection and management as a means to create heightened awareness of violence and discrimination based on sexual orientation and gender identity' A/HRC/41/45 at paragraph 17.

55 Independent Expert SOGI, note 54 at paragraph 22.

56 Report of the Independent Expert on protection against violence and discrimination based on sexual orientation and gender identity, Victor Madrigal-Borloz, 'Peace and Security' A/77/235 at paragraph 52.

which will need to be confronted in the development of an effective regulatory framework.

7.1 *Limitations in Regulatory Frameworks*

One of the principal issues that will need to be confronted in the development of measures and frameworks for protecting human rights in the context of offensive cyber operations is the refinement of our understanding of the nature and the implementation of cyber operations, and their effects on civilian populations, both in the immediate and longer term. Without such an understanding it is difficult to establish exactly how particular human rights can be violated. There will also need to be some conceptual work undertaken, both in the context of particular actions and litigation, but also extra-judicially, in mapping cyber operations and the effects on our existing understanding and application of human rights norms and standards.

7.2 *Attribution*

A particular issue that will arise in the context of establishing human rights violations and in bringing actions against perpetrators, either in court or through other mechanisms, is the issue of attribution. As identified above, one of the particular benefits of cyber operations for states, and particularly those carried out on behalf of states by PMSC and mercenaries, is the difficulty or even the impossibility of such operations being attributed to the state. This is a consequence of the fact that such operations are conducted remotely from a distance and by means that are often deliberately concealed from tracing. The use of third parties such as PMSC and mercenaries also creates a further degree of separation, and one that is potentially unbridgeable from the originator of the cyber operation. As one report frames it:

> attribution of cyber operations to states is notoriously difficult. On the one hand, despite advances in cyber forensics, it is often impossible to trace with confidence the factual origin of certain operations, given the Internet's decentralized nature, user anonymity and the use of spoofing techniques. On the other hand, the legal standard for attributing the conduct of private groups or individuals to states is exacting.[57]

57 Priya Urs and others, 'The International Law Protections against Cyber Operations Targeting the Healthcare Sector' (Oxford Institute for Ethics, Law and Armed Conflict (ELAC) 2023) <https://www.elac.ox.ac.uk/new-research-report-the-international-law-protections-against-cyber-operations-targeting-the-healthcare-sector/> accessed 11 July 2024 note 39, pp. 170–171.

In a final example, the LGBTI+ community is at particular risk from both data theft and surveillance. In a 2019 report to the Human Rights Council, the Independent Expert on Sexual Orientation and Gender Identity highlighted that there are often particular risks around data collection and management for LGBTI+ persons noting that 'the risks are exacerbated owing to the associated stigmatization in certain social contexts, which might create a motivation to hack or steal the data or otherwise unlawfully access it.'[54] It follows, therefore, that data theft by PMSC or mercenaries in cyber operations render LGBTI+ persons particularly vulnerable as it is already well known that such data may be used 'as the basis for surveillance, harassment, entrapment, arrest and persecution by government officials.'[55] In addition, civilian displacement caused by cyber operations that damage State infrastructure can result in heightened human rights risks for LGBTI+ persons such as 'stigmatization, sexual and gender-based violence, abuse by or lack of protection from security forces, arbitrary detention and exclusion from access to essential basic services.'[56]

7 Regulatory and Accountability Challenges

The chapter so far has considered the evolution of cyber operations as an addition or alternative to traditional kinetic means of conducting hostilities, attacks and warfare, the role of PMSC and mercenaries in cyber operations, the nature and impact of various operations, and the impact on human rights protections. This final section briefly identifies and considers some of the challenges which exist in relation to the regulation of cyber operations by PMSC and mercenaries and the enforcement of human rights norms and standards. Once again, the matters identified are not intended to be exhaustive but rather considers some of the key limitations of protective mechanisms, which will need to be subjected to more detailed analysis elsewhere, and the issues

54 Report of the Independent Expert on protection against violence and discrimination based on sexual orientation and gender identity Victor Madrigal-Borloz, 'Data collection and management as a means to create heightened awareness of violence and discrimination based on sexual orientation and gender identity' A/HRC/41/45 at paragraph 17.

55 Independent Expert SOGI, note 54 at paragraph 22.

56 Report of the Independent Expert on protection against violence and discrimination based on sexual orientation and gender identity, Victor Madrigal-Borloz, 'Peace and Security' A/77/235 at paragraph 52.

This can be even more difficult when dealing with notoriously opaque PMSC and mercenaries.

7.3 *Accountability*

In 2023 the UN Working Group on mercenaries concluded that 'accountability is rare' when seeking to hold mercenaries and PMSCs and their personnel to account for violations of human rights.[58] In addition to the general difficulties around establishing attribution and the originators of cyber operations, additional layers of complication surround PMSC and mercenaries and make accountability particularly problematic. These include:

(a) the secrecy and opacity surrounding the activities of mercenaries, mercenary-related actors and private military and security companies, as well as the lack of transparency and of access to information on their activities;
(b) complex business and corporate structures and issues related to jurisdiction; and
(c) national and international regulatory gaps.[59]

At the same time, international criminal law is insufficiently developed at present to play an effective role in ensuring criminal accountability for human rights violations by these types of actors. Similarly, criminal accountability via national courts is limited and there is negligible legal precedent despite appropriate legislative provisions in some states, including the States that are party to the UN Convention on mercenarism that criminalises mercenarism, and obliges State parties to investigate, prosecute, and sanction such crimes.[60]

These obstacles and regulatory gaps require urgent attention given the increasing rate of human rights violations perpetrated in the cyber sphere by PMSC and mercenaries.

---

58 Report of the Working Group on the use of mercenaries as a means of violating human rights and impeding the exercise of the right of peoples to self-determination, 'Access to justice, accountability and remedies for victims of mercenaries, mercenary-related actors and private military and security companies,' A/HRC/51/25 at paragraph 9.

59 Working Group on mercenaries, note 58.

60 International Convention against the Recruitment, Use, Financing and Training of Mercenaries UNGA Res. 44/34 New York, 4 December 1989.

8 Conclusion

This chapter has sought to contribute to an underexamined topic by highlighting the rise of PMSC and mercenaries involved in offensive cyber operations in armed conflicts. It has also explained some of the very specific ways in which PMSC and mercenaries engage in armed conflicts via cyber operations, and the serious human rights challenges arising from that engagement. An extensive assortment of human rights, ranging across civil, political, economic, social, and cultural rights, are at risk of violation from cyber operations carried out by mercenaries and PMSC, including the rights to life, health, and privacy, as well as the rights to freedom of expression, thought, and association. Given the narrow focus of the chapter and the breadth of the subject, it is evident that more research needs to be undertaken, and more academic attention paid to the topic.

What is also clear is that the particularities of cyber operations coupled with the specificities of PMSC and mercenaries put human rights at great risk during armed conflicts, and those risks of abuse are exacerbated greatly for civilians in vulnerable situations such as children, persons with disabilities, displaced persons, and LGBTI+ persons. Heightened risks of violations and subsequent impacts during cyber operations are therefore of great concern to these marginalised groups.

At the same time, regulatory gaps, difficulties in establishing attribution, and scant human rights or criminal accountability are particularly problematic. States need to discontinue or prevent the use of PMSC and mercenaries for this type of cyber warfare in order to prevent egregious violations of human rights. Filling regulatory gaps and establishing effective mechanisms for accountability are vital and critical to ensure deterrence and access to justice for impacted civilians. States ought to be demonstrating their commitment to prevention of violations of human rights by mercenaries and PMSC generally, and more specifically during cyber operations, by ratifying existing international treaties and/or publicly committing to other regulatory standards. This commitment could be shown, for example, by ratifying the UN Convention on mercenarism which requires national criminalisation of mercenary activities by State Parties. Similarly, adhering to the Montreux Document which articulates how international law applies to the activities of private military and security companies during armed conflict and sets out good regulatory practices would demonstrate that a state is taking the issue seriously.[61] Additionally, going

61 Sorcha MacLeod and Rebecca DeWinter-Schmitt, "Certifying private security companies: effectively ensuring the corporate responsibility to respect human rights?", *Business and Human Rights Journal*, vol. 4, No. 1 (2019), pp. 55–77.

forward, States must ensure that the provisions of the draft instrument of the UN Open-ended Intergovernmental Working Group on PMSC fully address the human rights challenges of cyber operations by recognising the diversity and gravity of possible violations. They must also make special efforts to ensure that any final instrument guarantees protection to persons in the most vulnerable situations who are susceptible to the most egregious harms and violence from cyber operations. Absent acknowledgement of and concrete action on cyber operations by mercenaries and PMSC, civilian populations will suffer ever increasing harms with impunity.

CHAPTER 13

Cyber Espionage and the Nordics: Between Principles and Pragmatism

Asbjørn Thranov[1]

1 Introduction

Cyber espionage has become a prevalent method for states to gather confidential information online. The vast interconnectedness of the Internet provides a target-rich environment for states to collect large amounts of data at an unprecedented speed and scale.[2] Cyber espionage is also characterised by being a relatively risk-free enterprise.[3] States have a global reach to spy on other states without needing physical proximity to the target.[4] In addition, the inherent anonymity offered by the Internet makes it extremely challenging to trace cyber espionage activities back to their perpetrators, allowing states to conceal or eliminate their digital footprints easily.[5] Consequently, the political and diplomatic repercussions of getting caught engaging in cyber espionage are significantly lower compared to traditional forms of physical espionage.[6]

Unsurprisingly, the Nordic countries[7] have embraced cyber espionage as a method to collect information.[8] Cyber espionage is a force multiplier for these

1 Asbjørn Thranov holds a PhD in international law from the University of Copenhagen. He previously worked as a legal advisor and cyber security analyst for the Danish Defense.

2 See generally, *Offensive cyber-programmes – An ideal business model for states*, technical report (General Intelligence and Security Service of the Netherlands, February 2020), 4–5, https://english.aivd.nl/publications/publications/2020/02/26/publicationaivdoffensivecyber-programmes---an-ideal-business-model-for-states.

3 See generally, *Offensive cyber-programmes – An ideal business model for states*, 4–5.

4 *Intelligence Outlook 2022*, technical report (Danish Security and Intelligence Service, December 2022), 35, https://www.feddis.dk/globalassets/fe /dokumenter/2022 /udsyn2022/-fe_udsyn_22_uk-.pdf.

5 See generally *Offensive cyber-programmes – An ideal business model for states*, 4–5.

6 See generally, *Offensive cyber-programmes – An ideal business model for states*, 6.

7 In this chapter, the Nordic states refer to Denmark, Finland, Norway and Sweden.

8 All of the Nordic states, except Sweden, have publicly admitted using cyber espionage to gain unauthorised access to other countries' computer networks to gather information. See Section 1.3 below.

 | DOI:10.1163/9789004703933_014

small but high-tech countries, giving them more strategic power through intelligence insights.[9]

Yet the Nordic states face a well-known dilemma regarding cyber espionage. On the one hand, they want to adopt this new technology to tackle emerging threats and gather intelligence. On the other hand, highly digitised societies are vulnerable to cyber espionage, which puts them at risk of losing valuable information to strategic competitors.[10]

This chapter analyzes how the Nordic states balance the need for operational flexibility to conduct peacetime cyber espionage with the aim of establishing some normative guardrails for state activities in cyberspace. Using Nordic legal pragmatism as a lens, this chapter explores the Nordic states' views on the interaction between (cyber)[11] espionage and international law. It is argued that the Nordic states do not give much importance to international law, particularly the principle of territorial sovereignty, when it comes to their own and others' cyber espionage activities.

The Nordic approach might not result from deliberate pragmatic legal thinking but aligns with a pragmatist view of international law. Under this view, legal rules are just one of several factors that states consider when conducting their international affairs. The Nordic countries seem to prioritize factors beyond international law when it comes to cyber espionage.

This chapter is structured accordingly. Section 2 presents a working definition of cyber espionage and introduces Nordic legal pragmatism as a viable framework to study the Nordic states' views of cyber espionage under international law. Section 3 illustrates that most Nordic countries have publicly acknowledged their engagement in cyber espionage through scrutiny of their national intelligence laws and other available information. In Section 4, I analyse the Nordic states' perspective on the legality of peacetime (cyber) espionage under international law. To gain a more honest understanding of

9 See e.g., David A. Wallace, Amy H. McCarthy, and Mark Visger, "Peeling Back the Onion of Cyber Espionage after Tallinn 2.0," *Maryland Law Review* 78, no. 2 (2019): 212; Mikkel Storm Jensen, "Småstater og cybervåben – nye muligheder og nye begrænsninger," *Økonomi & Politik* 93. Årgang, no. 3 (2020): 17–18; Joseph S Nye Jr, "Cyber power," *Harvard Kennedy School,Belfer Center for Science and International Affairs*, May 2010, 19.

10 Kubo Macak has labelled this tension a 'glass house dilemma' as states try to navigate their need for operational flexibility with restrictive rules to protect themselves from other states' malicious cyber activities. See Kubo Macak, "On the Shelf, but Close at Hand: The Contribution of Non-State Initiatives to International Cyber Law," AJIL *Unbound* 113 (2019): 82–84.

11 In this chapter, brackets around the word 'cyber' indicate that a given statement applies to both cyber espionage and traditional intelligence collection more broadly.

the Nordic states' position on international law as it applies to cyberspace, I examine official national documents that have received little attention from international legal experts. Section 5 analyzes the Nordic states' interpretation of the principle of territorial sovereignty in the context of cyberspace. It highlights the discrepancy between the Nordic states' public stance on sovereignty as a primary rule of international law and their real-world implementation with regard to (cyber) espionage. Section 6 claims that the political norm against economic cyber espionage for commercial gains, which the Nordic states have sought to promote with other like-minded Western countries, is ineffective in curbing economic cyber espionage. Section 7 asserts that international and domestic law provides little protection and deterrence against espionage, including cyber espionage, a reality known and seemingly accepted by the Nordic states. Section 8 presents conclusions.

2 Definition of Cyber Espionage and Conceptual Framing

2.1 *Cyber Espionage: Collection of Information in Cyberspace*

There is currently no universally accepted definition of intelligence or espionage, including cyber espionage that is recognised on an international level.[12] This lack of an internationally agreed definition of espionage poses challenges for the legal classification and examination of cyber espionage as states use different terms to describe their information collection. For instance, the term 'intelligence activity' can encompass all intelligence-related activities, including intelligence collection and covert operations carried out by a state's intelligence services.[13] By contrast, espionage is often defined more narrowly than intelligence[14] although a firm distinction cannot be drawn between these two terms.

---

12 See, e.g. Ido Kilovaty, "World Wide Web of Exploitations – The Case of Peacetime Cyber Espionage Operations under International Law: Towards a Contextual Approach," *Columbia Science and Technology Law Review* 18, no. 1 (2016): 46 (noting that 'definition is prone to becoming outdated almost instantaneously'); Glenn Sulmasy and John C Yoo, "Counterintuitive: intelligence operations and international law," *Michigan journal of international law* 28, no. 3 (2007): 637 637 ([There is] 'no internationally recognised and workable definition of "intelligence collection").

13 Ashley S Deeks, "Confronting and adapting: Intelligence agencies and international law," *Va. L. Rev.* 102 (2016): 600 at footnote 1.

14 'Espionage is a much narrower topic than "intelligence," much of which is collected via open source information, voluntary exchanges of information among nations, and technical means such as satellite imagery and signals intelligence that are generally accepted as legal by the international community'; US Department of Defense Office of

According to the Norwegian Intelligence Service (NIS), 'intelligence' refers to 'both the activity and the product of state-sanctioned collection, analysis and assessment of data and information, either openly or covertly, to gain advan-tages in decision-making processes.'[15] This concise definition provides a valid starting point for defining cyber espionage as it includes three key elements often associated with states' digital spying:

1. The Norwegian definition focuses on '*state-sanctioned collection*' of information. Espionage is mainly an interstate phenomenon in which states spy against each other. Since espionage is largely state-led, it naturally brings this activity within public international law.
2. Espionage is often conducted '*covertly*', distinguishing spying from other open methods of gathering information, such as the consensual exchange of information between states through diplomatic channels. Cyber espionage is by nature almost always conducted covertly as the sole purpose is to hide the intrusion itself and the author behind.[16]
3. Espionage is conducted to collect data and information '*to gain advantages in decision-making processes*'. The primary objective of cyber espionage is to exfiltrate confidential data from the target network or to map the targeted system. States use cyber espionage to gain an advantage or even superiority in information over their competitors. This helps them advance their national interests and improve their relative power position on the international stage.[17] The difference between cyber espionage and offensive cyber operations is that the former focuses on collecting data, while the latter is intended to cause destructive or disruptive effects on target systems or connected infrastructure.

General Counsel, *Assessment of International Legal Issues in Information Operations*, 1999, 45. See also Geoffrey B. Demarest, "Espionage in International Law," *Denver Journal of International Law and Policy* 24, no. 2 (1995): 347 ('Espionage should be narrowly defined to exclude acts of technical intelligence gathering').

15 *FOCUS 2022 – The Norwegian Intelligence Service's assessment of current security challenges*, technical report (Norwegian Intelligence Service, January 2022), 18, https://www.etterretningstjenesten.no/publikasjoner/fokus/focus-english/Focus%202022%20%20-%20english.pdf/_/attachment/inline/dc86257779cb4f0abc4c9883c32fb65a:161a477e1ab332bdf02ed556e6c963251537bf22/Focus%202022%20%20-%20english.pdf.

16 'Secrecy is often a defining feature of cyber espionage, and the consequences are thus difficult to detect; Danish Defense Intelligence Service, *Intelligence Outlook 2022*, December 2022, p. 39.

17 The 2022 annual threat assessment of the Danish Defence Intelligence Service predicted that as 'the competition intensifies between state actors, rival states will increasingly try to steal information through espionage, in particular, cyber espionage'; *Intelligence Outlook 2022*, 35.

For this chapter, NIS's definition needs slight modification to capture the technical aspect of cyber espionage, which involves hacking into another state's computer systems to gather information in cyberspace. As such, this chapter defines cyber espionage as a state-sponsored covert collection of data and information from another state's computer systems to gain political, military or economic advantages.

2.2 *A Nordic Pragmatist Approach to International Law*

This chapter views the Nordic states' approach to cyber espionage under international law through the lens of Nordic legal pragmatism. Legal pragmatism is a broad approach to law that emphasises the practical consequences of legal interpretation and the importance of context.[18] Legal pragmatism is not a distinct legal theory, but rather a method that evaluates the efficacy of rules by analysing their practical consequences and success in fulfilling objectives.[19] Its focus lies on the practical and actual application of legal principles, rather than solely on the underlying good intentions.

Legal pragmatists, informed by the work of justice Oliver Wendell Holmes – a pivotal figure in both legal pragmatism and realism – emphasise the importance of critically evaluating legal concepts. Holmes famously argued that abstract legal principles are insufficient for resolving complex legal issues.[20] By this, he meant that general principles lack practical application until they are grounded in the specificities of a given case. He advocated for a rigorous examination of these abstract principles, metaphorically described as applying a healthy dose of 'cynical acid' to determine their effectiveness in real-world scenarios.[21]

In the same way, this chapter aims to provide an acid bath for the Nordic states' approach to cyber espionage under international law. This chapter argues that the Nordic countries apply international law, precisely the principle of sovereignty, to cyber espionage more pragmatically than what is expressed in their 'black letter' approaches to applying international law to cyberspace.

---

18 For contemporary explanations of pragmatism, generally see Michael J. Glennon, *The fog of law: pragmatism, security, and international law* (Washington, D.C: Woodrow Wilson Center Press, 2010); Tor-Inge Harbo, "Folkerettspragmatisme," *Kritisk juss* 46, no. 3 (December 2020): 222–235; Sverre Blandhol, *Nordisk rettspragmatisme: Savigny, Ørsted og Schweigaard om vitenskap og metode* (Copenhagen: DJØF, 2005).

19 Michael M Lieberman, "The pragmatic method and international law in the fight against terrorism," *Martinus Nijhoff Publishers*, 2008, 195; Blandhol, *Nordisk rettspragmatisme*, 47ff.

20 This is the idea that Holmes emphasised in his famous quote: 'General principles do not decide concrete cases'; Lochner v. New York, 198 U.S. 45, 76 (1905) (Holmes, J., dissenting).

21 Oliver Wendell Holmes, "The Path of the Law," *Harvard Law Review* 457 (1897): 5.

As such, legal pragmatism is a model that explains how the Nordic countries view cyber espionage vis-à-vis international law, even though this approach may not be actively chosen or even recognised by Nordic states themselves.

Legal pragmatism has a deep-rooted tradition in Nordic legal culture.[22] Nordic legal pragmatism is characterised by its emphasis on utility and the resolution of practical legal issues, without reference to philosophical ideas, morality, or will.[23] This pragmatic approach has undoubtedly influenced significant parts of Nordic legal thought and the practical application of the law.[24] Yet legal pragmatism is likely more commonly used in the Nordic countries when applying national law, but less common when approaching international law.[25]

There is no single definition that can capture all of the nuances of Nordic legal pragmatism, but it can be characterised by at least four main tenets[26] which are:

- *Anti-fundamentalism*: Legal pragmatism is antifoundational in rejecting the idea that there is a single, objective truth about the law.[27] Legal pragmatists often cast doubt on whether abstract legal categories and principles truly yield the intended outcomes they claim to achieve.[28]
- *Contextualism*: Legal pragmatism emphasises the importance of context in legal reasoning. Pragmatists argue that legal assessments

22 See generally, Sverre Blandhol, "Rettspragmatismen i perspektiv," *Kritisk juss (Online)* 46, no. 3 (2020): 166–178. Some scholars believe that there is a unique Nordic approach to legal pragmatism. See, e.g., Blandhol, *Nordisk rettspragmatisme*, while others argue that this approach is not sufficiently distinct from other forms of legal pragmatism. See, e.g., Jens Evald and Sten Schaumburg-Müller, eds., *Retsfilosofi, retsvidenskab og retskildelære*, 1. udg., 1. opl (København: Juristog Økonomforbundets Forl, 2004), 93; Jørgen Dalberg-Larsen, "Sverre Blandhol: Nordisk rettspragmatisme. Savigny, Ørsted og Schweigaard om vitenskap og metode," *Tidsskrift for Rettsvitenskap* 119, nos. 4–5 (November 2006): 652.

23 Carsten Munk-Hansen, *Retsvidenskabsteori*, 1. udgave. (Kbh: Juristog Økonomforbundet, 2014), 162.

24 Evald and Schaumburg-Müller, *Retsfilosofi, retsvidenskab og retskildelære*, 69–99; Blandhol, *Nordisk rettspragmatisme*; Jonas Christoffersen, "Pragmatisme i spændingsfeltet mellem ret og retfærdighed," *Kritisk juss* 46, no. 3 (December 2020): 179–192, http://www.idunn.no/doi/10.18261/issn.2387-4546-2020-03-03; Harbo, "Folkerettspragmatisme." For a more sceptical stance on the spread of legal pragmatism in the Nordic region, see Mads Bryde Andersen, "Nordisk formueret mellem pragmatisme og principfasthed," *Tidsskrift for Rettsvitenskap* 133, no. 1 (March 2020): 47 (arguing that most legal systems could be characterised as pragmatic).

25 Harbo, "Folkerettspragmatisme".

26 See, e.g. Blandhol, "Rettspragmatismen i perspektiv".

27 Blandhol, 173.

28 Glennon, *The fog of law*, 9.

cannot be made in a vacuum but must be made in light of the legal question's specific social and political circumstances.[29]

- *Consequentialism*: It is also central to the pragmatic way of thinking that theories and concepts should be evaluated by their consequences.[30] Pragmatists do not simply evaluate the usefulness of a rule by looking at the rule itself or its underlying principles. Instead, they believe that the value of a rule or a legal concept is determined by how well it works in practice.[31]
- *Pluralism*: Legal pragmatism supports using various sources and theories to solve a specific problem. The law must be grounded in empiricism, ensuring its connection to concrete cases and the practical application in the field.[32]

These features make legal pragmatism a distinct approach to international law beyond everyday notions of practicality, opportunism, and problem-solving.[33] Legal pragmatism is both a way of conceptualising law from an external perspective and an approach for states and other legal actors to operate with law. This multifaceted method makes Nordic legal pragmatism a powerful explanatory framework for analysing the Nordic countries' approach to cyber espionage under international law.

First, Legal pragmatism is a method of analysing whether legal concepts and categories, such as the principle of territorial sovereignty, are still relevant in today's times and technological changes.[34] This approach considers the incentives and disincentives that the Nordic states weigh regarding a particular interpretation of the law, as well as how likely these states are to comply with such rules. Considering these factors, we can determine whether a legal concept or category is still valuable and effective.

Second, legal pragmatism lends well to the relationship between 'high politics' and international law.[35] High politics are those matters that concern the most important and existential issues facing states, such as national security and defence. In such matters, state behaviour tends to be determined by social

29 Blandhol, "Rettspragmatismen i perspektiv," 177.

30 Blandhol, 175.

31 Glennon, *The fog of law*, 10; Blandhol, "Rettspragmatismen i perspektiv," 175.

32 Blandhol, 176–177.

33 Siegfried Schieder, "Pragmatism and International Law," in *Pragmatism in international relations*, ed. Elisabetta. Brighi and Harry Bauer (Routledge, 2009), 125–126.

34 Michael J Glennon, "The road ahead: Gaps, leaks, and drips," *Leaks, and Drips (April 4, 2013)* 89 (2013): 378.

35 See generally, Glennon, *The fog of law*.

and power-related factors rather than international law rules.[36] Legal pragmatists advocate for an open and honest examination of these considerations, rather than hiding behind legal jargon.[37] As Michael Glennon, a leading proponent of legal pragmatism, forcefully argues, international law in the 'high politics' of state security is 'more effect than cause' subject to 'cultural, historical, and power-related factors'.[38]

Third, cyber espionage is ultimately a matter of 'high politics', and the legal status of cyber espionage is deeply entangled with the role that spying plays in international affairs. To fully understand the complex relationship between law and espionage, we must seek alternatives to the more rigorous formalistic, positivist approach in interpreting and applying the law to find answers to questions that have no doctrinal answers.[39] Ultimately, '[i]ntelligence activities are a prime candidate for legal pragmatism – and especially its scepticism toward doctrine'.[40]

A potential criticism of legal pragmatism is the risk of depriving international law of the features that make it a distinctive enterprise in international affairs by focusing too much on external non-legal factors. However, acknowledging these realities does not necessarily mean that pragmatic legal reasoning is deprived of any normative or doctrinal analyses of international law. Legal pragmatism is neither opposed to legal doctrine nor a blanket rejection of traditional sources of international law.[41] Pragmatism is also not simply a different label for an international relations realism that claims that power politics is everything and denies any normative effect of international law.[42]

A pragmatic analysis begins from international legal rules, principles, and precedents and is then driven by experience and the actual behaviour of states.

---

36 See generally, Glennon, 37–38. See also Craig Forcese, "Pragmatism and Principle: Intelligence Agencies and International Law," *Virginia law review* 102 (2016): 67 ('International law colors state discourse without governing the outcomes of state decisions, at least for matters of high politics').

37 Glennon, *The fog of law*, 20.

38 Glennon, 37–38.

39 For a similar view see Asaf Lubin, "SolarWinds and the International Law of Peacetime Intelligence Operations," in *The Oxford Process on International Law Protections in Cyberspace: A Compendium* (Oxford Institute for Ethics, Law / Armed Conflict, 2022), 315. While I agree with Lubin's anti-formalist approach to espionage, I find his New Haven School grounded appreciation for human dignity less convincing.

40 Craig Forcese, "Pragmatism and Principle: Intelligence Agencies and International Law," 67.

41 Emmanuel Roucounas, *A landscape of contemporary theories of international law* (Leiden Boston: Brill Nijhoff, 2019), 177; Schieder, "Pragmatism and International Law," 128.

42 Schieder, 125; Harbo, "Folkerettspragmatisme," 222.

Thus, applying a pragmatic legal approach to international law is possible without sacrificing the normativity of international legal rules or linking it to power politics.[43] Seen in this light, Nordic legal pragmatism is, as I intend to show in this chapter, a particularly suitable approach to understanding how the Nordic states approach the intricate relationship between international law and the political realities surrounding cyber espionage.

3 Small but Robust Cyber Intelligence Actors

Like all other nations, the Nordic countries depend on intelligence gathering to inform their national security policies and protect their national interests. Their information-gathering methods encompass a variety of traditional approaches, including human intelligence and signal intelligence. Additionally, they have adopted cutting-edge technologies for intelligence gathering and analysis, further strengthening their espionage operations.

The Nordic countries have historically maintained a veil of secrecy around their cyber operations capabilities. However, recent years have seen the enactment of new domestic legislation governing foreign intelligence operations in all of these countries. All Nordic states, excluding Sweden, have now openly admitted to possessing the capacity and legal authorisation to conduct so-called computer network exploitation (CNE), another term for cyber espionage.

The Danish Defence Intelligence Service (*DDIS*) *Act* authorises Denmark's foreign intelligence service to collect and obtain information which may be important to the performance of its intelligence-related activities.[44] According to the explanatory notes to the DDIS Bill, the DDIS can use all types of collection methods and adapt continuously to technological developments.[45] The DDIS has publicly acknowledged since 2016 that it uses CNE operations, in

43 ('[P]ragmatism turns not just against the view of international law as a mere set of norms, but also against the other extreme of reducing international law to a question of power'); Schieder, "Pragmatism and International Law," 132.

44 *The Danish Defence Intelligence Service* (*DDIS*) *Act* (*Consolidated Act No. 1287 of 28 November 2017, as amended* (*most recently by Act No. 1706 of 27 December 2018*) (*the DDIS Act*), Section 3.

45 *L 163 – svar på spm. 3 om lovforslaget ikke giver mulighed for at kontrollere, om Forsvarets Efterretningstjeneste overholder folkeretten, når FE opererer i udlandet, fra forsvarsministeren*, May 2013, Section 4.3.2. https://www.ft.dk/samling/20121/lovforslag/ l163/spm/3/svar/1051114/1245717/index.htm.

which hackers gain unauthorised access to computer systems, closed forums, or IT systems to gather information.[46]

The Norwegian Intelligence Service Act also authorises the Norwegian Intelligence Service (NIS) to conduct so-called 'end-point collection', which is to 'observe and collect electronic information that is not openly available in computer systems or similar systems or services possessed by or expected to be used by intelligence targets'.[47] In other words, the Norwegian Intelligence Service also has a clear legal mandate to conduct cyber espionage against other states.

Finland's military intelligence (Finnish Defence Intelligence Agency, FDI) is also legally mandated to conduct foreign computer network exploitation outside Finland. In June 2019, new and comprehensive intelligence legislation on military and civilian intelligence entered into force in Finland. *The Act on Military Intelligence* enables the FDI to use new intelligence collection methods that it was previously unable to perform. Under Section 62 of the Act, the FDI 'may target foreign computer network exploitation at an information system if such exploitation can be expected to be of particular importance to obtaining information for an intelligence task'.[48]

Sweden is the only Nordic country that has not publicly disclosed whether it engages in computer network exploitation. In 2008, Sweden's government passed a new *Signals Intelligence Act* that allows the National Defence Radio Establishment (FRA) to listen to and read communications that travel through cables.[49] The FRA is Sweden's SIGINT agency and the most likely government actor to conduct cyber espionage. However, the *Signals Intelligence Act* does not specify whether FRA is authorised to hack into foreign computer systems to collect information. In a 2008 parliamentary defence committee meeting,

46 *Beretning 2013–2014*, technical report (Forsvarets Efterretningstjeneste, October 2016), 36, https://www.fe-ddis.dk/da/produkter/beretning/beretningsarkiv/beretning-2013-2014/; *Indblik: Beretning 2019–2020*, technical report (Forsvarets Efterretningstjeneste, December 2021), 23, https://www.fe-ddis.dk/da/produkter/beretning/beretningsarkiv/beretning-2019-2020/.

47 *Act on Military Intelligence (590/2019) (Translation from Finnish)*, Section 6–10, https://finlex.fi/en/laki/kaannokset/2019/en20190590.pdf.

48 *Act on Military Intelligence (590/2019) (Translation from Finnish)*, Section 62. See also *Finnish Military Intelligence review 2023*, technical report (The Finnish Defence Forces, 2023), 12, https://puolustusvoimat.fi/documents/1948673/73396483/EN_Sotilastiedustelun_julkinen_katsaus_2023.pdf/8f9b081a-34f3-aa7a-a82d-c0f73a50bb53/EN_Sotilastiedustelun_julkinen_katsaus_2023.pdf?t=1674123050373.

49 *Lag (2008:717) om signalspaning i försvarsunderrättelseverksamhet*, https://www.riksdagen.se/sv/dokumentochlagar/dokument/svenskforfattningssamling/lag2008717omsignalspaning-i_sfs-2008-717/.

Ingvar Åkesson, the then Director-General of FRA, publicly stated that FRA would not engage in so-called active signals intelligence (*'aktiv signalspaning'*), which involves the collection of information from computer systems through hacking.[50] However, documents leaked by Edward Snowden, a former employee of a service provider for the National Security Agency (NSA), suggested that the FRA was cooperating with the NSA in carrying out computer network exploitation.[51] Neither Runar Viksten, the former judge of the Swedish Defence Intelligence Court,[52] nor an official FRA spokesperson have been willing to confirm or deny whether the *Signals Intelligence Act* itself gives the FRA the right to hack into computers to collect information. Professor Mark Klamberg, a leading expert on FRA's statutory authorities at Stockholm University, has confirmed that the *Signals Intelligence Act* and its preparatory works do not specifically address the issue of whether FRA is authorised to hack into computers.[53] The lack of publicly accessible data hinders a definitive conclusion on Sweden's involvement in cyber espionage operations.

With statutory powers to conduct cyber espionage abroad, the limitations for the Nordic countries' digital spying activities appear to be non-legal. Needless to say, workforce, technology, and money are limiting factors for the Nordic states' overall capacity to conduct cyber espionage. Therefore, the Nordic countries are likely not able to match the cyber espionage capabilities of larger and more powerful states such as the United States, China, and Russia.[54] For instance, out of all the Nordic countries, only Sweden is listed in the top 30 of the most powerful countries in cyberspace in the 2022 National Cyber Power Index published by the Belfer Center.[55] The index measures cyber power based

---

50 Monica Kleja, "FRA: – Vi kommer inte hacka," May 2008, accessed October 20, 2023, https://www.nyteknik.se/nyheter/fra-vi-kommer-inte-hacka/608387.

51 Gunnar Rensfeldt, "FRA hackar datorer – topphemligt projekt med NSA," *SVT Nyheter*, December 2013, accessed October 20, 2023, https://www.svt.se/nyheter/granskning/ug/frahackar-datorer.

52 Monica Kleja, "FRA saknar riksdagsmandat att hacka," Section: nyheter, *Nyteknik*, December 2013, accessed October 20, 2023, https://www.nyteknik.se/nyheter/frasaknarriksdagsmandat-att-hacka/606730.

53 E-mail from professor Mark Klamberg to author on 19 October 2023 21:16 (on file with author).

54 'As a rule of thumb, larger countries with geopolitical ambitions tend to have more intelligence capabilities (agencies, workforce, budget and capacities)'; Dennis Broeders and Camino Kavanagh, *Shades of Grey: Cyber Intelligence and (Inter)national Security*, technical report (EU Cyber Direct, October 2023), 18, accessed October 17, 2023, https://eucyberdirect. eu/research/shades-of-grey-cyber-intelligence-and-inter-national-security.

55 Julia Voo, Irfan Hemani, and Dan Cassidy, *National Cyber Power Index 2022*, technical report (Belfer Center for Science and International Affairs, Harvard Kennedy School,

on metrics such as intelligence collection, finance, and defence. This ranking is somewhat surprising given that Sweden has not publicly acknowledged that it conducts cyber espionage. Although it is impossible to determine the extent of the cyber espionage capabilities possessed by each Nordic state in this chapter, it can be assumed that they possess strong cyber and intelligence capabilities. This raises the question of whether Nordic states consider cyber espionage subject to international law constraints. The following section will explore and analyse this question.

4 Unpacking the Nordic Legal Discourse on Cyber Espionage

The legal status of espionage under international law has long been relatively unsettled.[56] The practice of spying is not directly nor specifically regulated by any international treaty, and there is no customary norm that prohibits traditional espionage or cyber espionage *per se*. This lack of specific regulation has led a majority of international legal experts to conclude that intelligence gathering is not explicitly prohibited by international law.[57]

Traditionally, states have hesitated to publicly articulate their legal stances on the applicability of international law to their espionage activities. However, a growing number of states are now exhibiting greater transparency regarding their positions on the interplay between cyber espionage and international law.[58] This development was stimulated by Edward Snowden's revelations in 2013, and the ensuing global discussion about the boundaries of states' surveillance activities.[59] The increased openness is also advanced by the ongoing debate between states about the application of international law to cyberspace and the increasing number of official national position papers addressing this

September 2022), 10, https://www.belfercenter.org/publication/national-cyber-power-index-2022.

56 See, e.g., David P. Fidler, *Advanced introduction to cybersecurity law*, Elgar advanced introductions (Edward Elgar Publishing, 2022), 80; Darien Pun, "Rethinking Espionage in the Modern Era Comments," *Chicago Journal of International Law* 18, no. 1 (2017): 360.

57 See, e.g., Russell Buchan, *Cyber Espionage and International Law* (Bloomsbury Publishing, 2019); Michael N. Schmitt, ed., *Tallinn manual 2.0 on the international law applicable to cyber operations*, Second edition (Cambridge University Press, 2017), Commentary to Rule 32, para 5 ('The International Group of Experts agreed that customary international law does not prohibit espionage').

58 For an overview, see, e.g., Asbjørn Thranov, *Cyber espionage: how the competition for intelligence challenges international law* (Danish Institute for International Studies, 2023), https://pure.diis.dk/ws/files/23085537/Cyber_espionage_DIIS_Report_2023_04.pdf.

59 Fidler, *Advanced introduction to cybersecurity law*, 82–83.

issue. These national statements offer critical insights into states' views on applying international law to cyber operations. All the Nordic countries have released individual position papers outlining their interpretation of international law in the context of cyber operations.[60]

At first glance, the Nordic states do not appear to provide much clarity about the legal status of cyber espionage under international law in their national statements. The Norwegian statement expressly states that it 'does not contain any specific analysis of cyber espionage.'[61] Similarly, the Danish statement also mentions explicitly that the 'sector specific issues' of 'intelligence gathering' is excluded from the legal analysis.[62] Neither the Finnish nor Swedish statements make any specific mention of cyber espionage or other forms of intelligence gathering.

Upon closer scrutiny, however, the Nordic states have more to say about international law and cyber espionage than meets the eye in their official statements on international law in cyberspace. As we progress through this chapter, we will discover that the Nordic countries have expressed their views on the interplay between international law and espionage through official documents such as legal analyses and memoranda. These documents were primarily created and published in relation to parliamentary work on new intelligence legislation, as mentioned in Section 3 above. From a legal pragmatic perspective, it is less important whether these documents are considered formal evidence

60 Jeppe Mejer Kjelgaard and Ulf Melgaard, "Denmark's Position Paper on the Application of International Law in Cyberspace: Introduction," *Nordic Journal of International Law*, July 2023, 1–10, https://doi.org/10.1163/1571810720230001, https://brill.com/view/journals/nord / aop/ article10.116315718107-20230001 / article-10.1163-15718107-20230001. xml; Marja Lehto and Ministry of Foreign Affairs of Finland, "Finland's views on International Law and Cyberspace," Place: Leiden, The Netherlands Publisher: Brill | Nijhoff, *Nordic Journal of International Law*, 2023, 1–14, https://brill.com/view/journals/nord/aop/article10.1163-15718107-20230002/article-10.1163-15718107-20230002.xml; Vibeke Musæus, "Nor-way's Position Paper on International Law and Cyberspace," Place: Leiden, The Netherlands Publisher: Brill | Nijhoff, *Nordic Journal of International Law*, 2023, 1–19; Ola Engdahl and Government of Sweden, "Sweden's Position Paper on the Application of International Law in Cyberspace," Place: Leiden, The Netherlands Publisher: Brill | Nijhoff, *Nordic Journal of International Law*, 2023, 1 –9, https://doi.org/https://doi.org/10.1163/15718107-20230004, https:// brill. com/ view/ journals/ nord/ aop/ article10.1163-15718107-20230004 / article-10.1163-15718107-20230004.xml.

61 Musæus, "Norway's Position Paper on International Law and Cyberspace," p. 6 at footnote 15.

62 Kjelgaard and Melgaard, "Denmark's Position Paper on the Application of International Law in Cyberspace: Introduction," 2.

of verbal state practice and/or *opinio juris*.[63] What matters is whether one can derive legal reasoning from these sources.[64]

Norway and Finland have provided the most precise and detailed legal views on the legal status of peacetime (cyber) espionage.

In 2018, the Norweigan Ministry of Defence drafted a memorandum (*høringsnotat*) as part of the legislative work to create a new intelligence service act for the Norwegian Intelligence Service.[65] In a section about the international legal framework for states' intelligence activities, the memorandum asserts that espionage is not as such prohibited under international law.[66] The reason for this position is, according to the memorandum, that espionage is such a common and widespread activity among states that state practice has accepted spying, at least tacitly.[67]

Finland also justifies the legality of espionage with direct reference to the fact that most states engage in intelligence collection. In the official working group report *Guidelines for Developing Finnish Intelligence Legislation*, the Finnish Ministry of Defence argued that:

> It may be assumed that intelligence operations are not universally acceptable under international law because governments frequently indicate that they do not approve of such operations by declaring persons *persona non grata* or by other means. On the other hand, it cannot be assumed that intelligence operations should be considered prohibited under international law because nearly all governments engage in such operations. Intelligence operations are well established worldwide, and the attitude of any given country to such activities is determined according to whether it is an intelligence-gathering country or a target country, as the case may be.[68]

---

63 This is undoubtedly the case as the official records were drafted by executive or legislative state organs and subsequently made publicly available. See *'Committee on Formation of Customary (General) International Law'* (2000) *69 Int'l L Ass'n Rep Conf 712*, See 725ff.

64 See Blandhol, "Rettspragmatismen i perspektiv," 177.

65 *Høringsnotat: Forslag til ny lov om Etterretningstjenesten*, November 2018, https://www.regjeringen.no/contentassets/556459ec77bd448f828af034dd573e11/horingsnotat---forslagtil-ny-lov-om-etterretningstjenesten.pdf.

66 *Høringsnotat: Forslag til ny lov om Etterretningstjenesten*, 25.

67 'Statspraksis [...] viser at statene i utgangspunktet aksepterer etterretningsvirksomhet';*Høringsnotat: Forslag til ny lov om Etterretningstjenesten*, 25.

68 *Guidelines for developing Finnish intelligence legislation: Working group report*, technical report (Ministry of Defence, March 2015), 77, https:// www . defmin . fi/ files/ 3144 / GUIDELINES_FOR_DEVELOPING_FINNISH_INTELLIGENCE_LEGISLATION.pdf.

Norway and Finland seem to believe that the widespread use and acceptance of espionage in the international community makes it lawful *per se*. However, neither country provides a thorough legal analysis to support espionage's lawfulness under customary international law.

Some international lawyers would disagree with the claim that espionage is legal under customary international law because states widely practise it.[69] They will argue that states rarely publicly assert that international law permits espionage, which is a critical shortcoming, as customary international law requires both state practice and *opinio juris* to be established. Therefore, the mere fact that espionage is commonplace does not establish a permissive customary international law norm for this activity.[70] Additionally the same lawyers will argue that some states have explicitly condemned espionage as unlawful, which provides a strong indication of *opinio juris* pointing towards the illegality of espionage under customary international law.[71]

By contrast, legal pragmatists would argue, based on their rejection of absolute foundations and formalism, that the legality of espionage under international law could not be determined solely by state practice and *opinio juris*. An international lawyer with a pragmatic approach would argue that, in reality, it is complicated to establish whether a customary international law norm exists that either permits or prohibits espionage. This is because the threshold for proving the existence of such a norm is very high.[72] Instead, one must build from the empirical fact that espionage is a common practice in the international community and that most states accept this activity as a matter of both

69 See e.g. Russell Buchan, "Cyber Espionage, International Law and the Protection of Digital Supply Chains," in *The Oxford Process on International Law Protections in Cyberspace: A Compendium* (Oxford Institute for Ethics, Law / Armed Conflict, 2022), 332–333; Naomi Hart, "Espionage and Elusive Rules of Customary International Law," in *The Oxford Process on International Law Protections in Cyberspace: A Compendium* (Oxford Institute for Ethics, Law / Armed Conflict, 2022), 302–303; Patrick Terry, "Absolute Friends: United States Espionage against Germany and Public International Law," Publisher: Société québécoise de droit international, *Revue québécoise de droit international/Quebec Journal of International Law/Revista quebequense de derecho internacional* 28, no. 2 (2015): 183; Kevin Jon Heller, *Low-intensity cyber operations and state sovereignty in cyberspace*, technical report (Djøf Publishing: Centre for Military Studies, 2022), 50.

70 See e.g. Buchan, "Cyber Espionage, International Law and the Protection of Digital Supply Chains," 332–333; Hart, "Espionage and Elusive Rules of Customary International Law," 302–303; Terry, "Absolute Friends: United States Espionage against Germany and Public International Law," 183; Heller, *Low-intensity cyber operations and state sovereignty in cyberspace*, 50.

71 See e.g, Heller, 50; Buchan, "Cyber Espionage, International Law and the Protection of Digital Supply Chains," 332–333.

72 Glennon, *The fog of law*, 78.

law and policy.[73] In the words of Glennon, '[i]n a voluntarist system, what States do has as much juridical effect as what States say, because deeds indicate even more reliably than words what rules States in fact accept'.[74] From a pragmatist's perspective, a rule in international law is considered binding when the prevailing incentive structure – a balance of incentives and disincentives – makes violating the rule excessively costly. This, in turn, leads to widespread compliance by a significant number of states, ultimately solidifying the rule's legal status.[75]

Assuming that a customary norm prohibits espionage, one would expect a higher level of global condemnation when states are caught spying. However, such condemnations are rare, even though espionage is a common practice.[76] Moreover, when states do respond to espionage activities by other states, they may not always base their actions on legal considerations.[77] Generally, governments tend to be less tolerant of foreign espionage against them than they are of their spying activities.[78]

Norway and Finland highlight this paradox of states protesting against being spied on while engaging in espionage.[79] When viewed through a legal pragmatic lens, Norway and Finland appear to base their views on the legality of espionage on the context and consequences of espionage rather than abstract legal categories. This understanding is underlined by the fact that Norway argues that the international community seems content with the tacit acceptance that spying is legal and mentions explicitly that this '*pragmatism*' is reflected in the fact that states' intelligence activities are not directly regulated

73 For a similar argument see Lubin, "SolarWinds and the International Law of Peacetime Intelligence Operations," 320–321 ('I encourage those [...] who are skeptical about the pos-sibility of evolving customary rules around espionage to quantifiably state how much more public conduct is necessary and of what variety before we can seriously consider the effects of state practice in this field').

74 Michael J Glennon, "Terrorism And International Law: The Case For Pragmatism," Publisher: Leiden, Koninklijke Brill NV, 2008, 89.

75 'States engage in a hard-headed, cold-blooded calculus, weighing the costs of violating the supposed rule against the benefits of complying with it.'; Glennon, 90.

76 Hart, "Espionage and Elusive Rules of Customary International Law," 305–306.

77 Hart, 305–306.

78 A. John Radsan, "The Unresolved Equation of Espionage and International Law Symposium: State Intelligence Gathering and International Law," *Michigan Journal of International Law* 28, no. 3 (2006): 606.

79 *Høringsnotat: Forslag til ny lov om Etterretningstjenesten*, 25 'Selv om stater har protestert når det har blitt kjent at de har vært utsatt for etterretningsvirksomhet fra andre stater, er protestene ofte preget av det faktum at den protesterende stat selv utfører lignende handlinger som det de blir utsatt for'.

in international law.[80] Moreover, Norway points out that few countries have proposed international regulation of espionage.[81] This position seems to suggest that most states accept that spying cannot and should not be directly regulated by international law.

Although, both Norway and Finland take the position that international law does not prohibit espionage as such, they clearly determine that specific rules and principles regulate the means and methods states use to collect intelligence.[82] This interpretation is, for instance, confirmed by Norway's statement on how international law applies to cyberspace. In a footnote, the statement offers the view that 'cyber operations whose purpose and effect is limited to the mere collection of information for use by the authorities, which is not illegal under international law. However, certain aspects of such intelligence operations could violate specific rules of international law.'[83] This view seems to be shared by Denmark, which has publicly stated that 'the Danish Defense Intelligence Service must, in its activities abroad, comply with Denmark's international obligations'.[84]

These statements support a prevailing view among states and academics that peacetime espionage, whether cyber or conventional, is not *per se* unlawful under international law, but that the means and methods to collect information may violate general principles of international law and specific legal regimes.[85] This legal view means that states are allowed to engage in (cyber) espionage unless there is a specific prohibition – such as the laws protecting

---

80 'Det internasjonale samfunn synes tilfreds med å opprettholde en stilltiende enighet om at etterretningsvirksomhet ikke er folkerettsstridig. Denne *pragmatismen* gjenspeiler seg i at utenlandsetterretningsvirksomhet er lite regulert i den skrevne folkeretten.';*Høringsnotat: Forslag til ny lov om Etterretningstjenesten*, 25 (original emphasis).

81 Selv om enkeltaktører har tatt til orde for at etterretningsvirksomhet helt eller delvis burde reguleres nærmere, har få om noen stater argumentert for dette.';*Høringsnotat: Forslag til ny lov om Etterretningstjenesten*, 25.

82 'Selv om etterretning ikke er ulovlig etter folkeretten, må måten man gjennomfører etterretningsvirksomhet på, likevel vurderes konkret opp mot folkerettslige normer.';*Høringsnotat: Forslag til ny lov om Etterretningstjenesten*, 26.

83 Musæus, "Norway's Position Paper on International Law and Cyberspace," p. 6 at footnote 15.

84 'Forsvarets Efterretningstjeneste (FE) skal ved sin virksomhed i udlandet overholde Danmarks internationale forpligtelser.'; *L 163 – svar på spm. 3 om lovforslaget ikke giver mulighed for at kontrollere, om Forsvarets Efterretningstjeneste overholder folkeretten, når FE opererer i udlandet, fra forsvarsministeren*.

85 See, e.g., Schmitt, *Tallinn manual 2.0 on the international law applicable to cyber operations*, Rule 32. For states that have expressed a similar view, see Thranov, *Cyber espionage*, 16.

diplomats and consulates and diplomatic premises and communications.[86] In other words, the view is that (cyber) espionage is not conducted in a legal vacuum but within some international law constraints that may be violated depending on the methods and techniques used to gather intelligence.

The following section examines whether the Nordic states consider that the principle of territorial sovereignty prohibits (cyber) espionage and, if so, under what circumstances.

5 The Nordic Approach to Sovereignty in Cyberspace

5.1 *A Principled Approach to Sovereignty*

Sovereignty is considered a fundamental concept in international law. However, there is disagreement among states and scholars about whether it is a political principle or a binding legal rule.[87] If sovereignty is a binding legal rule, then states that violate it may commit an internationally wrongful act.[88] The United Kingdom is the only state that explicitly has stated and maintained the view that sovereignty is an important political concept, but it does not see it as a legally binding rule.[89]

Most states interpret sovereignty as a legally binding rule of international law.[90] The Nordic states have also firmly located themselves in this camp when they explain that sovereignty is a primary rule of international law and that its

86 Dan Jerker B Svantesson et al., *The Developing Concept of Sovereignty: Considerations for Defence Operations in Cyberspace and Outer Space* (Technology / Jurisdiction Legal Research Team, 2021), 41; Buchan, *Cyber Espionage and International Law*, 70ff.

87 See, e.g., Gary P. Corn and Robert Taylor, "Sovereignty in the Age of Cyber Symposium on Sovereignty, Cyberspace, and Tallinn Manual 2.0," *AJIL Unbound* 111 (2017): 207–212; Michael N Schmitt and Liis Vihul, "Respect for sovereignty in cyberspace," *Tex. L. Rev.* 95 (2016): 1639.

88 Schmitt, *Tallinn manual 2.0 on the international law applicable to cyber operations*, 17–27.

89 Jeremy Wright, *Cyber and International Law in the 21st Century*, May 2018, https://www .gov .uk/government/speeches /cyber-and-international-law-in-the-21st-century; Suella Braverman, *International Law in Future Frontiers*, May 2022, https://www.gov.uk/ government/speeches/international-law-in-future-frontiers.

90 See e.g., *China's Views on the Application of the Principle of Sovereignty in Cyberspace*, 2021, https://documents.unoda.org/wp-content/uploads/2021/12/Chinese-Position-Paper-on -the-Application-of-the-Principle-of-Sovereignty-ENG.pdf; *Costa Rica's position on the application of international law in cyberspace*, July 2023, https://docs-library.unoda.org/ Open-Ended_Working_Group_on_Information_and_Communication_Technologies_-_ (2021) /Costa _ Rica_ - _Position _ Paper_ - _International _ Law _ in _ Cyberspace . pdf; *Italian position paper on International law and cyberspace*.

violation constitutes an internationally wrongful act.[91] According to this perspective, a foreign state's cyber operations conducted remotely against cyber infrastructure located within the territory of another state may constitute a violation of sovereignty and therefore an internationally wrongful act.[92]

The Nordic states agree that determining whether a cyber operation violates sovereignty should be based on two criteria:[93] (1) the degree to which it

91 'Denmark is of the view that sovereignty is not only a principle but a primary rule of international law a breach of which amounts to an internationally wrongful act and if attributable to a State it may give rise to State responsibility.'; Kjelgaard and Melgaard, "Denmark's Position Paper on the Application of International Law in Cyberspace: Introduction," 2–3; 'The argument has been raised recently that no legal consequences could be attached to sovereignty as a general principle, at least for the purposes of cyber activities. It is not only difficult to reconcile such an idea with the established status of the rule prohibiting violations of sovereignty in international law but it also gives rise to policy concerns.'; 'Finland disagrees with the claim that no rights and obligations would flow from the principle of sovereignty as such, or that no rule prohibiting violations of sovereignty would have crystallized in respect of cyber activities'; Lehto and, "Finland's views on International Law and Cyberspace," 3; 'Norway has therefore considered it important to make it clear that in its view, sovereignty is both a principle and a primary rule of international law that is applicable in cyberspace.'; Musæus, "Norway's Position Paper on International Law and Cyberspace," 3; 'States also have an obligation to respect the sovereignty of other States, and a breach of this obligation would amount to a wrongful act and give rise to State responsibility'; Engdahl and, "Sweden's Position Paper on the Application of International Law in Cyberspace," 4.

92 Schmitt, *Tallinn manual 2.0 on the international law applicable to cyber operations*, 17–27.

93 'Denmark supports the view that the lawfulness of a cyber operation should be assessed based on two different bases: the degree of infringement upon the target State's territorial integrity, and whether there has been an interference with or usurpation of inherently govern-mental functions.'; Kjelgaard and Melgaard, "Denmark's Position Paper on the Application of International Law in Cyberspace: Introduction," 3; 'a non-consensual intrusion in the computer networks and systems that rely on the cyber infrastructure in another State's territory may amount to a violation of that State's sovereignty [...] an unauthorized intrusion by cyber means may be seen as a violation of the target State's territorial sovereignty if it interferes with data or services that are necessary for the exercise of inherently governmental functions.'; Lehto and, "Finland's views on International Law and Cyberspace," 7; 'Norway has also expressly recognised that States can violate sovereignty in two ways. First, on the basis of territoriality, and second on the basis of interference with or usurpation of the inherently governmental functions of another State.'; Musæus, "Norway's Position Paper on International Law and Cyberspace," 3; 'In general, Sweden is of the view that violations of sovereignty may arise from cyber operations that result in damage or loss of functionality. [...] Interference with a State's inherently governmental functions may also constitute a violation of State sovereignty, including when undertaken with cyber means.'; Engdahl and, "Sweden's Position Paper on the Application of International Law in Cyberspace," 4.

infringes on the target state's territorial integrity, and (2) whether it interferes with or usurps inherently governmental functions.

Regarding the first basis (territorial integrity), the Nordic states agree that the consequences of a cyber operation are crucial in determining whether it violates sovereignty. They all agree that a violation of sovereignty occurs when it causes physical damage or injury, as well as loss of functionality to cyber infrastructure.[94] In addition to physical damage and loss of functionality, tampering with or deleting data may also constitute a breach of sovereignty, even if there is no physical harm or loss of functionality.[95]

Therefore, the Nordic states incorporate a *de minimis* threshold into their interpretation of the principle of sovereignty, whereby a certain level of harm is required for a violation of international law to occur. This *de minimis* threshold is most clearly expressed in the Danish statement, according to which '[c]yber activities causing negligible physical effects or loss of functionality would generally not be considered a violation of sovereignty'.[96] By adopting a *de minimis* approach, the Nordic states have rejected the view that any unauthorized intrusion into a state's computer systems is a violation of that state's territorial sovereignty. The Nordic states' approach differs from other states such as France[97] and

94 'Concerning infringements on a State's territory Denmark generally shares the view that cyber operations which result in physical damage or injury constitute a violation of a State's sovereignty'; Kjelgaard and Melgaard, "Denmark's Position Paper on the Application of International Law in Cyberspace: Introduction," 4; 'In addition to material harm that may be caused by such an operation, other relevant considerations include whether an intrusion in the cyber infrastructure triggers a loss of functionality of the equipment relying on it, or modifies or deletes information belonging to the target State, or to private actors in its territory'; Lehto and, "Finland's views on International Law and Cyberspace," 7; 'Causing physical damage by cyber means on another State's territory may easily qualify as a violation of territorial sovereignty. [...] In addition to physical damage, causing cyber infrastructure to lose functionality may also be taken into consideration and may amount to a violation.'; Musæus, "Norway's Position Paper on International Law and Cyberspace," 8; 'In general, Sweden is of the view that violations of sovereignty may arise from cyber operations that result in damage or loss of functionality'; Engdahl and, "Sweden's Position Paper on the Application of International Law in Cyberspace," 4.

95 Kjelgaard and Melgaard, "Denmark's Position Paper on the Application of International Law in Cyberspace: Introduction," 4; Lehto and, "Finland's views on International Law and Cyberspace," 7; Musæus, "Norway's Position Paper on International Law and Cyberspace," 8; Engdahl and, "Sweden's Position Paper on the Application of International Law in Cyberspace," 4.

96 Kjelgaard and Melgaard, "Denmark's Position Paper on the Application of International Law in Cyberspace: Introduction," 4.

97 *International Law Applied to Operations in Cyberspace*, September 2019, 10–11.

Iran,[98] who consider any cyber operation, no matter how minor, as a breach of sovereignty.

Regarding the second criterion, the Nordic states have all adopted the position that a cyber operation can also violate the principle of sovereignty if it interferes with or usurps a state's inherently governmental functions. This criterion for a sovereignty violation was proposed by the Tallinn Manual 2.0.[99] Inherently governmental functions are those functions that are solely performed by the state. Only Norway has provided specific examples of cyber operations that can interfere with or usurp such functions. These examples include altering or deleting data or blocking digital communication between public bodies and citizens in order to disrupt the delivery of social services, the conduct of elections, the collection of taxes, or the performance of key national defence activities.[100] Finally, all Nordic states believe that whether a cyber operation constitutes a violation of sovereignty must be assessed on a case-by-case basis, taking into account the nature, circumstances, and consequences of the operation.[101]

The Nordic states' approach to sovereignty could be said to be principled. Principled because they conceptualise sovereignty as a standalone rule with some defined legal boundaries and thresholds for violation in the cyber context. In light of their commitment to a rules-based international order, it is unsurprising that the Nordic states have embraced the principled view that sovereignty is a primary rule of international law. This view provides response options, such as countermeasures, to address hostile cyber operations that Nordic states view as a violation of their sovereignty.[102]

A crucial question is how the Nordic countries' emphasis on sovereignty-as-a-rule translates into their view of cyber espionage. Do they consider espionage a violation of a country's territorial sovereignty, whether by themselves or others? Is there a legal difference between physical and digital spying in terms of intrusion into a country's territory? The following subsections will explore these questions.

---

98 *Declaration of General Staff of the Armed Forces of the Islamic Republic of Iran Regarding International Law Applicable to the Cyberspace*, August 2020.

99 Schmitt, *Tallinn manual 2.0 on the international law applicable to cyber operations*, 21–22.

100 Musæus, "Norway's Position Paper on International Law and Cyberspace," 9.

101 Kjelgaard and Melgaard, "Denmark's Position Paper on the Application of International Law in Cyberspace: Introduction," 3; Lehto and, "Finland's views on International Law and Cyberspace," 8; Musæus, "Norway's Position Paper on International Law and Cyberspace," 9; Engdahl and, "Sweden's Position Paper on the Application of International Law in Cyberspace," 8.

102 Heller, *Low-intensity cyber operations and state sovereignty in cyberspace*, 18.

5.2 *Sovereignty and Cyber Espionage*

The Nordic countries' national position papers on international law in cyberspace do not explicitly discuss the relationship between cyber espionage and sovereignty. This reluctance to directly address the issue of sovereignty and cyber espionage contrasts with the views of other Western states, which have recently explicitly stated that remote-access cyber espionage operations do not violate sovereignty such as Canada[103] and New Zealand.[104]

The Nordic countries' approach to sovereignty suggests that they likely believe that cyber espionage involving only unauthorised access to computer systems or networks does not violate sovereignty. This proposition is based on the interpretation of sovereignty by the Nordic states, which is that cyber operations will only be considered a violation if they cause harmful effects which disrupt the operation of the targeted computer systems or interfere with and/or usurp inherently governmental functions through deletion or alteration of data.

Some actual instances from each country can be given to support this claim. These examples demonstrate that the Nordic countries do not invoke the principle of sovereignty when they become the targets of cyber espionage conducted by other nations.

In April 2017, a state-sponsored Russian hacking group was discovered to have hacked into the Danish Defence, gaining access to the emails of specific staff members to steal information. Denmark's defence minister characterised the incident as 'part of a continuing war from the Russian side in this field, where we are seeing a very aggressive Russia'.[105] Yet Denmark did not claim its territorial sovereignty had been violated.

In March 2021, the Norwegian parliament disclosed that Chinese cyber actors had compromised its email systems. Norwegian Foreign Minister Ine Eriksen Søreide firmly asserted 'such malicious cyber activities to take place is in contradiction of the norms of responsible state behaviour endorsed by

103 'Some cyber activities, such as cyber espionage, do not amount to a breach of territorial sovereignty, and hence to a violation of international law'; *Canada's National Position: International Law Applicable in Cyberspace*, April 2022, para 10, https://www.international.gc.ca/world-monde/issues_development-enjeux_developpement/peace_security-paix_securite/cyberspace_law-cyberespace_droit.aspx?lang=eng.

104 'There is a range of circumstances—in addition to pure espionage activity—in which an unauthorised cyber intrusion, including one causing effects on the territory of another state, would not be internationally wrongful'; *Canada's National Position: International Law Applicable in Cyberspace*, para 14.

105 "Denmark Says Russia Hacked Defense Ministry E-Mails," *Radio Free Europe*, April 2017, https://www.rferl.org/a/russia-denmark-defense-ministry-hacking/28448928.html.

all UN Member States'.[106] Despite her condemnation of the cyber activities, the foreign minister refrained from explicitly identifying the specific 'norms of responsible state behavior' that had been breached, nor did she assert that Norway's sovereignty had been violated.

In a similar vein, in March 2021, the Finnish Security and Intelligence Service, Supo, exposed a state-sponsored cyber espionage operation that targeted the country's parliament in the previous year.[107] Anu Vehvilainen, the speaker of the house, characterized the espionage operation as 'a severe threat to our democracy and Finnish society',[108] but not as a breach of Finnish sovereignty. In May 2021, the Swedish authorities disclosed that Russia had conducted a cyber espionage operation against the Swedish Sports Confederation from December 2017 to May 2018. In response to a parliamentary inquiry, the Swedish Foreign Minister, Ann Linde, merely described the cyber operations as an unacceptable violation of agreed norms for responsible state conduct in the cyber domain but not as a violation of sovereignty.[109]

Notably, none of the Nordic countries have directly asserted that their sovereignty has been infringed upon by the cyber espionage operations listed above, but rather, as in the case of Norway and Sweden, have implied that these operations violate unspecified norms of responsible state conduct in cyberspace. It is somewhat perplexing that the principle of sovereignty is not referred to in the context of cyber espionage, as the Nordic states consider sovereignty a standalone rule. Assuming the rule has been violated, one would expect the Nordic states to claim that their sovereignty had been violated. Instead, their reactions suggest that sovereignty is not considered an operative rule in the context of cyber espionage.

---

106 *Cyber operation against the Storting*, accessed November 9, 2023, https://www.regje ringen.no/en/historical-archive/solbergs-government/Ministries/ud/news1/2021/cyber_operation/id2866410/.

107 *Supo identified the cyber espionage operation against the parliament as APT31*, accessed November 9, 2023, https://supo.fi/en/- /supo- identified- the- cyber- espionage - operation- against-the-parliament-as-apt31.

108 "Finland says Chinese hackers behind parliament attack," *The Economic Times*, March 2021, accessed November 9, 2023, https://economictimes.indiatimes.com/news/international/ world- news/finland- says- chinese- hackers- behind- parliament- attack/articleshow/81592545.cms.

109 'Det grova dataintrång som Åklagarmyndigheten pekat ut en rysk statlig aktör som ansvarig för, är en oacceptabel överträdelse av överenskomna normer för staters ansvars- fulla uppträdande på cyberområdet.'; *Dataintrång mot Riksidrottsförbundet: Skriftlig fråga 2020/21:2704 av Pål Jonson (M)*, May 2021, accessed November 9, 2023, https://www.riksdagen.se/sv/dokument-och-lagar/dokument/skriftlig-fraga/dataintrang-mot-riksidrottsforbundet_h8112704/.

It is also peculiar that none of the Nordic states have attempted to interpret the principle of sovereignty in a manner that would prevent certain forms of cyber espionage. The Nordic states could, for instance, have explicitly stated that cyber espionage against certain types of confidential governmental data may potentially violate the principle of sovereignty because it interferes with inherently governmental functions. For instance, Poland advocates for such an interpretation, asserting that cyber operations that involve the 'theft' of government data belonging to state organs may violate the principle of sovereignty.[110] However, this interpretation is a double-edged sword, as it would also restrict the Nordic states from stealing other states' sensitive governmental data, according to the principle of sovereign equality.[111]

Additionally, the Nordic states could also have argued that the legality of cyber espionage should be assessed based on criteria such as the scale, intensity, severity, and potential negative consequences of the operation. This contextual approach was, for instance, suggested in a 2015 report by the Norwegian Committee of Digital Vulnerabilities in Society (the so-called *Lysneutvalget* named after the Professor and head of the committee Olav Lysne).[112] In discussing the international legal framework for cross-border intelligence collection, the Committee suggested that certain forms of cyber espionage, such as economic cyber espionage, could so severely damage a state's economy that they would constitute a violation of sovereignty.[113] The Committee also

110 *The Republic of Poland's position on the application of international law in cyberspace*, December 2022, https://www.gov.pl/attachment/3203b18b- a83f -4b92-8da2-fa0e3b449131. For an interpretation of the Polish statement, see Roguski Prezemyslaw, *Poland's Position on International Law and Cyber Operations: Sovereignty and Third-Party Countermeasures*, Just Security, January 2023, https:// www . justsecurity . org / 84799 / polands- position- on- international-law-and-cyber-operations-sovereignty-and-third-party-countermeasures/.

111 'Whatever is lawful, just, or equitable for one State in a particular situation, should be equally lawful, just, and equitable for all other States in that situation'; Juliane Kokott, "States, Sovereign Equality," in *Max Planck Encyclopedias of International Law* [*MPIL*] (April 2011), para 23. See also Michael Schmitt, "The Law of Cyber Conflict: Quo Vadis," *Articles of War, Lieber Institute, West Point*, July 2022, https://lieber.westpoint.edu/law-cyber- conflict- quo- vadis/ ('The obstacle [of firm stands] is the principle of sovereign equality, by which an interpretive position that limits the hostile activities of other States also restrains the State that adopts it from employing cyber means in pursuit of its own national interests').

112 *Folkerettslige rammer for grenseoverskridende informasjonsinnhenting*, technical report (Lysneutvalget, May 2015), https://www.regjeringen.no/contentassets/fe88e9ea8a354b d1b 63bc0022469f644/no/sved/2.pdf.

113 *Folkerettslige rammer for grenseoverskridende informasjonsinnhenting*, 3.

suggested that the purpose and methods of the intelligence gathering may be relevant to this determination.[114]

This suggestion appears to be consistent with the Nordic states' view that whether an unauthorised cyber intrusion violates a state's sovereignty depends on its nature and consequences and must be assessed on a case-by-case basis.

It remains to be seen whether the Nordic states will claim that certain types of cyber espionage violate the principle of territorial sovereignty. However, based on their present stance on the topic, they seem to agree that merely collecting data from foreign actors is unwelcome, but not considered a violation of sovereignty in itself.

5.3 *Sovereignty and Physical Espionage*

The Nordic states' apparent view that cyber espionage does not violate sovereignty raises another question: Do the Nordic states have a different approach to sovereignty regarding espionage in cyberspace compared to the physical world? To put it another way, does a foreign state's unauthorised intrusion into a Nordic country's airspace, territorial waters, or land territory constitute a violation of sovereignty, even if the intrusion does not produce any significant effects within the country?

From an academic point of view, some international lawyers have argued that customary international law suggests that the principle of sovereignty offers equal protection to a country's physical and virtual territories. As Russel Buchann and Iñaki Navarrete argue 'there seems [...] no *principled* reason for regarding the rule of territorial sovereignty as providing a State's sovereign cyber infrastructure with less protection from intrusion than a State's sovereign physical territory'.[115] To Kevin Heller the position that remote cyber espionage is not a violation of the principle of territorial sovereignty 'makes little *logical* sense, given that the penetrated computer system is physically located on the territory of the targeted State.'[116]

A legal pragmatist would reject an absolutist view on sovereignty, which considers any non-consensual digital or physical incursion into another state's territory as a violation of its sovereignty. Pragmatists believe that the question of sovereignty violations should not be answered through a purely logical

---

114 *Folkerettslige rammer for grenseoverskridende informasjonsinnhenting*, 3.

115 Russell Buchan and Iñaki Navarrete, "Cyber espionage and international law," in *Research handbook on international law and cyberspace*, ed. Nicholas Tsagourias and Russell Buchan (Edward Elgar Publishing, 2021), 247 (emphasis added).

116 Kevin Jon Heller, "In Defense of Pure Sovereignty in Cyberspace," *International Law Studies* Volume 97 (2021): 1481 (emphasis added).

exercise based on abstract and absolute legal principles.[117] They would argue that whether a physical trespass by another state's agents is a breach of sovereignty depends on the specific circumstances.

The Nordic states seem to accept that the principle of sovereignty does not prohibit foreign states' intelligence collection activities. Again, Finland and Norway express this view most clearly.

At first, Finland seems to take the view that physical intrusions into the territory of another state constitute a breach of sovereignty. Based on the jurisprudence of the International Court of Justice, Finland explicitly states in its position papers on international law and cyberspace that it is a violation of a state's territorial sovereignty when a foreign state conducts 'unauthorized intrusions to physical spaces such as overflight of a State's territory by an aircraft belonging to another State or under its control, penetration of territorial waters by foreign warships, conducting certain activities in another State's territory without its consent.'[118]

However, Finland also seems to tolerate some foreign intelligence gathering on its territory, even when it is not authorised. It is mentioned explicitly in Finland's *Guidelines for Developing Finnish Intelligence Legislation* that 'most governments, up to a point, tolerate or even accept the activities of foreign intelligence officials in their territory.'[119] Whether foreign intelligence gathering on another country's territory can be tolerated depends on the circumstances, according to the legal memo. For example, it may be acceptable if the two countries exchange information that benefits them or if the foreign power is openly gathering general information about the target country that does not harm anyone. However, suppose the foreign power is engaged in covert activities, or the information they collect is sensitive or harmful. In that case, the target country may take a dim view of this and even prosecute the foreign officials involved.[120]

My reading of Finland's position is that espionage conducted by sending an agent into another state's physical territory is not necessarily a violation of that state's territorial sovereignty.

117 '[A pragmatist] turns away from abstraction and insufficiency, from verbal solutions, from bad a priori reasons, from fixed principles, closed systems, and pretended absolutes and origins.'; William James, *Pragmatism – a New Name for Some Old Ways of Thinking by William James: With a Critical Introduction by Eric C. Sheffield*, ed. Eric C. Sheffield (Myers Education Press, 2019), 33.

118 Lehto and, "Finland's views on International Law and Cyberspace," 7 (footnotes omitted).

119 *Guidelines for developing Finnish intelligence legislation: Working group report*, 75.

120 *Guidelines for developing Finnish intelligence legislation: Working group report*, 75.

Norway appears to share Finland's view that physical espionage does not violate the target state's territorial sovereignty. According to Norway's official defence intelligence doctrine (*Forsvarets Etterretningsdoktrine 2021*), states generally accept foreign intelligence activities on their territory as a default assumption, and the international community tacitly agrees that such activity does not violate international law.[121] According to the intelligence doctrine, states tolerate espionage due to their reluctance to forbid an activity in which they engage.[122]

Some scholars will likely view Norway's and Finland's statements as an expression of the view that the long-standing practice of espionage constitutes a customary exception or 'carve-out' to the rule of sovereignty.[123] Other scholars will argue that there is insufficiently clear and convincing evidence in the form of public state practice and *opinio juris* to establish a customary exception to the principle of territorial sovereignty.[124]

By contrast, legal pragmatists focus more on how sovereignty operates in reality rather than whether espionage is a customary exception to the principle of territorial sovereignty. When we observe the actual behaviour of the Nordic states, it becomes even more evident that they do not consider sovereignty an operative rule in relation to either physical spying or cyber espionage.

To illustrate this point, consider a recent case from Denmark, where three members of ASMLA (Arab Struggle Movement for the Liberation of Ahwaz), an opposition movement to Iran, who were residing in Denmark, had conducted intelligence activities in Denmark on behalf of a Saudi intelligence service in February 2020.[125] Despite the gravity of the situation, where Saudi Arabia and

---

121 'Man kan dermed argumentere for at statspraksis viser at statene i utgangspunktet aksepterer fremmed etterretning på eget territorium, og at det internasjonale samfunn opprettholder en stilltiende enighet om at slik virksomhet ikke er folkerettsstridig'; *Forsvarets efterretningsdoktrine 2021*, March 2021, 10, https: //www.etterretningstjenesten .no/publikasjoner/etterretningsdoktrinen.

122 'Begrunnelsen for en slik toleranse er blant annet at man ikke ønsker å forby noe man gjør selv.'; *Forsvarets efterretningsdoktrine 2021*, 10.

123 See e.g., Ashley Deeks, "An International Legal Framework for Surveillance," *Virginia Journal of International Law* 55, no. 2 (2015): 291. This view was also represented by a minority of the Tallinn Manual 2.0 experts, who considered that acts of espionage represent a customary exception to the rules of sovereignty and non-intervention; Schmitt, *Tallinn manual 2.0 on the international law applicable to cyber operations*, See commentary to rule 32, para. 9.

124 See, e.g., Buchan, *Cyber Espionage and International Law*, 174ff; Schmitt and Vihul, "Respect for sovereignty in cyberspace," 1645.

125 *Assessment of the espionage threat to Denmark*, technical report (Danish Security and Intelligence Service, 2022), 16, https:// pet. dk / en/- /media/ mediefiler / pet/ dokumenter/ analyser-og-vurderinger/vurdering-af-spionagetruslen-mod-danmark/vsd_uk.pdf.

Iran brought their rivalry to Denmark, the Danish authorities' response was merely a diplomatic reaction. The Danish Ministry of Foreign Affairs issued a press statement stating that espionage on Danish soil is entirely unacceptable.[126] However, Denmark did not accuse Saudi Arabia of violating its territorial sovereignty.

While the Nordic states do not claim sovereignty violations when targeted by digital or physical espionage, they often condemn Russian intrusions into their territorial waters and airspace. For example, in the spring of 2022, Denmark characterised Russian military vessels and fighter aircraft entering its territorial waters and airspace as infringements on its territory and accused Russia of violating international law.[127] Similarly, Swedish Defense Minister Peter Hultqvist condemned the brief incursion of a Russian spy plane into Swedish airspace in March 2022 saying that '[t]he Russian violation of Swedish airspace is, of course, completely unacceptable [...] Swedish sovereignty and territory must always be respected'.[128]

However, Sweden does not use the same vernacular of the violation of territorial sovereignty when Danish military aircraft occasionally cross into Swedish airspace. In fact, Danish fighter jets violated Swedish airspace more often than Russian aircraft during the period 2016–2018.[129]

Why do the Nordic states only invoke a breach of sovereignty when Russian military ships and planes encroach on their airspace and territorial waters but not when they catch foreign spies on their land or detect cyber espionage?

---

126 *Jeppe Kofod: Spionage på dansk jord er fuldstændigt uacceptabelt*, accessed October 31, 2023, https://via.ritzau.dk/pressemeddelelse/13587489/jeppe- kofod- spionage- pa-dansk- jord-er-fuldstaendigt-uacceptabelt?publisherId=2012662.

127 See *Krænkelser af dansk territorialfarvand: Ruslands ambassadør til samtale i Udenrigsministeriet*, accessed October 31, 2023, https: / / via . ritzau . dk / embedded / release / 13653753 / kraenkelser - af - dansk - territorialfarvand - ruslands - ambassador - til - samtale - i - udenrigsministeriet? publisherId= 2012662 & lang =da& widget=true; *Ruslands ambassadør til samtale i Udenrigsministeriet efter uacceptabel krænkelse af dansk luftrum Udenrigsministeriet*, accessed October 31, 2023, https: // via. ritzau. dk / embedded/ release/ 13650339 / ruslands- ambassador- til - samtale- i - udenrigsministeriet- efter - uacceptabel- kraenkelse- af - dansk-luftrum?publisherId=2012662&lang=da&widget=true.

128 "Swedish defence minister calls Russian violation of airspace 'unacceptable'," *Reuters*, March 2022, chap. Europe, accessed November 1, 2023, https://www.reuters.com/world / europe/swedish- armed- forces- says- russian- fighter- jets- violated- swedish- airspace-2022- 03- 02/.

129 *Denmark encroaches on Sweden's airspace more often than Russia*, accessed November 11, 2023, https://www.thelocal.se/20190410/denmark-encroaches-on-swedens-airspace -more-often-than-russia.

The principle of sovereignty cannot explain this difference; only the specific context can.[130] Eric Talbot Jensen offers a possible explanation when he notes that '[s]overeignty is a principle that depends on the domain and the practical imperatives of states and is subject to adjustment in interstate application'.[131]

Jensen also explains that states apply 'sovereignty to particular sets of facts or instances of state interaction', giving the example that states do not consider 'espionage to be a per se violation of sovereignty, even when those actions take place in and/or have effects in another state'.[132]

This understanding of sovereignty resonates with pragmatic reasoning.[133] The principle of sovereignty is not a clear-cut or hand-and-fast rule that is applied equally to the case of all foreign intrusions into a state's physical or virtual domains. Instead, sovereignty has both a rule-like and principle-like character that apply differently to various domains and forms of intrusions.[134] States may have different interpretations of sovereignty depending on who they are interacting with (friend/adversary) and the degree of the intrusion (military aircraft, navy vessels or individual spies).

From this point of view, states' interpretations of sovereignty may vary depending on the power dynamics, interests, and a multitude of other factors at play when they interact with other states.[135] The context is important for whether or not a state breaches the sovereignty of another state through its intrusive activities. A state aircraft briefly entering another state's airspace is sometimes considered a violation of sovereignty, while a foreign state stealing massive amounts of sensitive data from a state's computer systems is not.

Despite their claims that sovereignty is a primary rule of international law, Nordic countries do not treat it as such in the context of espionage, cyber or otherwise. If they genuinely considered sovereignty an operative rule, they would be more likely to condemn foreign espionage as illegal, whether carried out by spies physically present in their territories or by cyber means. While the Nordic states publicly express their commitment to a rule of sovereignty,

130 Goldsmith and Loomis offer the same view and add that '[t]he naked principle of "sovereignty" cannot tell us why some border crossings are unlawful and some not'; Kristen E. Eichensehr, "Defend Forward and Attribution," in *The United States' Defend Forward Cyber Strategy* (Oxford University Press, March 2022), 154.

131 Eric Talbot Jensen, "The Tallinn Manual 2.0: Highlights and Insights," *Geo. J. Int'l L.* 48 (2016): 741–742.

132 Jensen, 741–742.

133 Glennon, "The road ahead: Gaps, leaks, and drips," footnote 30.

134 For this view see Svantesson et al., *The Developing Concept of Sovereignty: Considerations for Defence Operations in Cyberspace and Outer Space*, 19.

135 Svantesson et al., 22.

their actions contradict this stance. Said differently, they pay lip service to the idea that sovereignty is a standalone rule of international law, but their actual behaviour does not align with it.

From a pragmatic perspective, the hesitation of the Nordic countries to fully embrace the principle of sovereignty in the context of cyber espionage sheds light on its limitations as a binding rule in international law. A rule of international law is only binding because the system of incentives and disincentives makes it too costly for states to violate, and so most states comply with it most of the time.[136] Yet states are strongly incentivised to collect intelligence from other states, even if this is considered a violation of their territorial sovereignty. It is safe to assume that most states violate the principle of territorial sovereignty daily through spying activities. These frequent violations are compelling evidence that sovereignty is not a binding rule under international law. Ultimately, sovereignty is a 'paper rule' that has no legal consequences in the context of cyber or physical espionage.[137]

Another 'paper rule' that has proven ineffective to stop cyber espionage is the so-called norm against ICT-enabled theft of intellectual property for commercial gain. The following section addresses the Nordic states' unsuccessful attempt to promote this non-binding political norm.

6 The Ineffective 'Norm' against Economic Cyber Espionage

Even though the Nordic countries generally view cyber espionage as legal under international law, they have supported a political, non-legally binding norm prohibiting economic cyber espionage for commercial gain.

This norm first emerged in the 2015 bilateral cyber agreement between China and the United States, where they agreed that 'neither country's government will conduct or knowingly support cyber-enabled theft of intellectual property, including trade secrets or other confidential business information, with the intent of providing competitive advantages to companies or commercial sectors'.[138] The norm was later endorsed by the G-20 countries in 2015 and the G7 countries in 2016.

136 Glennon, "The road ahead: Gaps, leaks, and drips," 378.

137 For the distinction between 'real rules' and 'paper rules' see Glennon, *The fog of law*, 126.

138 *FACT SHEET: Imposing Costs for Harmful Foreign Activities by the Russian Government*, April 2021, https://www.whitehouse.gov/briefing-room/statements-releases/2021/04/ 15/fact-sheet-imposing-costs-for-harmful-foreign-activities-by-the-russian-government/.

The Nordic states endorsed this norm in the 2016 *Joint Statement on Third Annual Nordic-Baltic + U.S. Cyber Consultations.*[139] By adopting this norm, the Nordic countries and other like-minded liberal countries sought to differentiate between legitimate espionage for national security and illegitimate economic espionage for commercial gains.

Norway has adopted and implemented the norm of prohibiting economic espionage more thoroughly than any other Nordic country. On the recommendation of the Norwegian Ministry of Defense, the 2020 *Norwegian Intelligence Act* was amended to include a ban on so-called industrial espionage.[140] The Act explicitly states that the Norwegian Intelligence Service 'shall not collect or assist in collecting, process or disclose information to give companies or other commercial entities or sectors a competitive advantage'.[141]

The Norwegian Ministry of Defense argued that the norm prohibiting economic espionage has gradually evolved into a binding customary international norm through the practice and *opinio juris* of so-called 'central states'.[142] Norway's statement on international law in cyberspace also promotes the norm against economic espionage. The statement asserts that cyber espionage is only lawful if used to collect information for 'authorities', which can be understood as only state agencies and governmental bodies, not private companies.[143]

However, Norway's ban on economic espionage extends only to acquiring commercial information that provides a competitive edge in the business realm. The preparatory works of the *Norwegian Intelligence Act* stipulate that the intelligence service is authorised to collect economic intelligence about the governmental sphere (*'statsvitenskapelig kontekst'*).[144] Thereby, Norway

139 ('[N]o state should conduct or knowingly support cyber-enabled theft of intellectual property, including trade secrets or other confidential business information, with the intent of providing competitive advantages to companies or commercial sectors'); *Joint Statement on Third Annual Nordic-Baltic + U.S. Cyber Consultations*, September 2016, accessed November 6, 2023, https://2009-2017.state.gov/r/pa/prs/ps/2016/09/262038.htm.

140 *Høringsnotat: Forslag til ny lov om Etterretningstjenesten*, 143.

141 *Act on Military Intelligence (590/2019) (Translation from Finnish)*, Section 4–9.

142 'De senere år har man sett en gryende sedvanerettsutvikling knyttet til et folkerettslig forbud mot såkalt industrispionasje mellom stater [...] De bilaterale avtalene som de senere år er inngått, samt felleserklæringene som er avgitt, kan sies å reflektere en mellomstatlig regel som har oppstått som følge av en felles forståelse blant et økende antall sentrale stater'; *Høringsnotat: Forslag til ny lov om Etterretningstjenesten*, 143.

143 Musæus, "Norway's Position Paper on International Law and Cyberspace," p. 6 at footnote 15.

144 'Begrepet konkurransemessige fortrinn må forstås i en kommersiell kontekst, og ikke for eksempel i en statsvitenskapelig kontekst'; *Prop. 80 L (2019–2020): Lov om*

differentiates between economic espionage aimed at gaining an unfair competitive advantage for Norwegian firms and economic intelligence gathered to inform decision-makers on matters such as foreign nations' budgets and the global financial landscape.

Denmark, Finland, and Sweden have seemingly not taken steps as specific as Norway to implement the norm against economic cyber espionage in their national intelligence legislation or publicly available policies. Nevertheless, these states draw the same distinction between economic espionage for commercial advantages and the collection of strategic economic intelligence as evidenced by the *Joint Statement on Third Annual Nordic-Baltic + U.S. Cyber Consultations*. The Nordic countries' decision to abstain from economic espionage is likely driven more by a practical evaluation of their self-interests rather than a moral conviction against such practices. The economic prosperity of the Nordic countries hinges heavily on innovation and intellectual property, so they have a significant stake in upholding an international norm against commercial (cyber) espionage. Moreover, they lack a robust mechanism to transform stolen economic intelligence into marketable products for domestic businesses.

These factors explain why the Nordic states have singled out economic espionage for denunciation through official condemnation to discourage it. For example, in December 2018, the Danish Ministry of Foreign Affairs (MFA) joined the United Kingdom in condemning a Chinese cyber espionage campaign. In a (then) Twitter statement, the Danish MFA wrote, 'DK shares concern about commercial espionage, including from China, which goes against the rules-based international order and threatens to undermine our economy. We will continue to promote responsible state behavior in cyberspace'.[145]

The norm against economic cyber espionage aims to differentiate between economic espionage and espionage conducted for national security purposes. Professor Gary Brown, a former senior legal counsel for U.S. Cyber Command, refers to this distinction as being between 'good' and 'bad' espionage, although he disagrees that such a clear distinction can be made.[146]

To a pragmatist, the question is not whether economic espionage can be denounced as 'bad'. Again, a pragmatist assesses rules and norms based on

---

Etterretningstjenesten (*etterretningstjenesteloven*), Til § 4–9, accessed November 8, 2023, https://www. regjeringen.no/no/dokumenter/prop.-80-l-20192020/id2698600/?ch=17.

145 *DK shares concern about commercial espionage*, accessed November 7, 2023, https:// twitter.com/DanishMFA/status/1075842890461532161.

146 Gary Brown, "Spying and Fighting in Cyberspace: What Is Which," *J. Nat'l Sec. L. & Pol'y* 8 (2016): 624.

whether they work rather than measuring them against some abstract morality or other ideas. In practice, the norm against economic espionage has not been effective in stopping states from stealing each other's trade secrets and intellectual property. In a pragmatist world, states follow or violate norms based on their economic, political, or military interests.

Despite the efforts of the Nordic states and other Western states to promote the norm, it has neither emerged as a universally accepted political norm nor crystallised into customary law.[147] Most importantly, the norm against economic cyber espionage has not discouraged states like China, which is the primary target of this norm, from engaging in such activities.[148]

In their effortless attempt to restrict other countries from engaging in economic espionage, the Nordic states, notably Norway, have imposed normative limitations on their ability to participate in such activities. In a global landscape characterised by heightened geopolitical rivalry for technological advancements, adhering to unilateral self-restrictions while other nations remain unconstrained appears undesirable from a normative perspective.

The ineffectiveness of the norm against economic cyber espionage underscores a broader issue that neither legal frameworks nor non-binding norms may be effective means to deter cyber espionage. The following section discusses the Nordic countries' perspective on law's deterrent effects.

7 Feckless Norm Deterrence against Cyber Espionage

As cyberspace evolved, governments recognized the need for cyber deterrence to prevent adversarial actions. Deterrence is widely understood as a way to

---

147 Duncan B Hollis and Jan Neutze, "Defending Democracies via Cybernorms," in *Defending Democracies: Combating Foreign Election Interference in a Digital Age*, ed. Jens David Ohlin (Oxford University Press, 2021), 342; Jack Goldsmith and Robert Williams, *The Chinese Hacking Indictments and the Frail "Norm" Against Commercial Espionage*, November 2017, https://www.lawfareblog.com/chinese-hacking-indictments-and-frail-norm-against-commercial-espionage. For a more optimistic view on the viability of the norm, see Gatra Priyandita, Bart Hogeveen, and Ben Stevens, "State-sponsored economic cyber-espionage for commercial purposes," Publisher: International Cyber Policy Centre, December 2022, https://www.aspistrategist.org.au/state-sponsored-economic-cyber-espionage-for-commercial-purposes-on-the-rise/.

148 See e.g., *Intelligence Outlook 2022*, 57 ('China employs an extensive array of instruments to map and transfer foreign technology [including] espionage, in particular cyber espionage. China highly likely also targets Danish companies and research institutions for information and technology.').

dissuade other states from taking unwanted actions.[149] Classical deterrence theory differentiates between *deterrence by denial*, which relies on the threat of effective defences to prevent an attack from succeeding, and *deterrence by punishment*, which relies on the threat of retaliation to make an attack too costly to be worthwhile.[150]

It has also been suggested that international law and norms can deter states from engaging in hostile cyber activities.[151] So-called *deterrence by norms* increases the reputational cost of bad state behaviour, which may discourage states from violating international law, as they do not want to be labelled as law-breakers. Additionally, international law can be used to hold states accountable for violations by providing legal grounds for victims of hostile cyber activities to take countermeasures.[152] For instance, Kevin Heller proposes that small states with limited cyber capabilities should adopt a stricter interpretation of sovereignty, which would enable them to take countermeasures against other states' cyber espionage operations, which would have a greater deterrent effect.[153]

However, there are reasons to doubt the effectiveness of international law in deterring cyber espionage. As David P. Fidler correctly notes: 'The deep and intense government interest in cyber espionage underscores the lack of legal rules and deterrence that have long characterized this area'.[154] The argument behind this view is that cyber espionage is a persistent reality of international politics and increased geopolitical competition, and therefore, it cannot be deterred by law or other defensive means.[155]

---

149 Joseph S Nye, "Deterrence and Dissuasion in Cyberspace," *International security* 41, no. 3 (2017): 52.

150 See generally, Jon R Lindsay, "The Impact of China on Cybersecurity: Fiction and Friction," Place: Cambridge Publisher: The MIT Press, *International security* 39, no. 3 (2015): 53.

151 See generally, Nye, "Deterrence and Dissuasion in Cyberspace," 60f; Tim Stevens, "A Cyberwar of Ideas? Deterrence and Norms in Cyberspace," *Contemporary Security Policy* 33, no. 1 (April 2012): 155f.

152 Michael N. Schmitt, "Taming the Lawless Void: Tracking the Evolution of International Law Rules for Cyberspace," *Texas National Security Review:* Volume 3, Issue 3 (2020): 42 ('The growing number of states that accept the rule as "hard law" is further indication of a trend towards treating international law as an effective tool in deterring harmful cyber activities').

153 Heller, *Low-intensity cyber operations and state sovereignty in cyberspace*, 65.

154 Fidler, *Advanced introduction to cybersecurity law*, 80.

155 'Deterrence is mostly irrelevant in an intelligence contest. No combination of threats and promises will stop a rival intelligence service from collecting information.' Joshua Rovner, *The Intelligence Contest in Cyberspace*, https://www.lawfareblog.com/intelligence-contest-cybers pace. See also Fidler, *Advanced introduction to cybersecurity law*, 90 'The lack of deterrence by norms and by punishment means that countries create patchworks of legal

The Nordic states appear to agree that neither domestic nor international law effectively deter foreign cyber espionage.

Regarding domestic legislation, the Nordic states do not appear to be concerned about the possibility that their intelligence activities may violate the target states' domestic legislation. In the legal memo *Guidelines for Developing Finnish Intelligence Legislation*, Finland asserts that whether an intelligence operation violates domestic legislation is a potential risk factor to consider but not a legal barrier to conducting the operation.[156] It also notes that no other comparable Western countries have enacted laws requiring foreign intelligence operations to be accepted by the target country or to comply with the target country's laws.[157] The Danish Defense Intelligence Service also flatly states that it uses methods that may be illegal in the target countries.[158]

These statements are surprisingly revealing for states that traditionally seek to promote the rule of law, both domestically and internationally. Of course, there is a significant distinction between domestic legal systems and the international legal system. The international legal system is based on consent and is voluntary. This means that states are obligated only to follow the rules to which they have consented. Nevertheless, violating the domestic laws of another state could be interpreted as disregarding the rule of law in general.

The Nordic states also appear to question whether their domestic law provides much protection against cyber espionage. This view is most clearly expressed in Norway's official defence intelligence doctrine, which explains that national criminal law is ineffective against modern intelligence collection.[159] It also explains that new technologies and an increasingly digitized world have made it easier for states to conduct intelligence operations against other states from their own territory, making it difficult for states to use national legislation to protect themselves from activities that do not occur within their jurisdiction.[160]

---

measures to protect and defend against cyber espionage. The effectiveness of defensive measures is questionable.'

156 *Guidelines for developing Finnish intelligence legislation: Working group report*, 75.

157 *Guidelines for developing Finnish intelligence legislation: Working group report*, 75.

158 'For at skaffe den viden kræver det ofte, at vi benytter metoder, som normalt ville ligge uden for lovens rammer. Eller sagt med andre ord metoder, som kan være ulovlige i de lande, vi benytter dem i.'; *Indblik: Beretning 2019–2020*, 10.

159 'En stats nasjonale lovgivning har imidlertid begrenset effekt mot moderne etterretning. Som en følge av ny teknologi og en stadig mer digitalisert verden kan stat A lettere gjennomføre etterretningsoperasjoner mot stat B fra eget territorium. Stat B vil vanskelig kunne beskytte seg med nasjonal lovgivning mot aktivitet som ikke foregår innenfor statens jurisdiksjonsområde.'; *Forsvarets efterretningsdoktrine 2021*, 10.

160 *Forsvarets efterretningsdoktrine 2021*, 10.

Moreover, none of the Nordic states, as far as I know, have attempted to use criminal indictments of foreign hackers under domestic law to deter cyber espionage, a strategy that has largely failed for the United States.[161] For example, the Swedish Prosecution Authority discontinued its investigation into the 2018 cyber espionage operation against the Swedish Sports Federation mentioned above because the legal prerequisites for prosecuting or extraditing Russian state-sponsored hackers to Sweden were absent.[162] This case illustrates that perpetrators of cyber espionage are highly unlikely to face prosecution due to the uncooperative nature of the purported country of origin, which often refuses to provide any assistance in elucidating the affair.

The Nordic states do not seem to view international law as a normative barrier protecting their interests by deterring cyber espionage. As mentioned above, the Nordic states do not believe that espionage is illegal *per se* under international law, nor do they invoke the principle of sovereignty when they have been the target of other states (cyber) espionage operations. Instead, they prefer non-legal responses to other states' cyber espionage. This approach is most clearly seen in Denmark's statement on international law in cyberspace, which mentions that:

> States may be subject to unfriendly or hostile cyber acts or omissions that do not rise to the level of illegality under international law. These may be met with responses of a diplomatic, economic, or political nature intended to deter and hold accountable such States, irrespective of the fact that those acts are not illegal under international law. Such responses are generally termed retorsions.[163]

The statement does not explicitly mention cyber espionage. Still, it likely refers to it since espionage is generally considered an unfriendly act between

161 'it is hard not to conclude that the Justice Department's deterrence-by-indictment efforts have failed. And the scale of the failure is large'; Jack Goldsmith and Robert D. Williams, "The Failure of the United States' Chinese-Hacking Indictment Strategy | Lawfare," *Lawfare*, December 2018, accessed November 3, 2023, https://www.lawfaremedia.org/article/ failure-united-states-chinese-hacking-indictment-strategy.

162 *Investigation into serious breach of data secrecy by Russian intelligence agency discontinued*, April 2021, accessed November 9, 2023, https://www.aklagare.se/en/media/press-releases/2021/april/1/january/investigation-into-serious-breach-of-data-secrecy-by-russian-intelligence-agency-discontinued/.

163 Kjelgaard and Melgaard, "Denmark's Position Paper on the Application of International Law in Cyberspace: Introduction," 8.

nations.[164] Denmark suggests responding to such hostile actions with legally permissible unfriendly acts known as retorsions. Because retaliatory measures are primarily political, they are not subject to the same strict legal constraints as other types of responses, such as countermeasures. Examples of retorsive measures include declaring diplomats *personae non gratae*, taking economic or other measures against individuals involved in unfriendly cyber activities, or as Norway suggests merely publicly declaring that another state is responsible for a cyber operation.[165]

While assessing the deterrent effect of retorsions is difficult, there is good reason to doubt whether they or other political responses to cyber espionage have any such impact. Expelling foreign spies working under diplomatic cover may limit their ability to conduct physical espionage in the target country.

However, this could ironically lead the spying country to collect intelligence remotely, which is more difficult to detect and deter. For instance, in April 2022, Denmark's Security and Intelligence Service (PET) concluded that expelling 15 Russian intelligence officers had significantly affected. Russia's ability to spy on Denmark using human sources. PET also assessed that Russia would continue to spy, albeit using different methods.[166]

It is also widely acknowledged that the United States' use of sanctions and criminal charges against foreign hackers to deter Chinese and Russian cyber espionage has shown limited success.[167] If the United States, with its vast resources and capabilities, cannot deter other states from cyber espionage

164 See, e.g. Demarest, "Espionage in International Law," 347 ('While clandestine information gathering will continue to be considered an unfriendly act between nations, such activity does not violate international law').

165 'Publicly declaring that another State is responsible for a cyber operation is in itself an act of retorsion.'; Musæus, "Norway's Position Paper on International Law and Cyberspace," 15.

166 *Krigen i Ukraine har øget Ruslands spionagebehov i Danmark*, technical report (Danish Security and Intelligence Service, 2023), accessed November 6, 2023, https://pet.dk/pet/nyhedsliste/krigen-i-ukraine-har-oeget-ruslands-spionagebehov-i-danmark/2023/05/02.

167 'US sanctions and criminal indictments imposed after previous acts of cyber espionage had not deterred Russia and China from spying on the United States.'; David P. Fidler, "SolarWinds and Microsoft Exchange: Hacks Wrapped in a Cybersecurity Dilemma Inside a Cyberspace Crisis," *Georgetown Journal of International Affairs*, April 2021, https://gjia . georgetown. edu/ 2021 / 04 / 12 / solarwinds-and-microsoft-exchange-hacks-wrapped-in-a-cybersecurity-dilemma-inside-a-cyberspace-crisis/. See also Jon R. Lindsay, "Tipping the scales: the attribution problem and the feasibility of deterrence against cyberattack" [in en], *Journal of Cybersecurity*, November 2015, 57 ('China conducts pervasive cyber espionage against Western interests, and there is good evidence available publicly and in US intelligence circles that the Chinese state is responsible, but so far naming and shaming actions have had little effect').

through a comprehensive, multi-pronged response, it is difficult to believe that the small Nordic states can.[168]

Given the above, the best defence against cyber espionage is technical rather than legal or political. The only effective way to deter cyber espionage is to prevent other states from gaining access to sensitive information by hardening targets. This 'harden the target' approach can prevent states from conducting cyber espionage by making it more difficult and costly.[169] But even strong cyber security measures have their limits against state actors with the resources to launch sustained and sophisticated attacks.

8 Conclusion

The Nordic countries have traditionally demonstrated an unwavering commitment to the rule of law at both domestic and international levels. They seek to foster a so-called 'rules-based international order' and uphold compliance with international law in the physical world and cyberspace. This belief in a global rule of law for cyberspace is clearly expressed in the Nordic countries' statements on applying international law in cyberspace.

This chapter has challenged the Nordic states' apparent principled and formal approach to international law in cyberspace as expressed in their national statements. Through the lens of Nordic legal pragmatism, the chapter has explored how the Nordic states balance the need for operational flexibility to conduct peacetime cyber espionage with the need to have some general normative guardrails for states' activities in cyberspace.

In doing so, it has provided the central insight that the Nordic states' view on the interaction between international law and cyber espionage is shaped more by real-world policy and pragmatic concerns than by formal rules. This pragmatism is perhaps unintended but nonetheless most clearly witnessed by the Nordic states' actual (non) use of the principle of territorial sovereignty in relation to (cyber) espionage. While the Nordic states agree that sovereignty is a standalone rule of international law that can be violated, they do not, in their actual practice, treat it as an operative rule that puts any normative limits on their own or other states' cyber espionage activities.

168 '[W]ithin "classical deterrence" it is close to impossible for small states to unilaterally generate the necessary capability and credibility.'; Marius Kristiansen and Njaal Hoem, "Small players in a limitless domain: Cyber deterrence as small state strategy," *Comparative Strategy* 41, no. 1 (January 2022): 21.

169 Fidler, *Advanced introduction to cybersecurity law*, 8.

The Nordic countries are likely to consider international rules and norms when deciding whether cyber espionage activities, including their own and those of other nations, are legal. However, these factors are of lesser importance when compared to the strategic necessity of gathering information in cyberspace and the understanding that espionage is a lawful and accepted practice in international affairs. In other words, the Nordic states have opted for a pragmatic approach to cyber espionage under international law rather than a principled one.

Index

Printed in the United States
by Baker & Taylor Publisher Services